MONASTIC LANDSCAPES

MONASTIC LANDSCAPES

JAMES BOND

TEMPUS

First published 2004
1004629580
Tempus Publishing Ltd
The Mill, Brimscombe Port
Stroud, Gloucestershire GL5 2QG
www.tempus-publishing.com

British Library Cataloguing in Publication Data.
A catalogue record for this book is available from the British Library.

ISBN 0 7524 1440 2

Typesetting and origination by Tempus Publishing.
Printed and bound in Great Britain.

Contents

Acknowledgements

If I could name all those who have contributed to this study over its many years of gestation, my list of acknowledgements would be almost as long as the book itself. I would, however, particularly like to thank friends and colleagues whose work on monastic matters or in the general field of landscape history has been of special assistance, notably Grenville Astill, Mick Aston, Joe Bettey, Ian Burrow, Jenni Butterworth, Glyn Coppack, Nick Corcos, Michael Costen, Chris Currie, Robert Dunning, Chris Dyer, Martin Ecclestone, Roberta Gilchrist, Patrick Greene, Teresa Hall, Fred Hartley, John Harvey, Dick Holt, Graham Keevill, Steve Moorhouse, Eddie Price, Pat Preece, Steve Rippon, David Robinson, Tony Scrase, Terry Slater, Chris Taylor, Martin Watts and Brian Weller. The examples set by Robin Donkin and David Williams in their publications on the Cistercians have been particularly inspirational. Students of the former Department for Continuing Education of Bristol University who have followed me on related courses over many years have taught me far more than I have ever taught them.

I owe debts of gratitude to numerous librarians, record office staff, site custodians, farmers and owners and occupants of former monastic buildings, and apologise to them for their anonymity. Six people deserve special mention: Peter Kemmis Betty, who invited me to write this book, for his understanding and patience over a long-overdue manuscript which turned out to be twice the length that either of us had anticipated; Emma Parkin, Alex Cameron, Nadia Stone and Margaret Haynes for seeing the book through production; and my wife, Tina, who has tolerated many holidays spent in trudging over muddy, bumpy fields and clambering through cobwebby buildings, has read and made many constructive comments on my early drafts, has done incomprehensible things with a computer to produce final versions of my maps and text, has helped with the index, and has been immensely supportive throughout. All errors of fact, interpretation or judgement are my responsibility alone.

Foreword

James Bond has been interested in aspects of monastic landscape for all the time that I have known him, since we were postgraduates sharing an office in the Geography Department of Birmingham University in the 1960s. James went on to carry out seminal research on the monastic estates of Evesham Abbey, Abingdon Abbey, and Dorchester Abbey. Latterly, he has been looking at the estates of Glastonbury Abbey, arguably the most famous and certainly the most wealthy of medieval monastic institutions.

His work on monastic estates has always been wide ranging and this is reflected in the contents of this book. Monastic and religious institutions were immensely important and influential in the Middle Ages. They owned vast tracts of land and affected the lives of many millions of medieval people. Indeed, there were few areas of life or parts of the country where their influence was not dominant. A large proportion of the landscape was created, developed and defined by them in this period. Whether we look at medieval towns, rural settlements, churches, water mills, former parks or gardens, or the origins of later industrial activity, we are often seeing the impact and interest of monastic houses.

In this monumental book, James Bond has gathered and ordered all this material and marshalled the information to give us a very full and comprehensive survey of the monastic contribution to the medieval landscape. This work is destined to become the seminal work on this topic. Few who are interested or involved with research on early landscape development, or who are interested in the role and influence of the monastic and religious institutions in the medieval period will not find new material or interpretation in it. But it will also be useful to field archaeologists who daily dig up aspects of this topic, medieval archaeologists for whom this subject is a dominant force, and historians. For while monasteries and their activities are generally well-documented, so often references to developments out on their estates are not so well known and so often have not been related to features on the ground.

There is much of inspiration for many scholars here.

Professor Mick Aston

Illustration credits

Colour plates

9, **11**, **14**, **21**, **32**: Mick Aston
30: Public Record Office E 164/25, fo.222r

Text figures

1: British Library, MS Cotton Augustus ii, 33
11, **39**, **60**, **76**, **81**, **104**, **105**, **114**: Mick Aston
19, **28**, **79**, **80**: Copyright reserved, Cambridge University Collection of Air Photographs: BPJ 40, BEY 14, BSB 70, AFL 71
29, **55**, **56**, **78**, **109**, **113**: These photographs, which are Crown Copyright, are published by permission of the Ministry of Defence and of the Controller of Her Majesty's Stationery Office: BY 9, EA 49, SP 72, UC 66, AZ 68, NB 8
21: From N. Whittock, *The Microcosm of Oxford* (Oxford, 1830)
30: Engraving accompanying a letter by James Hunt to the *Gentleman's Magazine*, Vol.86 (February 1816), p.105
38, **45**: Tina Bond
53: Westminster Abbey Muniment 432, Copyright Dean & Chapter of Westminster

All other photographs, maps and line drawings are by the author.

Preface

This is a book I have wanted to write for thirty years. Oddly, not everyone shares my enthusiasm. I have discovered that, in almost any gathering, if I happen to mention that I am interested in medieval monastic estates, there is a moment of silence and expressions become glazed; then the apprehension that I might be about to expound further quickly prompts my companions to begin talking about car maintenance, horse-racing or stock market prices. I find this curious. If we have any interest at all in our surroundings as we travel around the English countryside, we cannot avoid encountering features created or modified by monastic landowners in the Middle Ages. Yet, while popular folklore credits monks with digging 'secret tunnels' over prodigious distances (frequently with nunneries as their destination), there almost seems to be a conspiracy of silence about their real achievements. How many coach parties touring round the Cotswolds are told that Stow-on-the-Wold is an early twelfth-century new town developed by Evesham Abbey, or that Broadway was an unsuccessful town promotion attempted by the monks of Pershore in the thirteenth century? How many holidaymakers on the Norfolk Broads realise that they are sailing over the flooded turbaries of Norwich Priory and St Benet's Abbey? How many modern pilgrims to Glastonbury are aware of that great abbey's part in canalising the watercourses and draining the marshes of the surrounding levels?

My own eyes were opened to the possibilities in this field by a lucky encounter with the chronicle of Evesham Abbey while in my first job as Archaeological Officer at the Worcestershire County Museum back in the early 1970s. Reading through the chronicle, I became excited by the number of references to the construction of houses, barns and dovecotes, mills and fishponds. Although the source had long been known to historians, I could not understand why no one seemed to have followed it up by trying to find out how many of those earthworks and buildings survived in the present landscape. As soon as I began exploring the Evesham manors on the ground, I found myself stumbling across other medieval features mentioned neither in the chronicle nor in other documents. So, a conviction in the value of multi-disciplinary approaches to the landscape was born, together with a lifelong interest in monastic estates, where the potential for combining documentary and fieldwork approaches can be so rewarding.

Unfortunately the need to earn a living has a nasty habit of getting in the way of real work, and opportunities to pursue this interest have been somewhat spasmodic. In reality, of course, to do full justice to such an enormous topic would require several lifetimes and a range of skills that no individual can hope to possess. Quite a lot of the material in this book is, therefore, a product of the intermittent and sometimes accidental gleanings of three decades rather than a set period of concentrated research. Yet, perhaps that is itself not such a bad thing. In times when professional requirements so often demand complete answers yesterday, pottering about with a long-term project has its own virtues and its own rewards.

The prospects for studying monastic estates on the continental scale are enormously inviting, but for the purposes of this book I have had to restrict my attentions to England and Wales; even then, I have still found myself trying to cram several gallons into a pint pot. What is offered here is an exploratory introduction, not a presentation of definitive conclusions. Despite a vast literature on monasticism, relatively few monastic estates have yet been subjected to detailed topographical examination. If this encourages others to investigate further the monastic role in the landscape, it will have achieved its aims.

A few decisions on matters of presentation need some explanation. Simply because there has been no comprehensive nationwide survey of monastic estates, all distribution maps offered here should be regarded as provisional. For the sake of clarity, most quotations from early documents are rendered into modern spelling. However, I have decided to retain imperial measurements rather than use the metric system, partly because this inherently makes more sense when dealing with a medieval topic, partly because I suspect that the majority of readers will still relate more readily to miles, acres and gallons rather than kilometres, hectares and litres.

Many places are mentioned which will be unfamiliar to most readers. In the interests of saving space and avoiding repetition, I have employed the index to identify the county in which they lie, quoting this in the text only where place-names are duplicated, or where otherwise it seemed essential. I decided to use the pre-1974 counties for this purpose, again partly because they remain familiar to most readers and bear a closer relationship to the administrative geography of the Middle Ages, whereas modern administrative units are so ephemeral as to be worthless in historical terms. I have also made the index serve as an aid to the text by identifying there the order of every monastic house and the dates of every abbot mentioned. I have generally modernised the spelling of medieval personal names except in cases where a Latin or archaic form (such as Giraldus Cambrensis or Jocelin of Brakelond) has become hallowed by familiarity.

This book is aimed at the interested general reader rather than the academic, and to avoid inflating still further a text which has grown well beyond the dimensions specified on my contract I have, reluctantly, abandoned any thought of providing comprehensive references to the many hundreds of miscellaneous sources used. However, I hope that the general bibliography and chapter bibliographies will serve at least some of the needs of those who wish to explore any topics further.

Finally, although some of the buildings mentioned are in the care of English Heritage, Cadw or the National Trust, and many other sites may be visible from public roads or footpaths, much of what is described in the text lies on private land, and it must not be assumed that there is any right of public access.

1
Monasteries in the landscape: approaches and sources

Introduction

Monastic buildings are among our greatest architectural legacies from the Middle Ages. Few visitors can fail to be awed by the soaring majesty of the great churches of Canterbury, Gloucester or Worcester, or to be moved by the magnificent setting and picturesque ruins of Fountains, Rievaulx or Tintern. Yet, for most of us today, the way of life which generated them seems as remote as the moon. Why were they built, how were they used, and how were they paid for?

Many books have been written about the history, the architecture, the art and the archaeology of monasteries, and it is not difficult to find the answers to some of these questions. However, if we are to understand the full extent of the impact of the monastic orders during the Middle Ages, we have to realise that the churches and claustral buildings, grand though they may be, are only the tip of the iceberg.

Many monasteries (and nunneries) were endowed from their first foundation with extensive lands, which were intended to provide sustenance and income to support the community. At the time of the Dissolution in the sixteenth century, monasteries were alleged to hold one-third of all the land in England – an exaggeration, but modern estimates would still place the figure between 20 and 25 per cent. Monasteries were relatively immune from the mishaps which so often disrupted the inheritance of lay estates, such as confiscation, or failure of the male line. As permanent corporations, they were able to maintain a continuity of ownership, in some cases spanning up to seven centuries, in a way that few secular landowners could match. They could afford to take the long-term view, and had both opportunity and incentive to invest part of their capital in developing their landed properties. We thus find monastic communities actively involved in improving agricultural production, clearing woodland, draining marshes, enclosing parks and gardens, creating rabbit warrens, planting orchards and vineyards, altering watercourses, constructing mills and fisheries, building churches, houses, barns and dovecotes, removing or replanning villages and even founding new towns on their estates. Many traces of these activities can still be seen today; yet the true scale of the contribution of the monastic orders remains very little appreciated. The aim of this book is to explore the impact of the monasteries upon the wider landscape beyond the claustral buildings.

Approaches

The study of monastic estates demands a multi-disciplinary approach. The skills of documentary historians, field archaeologists, architectural historians and other specialists all have a vital part to play, but employed in isolation they can only ever produce an incomplete and sometimes misleading picture. Many case studies of the economy of particular monasteries have been produced by historians studying written records, and these are often excellent on their own terms; yet their authors rarely seem to have been inspired by their researches to follow Professor Tawney's much-quoted injunction to get their boots on and to investigate further on the ground.

Equally, architectural historians have sometimes examined medieval houses and barns down to the most intimate details of stone mouldings and carpentry joints, without ever seeming to appreciate that such buildings stood on monastic property, and that there may be relevant documentation and structures for comparative study elsewhere on the same estate. These are extremes, and perhaps it is unfair to castigate investigators for not asking wider questions when this would have involved stepping beyond the bounds of their own specialisms. Nevertheless, efforts to integrate the evidence from archaeology, architecture and the documentary record remain few in number, and unless we attempt to do this, our understanding will remain limited.

Written sources

In any study of a monastic estate, our first need is to identify the nature and extent of its landed property and then, if possible, to define its bounds and to assess its resources. This can only be commenced through documentary research, and there are three main groups of sources which can help us: records of monastic property compiled by external agencies for taxation or valuation purposes; property transactions between lay individuals and monasteries; and documents generated internally within the monastery to serve its own needs.

The first group includes three particularly important sources. The Domesday Survey of 1086 is the best-known of the governmental records. In part a feudal reckoning, in part an assessment of taxable resources, it lists the properties of 50 English abbeys and priories (including eight nunneries) in addition to lands in England owned by 30 continental monastic houses. These range from the vast estates of Glastonbury Abbey, scattered through five counties, yielding a gross annual income of well over £800, down to the small alien priory of Swavesey, whose Cambridgeshire property produced just £2. In addition to listing the number of ploughs and extent of woodland, pasture and meadow belonging to each manor, Domesday Book provides a miscellany of information on mills, fisheries, vineyards, markets and other resources.

Whereas the Domesday Survey was a royal inquisition covering monastic, episcopal and lay property alike, the Ecclesiastical Taxation authorised by Pope Nicholas IV in 1291 to finance Edward I's projected Crusade applied only to clerical, episcopal and monastic income. Two categories of information were recorded: *Spiritualities*, consisting of taxable clerical income from each parish through tithes, glebe land and mortuary fees, and *Temporalities*, income from demesne lands, including rents, arable lands, mills, livestock and occasionally miscellaneous items such as dovecotes, gardens and fishponds.

When Henry VIII repudiated the authority of Rome in 1534, taxes which had formerly gone to the pope were diverted to the crown, and Parliament authorised a new annual tax on the church. The chancellor, Sir Thomas Audley, sent inquisitors into every diocese to discover the income of all churches and monasteries. The information collected was brought together in 1535 in a record called the *Valor Ecclesiasticus*. For each monastic house the *Valor* lists the gross income from all manors, farms, rents and temporal revenues and all rectories, vicarages, tithes, glebes, oblations and other spiritual revenues, deducting various outgoings such as alms, pensions and wages of bailiffs, stewards and auditors to arrive at a net income to be taxed. Returns from several monasteries are missing. However, for the majority of houses it provides a valuable insight into the management of their estates on the eve of the Dissolution, underlining the extent to which direct exploitation had given way to farming out resources in exchange for fixed payments. Cromwell's commissioners made more detailed surveys of the demesnes of those smaller monasteries which were to be suppressed in 1536, and there are also a number of surveys of former monastic demesnes made immediately after the Dissolution which may amplify the details contained in the *Valor*.

Property transaction records include charters and wills, which record grants of lands and rents from lay individuals to monasteries. Later on, grants and leases from monasteries to tenants are found. Many ancient religious foundations were supported by grants of land from the king. These were recorded in charters which conveyed security of possession, and excused the recipient from a range of tributes and duties formerly owed from the estate. Numerous pre-Conquest charters survive with nominal dates from the seventh century onwards (1). Stephen Morland has listed 63 charters covering lands belonging to Glastonbury Abbey in Somerset, 16 in Wiltshire, seven in Dorset, two in Devon and one each in Berkshire, Gloucestershire and Hampshire, along with

1 *Charter recording grant of land at Cuddesdon (Oxfordshire) by King Edwy in 956 to his ealdorman Aelfhere, who passed the property on to Abbot Aethelwold of Abingdon. The terms of the grant are recited in Latin, followed by a detailed boundary perambulation in Old English (beginning half-way down the page in slightly smaller script), terminating in a list of witnesses. The extant document is believed to be slightly later than the date of the grant*

66 other charters relating to properties lost by the abbey before the Norman Conquest, or covering lands in which it never had a genuine claim.

Quite apart from their basic value in identifying what estates were granted to the monasteries, many charters have attached boundary perambulations which offer some hope of reconstructing the precise limits of each property. Such perambulations are themselves often of great interest, featuring many aspects of the contemporary landscape (**5, 6** and **colour plate 1**). However, charters are notoriously dangerous documents to take at face value. Very few of the earliest charters survive in their original form. Many of the extant documents are later copies which, while containing authentic material, often also include errors and inserts. Some of them were concocted to replace long-lost originals, particularly where an abbey needed to support claims to possessions which had been challenged. Others were deceitfully manufactured in the hopes of establishing claims to land over which the abbey had no legitimate rights. Crowland Abbey lost all its records in a disastrous fire in 1091, and attempted to redeem the situation by making a complete series of forgeries. Forged charters can often be detected through anachronisms in form, content or language. Sometimes boundary perambulations were added at a date subsequent to that of the original grant, and occasionally boundary clauses later became wrongly attached to a different charter. Many monastic houses provided a depository service, storing charters relating to land in which they had no direct interest on behalf of benefactors and other laymen. Despite the undeniable problems in dealing with them, however, charters remain an invaluable source for reconstructing the early medieval landscape.

As the number of grants increased, it became ever more difficult to store the accumulated rolls of charters so that they were accessible when needed. By the eleventh century, the greater monasteries were finding it imperative to devise some more efficient form of filing the information, and the practice developed of compiling land registers or cartularies which could be kept up to date as further gifts accrued. The earliest surviving English monastic cartulary, from Worcester Cathedral Priory, was commenced in the time of Bishop Wulfstan I (1003-16). Bound in with this volume is a transcript of 23 further charters including 11 sets of bounds compiled at the end of the eleventh century by the sub-prior Hemming. Today the whole text is usually, though incorrectly, referred to as Hemming's Cartulary. It relates the ancient history of the church of Worcester, lists many grants and donations made to it, and bewails its subsequent losses at the hands of the Danes and Normans. The next major monastic cartulary to survive is the *Codex Wintoniensis*, compiled in the second quarter of the twelfth century for the use of the cathedral priory of St Swithun at Winchester. This contains transcripts of 218 pre-Conquest land charters going back to the 680s, the largest single extant collection. Probably half of the charters dated before the 920s are spurious or show signs of modification, but 90 per cent of the later charters appear genuine.

Glastonbury Abbey compiled its first landbook, the *Liber Terrarum*, somewhere around 1200. This contained transcripts of 136 pre-Conquest charters. The original book is no longer extant, but fortunately a summary of its contents was made when the abbey library was catalogued in 1247. Another collection of Glastonbury documents, including the texts of 49 pre-Conquest charters, was transcribed into a volume known as the Great Chartulary in around 1348. A further copy, made for the personal use of Abbot Walter Monington (1342-75), contains several additional later deeds, but the main text is inferior, the scribal errors of the original being compounded by the copyist. A cartulary for Burton Abbey was compiled some time between 1230 and 1241; a few years later all known pre-Conquest charters for this abbey were copied into a volume of miscellaneous historical records, while a third Burton cartulary contains exclusively post-Conquest texts. Records of rights over land continued to be compiled up to the end of the Middle Ages. Peterborough Abbey's *Carte Nativorum* is unusual in documenting land

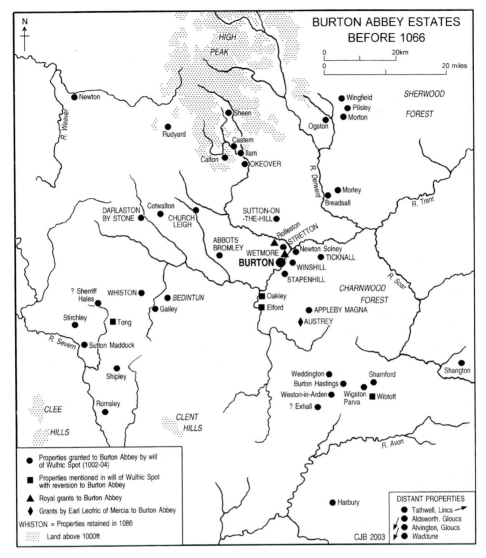

BURTON ABBEY ESTATES BEFORE 1066

N

0   20km
0   20 miles

HIGH PEAK

SHERWOOD FOREST

Newton

R. Weaver

Sheen

Rudyard

Castern

Calton • Ilam
OKEOVER

Wingfield
Pilsley
Morton
Ogston

R. Derwent

Morley
Breadsall

R. Trent

DARLASTON BY STONE
Cotwalton
CHURCH LEIGH

SUTTON-ON-THE-HILL

ABBOTS BROMLEY
WETMORE
BURTON
Rolleston
STRETTON
Newton Solney
TICKNALL
WINSHILL
STAPENHILL

R. Scar

CHARNWOOD FOREST

? Sherriff Hales
WHISTON
BEDINTUN
Gailey

Stirchley
Tong

R. Severn
Sutton Maddock

Shipley

CLEE

Romsley

HILLS

CLENT HILLS

Oakley
Elford
APPLEBY MAGNA
AUSTREY

Weddington
Burton Hastings
Weston-in-Arden
? Exhall
Sharnford
Wigston Parva
Wibtoft

Shangton

R. Avon

Harbury

Properties granted to Burton Abbey by will of Wulfric Spot (1002-04)

Properties mentioned in will of Wulfric Spot with reversion to Burton Abbey

Royal grants to Burton Abbey

Grants by Earl Leofric of Mercia to Burton Abbey

WHISTON = Properties retained in 1086

Land above 1000ft

DISTANT PROPERTIES
Tathwell, Lincs →
Aldsworth, Gloucs
Alvington, Gloucs
Waddune

CJB 2003

2 Estates of Burton Abbey (Staffordshire) before 1066

transactions of the abbey's villein tenants, mostly from the thirteenth and four-teenth centuries.

Wills often record bequests to monastic houses. The will of Wulfric Spot, founder of Burton Abbey in 1004, lists his endowment, comprising lands in 15 places in Staffordshire, 12 in Derbyshire, five in Shropshire, three in Leicestershire, three in Warwickshire, plus nine other places whose names are ambiguous or unrecognisable, plus livestock and other interests (**2**). Either Wulfric's good intentions were never carried through, or the abbey lost control of much of its property during the Danish occupation, for the Domesday survey identifies a much-diminished estate reduced to 11 manors in

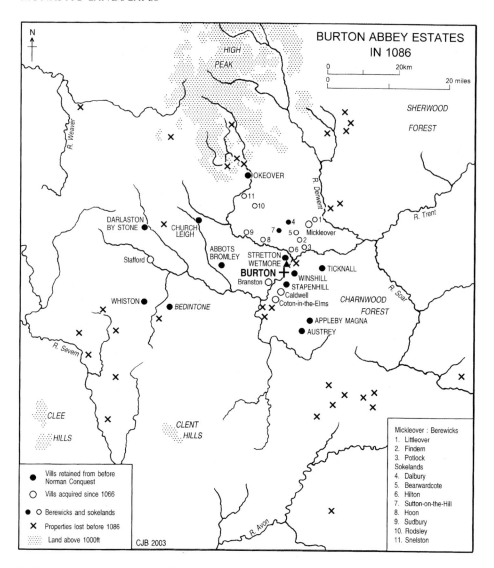

3 *The depleted estates of Burton Abbey in 1086, showing properties lost before the Domesday survey*

Staffordshire, four in Derbyshire and one in Leicestershire (**3**). Bequests of cash became more common in the later Middle Ages, sometimes earmarked for particular building projects, as when William Wenard in 1441 left 100 marks to the Greyfriars of Exeter for making a new cloister and 80 marks to the nuns of Polsloe for a new belfry tower.

The third group of written sources consists of documents generated within the abbey to serve its own purposes, particularly internal administrative needs. These often illuminate the ways in which monastic property was used and the nature of the abbey's investment in it. For some houses – Canterbury Cathedral Priory, Durham, Westminster, Norwich, Worcester, Glastonbury – there is an embarrassment of riches, while for many smaller houses surviving records are sparse. Internal records are of many different kinds, which sometimes overlap, and only a brief outline can be given here.

Monasteries had a long tradition of historical scholarship, going back to the time of Bede. After the Norman Conquest this took on a keener edge, as they found themselves needing to bolster their reputation as places of great antiquity and sanctity in order to defend their possessions against episcopal and secular rivals. Chronicles and annals, along with hagiographies of local saints, emphasising continuity with the past, became popular. An early twelfth-century history attributed to Symeon of Durham drew upon earlier sources describing the wanderings of the monks displaced from the island of Lindisfarne and their eventual arrival at Durham with the relics of St Cuthbert, emphasising the special protection given by the saint to the monks and their lands, and describing the estates of the church with its bounds in meticulous detail. The monks of Glastonbury commissioned William of Malmesbury to write up the foundation traditions and early history of their house in the late 1120s, probably on the strength of his earlier work in translating the Anglo-Saxon biography of St Wulfstan into Latin for the monks of Worcester. The Glastonbury story was updated by subsequent chroniclers, Adam of Damerham writing in the early 1290s, John of Glastonbury continuing up to 1342, and William Wyche up to 1493. The *Liber Eliensis* compiled at Ely in the later twelfth century related the history of the church at Ely from its foundation by St Aetheldreda in the seventh century up to the time of Henry II; it incorporates an earlier chronicle describing the refoundation of the house by Bishop Aethelwold and listing the properties with which he endowed it. Other monastic chroniclers were more concerned with wider historical events, and are less useful for our purposes.

At their best, monastic chronicles can be a gold mine of topographical information. The chronicle of Evesham Abbey is a composite document, the first part recording the history of the abbey from its foundation up to the early twelfth century. This was continued by Thomas Marlborough, who was successively dean, sacrist, prior and finally abbot (1229-36), and then carried on by an anonymous chronicler up to the death of Abbot Roger Yatton in 1418. The fourth and final section, continuing the story up to the Dissolution, is much thinner. The second and third sections of the Evesham chronicle are especially valuable for the detail they provide on building works and estate management. Thomas Marlborough, for example, listed the achievements of Abbot Randulf (1214-29), including the replacement of barns on five of the abbey's manors, the building of five new dovecotes, the construction of eight fishponds, the building of two new mills and the purchase of two more, the clearance of woodland and the ploughing-up of new land. John of Glastonbury's account of the deeds of Abbot Robert Petherton (1261-74) and Matthew Paris' description of the achievements of John Hertford, Abbot of St Albans (1235-63) are equally informative.

Biographies of individual abbots form a special category, the supreme example of which is the chronicle of Jocelin of Brakelond, abbot's chaplain and later guest-master and almoner at Bury St Edmunds, which describes the career of Abbot Samson (1182–1211). Quite apart from his vivid character sketches and the glimpses of the internal politics of the monastery, Jocelin provides much information on the management of the abbey's extensive properties, and on the town of Bury St Edmunds itself. Towards the end of the Middle Ages we have the unique survival of a personal journal kept by William More, prior of Worcester from 1518 to 1535, detailing his daily expenses and his amiable life as a country gentleman on his rural properties. This provides invaluable information on the repair of his manor houses, the management of his fishponds and the upkeep and yields of his deer parks, rabbit warrens and dovecotes.

The tradition of compiling chronicles was especially characteristic of the older Benedictine houses. However, at the end of the fourteenth century the Cistercian abbey of Meaux found an outstanding chronicler in the person of Thomas Burton, bursar and subsequently abbot. Burton described in vivid detail the difficulties experienced by the monks in coping with coastal erosion, silting and flooding in the Humber estuary. Part of his concern was to seek tax relief on lands inundated by the sea; but the level of topographical detail he provides leaves no room for doubting the essential accuracy of his account.

Manorial surveys and custumals, terriers, rentals and court rolls provide another range of evidence. An unusually full sequence of surveys is available for the Glastonbury Abbey estates. An inquest into the abbey's income drawn up in 1171 by Hilbert, precentor of Wells, compares the situation then with the results of earlier surveys made before 1135 but no longer extant. A second inquisition drawn up in 1189 when Henry Sully became abbot contains 35 manorial surveys recording how much land each tenant held and the customary services and payments due from each. A further survey survives only in a fourteenth-century copy, where it is misdated 1128, though internal evidence shows that it was probably compiled by order of Abbot Savaric in 1198. Yet another inquest was carried out in 1201. The period between 1192 and 1219, when Glastonbury was united with the see of Bath, was a low point in the abbey's fortunes, and further manorial surveys, rentals and custumaries were drawn up as Abbot Michael Amesbury (1235–52) and his successor Roger Ford (1252–61) reorganised the estates and initiated a period of recovery. Finally, in 1516–17 a terrier was drawn up for Abbot Richard Beere, consisting of a very thorough and detailed series of manorial visitations.

A final important group of sources is the *compoti* or accounts recording balances of income and expenditure. The earliest English monastic farming record known is a single page of notes jotted down by four different individuals at Ely Abbey in the first quarter of the eleventh century. This was a rough draft made in preparation for compiling the formal accounts, and includes an inventory of livestock on the abbey's farms, a list of rents in eels due from the abbey's fenland properties, and a list and valuation of livestock, seed, farm implements, boats and nets sent to Thorney Abbey. After the Dissolution this page was cut into three strips and recycled for bookbinding, and it is only relatively recently that the three parts have been reunited.

The complexities of monastic accounting cannot be considered fully here, but broadly the documents fall into two groups, the internal departmental accounts of the obedientiaries (that is the more senior members of the community who were charged with special responsibilities, such as the cellarer, granger, kitchener, sacrist and infirmarian), and the accounts of individual manors on the estates. In larger Benedictine monasteries such as Durham, Selby, Worcester, Peterborough, Norwich, Abingdon and Glastonbury, separate accounts were maintained by each of the obedientiaries, but the survival of account rolls from individual offices or departments is often erratic. No manorial accounts survive from before the thirteenth century, but a vast mass of accounts of the stewards and reeves on Glastonbury Abbey's manors, dating from the later thirteenth century to the Dissolution, survive unpublished and still not fully explored. In smaller houses the financial system tended to be more centralised, as in the Augustinian Priory of Bolton, where an unusually comprehensive book of accounts survives from the period 1286-1325. A single annual account from Beaulieu Abbey, dated from internal evidence to 1269-70, contains the year's income and expenditure for each grange, manor, department and workshop, interspersed with rules and tables for checking each account at the audit.

Maps

Surveys of lands in the Middle Ages were normally relayed by means of written descriptions, and maps were rarely employed. Nevertheless, a significant proportion of the medieval maps which do exist come from monastic archives. The most detailed examples are those concerned with the water supply to individual precincts. The first known large-scale English plan is the famous depiction of Prior Wibert's water system at Christ Church, Canterbury, dating from around 1150-60. A more diagrammatic survey of the water supply from Wormley to Waltham Abbey dates from the 1220s, and there is an elaborate early sixteenth-century map of the water conduits at the London Charterhouse.

In the middle of the thirteenth century Matthew Paris of St Albans Abbey produced the earliest known medieval map of the whole of Britain. Four versions survive. The level of accuracy is not high, and one copy bears the delightful admission that 'if the size of the page had permitted, the island would have been shown longer than it is'. The basis of the map was clearly a written itinerary, a vertical string of 17 place-names from Dover to Newcastle-upon-Tyne, around which other details are fitted. The selection of places depicted is idiosyncratic, with important Benedictine monasteries figuring prominently, as well as five cells of St Albans Abbey itself.

Between these two extremes a handful of maps depict parts of monastic estates. The Chronicle of St Augustine's, Canterbury, includes a plan of the Isle of Thanet made around 1400 by Thomas Elmham, a monk at the abbey, illustrating the foundation of the seventh-century nunnery of Minster-in-Thanet, a site which later became one of the principal granges of St Augustine's. According to legend, the founder of the early house, Domneva, niece of King Egbert of Kent, had a pet deer which was released to run round the island, and the nunnery was endowed with all the land that lay within the deer's track. A green line on the map shows the path taken by the deer.

A significant proportion of monastic maps were produced in connection with disputes or lawsuits between an abbey and its tenants or neighbours. A map of Wildmore Fen copied into a psalter at Kirkstead Abbey in or before 1249 is almost certainly a product of the abbey's concern to protect its grazing rights there. The Chertsey Cartulary includes a mid-fifteenth-century map drawn up during a protracted disagreement with some of the abbey's tenants over rights in the Thames meadows between Chertsey and the village of Laleham; it shows the meadows concerned, along with a barn, two undershot watermills and a bridge (**colour plate 30**). Another pasture dispute between the monks of Durham and their tenants at Elvet is illustrated by a rough map made in the 1440s. Two equally sketchy diagram maps in the Westminster archives, drawn by the same scribe some time in the 1470s, depict lands at Staines and fishing rights on the River Colne between Harefield and Denham which were in dispute between the abbey and its tenants (**53**). A map hanging in the Guildhall in Abingdon, dating from around the time of the Dissolution with later annotations, depicts some 3 miles of the River Thames from the southern end of the town up to Radley. It was probably made in connection with disputes over the use of the river involving Abingdon Abbey, and is of interest for its depiction of the abbey moat and fishponds, the weir in the river, the abbey's farm at Barton Court (**20**), and the daubing over with mauve paint of all abbey buildings demolished after the Dissolution.

Buildings, landscape archaeology and the synthesis of evidence

The amount of information which documentary sources can give us about monastic estates is immense, indeed, almost overwhelming. Yet, as Professor Hoskins instructed many years ago, we have a still richer record in the landscape itself. If we can learn to identify the surviving monastic farm

	Manor-house	Barn	Dovecote	Corn-mill	Fulling-mill	Church/parochial chapel	Domestic chapel/oratory	River-fishery	Fishpond	Stone-quarry	Vineyard	Park	Warren	Wood
Abingdon			○	◉	◉	●		◉	●○					
Appleford	◐			○		●		◉					?	
Barton Court	◉	◉	◉										?	
Boxford				◉	◉	●								●○
Charney Basset	◉			◉		●	●							○
Chieveley						●							?	●○
Cuddesdon	○			◉		●	○	○		●○			?	◉
Culham	●	○				●		◉					◉	●○
Cumnor	◉			◉		●		○		●○			?	◉
Drayton		○		◉		●								
Dumbleton	○			◉		●								●○
East Hanney				◉					●					
East Lockinge		○		○		●				●○				
Farnborough						●								●○
Garford	○			◉		●								
Goosey	◐					●			●					
Lewknor	●	○	○	○		●								●○
Little Wittenham				○		●		○						◉
Longworth	◐					●		○					?	
Marcham			●○	◉		●								◉
Milton				◉		●								
Northcourt	○	●												
Radley	○					●						◉		◉
Shellingford	○		○	○		●			●				?	○
Shippon	○	●	○			○		○						○
Sutton Courtenay	●			◉		●								
Tadmarton		●		◉	○	●							?	
Uffington	?			●○		●							?	
Watchfield				●○							?			
Welford				◉		●							?	●○
West Ginge				○										
Whistley	?			◉		○		○						●○
Winkfield						●								●○

● Field evidence only
◉ Field and documentary evidence: identity undoubted
●○ Field and documentary evidence: identity uncertain
◐ Site known but no upstanding remains
○ Documentary evidence only

4 *Abingdon Abbey (Berkshire): concordance of field and documentary evidence for features on estate manors*

buildings, the earthworks of their mills and fishponds and industrial remains, if we can unravel the meaning of the subtler traces of woodland management and agricultural exploitation, and read the clues embedded in the plans of monastic towns and villages, a new dimension will be added to our understanding.

To achieve as rounded a picture as possible, we must in the end try to bring together the results of documentary and field investigation. However, this is not as straightforward as it sounds. With both classes of evidence we face the problems of erratic survival and the risks of misinterpretation. As soon as we begin exploring the landscape, we discover sites for which there appears to be no documentary evidence; equally, sites are recorded in the written sources which cannot be located on the ground. Even where documentary evidence and field evidence for a structure such as a barn, or mill, or dovecote, coincide within a particular location, there may still remain considerable uncertainty as to whether the building we now see is identical to that mentioned in the documents (**4**). There are no easy answers to these problems; the challenges are formidable, but the rewards are great.

2
Acquisition and exploitation of monastic estates

Introduction

The basis of economic stability and power in the Middle Ages was land. However, monastic communities lived off their lands in a variety of ways, and the precise form of exploitation depended upon a number of factors. Whether the house was located in an area more suited to arable or to pastoral farming was obviously important. Large, wealthy houses with extensive landed properties had more options and more flexibility than small, poorly-endowed ones. There were significant differences between the monastic orders. Finally, patterns of exploitation changed significantly through time in response to broader social and economic trends.

The acquisition of land

How did the abbeys acquire their land in the first place? We live in a deeply cynical age, and many people today find it difficult to comprehend the notion of simple piety as a motive for giving land to a monastery. If piety alone was not enough, fear of the consequences of one's worldly conduct in the afterlife made the idea of 'spiritual insurance' very attractive. Donations were not necessarily a sacrifice, even in material terms. Often land given was immediately taken back on lease by the donor, who continued to enjoy most of the income from it for the term of his own life, with the permanent transfer taking effect only after his death. Convention was also important: for many great families in the couple of centuries after the Norman Conquest, the endowment and support of monasteries was seen as a lordly duty, and successive monastic reforms saw different orders benefit in turn. The foundation of monasteries was also employed as a political instrument. During the Anarchy, when both sides were seeking support, King Stephen contributed to the foundation of several Savignac houses, while Matilda favoured the Cistercians. The English crown and the marcher lords both saw the plantation of English monks in Wales as part of the policy for the colonisation and pacification of that country; but whereas Benedictine houses were confined to the English-controlled borderlands, the Cistercians also found favour with the independent Welsh princes. Cistercian marcher abbeys risked losses in wartime, but were able to benefit from both English and Welsh lords, who may have been glad to offload vulnerable outliers of their estates to them.

Monastic chronicles and foundation charters understandably tend to emphasise the piety of donors and the high respect in which the community was held, but there is perhaps another side to the story. It is difficult to see how even the old-established Benedictine houses could have accumulated their extensive estates, containing a balance of land use potential, without some degree of coercion. The reformed orders of the twelfth century, notably the Cistercians, had a very clear vision of what they needed, and gained a reputation for ruthlessness because of the way in which they built up large consolidated holdings out of numerous small plots given by a multiplicity of owners. A few houses like Cirencester Abbey, unusually richly endowed from the outset, added little to their initial land grants. However, most monasteries took every opportunity to improve and expand their holdings over a prolonged period, adopting a policy of exchanging or purchasing land when donations began to dry up.

The earliest monastic lands

Little can be said about the endowments of the first monastic communities. Ascetic monasticism played an important part in the revitalisation of the British church in the late fifth and sixth centuries, and this tradition lingered on in the west, particularly in Wales, Cornwall and Cumbria. It is uncertain how much continuity there may have been between the Celtic and early English foundations at places like Glastonbury, Shaftesbury, Sherborne and Malmesbury, but it is unlikely that such communities were lavishly endowed with land, before or after the English settlement.

The earliest Anglo-Saxon religious communities, following the missionary activities of Augustine of Canterbury and his colleagues, were diverse and often unstable in character. During the pioneering era of the seventh century the original foundations were often for nuns or contained a mixed community. No clear distinction can be made at this time between *monasteries*, containing monks pursuing a contemplative way of life, and *minsters*, served by secular clerics having a more evangelical role – indeed, both words come from the same root. Moreover, some of the documented foundations may have been no more than fictional devices for evading payment of secular dues. Augustine's first Kentish foundation in Canterbury, settled around 598, was followed over the next century by Westminster, Chertsey and Barking within the kingdom of Essex, by Bury St Edmunds in East Anglia, by the Old Minster at Winchester, Abingdon, Glastonbury, Malmesbury and Muchelney in Wessex, by Peterborough, Thorney, Bath, Gloucester, Worcester, Pershore, Bardney and Evesham in Mercia, and in Northumbria by Lindisfarne, Hartlepool, Whitby, Ripon, Hexham, Monkwearmouth and Jarrow. Bede records King Ethelbert of Kent and the Northumbrian kings Oswald, Oswy and Aldfrith all giving lands and endowments for the support of the new bishoprics and monasteries within their kingdoms, and occasionally he records the extent of land given. Abbess Hilda of Hartlepool received ten hides for her foundation of Whitby (a hide at that time being reckoned as enough land to support a family), King Aldfrith gave 30 or 40 hides for Wilfrid's monastery at Ripon, King Wulfhere of Mercia gave Bishop Chad 50 hides for a monastery at Barrow in Lindsey, and King Aethelwalh of Sussex gave Bishop Wilfrid 87 hides at Selsey.

Donations of land to the church were facilitated when the form of tenure known as *bookland* was devised in the seventh century. In contrast to normal inherited property, the disposal of which was limited by the customary rights of kinsmen, bookland was created by royal charter conveying outright perpetual tenure to the individual, free of most secular obligations, with the right to bequeath the land away. It was designed specifically as a means of providing religious houses with stable endowments. In Wessex many of the greater churches, Abingdon, Malmesbury, Winchester Old Minster, Sherborne and Glastonbury, acquired considerable endowments in this form. The distinction between bookland and inherited land had disappeared by the time of the Norman Conquest.

The point was made in chapter 1 that the authenticity of many early charters recording grants of land to monasteries is debatable. Nevertheless, examples where simple boundary clauses are concisely expressed in Latin, using the cardinal points of the compass, may be of genuinely early date. A grant of land around Dagenham made in around 690 to Abbess Aethelburh, founder of Barking Abbey, contains a boundary clause naming just four landmarks, one of which is the River Thames (**5a**). A charter granted by King Ine of Wessex probably in 693 confirming land around Brent Knoll to Abbot Haemgils of Glastonbury records the property as bounded by the Severn estuary to the west, the River Axe to the north, Tarnock to the east and the lost River Siger, which still holds water in time of flood, to the south (**5b**). In 736 King Aethelbald of Mercia granted part of the district anciently known as Ismere in Worcestershire to one of his followers for the foundation of a monastery, which was said to be bounded on two sides by the River Stour, on the north by Kinver Wood and on the west by Morfe Wood. This religious house was short-lived, but is remembered in the name of Kidderminster.

Sometimes the construction of the nucleus of a more substantial home estate can be traced. Nicholas Brooks, by working backwards from the Domesday

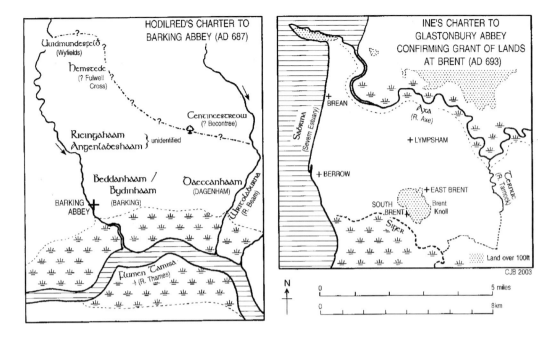

5 *Bounds of early charters.* Left (a) *Hodilred's charter to Barking Abbey (Essex), c.687.* Right (b) *Ine's charter to Glastonbury Abbey confirming grant of land at Brent (Somerset), c.693*

record and eliminating all properties known to have been granted between the ninth and eleventh centuries, has conjectured that the monks of Christ Church, Canterbury already held a considerable estate by the late eighth century, and that some of its Kentish manors, including East Peckham, East Farleigh, Eastry and Adisham, may even date back to the earliest bequests of the Kentish kings. Sir Frank Stenton showed that the first endowments of the monastic community at Abingdon extended northwards from the abbey over the wooded hills within the great bend of the Thames. Glastonbury Abbey appears to have had several distinct blocks of land in Somerset before the middle of the eighth century, the largest, spanning the Polden Hills, being first documented in a royal grant in 729, followed by the Brent Knoll property mentioned above, with smaller scattered areas up to 16 miles away.

The first enthusiasm for monastic foundations in England lasted for barely a century. By around 850 many of the early communities had ceased to exist. Some had been destroyed by the Vikings; others had decayed through complacency and apathy. Even those few communities which managed to survive in some form retained little effective control over their lands. The tide of English recovery against the Danes offered no immediate prospect of improvement. Although King Alfred founded a new monastery at Athelney and a nunnery at Shaftesbury, he was impelled to give away the lands of many abandoned monasteries as a reward for military support.

The tenth-century Benedictine reform

At the beginning of the tenth century, monastic life was at a very low ebb. However, the period between 940 and 1020 witnessed a major resurgence of monasticism in the south and the midlands. The movement to reform the English monasteries along strict Benedictine lines was spearheaded by Dunstan at Glastonbury, Oswald at Worcester and Aethelwold at Abingdon, with the active support of the West Saxon kings Edmund (939-46), Eadred (946-55) and Edgar (959-75), who made numerous restitutions of monastic property and many new grants of land (**6**).

One of the peculiar products of the tenth-century reform was the replacement of secular clerics by Benedictine monks in four English cathedrals (Canterbury, Winchester, Worcester and Sherborne). The estates of those churches in due course became divided, one part being designated for the support of the bishop, the other part being allocated to the monastic chapter. Domesday Book shows that the distinction had already been made before 1086.

At the same time, another important organisational change seems to have occurred, through the dismembering of large multiple estates, previously composed of economically-specialised components, into individual, self-contained vills or manors, each with their own field system and village nucleus. Glastonbury Abbey's estate on the Polden Hills, enlarged since the original grant of 729, had been fragmented into ten separate land units by the time of the Norman Conquest. Each portion then contained a separate village, some of which show clear evidence of planning, so the reorganisation of the estate may also have produced some major changes in the rural landscape.

A brief anti-monastic reaction followed King Edgar's death, particularly in western Mercia, where some communities were again dispersed and others were deprived of parts of their lands. By the end of the tenth century, the movement had recovered its strength but, as yet, it was confined to the southern half of England, no monasteries surviving north of the Wash.

The construction of monastic estates

Embedded within the Rule of St Benedict is an assumption that each monastery should attempt to be self-sufficient, drawing upon the resources of its own property for all its needs. The estates of the ancient Benedictine abbeys tended to span different types of countryside, thereby allowing for experiments in regional agricultural specialisation. As a matter of convenience, the home manors around the abbey itself were normally the main cereal production area, the source of most of the community's day-to-day requirements which needed

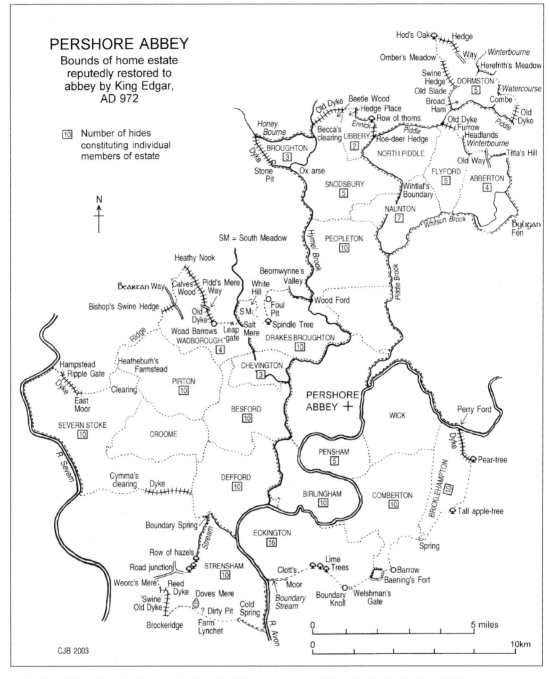

PERSHORE ABBEY
Bounds of home estate
reputedly restored to
abbey by King Edgar,
AD 972

[10] Number of hides
constituting individual
members of estate

N

SM = South Meadow

Hod's Oak — Hedge
Omber's Meadow — Way / Winterbourne
Herefrith's Meadow
Swine Hedge — DORMSTON [5]
Old Slade — Watercourse
Broad Ham — Combe
Beetle Wood — Old Dyke
Hedge Place — Old Dyke / Piddle
Old Dyke — Row of thorns
Ennick — Old Dyke — Furrow
Becca's clearing — LIBBERY [2] — Piddle — Headlands
Roe-deer Hedge — Winterbourne
Honey Bourne — NORTH PIDDLE — Old Way — Titta's Hill
BROUGHTON [3] — FLYFORD [5] — ABBERTON [4]
Dyke — Wihtlaf's Boundary
Stone Pit — Ox arse — Byrigan Fen
SNODSBURY [5] — NAUNTON [7] — Whitsun Brook

Heathy Nook — PEOPLETON [10]
Beartan Way — Pidd's Mere Way — Beornwynne's Valley
Calves Wood — White Hill — Wood Ford
Bishop's Swine Hedge — Old Dyke — Foul Pit — Spindle Tree
Woad Barrows — Leap-gate — Salt Mere — DRAKES BROUGHTON [10]
WADBOROUGH [4] — SM — CHEVINGTON [3]
Ridge — Heatheburh's Farmstead
Hampstead Ripple Gate — Clearing — PIRTON [10]
East Moor — BESFORD [10]
Dyke — PERSHORE ABBEY + — WICK — Perry Ford
SEVERN STOKE [10] — CROOME — Dyke — Pear-tree
PENSHAM [5] — BRICKLEHAMPTON [10] — Tall apple-tree
Cymma's clearing — Dyke — DEFFORD [10] — BIRLINGHAM [10] — COMBERTON [10]
R. Severn — ECKINGTON [16] — Spring
Boundary Spring — Lime Trees — Barrow
Row of hazels — Stream — Clott's — Baening's Fort
Road junction — STRENSHAM [10] — Moor — Welshman's Gate
Weorc's Mere — Reed Dyke — Doves Mere — Boundary Stream — Boundary Knoll
'Swine' Old Dyke — ? Dirty Pit — Cold Spring
Brockeridge — Farm Lynchet — R. Avon

0 ___ 5 miles
0 ___ 10km

CJB 2003

6 *Pershore Abbey (Worcestershire): detailed bounds of the home estate in 972. After Della Hooke, 1990*

the greatest attention. Resources which were poorly represented or unavailable within the home estate, such as pasture, woodland, and perhaps also fisheries and minerals, would be acquired at a greater distance. This characteristic pattern of complementary land use is well illustrated by a group of abbeys in the west midlands. St Peter's Abbey, Gloucester, had valuable properties in the Cotswolds and the Forest of Dean as well as much land in the Severn Valley. Evesham Abbey had about a dozen manors close by in the Avon Valley, a further concentration of property around Stow-on-the-Wold in the Cotswolds and one or two scattered manors elsewhere (**7**). Pershore Abbey also had lands both in the Avon Valley and up on the Cotswolds. Worcester Cathedral Priory had 26 manors scattered through the Avon and Severn valleys and over the Cotswolds, with further lands in the less developed countryside of Feckenham Forest and the Teme Valley.

Sometimes the importance of the home estate was endorsed by special administrative arrangements. At the core of Glastonbury Abbey's property was a liberty known as the Twelve Hides, originating in land grants of the late seventh century, within which the abbey enjoyed valuable fiscal and jurisdictional privileges. Evesham Abbey's block of Vale properties was already constituted as a separate deanery by the 1030s.

By contrast, the ancient Benedictine nunneries of Shaftesbury, Wilton, Romsey and St Mary's, Winchester, all held their most valuable demesnes at a distance, sometimes more than 20 or 30 miles away, possibly simply in order to avoid the responsibilities and distractions involved in direct management of a large home estate (**8**).

Following the initial foundation endowments, most houses attempted to strengthen their position by attracting further donations, and many monastic holdings underwent considerable expansion between the tenth and thirteenth centuries. Concerns about the amount of land passing to the church and the consequent loss of feudal dues eventually led Edward I to enact the Statute of Mortmain in 1279. This was intended to limit the unauthorised donation of land to monasteries. In effect, however, it simply handed the prerogative over to the king, who remained willing to accept payments from monastic houses for licences permitting them to acquire land. Many such licences are recorded in the Patent Rolls. However, by this time few monasteries were any longer attracting substantial new donations, and the statute was aimed against a process which was already in decline.

When gifts of land began to dry up, there were other ways of extending or rationalising the estates, by exchange or purchase. Abbot Thomas Marlborough bought 100 acres of land at Abbots Morton, Lenchwick and Sambourne for Evesham Abbey in 1230, while Abbot John Ombersley paid £30 for various houses and lands to increase the abbey's holding in Ombersley. Barbara Harvey has shown that Westminster Abbey was also beginning to buy land on a significant scale from the 1230s onwards, and continued to do so to 1390.

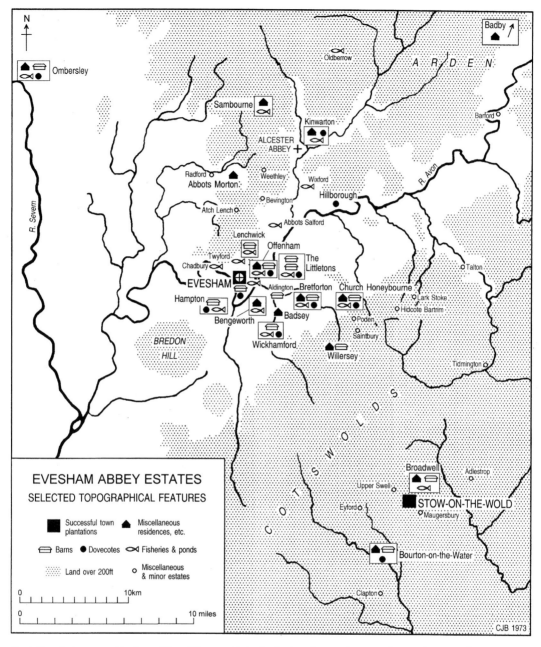

7 *A Benedictine estate: Evesham Abbey (Worcestershire), distribution of properties across the complementary farming regions of the Vale and the Cotswolds, showing selected topographical features*

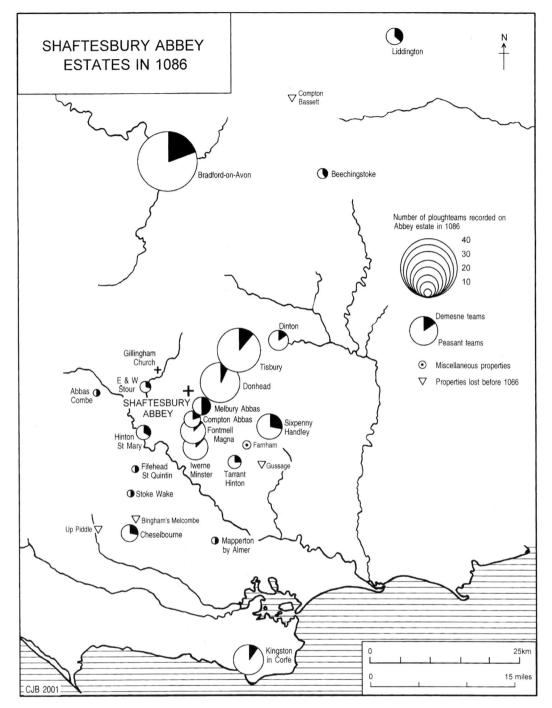

SHAFTESBURY ABBEY ESTATES IN 1086

N

Liddington

Compton Bassett

Bradford-on-Avon

Beechingstoke

Number of ploughteams recorded on Abbey estate in 1086

40
30
20
10

Demesne teams

Peasant teams

Miscellaneous properties

Properties lost before 1066

Dinton

Gillingham Church

Tisbury

E & W Stour

Abbas Combe

SHAFTESBURY ABBEY

Donhead

Melbury Abbas

Compton Abbas

Fontmell Magna

Sixpenny Handley

Hinton St Mary

Farnham

Fifehead St Quintin

Iwerne Minster

Tarrant Hinton

Gussage

Stoke Wake

Bingham's Melcombe

Up Piddle

Cheselbourne

Mapperton by Almer

Kingston in Corfe

0   25km

0   15 miles

8 *A nunnery estate: properties of Shaftesbury Abbey (Dorset) in 1086; the nuns' most valuable property, Bradford-on-Avon, was, characteristically, over 20 miles from the abbey*

Purchases in this period included some entire manors, such as Deerhurst in Gloucestershire and Hendon in Middlesex, which had been granted away in the twelfth century, and were now restored to the abbey demesnes. New purchases, such as Great Amwell in Hertfordshire, bought in 1270, or Stangraves in Kent, bought around 1315, lay in areas where the abbey already had considerable holdings, and must be seen as a process of consolidation. No purchases are recorded during the fifteenth century, but there was a final flurry of activity in the first decade of the sixteenth century, when Abbot John Islip bought a number of scattered manors with funds provided by Henry VII for the endowment of his chantry in the abbey church.

Differences between the monastic orders

Significant differences can be recognised between the various monastic orders in the nature and extent of the holdings they possessed. These differences arose partly through their differing ideological stances on the permissibility of various forms of income, partly through variations in the resources of those who endowed them, and partly through the times and places of their settlement, the later reformed orders tending to have more limited access to the best-quality arable land.

The older Benedictine estates tended to be concentrated in anciently-settled, fertile, low-lying countryside where there was a strong emphasis on arable farming. They were normally made up of a number of complete manors. Each manor included both demesne land worked on the abbey's behalf through the labour services of its peasant tenants under the supervision of a reeve or bailiff, and land farmed by the peasants for their own sustenance. The demesne tended to retain its integrity as a unit, even though it could from time to time be leased out for rent. On the more distant pastoral and woodland properties, management practices might be more flexible.

Nearly 200 more Benedictine monasteries and over 60 nunneries were endowed between 1066 and 1200, but with a few exceptions, such as Battle and Shrewsbury, the new foundations rarely matched the prestige or landed wealth of the pre-Conquest abbeys. Many of the new Norman lords preferred to give lands in England to continental houses such as Bec, Lyre, Séez and Fécamp. Managing English properties effectively from across the Channel was difficult, but endowments were sometimes included for the establishment of small dependent 'alien' priories.

The Augustinian Canons, whose rule was first adopted in England at Colchester soon after 1100, had some landed estates, but their relatively late arrival on the scene meant that they had generally missed out on the chance to acquire many grants of entire manors. Instead, Augustinian estates were usually made up by piecemeal gifts and purchases, improved by assarts and reclamation.

Their demesne lands were often relatively small, being formed around a nucleus of glebe-land belonging to appropriated churches (see chapter 12). A significantly higher proportion of their income (about 36 per cent on the eve of the Dissolution) was derived from their possession of churches.

The reformed orders such as the Cistercians, who first settled in England at Waverley in 1128, and the Premonstratensians, who first settled at Newhouse in Lincolnshire in 1143, were in a rather different position. Cistercian regulations initially forbade any revenue from churches, mills, courts or fairs. As relative latecomers, they too had little chance of acquiring substantial donations in the old-settled regions, and they tended to find most of their endowments in upland, marshland or woodland areas. The early statutes of the Cistercian order, which insist upon settlement 'remote from the concourse of men' were, in reality, doing little more than making a virtue out of necessity. The Cistercians were, therefore, cast in the role of pioneer farmers, often specialising in pastoral farming, in particular creating vast sheep-runs. They developed a distinctive form of management based upon *granges*, consolidated estate farms which lay entirely outside the manorial system, worked initially by lay brothers (**9**).

However, while there were significant differences between Benedictine and Cistercian estates, these should not be overemphasised. Despite their propaganda, it was rare for the Cistercians to settle in a complete wilderness. They still needed cultivable land nearby sufficient to support the community, and they usually compromised by seeking a site as secluded as possible on the margins of old-settled countryside. Many Cistercian granges specialised in arable farming, and came to develop ranges of buildings such as could be found on a Benedictine manor, while the Benedictines and Augustinians themselves learned from and imitated Cistercian practices. In later years, as more monastic estates were rented out, the differences receded still further.

The Dominicans, Franciscans and other orders of friars who appeared in the thirteenth century originated as mendicants, and were not supposed to hold even communal property, though in due course friary precincts with extensive gardens and orchards came to occupy significant areas within towns.

Finally, the English and Welsh endowments of the military orders, the Knights Templars and Knights Hospitallers, were acquired primarily to create profits which could be relayed on to the knights' main theatre of operations in the east and as places of recruitment and training. Most of their estates were organised through preceptories and commanderies which, in many ways, resembled the Cistercian granges.

Changes in management practices

During the first few hundred years of Benedictine monasticism in England some of the ideals of self-sufficiency persisted. Many of the greater

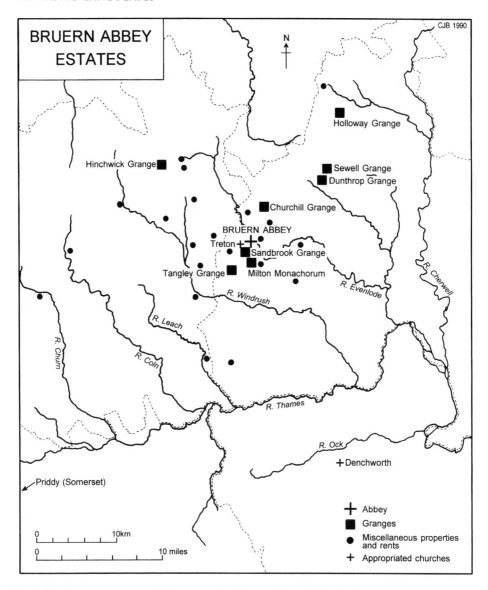

9 *A Cistercian estate: granges and other properties of Bruern Abbey (Oxfordshire)*

Benedictine houses had acquired sufficiently extensive landed estates to develop a food-farm system resembling that of the itinerant Anglo-Saxon royal household, whereby each constituent property was responsible for supplying produce for the maintenance of the monastic community for part of the year, usually for two or three weeks. There was, however, one significant difference: the monks were tied to their precinct, and, unlike kings, bishops or secular lords, were unable to move around their estates consuming the produce of each property in turn. The reorganisation of the ancient multiple estates into separate demesnes may have been carried out in order to manage some portions more intensively, thereby securing a more reliable food supply. Sometimes, as in the system organised for Ely by Abbot Leofsige in the 1030s, one group of properties was held as a contingency reserve in case any of the farms failed to deliver.

However, no monastic community could operate an entirely closed subsistence economy. The costs of transporting produce into the abbey from scattered distant demesnes and the risks of wastage could be high, and it made more sense to sell that produce and to use the cash to purchase necessities from markets nearer home. By the late eleventh century food renders in kind were generally in decline, being commuted into cash payments, though vestiges of the old system lingered on. By 1285 Canterbury Cathedral Priory had reorganised its manors into two groups, the tenants of the home estates in Kent continuing to supply corn and to carry it to the abbey's barns, the more distant manors rendering exclusively cash. On the Ely estates nearly 30 manors always seem to have lain entirely outside the food-farm system, and though some of them may have returned rents in kind, most of them served as cash farms.

As the Benedictine rule placed responsibility for food supply upon the cellarer, so Dunstan's reform gave the cellarer charge of all the abbey estates in order to save other monks from having to travel beyond the precinct. The cellarer often retained overall control of estate administration even after the Norman Conquest. However, either through the wishes of donors or as a result of administrative convenience, incomes from specific properties increasingly became earmarked for particular purposes. Firstly, some lands were allocated to the abbot for his personal use. Other manors were assigned towards the support of other monastic officials and their departments; while revenues from certain properties belonging to Canterbury Cathedral Priory and to the Old Minster at Winchester were reserved for the purpose of providing clothing to the monks.

Even before the Norman Conquest a practice had developed whereby properties were leased out, often for a term of two or more lives, in exchange for an initial sum and an annual render, either in cash or in kind. The advantage of this arrangement was that it stabilised the abbey's revenues, but the risk was that, as the descendants of the original lessees built up a bigger stake in the land, they came to think of it as their own, and the abbey often encountered difficulty in retrieving possession. The evidence for these processes is often open to alternative interpretations, as was demonstrated by a controversy between Professor M.M. Postan and Reginald Lennard in the 1950s. Postan believed that the surveys of the Glastonbury estates revealed a slow contraction in the abbey's demesne during the often disturbed times of the twelfth century, when the effective management of distant manors would have been difficult. The number of plough-teams employed by the abbot in 1201 was only 60 per cent of the total in 1086, the numbers of cattle had declined by the same amount, and the decline in sheep flocks was even greater, while labour services were also being commuted to cash rents. Lennard, however, argued that the decline in plough-teams indicated not a contraction of demesne arable, but a change in the terms of farming leases, and that the other phenomena noted by Postan were fortuitous and localised and did not represent a general trend of declining cultivation and rising rents.

During the more settled times of the late twelfth and early thirteenth centuries a growing population pushed up the demand for agricultural produce of all sorts, and prices rose. Direct management of land, for profit as well as subsistence, became increasingly attractive, and to take advantage of the rapidly expanding market many enterprising abbots began taking their demesnes back in hand. This period witnessed the zenith of Benedictine high farming, when the demesne acreages were increased by any means possible, including purchase, and productivity was improved through woodland clearance, drainage and reclamation. From the profits many abbeys embarked upon extensive building works.

The tide began to turn early in the fourteenth century, when population growth faltered. A series of bad harvests led to famine conditions in many areas, especially during the years 1315-17. The first outbreak of the Black Death, in 1349, reduced the population of Britain by between 30 and 50 per cent. Successive outbreaks in 1361 and 1369 prevented any rapid recovery. Declining prices for agricultural produce and rising labour costs now made it increasingly difficult for monasteries and secular lords alike to continue the direct farming of their demesnes, and it became more advantageous to lease them out to lay tenants in exchange for a fixed cash rent. On the Canterbury estates the leasing of virtually all of the manorial demesnes was achieved by the end of the fourteenth century. The leases, taken up by emerging yeomen and prosperous peasant farmers, sometimes by manorial officials, were initially often for a limited term of no more than ten years, and some vestiges of the old food-farm system continued on those Kentish manors where the farmers were required to send in a fixed annual quantity of wheat and barley as well as a cash rent. By the fifteenth century the priory was leasing out entire manors, not just the demesnes, on much longer-term leases, and the corn-rents were commuted for a cash equivalent. Durham Priory was leasing out a few of its demesnes by the 1370s, and between 1408 and 1416 all but two of its manors went out on lease. By the Dissolution most abbeys were leasing most of their property, often retaining only a single home farm in hand, and perhaps retaining for the abbot's use a small select group of isolated country residences, former manor-houses now divorced from their agricultural estates.

This paints a general picture of the main chronological changes in the ways in which monastic estates were managed, but in practice there was much variation. Idiosyncratic local decisions by abbots who failed to read the economic signs correctly, or who had some personal agenda of their own, often went against general economic trends. Worcester Priory continued to commute labour services and to lease out its demesnes well into the middle of the thirteenth century, and was selling most of its demesne crops and buying in most of its supplies from the market before the 1290s, while Westminster Abbey temporarily reverted to the practice of consuming its own demesne produce for a time in the fourteenth century. Some houses continued demesne farming long after it had been abandoned elsewhere. Permanent leasing of the demesnes on a large scale did not begin on the Canterbury Cathedral Priory estates before the 1370s, while the abbeys of Abingdon and Tavistock struggled on with direct exploitation well into the fifteenth century. Some blocks of land alternated between being kept in hand and farmed out, such as Bolton Priory's grange at Kildwick. At the same time as Canterbury Cathedral Priory was extending its leasehold system during the fifteenth century, it also introduced the innovation of keeping one or another of its Kentish manors in hand to be exploited directly.

Despite the general background of decline in the rural economy in the later Middle Ages, the upkeep of manorial property remained a seignurial responsibility, and some monastic houses still managed to maintain their demesnes in reasonable condition. A list of works undertaken by Prior John Fossor of Durham (1341-74) includes within the precinct a new larder, chapel, hay barn for the guesthouse, stables, forge, malthouse and granary, repairs to the brewhouse roof and the gable of a chapel over the gate, the rebuilding of the mill and the making of a new mill dam 140ft long, and further works on the outlying estates, including barns at Estrington and Allerton, two dairies, a byre and sheepcote at Beaurepaire and a stable and dairy at Pittington. Abbot Walter Monington of Glastonbury (1342-75) was still building barns and cowhouses at Butleigh, Lympsham, Walton, Street, Batcombe, East Pennard, Badbury, Ashbury and Sturminster Newton. Abbot William Boys (1345-67) continued to acquire tenements, cottages and land and to spend money on the great grange and summer hall at Evesham. The accounts of Merevale Abbey in the 1490s record repairs to the barns and stables within the precinct, to the barns on the granges at Moorbarn, Woodbarn, Witherley and Twycross and to the dovecotes at Orton-on-the-Hill and Mancetter. The priors of Canterbury, too, continued spending considerable sums on the upkeep and improvement of manorial farm buildings throughout the fifteenth century.

Conflicts over land

In the amassing of landed property it was inevitable that conflicts would occur, between abbeys and donors' families, between abbeys, tenants and commoners, and even between neighbouring abbeys. Disagreements were especially likely to occur where boundaries were ill-defined, in areas of marshland or upland pasture where intercommoning practices held sway. The medieval history of the Fenland is marked by disputes involving the Benedictine abbeys around its margins, as is the history of the Somerset moors by quarrels between Glastonbury Abbey and its neighbours. The Cistercians of Fountains and the Augustinians of Bolton and Bridlington were involved in a series of legal conflicts over grazing lands in the Yorkshire Dales throughout the fourteenth century

As a safeguard against such disputes, the Cistercian statutes required that none of their houses should be established within 10 Burgundian leagues (probably about 25 miles) of a pre-existing one, and that granges belonging to different abbeys should be at least 2 leagues apart. The Cistercians also entered into an agreement with the Premonstratensians in 1142 that neither order should establish a new house within two leagues of an existing house belonging to the other. In practice these instructions could be obeyed only by the earliest foundations, which still had a relatively clear field. After the middle of the twelfth century, as new Cistercian foundations proliferated, disputes became inevitable. Neath Abbey found its more westerly lands subject to frequent pillage by the Welsh, but was unable to expand its holdings in the other direction because of the foundation of Margam Abbey, only 8 miles to the east. The monks contemplated moving across the Bristol Channel to their Somerset property at Exford in 1199, but there found themselves baulked by the new foundation at Cleeve, only 12 miles away. Both Neath and Forde Abbeys had protested that the settlement of Cleeve would damage their interests, but without success. The monks of Salley raised similar objections in 1283 when the monks of Stanlaw, driven from their original site by coastal flooding, moved to Whalley, only 7 miles away; again the protests were unsuccessful. However, the Cistercians of Rievaulx did manage to enforce the removal of the Savignac monks who had settled nearby at Old Byland in 1143, and the younger community moved twice more before making its final settlement, though it retained Old Byland as a grange.

When the Cistercian abbey of Dieulacresse was founded in north Staffordshire in 1214, its abbot was permitted to accept lands within the nearby manor of Leek, but not to acquire any lands within a mile of the older-established Cistercian house of Croxden. Croxden was subject to no such restriction, and was exempted from payment of tithes on lands in Leek parish which it cultivated itself. In 1251 the terms of this agreement were broken when Dieulacresse acquired land at Fieldhead, a mile south-east of Croxden. The dispute was resolved only when Dieulacresse promised not to acquire any further land near Croxden or its grange of 'the Leyes' without its consent. Croxden allowed Dieulacresse to retain its new property and agreed not to accept any land there itself, in exchange for which it acquired freedom from tolls and market dues in Leek, and the right to enclose land at Onecote and Pithills.

It would be vain to hope that monasteries took a more philanthropic attitude to their tenants than lay landowners. When the foundation endowment of a new monastery consisted of a run-down estate where dues from peasants had not been pursued particularly energetically, the new regime often came as a considerable shock. Following the foundations of the Premonstratensian houses of Halesowen and Titchfield during the first half of the thirteenth century, their respective abbots, faced with large building bills, both embarked upon a policy of maximising incomes from rents, fines, and sales of corn and wool and insisted that traditional labour services were performed or commuted for cash. The resentment among the peasant tenants smouldered on for many years, occasionally breaking out into violence.

Alienations of monastic estates

The extent of monastic landholdings was never fixed and immutable, and there were losses as well as gains. Even ancient donations recorded by royal charter provided no real guarantee that a religious community could keep the lands it had been given. During the first period of Anglo-Saxon foundations, lands in frontier zones were especially vulnerable to the vagaries of political fortune. Some time around 750, King Aethelbald of Mercia gave the wealthy royal minster of Cookham in Berkshire to the cathedral church of Canterbury. After Aethelbald's death in 757 the Thames Valley passed to King Cynewulf of Wessex, who arranged for the deeds of Cookham to be stolen from Canterbury and brought to him so that he could regain the estate. Control of the Thames was then wrested back from Cynewulf by King Offa of Mercia, who, in his turn, refused to return the property to the church. Canterbury never regained Cookham, and Archbishop Aethelheard finally abandoned his claim to it in exchange for some lands in north Kent.

Inadequate custodianship, the depredations of the Danes and the anti-monastic reaction in Mercia after 975 all resulted in the alienation of much monastic property before the Norman Conquest. However, the losses were not irrevocable. Sometimes the lands of a defunct community were transferred to a new or resurrected one. Minster-in-Thanet, site of an early double community, was given by King Cnut to St Augustine's Abbey, Canterbury, and became its most important single property. A substantial part of the lands seized after 975 by Ealdorman Aelfhere of Mercia from the monasteries of Deerhurst and Pershore was later given by Edward the Confessor to Westminster Abbey. Pershore retained its autonomy, though in a reduced condition, shorn of half of its wealth; but Deerhurst never recovered from the blow, being reduced to a mere dependency of the Abbey of St Denis in Paris. The abandoned northern monasteries of Lindisfarne, Jarrow, Monkwearmouth and Stamford were all recolonised as dependencies of Durham during the 1080s, while

Hackness and, briefly, Lastingham, became part of the Whitby estate. The ancient monastic lands of Cholsey and Leominster were confirmed by Henry I to his new foundation at Reading in 1125, and Leominster was re-established some years later as a dependent priory. Conventual life was never resumed at Cholsey, but it became one of Reading's most valuable possessions (**30**).

After the Norman Conquest, King William imposed the obligation of supplying quotas of knights for the royal service on 24 of the larger English monasteries. Those which bore the greatest burden were Peterborough, required to supply 60 knights, Glastonbury and Bury St Edmunds with 40 knights each, followed by Abingdon (30), Winchester New Minster (20), Tavistock, Westminster and St Augustine's, Canterbury (each with 15 knights) and Coventry (10). Generally it was left to each abbey to work out the most effective way of meeting this requirement, and it was often achieved by allotting parts of the estates to the knights as military tenants. Small earthen castles sometimes distinguish such sites on the ground. Toot Hill in the Dean's garden at Peterborough is the motte of one such castle. On the outskirts of Abingdon is a much-eroded ringwork which lay at the centre of a five-hide property allocated to a knight called Owen, from one of whose descendants, Hugh FitzHenry, the property took its name of Fitzharris. This continued to function as a separate manor until 1248, when it was finally absorbed back into the abbey's estate.

The creation of royal forests sometimes prompted exchanges of land. Westminster Abbey was persuaded to relinquish lands at Windsor originally given to it by Edward the Confessor, but now required for afforestation by William the Conqueror, in exchange for several rather more valuable manors in Surrey and Essex. Further reorganisations became necessary when the system of cathedral priories was extended. The creation of a new see at Ely in 1109 resulted in a settlement whereby the monks retained control of two relatively compact blocks of manors in Cambridgeshire and Suffolk, while the bishop received lands scattered through 50 manors in six different counties.

Intermittent alienations of monastic lands recurred throughout the later Middle Ages. Properties belonging to houses in France were confiscated during periods of international conflict, in 1295-1303 and in 1374-1404, ending with the suppression of all the alien priories in 1414. The suppression of the Knights Templars in 1312 led to the sequestration of their property, and despite a papal decree that it should be handed on to the Hospitallers, King Edward II gave some of the land to his own favourites and creditors, while other portions were reclaimed by the heirs of the original Templar patrons. A number of smaller monastic houses failed to survive through the later Middle Ages for a variety of reasons.

However, these remain exceptional cases. On balance, monastic estates stood a much better chance of long-term continuity of ownership than those in secular hands.

3
Arable farming
on monastic estates

Monastic literature on farming and estate management

Medieval monastic libraries contained two types of literature on farming. The first was an inheritance from the classical world, copies of treatises by Roman authors. Abbot Wheathampstead of St Albans had a copy made of Cato's *De Agricultura*; although this text is largely concerned with olive plantations and other aspects of Mediterranean farming, its emphasis on self-sufficiency within the estate could be expected to appeal to the Benedictine mind. Copies of the agricultural manual of Columella existed in the libraries of St Augustine's Abbey in Canterbury, Durham, Waltham, Worcester and Byland. Whether such copies were made with any thought of practical utility or merely out of antiquarian or literary interest, we can only speculate.

The development of high farming in the thirteenth century promoted new concerns over the efficient management of estates, which in turn generated a new series of manuals on farming, estate management and accounting. Instructions on these topics were copied into the Gloucester cartulary in the time of Abbot John Gamages (1284-1306). Memoranda from the abbeys of Bury St Edmunds, Malmesbury, St Albans and Beaulieu show similar concerns. Most of the didactic writings on estate management were compiled for the use of lawyers, but the practical instructions on farming given by Walter of Henley, who later himself became a Dominican friar, had a wider appeal to monastic lords. Partial or entire copies of Walter's treatise are known from both great Benedictine houses in Canterbury, from Battle, Abbotsbury, Reading, Ramsey, Bury St Edmunds, Durham, Tynemouth and Luffield, and from the Augustinian priories of Mottisfont and Merton.

Bread and ale: the staples of a monastic diet

The purpose of farming was, of course, the production of food. Monastic rules and customs placed certain restrictions on what could be eaten, which varied from order to order. The Augustinian Rule imposed no extreme restraints, the Benedictine Rule forbade consumption of the flesh of four-footed beasts (although in later years this was relaxed), whereas the more austere orders such as the Carthusians and Grandmontines were subjected to a strict vegetarian diet. All orders, however, needed the produce of arable land for the two main staples of the monastic diet – bread and ale.

The Benedictine Rule permitted a daily allowance of 1lb of bread to each monk, though by the late Middle Ages consumption was sometimes twice that amount, and in Augustinian houses the allowance was even more generous. Several grades of bread were produced. The finest white wheat bread was consumed by the abbot and his guests; bread intended for the infirmary was also of superior quality; ordinary brown bread provided the monks' regular fare; while coarser bread, often made in part from oatmeal, rye or barley flour, was deemed sufficient for the hired labourers.

The daily allowance of ale for each monk or canon was often a gallon or more. However, if this sounds overindulgent, it must be remembered that little other drink was available. The quality of water was often suspect, and wine was costly. The basis of brewing was malt – grain in which the process of germination has been halted by heating in a kiln. Barley was the preferred cereal for malting, but where this was in short supply other grains, including wheat, oats and dredge (a mix of oats and barley) were used.

Assuming that a monastery lived up to the ideal of self-sufficiency, how much land would be needed to meet these basic needs? The standard conventual loaf weighed about 2lb after baking. Assuming production of 20 loaves from each bushel of grain, the average annual consumption of grain by each monk or canon would be in the region of 20 bushels. An acre of land could be expected to yield about 6 bushels of wheat a year in the Middle Ages, so an allowance of 2lb of bread a day would require around 3 acres of land for each member of the community. Similarly, 1 acre could be expected to give an annual yield of about 7 bushels of barley, and 1 bushel of unmalted barley might yield about 18-20 gallons of ale. Even at a consumption rate of 1 gallon per monk per day, this represents 20 bushels of barley a year; so the production of ale required around 2-3 acres of land for every member of the community. Assuming complete self-sufficiency in bread and ale, somewhere around 5 or 6 acres of land would be needed to supply each monk with these basic commodities. This estimate would be subject to considerable variation, depending upon the productivity of the soil. In reality, of course, matters were never that straightforward, because of the intervention of the market.

Buildings for producing bread and ale were normally located in the outer court of the monastery. Bakehouses with ovens have been excavated at Kirkstall, Thornholme, Mount Grace, Bradwell and Grove Priory, while brewhouses have been recognised at Waverley, Thornholme, Nuneaton and, less certainly, at Tintern, Waltham, St Neot's and the Templar preceptory at South Witham.

Cereal crops and their production

Most manors and granges practised, to a greater or lesser extent, a mixed farming economy. However, the vital necessity of ensuring adequate supplies of cereals, the labour-intensive nature of cereal cultivation and the need for adequate supervision meant that the main concentrations of arable land were often near the abbey.

Domesday Book, through its recording of demesne and peasant plough-teams, gives some impression of the relative importance of arable farming on monastic estates. Among the greater abbeys, Glastonbury retained the highest proportions of its land in demesne. On its valuable Wiltshire manor of Grittleton, there were 13 ploughs on the demesne, compared with seven operated by the peasant tenants. The overall proportion of demesne to peasant ploughs on the entire Glastonbury estate was around 1:1.6. However, this does not necessarily mean that the abbey's farming was more efficient or produc-tive. Michael Costen has shown that, compared with the lands of other local proprietors, the relationship of annual value to ploughlands remained relatively low on Glastonbury's property, and at this period the abbey seems to have responded to financial pressures by soliciting gifts of more land rather than exploiting its existing holdings more intensively. Ely Abbey had fewer large demesnes than Glastonbury, but nearly twice the number of smaller manors, where the proportion of demesne land was relatively high, the overall ratio of demesne to peasant ploughs here being about 1:1.9. Bury St Edmunds also emerges as an abbey with a strong interest in demesne farming at this time. By contrast, the records for Westminster Abbey and St Augustine's in Canterbury reveal much smaller proportions of their arable land held in demesne.

The 1189 survey of the Glastonbury estates records the ploughing-services owed to the abbey on its various manors. For example, at Winscombe each peasant holding half a virgate (a virgate might occupy between 15 and 40 acres) was required to plough three times during Lent with a complete team and to plough with as many oxen as he had at the abbot's plough-boons (extra labour services required from tenants at peak periods). A 'complete team' nominally comprised eight oxen throughout the early Middle Ages. A survey of Burton Abbey's home manor of around 1110-20 records two ploughs with 16 oxen, with four more oxen used for carting lime and a further four carting wood. However, both larger and smaller teams are recorded. The Gloucester cartulary records four teams of ten oxen each at Buckland near Broadway. Mixed teams and teams made up of horses alone were appearing in eastern England by the late twelfth century. Surveys of 23 manors of Ramsey Abbey during this period include 14 examples of mixed teams. When Abbot Samson of Bury St Edmunds leased out the manor of Semer around 1191, two of its three plough-teams consisted of six oxen and two horses apiece, while the third had eight horses. Though oxen were slower, they were hardier, demanded less fodder, and required less equipment such as collars, harness and shoes. They were still preferred for ploughing in the west of England long after horses had taken over in the east. The Evesham chronicle recounts how Abbot Thomas Marlborough 'provided ploughs in the Vale and at Ombersley, Morton, Sambourne and Badby, with a quality and number of oxen hitherto unknown in those parts'.

Through much of midland England regular open field systems prevailed, whereby the land of each township was divided into two or three large fields subdivided into furlongs and strips. The register of Winchcombe Abbey shows two-field systems operating on its manors of Cold Ashton and Sherborne, as does the cartulary of Bath Priory on its manors of Englishcombe and Weston. In 1396 extents were made of a number of manors belonging to Malmesbury Abbey, which show two fields at Brokenborough, Long Newnton and Cowfold with Norton, and three fields at Bremhill and Foxham, Charlton, Crudwell, Purton, Sutton and Kemble. Generally the basic arrangement of open fields remained stable, but on rare occasions it might undergo drastic reorganisation. Harold Fox has shown how Glastonbury Abbey replaced the old East and West Fields on its manor of Podimore by a new three-field arrangement between the harvest and autumn sowing of 1333, excavating a great ditch 6ft wide and 4ft deep to separate two of the new fields (**10**).

Sometimes the demesne land remained in scattered strips, intermingled with the strips of the peasant tenants, but often, as on the Bury St Edmunds manor of Worlingworth, it was concentrated in one area. Consolidated demesnes had the advantage of greater flexibility of use. Ramsey Abbey's demesne in Hemington in Northamptonshire consisted of 72 acres concentrated in a block called the Inlands at the west end of the vill, and by 1518 this had been enclosed and was down to a grass ley. The progressive farming developed by Battle Abbey on its Sussex estates in the fourteenth century was greatly assisted by the consolidation of most of its demesnes outside the common fields of its tenants.

Archaeological evidence of open-field strip farming can be seen in the corrugations of curved ridge and furrow which persist in many clayland areas beneath the superimposed patterns of later hedged enclosures. Here and there we also find indications of local pressures leading to intakes of marginal land. On the Glastonbury island the amount of land consumed by the abbey precinct, the town and the abbot's parks severely limited the space available for cultivation, and the tenants were forced to terrace even the steep slopes of Glastonbury Tor itself (**11**). Given the obvious difficulty of cultivating on such gradients, it is perhaps hardly surprising that 'alternative' interpretations of the 'Merlin's magic maze' variety have occasionally been mooted.

By contrast with the manorialised holdings of the Benedictines, in which the demesne was originally farmed by means of peasant labour services and

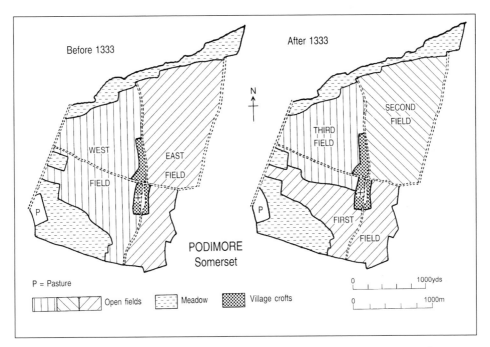

Before 1333   After 1333

SECOND
FIELD

THIRD
FIELD

WEST   EAST

FIELD   FIELD

P   P   FIRST

FIELD

N

PODIMORE
Somerset

P = Pasture

| | | | Open fields   Meadow   Village crofts

0   1000yds

0   1000m

10 *Podimore (Somerset): the reorganisation of the open fields from two to three fields in 1333.* After Harold Fox, 1986

11 *Glastonbury Tor (Somerset): medieval cultivation terraces on the steep slopes of the tor were a consequence of limited availability of land on the Glastonbury island*

remained subject to common grazing in the fallow year, and where common meadows and pastures were similarly shared between abbey and tenants, Cistercian granges were worked by lay brothers (and later by paid labourers) as exclusive, consolidated farms, unencumbered by communal rights. Granges were of varying size and character, but in areas of reasonably good farmland such as the Vale of York they regularly included 200-500 acres of arable land. Rievaulx Abbey's Kekmarish Grange in 1275-6 was estimated at 300 acres of arable and 300 acres of pasture. Meaux Abbey's grange at Tharlesthorpe consisted of 321 acres of arable, 152 acres of pasture and 100 acres of meadow a few decades later. In exceptional cases they could be much bigger. Meaux Abbey's Wharram Grange in 1396 included 1,100 acres of arable and 200 acres of meadow, while Fountains Abbey's Bradley Grange in 1497 consisted of 1,000 acres of arable, 2,000 acres of pasture, 1,000 acres of moor, 300 acres of wood and 100 acres of meadow.

For some years we can gain an idea of the proportions of crops grown over a whole monastic estate (**12**). In 1322 the four custodies of Christ Church, Canterbury, in south-east England included 2,677 acres under wheat, 2,385 acres under oats, 1,434 acres under barley and 367 acres under rye. Records of the quantities of grain threshed from four of the granges of Sibton Abbey in 1365, 1366 and 1367 amount to an average of 223 quarters of wheat, 214 quarters of barley, 204 quarters of oats and 18 quarters of rye per annum. Obviously the proportions of different crops varied, both according to location and year by year. On the Norwich Priory demesnes barley generally constituted 60 per cent of the crop, while wheat was more important on the Battle Abbey estates. From archaeological evidence, most of the wheat grown was bread wheat (*Triticum aestivum*), but there is also evidence for the cultivation of rivet or cone wheat (*Triticum turgidum*), which gave a softer mealy grain more suitable for biscuits or gruel.

Of the other cereal crops, oats mainly provided fodder for horses, but were also used to feed poultry and other livestock, while in times of shortage they could be used for malting or converted to meal or flour used in gruel, pottage or porridge. Oats were a particularly important crop on the granges of Strata Florida and Cwmhir in the colder, wetter areas of Wales, and in the north and west of England. They were also grown elsewhere, particularly on marginal land. Oats accounted for 44 per cent of Beaulieu Abbey's total arable production in 1269-70. On the Canterbury estates they comprised 29 per cent of the total arable acreage in 1322, but in the custody containing the manors around Romney Marsh the proportion rose to 40 per cent. Oats were an important crop on Crowland Abbey's estates in the early Middle Ages. On some of Ramsey Abbey's fen-edge manors, oats represented 50 per cent of all cereal production in the middle of the thirteenth century, but 50 years later they had almost disappeared from the rotation as the abbot turned large acreages over to sheep pasture.

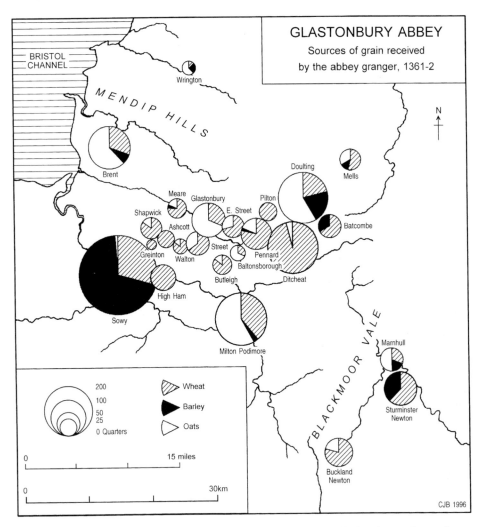

12 *Glastonbury Abbey: sources of grain received by the abbey granger, 1361-2.* Based upon figures from Ian Keil, 1961-7

Rye cultivation was quite widespread, particularly in areas of light soils, but it was the least important of the four main cereals. It accounted for only 3 per cent of the arable acreage on the Beaulieu estates in 1269-70, and only at the distant Coxwell grange did it cover over 100 acres. Similarly, only 4 per cent of the total arable acreage on the Canterbury estates was under rye in 1322, though the proportion was greater on the Essex manors (over 200 acres, comprising 11 per cent).

Wheat and rye were winter-sown crops; barley and oats were sown in the spring. Crop yields naturally varied greatly according to weather and soil conditions. Average sowings were of the order of 2-3 bushels per acre, and it was suggested by the author of one late thirteenth-century treatise that barley ought to yield eightfold, rye sevenfold, dredge, maslin (another mixed crop, wheat and rye), beans and peas sixfold, wheat fivefold and oats fourfold. These figures might be expected to represent ideal attainments, but on well-managed estates they were sometimes exceeded. Before 1350 the prior of Norwich's demesnes of Martham and Hemsby in east Norfolk regularly produced wheat harvests of 20 bushels per acre, in a good year as much as 30 bushels. Even in the later Middle Ages wheat yields on Battle Abbey's manor of Alciston regularly amounted to 12-16 bushels per acre. By contrast, yields on the Canterbury estates seem surprisingly low, averaging only 3:1 or 3.5:1 for wheat. Several abbeys used significantly higher sowing rates on their home demesnes than on their more distant properties. Christ Church, Canterbury, sowed barley on its Kentish manors at 5-6 bushels per acre, oats at 4-6 bushels and wheat at 3-4 bushels per acre, but only about two-thirds of those amounts elsewhere. Battle Abbey similarly employed much higher seeding rates in Sussex and Kent than on its distant estates in the Thames valley.

Crop rotations were quite flexible. Although on open-field manors one field would be left fallow in each year, the unit of cultivation on the other fields was normally the furlong, so that small areas of more specialised crops could be accommodated. The Huntingdonshire demesnes of Ramsey Abbey display a regular four-course rotation of barley, peas or vetches, wheat and fallow. Detailed surviving accounts of sowing and yields on individual furlongs on the Ramsey manor of Wistow in the later fourteenth century demonstrate the abbey's attempts at improvement, and its adjustments when things went wrong, as in 1393, when it was realised that the extension of wheat and barley at the expense of legumes had resulted in falling yields.

Whether demesne cereal produce went directly towards the sustenance of the community or was regarded as a cash crop varied from house to house and from period to period. Canterbury Cathedral priory was producing surpluses for market from an early period, and was shipping some of its corn abroad by 1207. Continental abbeys such as Bec naturally found it more convenient to sell the grain from their English estates. By contrast, almost all the grain produced by Bolton Priory in the early fourteenth century was consumed by the canons themselves. On another Augustinian estate, Oseney, near Oxford, most grain was consumed on the abbey's manors or sent in to the conventual granary, and only limited surpluses, unpredictable from year to year, reached the market.

In bad seasons even prosperous houses might be driven to look beyond their own estates for supplies. In the famine year of 1189 the Cistercians of Margam were forced to buy corn in Bristol and in Ireland, while the Abbot of Neath was buying corn in England in 1234. Several Cistercian and Premonstratensian houses in the north-west, Furness, Holm Cultram, and Cockersand, regularly imported grain from Ireland. A few houses, like Malton Priory in Yorkshire, elected to concentrate on pastoral farming, buying in most of their grain.

Peas, beans and vetches

Broad beans, peas and other legumes were grown as a field crop in many parts of England. They provided feed for horses, pigs and pigeons, and were an important constituent of soups and pottages consumed in the refectory. They were often dried for keeping through the year. Pulses had the additional virtues of replenishing nitrates in the soil and inhibiting weed growth, and they played a critical part in the improvement of agriculture during the high farming period. During the thirteenth century Battle Abbey began using legumes in rotation to reduce fallows on its Sussex coastal manors, particularly on its best arable land in Alciston and Lullington, where up to half of the arable acreage bore a continuous sequence of crops with no adverse effects on yields. The increasing amounts of corn sown on some of Ramsey Abbey's demesnes after 1320 can also be related to the increasing use of legumes.

Legumes accounted for 18 per cent of the total sown acreage of the Canterbury demesnes in 1322, rising to 28 per cent in East Kent. Peas were usually sown at a rate of 5 bushels per acre, beans and vetches at 4 bushels per acre. On Canterbury's manor of Agney and on Battle Abbey's land at Dengemarsh, both on Romney Marsh, legumes regularly occupied over a quarter of the demesne arable acreage in the later thirteenth and early fourteenth centuries. Beaulieu Abbey received 218 quarters of vetch, 127 quarters of peas and 97 quarters of beans from ten of its New Forest granges in 1269-70, and further purchases by the granarian suggest that this was insufficient to meet the need. Eight out of 11 Oseney Abbey barns contained some peas and vetches in the early fourteenth century, the quantities varying from 16 quarters up to 108 quarters.

Minor crops

Flax and hemp had been cultivated in small quantities since before the Norman Conquest, particularly near marshy areas, where water was available for retting (separating the fibres by soaking the harvested plants for a couple of weeks). Land at Westhoughton granted to the Premonstratensian canons of Cockersand around 1200 included a flax-retting pool. At the end of the fifteenth century, St Augustine's Abbey in Bristol was receiving tithes of flax from several low-lying manors in north Somerset and the Severn Valley. New crops introduced from the Low Countries made some appearance on monastic lands in east Norfolk: coleseed or rape was grown on Norwich Priory's demesne at Monks Grange, Pockthorpe, by about 1255, and over 55 stones of madder were sold from there in 1305-6. Buckwheat or brank, a crop of Asian origin, first appears in Norfolk in 1480, and small quantities were grown on the manor of Wroxham belonging to the nuns of Carrow by 1530.

Improving the land: weeding, manuring, marling and liming

Progressive Benedictine houses like Battle, Canterbury and Norwich made considerable efforts to improve the fertility of their soils. Animals grazing on fallow fields deposited dung randomly, but much of its value was lost through leaching and oxidisation. During the high farming period the practice of stall-feeding increased the supply of farmyard manure, which was collected, carted out to the fields, spread and ploughed in, thereby producing much greater benefit. Lime and marl were used on Canterbury's Romney Marsh manors to neutralise the acidity of the peat. Even at the small Benedictine cell of Earls Colne it is recorded that Prior William in the early thirteenth century improved all the unproductive land with a dressing of marl, while a payment for transport of marl at Jarrow Priory is recorded in 1357-8. Tavistock Abbey made considerable efforts to improve its stony, phosphate-deficient lands through the application of farmyard manure and sea-sand and the practice of beat-burning (burning pared turf and gorse and scattering the ashes before ploughing). On Cistercian estates too there are records of liming or marling from Tintern, Abbey Dore, Beaulieu and Fountains, and of muck-spreading at the granges of Tintern and Neath.

Grants made to the Premonstratensian canons of Beauchief in the late thirteenth century included liberty to cleanse their lands and those of their tenants of *goldae* (presumably some sort of yellow-flowered weeds, corn marigolds, charlock or coltsfoot), and if they found any fault with the cleansing they might take fines of their tenants.

4
Livestock farming on monastic estates

Introduction

Animals provided transport, draught power for ploughing and harrowing, meat, milk, hides or wool, and manure. These needs were universal, and some livestock were present on all monastic manors. However, monasteries also developed more specialised forms of livestock farming, which required more extensive grazing lands than could be provided by the fallow course of an arable rotation. They achieved this either by dedicating suitable parts of their own land to pasture for their exclusive use, or by acquiring grazing rights on commons. Two types of country in particular provided extensive pastures with little or no competition from arable farming: the low-lying marshlands of the Fens, Somerset Levels, Romney Marsh and Holderness; and the uplands of Wales, Mendip, the limestone and chalk scarplands, the Pennines, North Yorkshire Moors and Cheviots. The Cistercian houses of Fountains, Jervaulx and Furness in particular held vast tracts of upland moor around the Yorkshire Dales.

There was much competition for access to good pasture. Fountains Abbey and Bolton Priory both had grazing rights on the fells above Malham, and disputes between them in the thirteenth century were eventually resolved by building a boundary wall to divide the pasture, Bolton retaining exclusive rights to the east and Fountains to the west. In 1279 the tenants of the abbeys of Fountains and Salley accused each other of allowing their stock to graze over the other's pastures on Kilnsey, Arncliffe and Litton Moors, and the grangers of the two abbeys were ordered to erect great stones marked with crosses along the disputed boundary in order to delimit their respective rights. Bolton Priory was involved in further disputes with Bridlington Priory over pastures above Wharfedale in Washburn and Blubberhouses, and again with Fountains in 1300 after it purchased the manor of Appletreewick, in which Fountains also claimed pasture rights.

Seasonal movement of stock between upland and lowland pastures was especially common in the north, sometimes over considerable distances. Fountains

Abbey pastured some of its cattle in Allerdale, 60 miles away in Cumberland. In Wales transhumance of cattle exceeded that of sheep. In southern England similar movements of sheep flocks can be detected between the Cotswolds and the Severn Valley, and between the Weald, the Downs and Romney Marsh. Wayleave agreements were often needed to cross other proprietors' land, and in 1312 Fountains acquired right of free passage for its cattle throughout the Craven district of Yorkshire. It also negotiated the right to bring 460 sheep down Wharfedale for shearing and overwintering at Kettlewell. During the early thirteenth century the canons of Alvingham Priory had to give a landowner at North Conesby one sheep from their flocks in exchange for a right of access over his meadows to their sheepwash. Buildwas Abbey acquired access to a sheepwash on the River Severn in 1292.

Another feature of monastic stock farming was the excavation of ponds for watering: the monks of Salley Abbey acquired consent from another farmer in Barrowby shortly before 1300 to make a drinking pond for their cattle, 40ft square.

The balance between arable and pastoral farming, and between different types of livestock, was constantly changing. Until the middle of the twelfth century, when the primary task of the estates was still to provide subsistence, and when prohibitions on meat-eating were still generally observed, crop production was more important than pastoral farming, and cattle generally more valued than sheep. As the policy of direct demesne exploitation for the market developed during the later twelfth century, sheep numbers multiplied at the expense of cattle. This change can be detected over most of Britain, but is particularly evident amongst the Cistercian abbeys of Yorkshire which were beginning to export wool to the continent. Meaux Abbey was already converting some of its cattle-sheds to sheepcotes by the late twelfth century, and through the following century cattle pastures were increasingly being turned over to sheep. By the fourteenth century Meaux had between four and ten times more head of sheep than cattle. In Wales sheep farming became dominant in the more accessible parts of the south and north-east, but cattle remained important on the lands of the smaller, poorer Cistercian houses of mid-Wales.

West of the Pennines the size of monastic flocks was beginning to decline even before 1400, and cattle were once more gaining ground. In Yorkshire sheep remained important longer, but here too a fall in numbers is evident well before the Dissolution. As the export market dwindled, so pastoral farming once more became limited to serving the monastic community's own subsistence needs. Many of the stock farms were subdivided and leased, but the tenants were still often required to act as keepers of monastic flocks and herds, delivering agreed quantities of dairy produce, wool or hides to the abbey each year.

Cattle

Despite the rise of sheep farming, cattle remained important on Cistercian estates in mid-Wales, in the north-west and south-west of England, and in the Fenland. Cattle herds were numbered in the hundreds of heads rather than the thousands. Kirkstall Abbey had 618 cattle in 1301. Furness Abbey had about 600 oxen and 260 cows on its Cumberland, Lancashire and Yorkshire granges in 1297, compared to 5,000 sheep. Bolton Priory's cattle herd never exceeded 500 head during the early fourteenth century, while its sheep numbered over 3,000. Cattle numbers on the Meaux estate show a general decline from some 500-600 in the early fourteenth century down to about 270 in 1399. The herd belonging to Margam, most productive of the Welsh Cistercian abbeys, in 1291 consisted of only 425 cattle, but this was more than three times the size of the herd of its nearest Welsh rival. Cattle were individually four times the value of sheep, so even relatively modest numbers could represent a significant market value.

In the north of England specialised dairy farms and cattle-breeding stations known as *vaccaries* were often established at the heads of the dales, combining the complementary resources of enclosed valley hay-meadows and unenclosed fellside grazing. Byland Abbey's vaccary at Combe was founded in the late 1140s, while Meaux Abbey established its first vaccary before 1151. During the later thirteenth and early fourteenth centuries vaccaries were established in the Lake District by Fountains Abbey at Stonethwaite in Borrowdale, and by Furness Abbey at Brotherilkeld in Eskdale (**13** and **colour plate 4**). Calder Abbey began to consolidate a pastoral demesne in upper Calderdale during the second quarter of the thirteenth century, establishing four such farms there. Vaccaries might also be located where there was access to marshland grazing, generally more suited to cattle than to sheep, or in forests or chases where there was good pasture. Holm Cultram had a vaccary in Inglewood by 1215, and also grazed cattle on the Solway marshes.

Fountains Abbey developed a particularly well-organised system of vaccaries in Nidderdale. Cattle appear to have been kept throughout the year in Wharfedale and Nidderdale, but were also sometimes brought down to the lower granges and vaccaries. It is difficult to discern definite patterns of movement, but clearly some degree of transhumance between upland and lowland pastures was involved. Around the end of the eleventh century the monks of Fountains acquired rights to move their cattle through the township of Ripley between Cayton Grange, on the edge of the Vale of York, and the high summer pastures of Brimham overlooking Nidderdale, a distance of only 5 miles but a climb of some 600ft.

In the midlands, Merevale Abbey had organised its cattle into three separate herds by the end of the fifteenth century. The kitchen herd, grazed near the abbey, consisted of cattle destined for slaughter for consumption within the

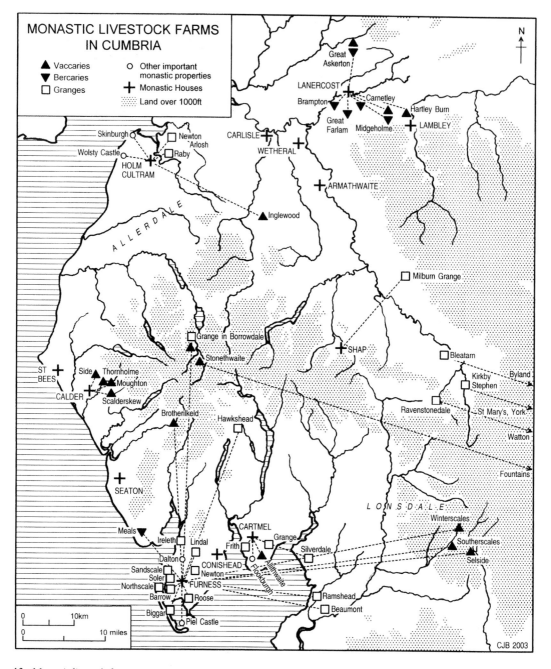

MONASTIC LIVESTOCK FARMS IN CUMBRIA

- ▲ Vaccaries
- ▼ Bercaries
- ☐ Granges
- ○ Other important monastic properties
- ✚ Monastic Houses
- ░ Land over 1000ft

N

Great Askerton

LANERCOST
Brampton
Carnetley
Hartley Burn

CARLISLE
WETHERAL
Great Farlam
Midgeholme
LAMBLEY

ARMATHWAITE

Skinburgh
Newton
Arlosh
Wolsty Castle
Raby
HOLM CULTRAM

Inglewood

ALLERDALE

Milburn Grange

Grange in Borrowdale
Stonethwaite
SHAP
Bleatarn

ST BEES
Side
Thornholme
Moughton
CALDER
Scalderskew
Brotherilkeld

Kirkby Stephen
Byland
Ravenstonedale
St Mary's, York
Watton

Hawkshead

Fountains

SEATON

LONSDALE
Winterscales

Meals
Ireleth
Lindal
CARTMEL
Frith
Grange
Silverdale
Southerscales
Selside

Dalton
CONISHEAD
Newton
FURNESS
Sandscale
Soler
Northscale
Barrow
Roose
Biggar
Piel Castle
Ramshead
Beaumont

Allithwaite
Flookburgh

0   10km
0   10 miles

CJB 2003

13 *Monastic livestock farms in Cumbria. Grazing rights were held by several abbeys across the Pennines in Yorkshire*

abbey. The dairy herd was also normally at Merevale. Most of the store beasts were also normally there, but parts of this herd were also maintained at Pinwall and other granges. It is difficult to ascertain how much the abbey was fattening cattle purely for its own needs and how much for commercial purposes, but many beef animals were probably sent to local markets. At the same time, however, the accounts record purchases of cattle at Atherstone fair and from tenants and from neighbouring villages.

Milk and butter were both difficult to keep, so cheese was the main dairy product. In the thirteenth century, it was estimated that one cow ought to produce sufficient milk for 98lb of cheese and 14lb of butter each year, but in reality cheese production ranged from 157lb of cheese per cow at Sibton Abbey in 1507-14, down to 32lb on the Tavistock Abbey estates. Cheese production from Canterbury Cathedral Priory's Romney Marsh dairy herds fluctuated, as from time to time reductions in the extent of available pasture or short-term needs to realise capital for projects such as improving sea defences caused proportions of the herd to be sold off.

Meat-eating was permitted only to the sick under the Benedictine rule, but some backsliding is evident even before the Norman Conquest, and in 1336 Pope Benedict XII bowed to the trend, issuing an edict permitting meat to monks of the order four days a week. By the fourteenth century the Cistercians too were abandoning a strict vegetarian diet, though the fast days and fast seasons were respected right up to the Dissolution. From the evidence of the kitchen midden at Kirkstall, consumption of beef there greatly outweighed any other meat, but it was mainly worn-out plough oxen and milk cattle no longer fit for lactation that found their way, well-stewed, onto the table. By contrast, the Augustinian canons of Norton Priory enjoyed a more discriminating diet, with no evidence for the consumption of elderly beasts and a preponderance of choice joints.

Sheep

In the early Middle Ages, sheep were kept primarily for milking, ten sheep producing as much butter and cheese as a cow. Medieval sheep were relatively small, so meat production was not initially a prime consideration, though by about 1500 mutton was making a significant contribution to the diet at Westminster and Winchester. Sheep were also valued for their dung, and skins were used for the production of vellum. However, it was the rising demand for wool which caused the great expansion of flocks after the twelfth century.

It is often difficult to get a clear idea of the size of monastic flocks. Grants of pasture often specified an upper limit on numbers in order to prevent regular overgrazing, but on the vast open moorlands of the north frequently no limits were fixed. Moreover, many abbeys developed the practice of moving portions of their flocks from manor to manor, so that the true numbers rarely emerge from individual manorial accounts. Numbers also fluctuated considerably from year to year through outbreaks of foot-rot, liver-fluke, murrain and other natural disasters. Annual losses of up to a third were common, and in bad years could rise much higher. In 1243 800 sheep died on Dunstable Priory's lands around Bradbourne in the Peak District. The St Albans Abbey records suggest that sheep-scab was imported with Spanish stock in 1274. Following the disastrously wet seasons of 1315–17 the Bolton Priory flock was reduced to 913 head, and it took eight years for it to recover to above 2,000. On Battle Abbey's Dengemarsh property 70 per cent of the young sheep died in 1321-2.

The Cistercians are often credited with the creation of large-scale commercial sheep farming in Britain, but some Benedictine houses were already running large flocks long before they arrived. The preliminary drafts of the Domesday Book which survive for some eastern and south-western counties include information on livestock which was omitted from the final version of the survey. From these records, Ely Abbey had about 9,000 sheep scattered over its demesnes in Norfolk, Suffolk and Essex, while the Norman abbeys of Caen, St Valéry and St Ouen had 883 sheep in the marshes of Essex. On the Glastonbury manors in Somerset a total of 3,338 sheep was recorded, of which 2,545 were on the abbey's own demesne properties.

During the twelfth century monastic flocks were often farmed out with their manors. Nevertheless, in 1125 Peterborough Abbey grazed just over 1,600 sheep and lambs, nearly half that number on its Northamptonshire estates. A survey of the English estates of the nuns of Holy Trinity, Caen, made shortly after 1106, also listed demesne flocks numbering 1,600 or more, concentrated on the Cotswold properties of Avening and Minchinhampton.

On the greater Benedictine estates, where arable or mixed farming predominated, sheep farming could nevertheless become a large-scale operation. Between 1250 and 1300 Glastonbury Abbey regularly had over 6,000 sheep scattered through 20-odd manors in Mendip, east Somerset, Dorset, Wiltshire and Hampshire, with about half that total concentrated on the chalk downlands of Buckland Newton, Monkton Deverill, Idmiston and Damerham. By the 1320s Christ Church, Canterbury, had a flock of 13,730 sheep, 10,000 of which were grazing in the Weald and the Kentish coastal marshes, with the remainder scattered through its manors in Surrey, Essex and Suffolk. The annual yield from Canterbury's flocks in 1322 was £300 from 50 sacks of wool, a further £50 from lambs' fleeces, £150 from lambs, £96 from the milk of 6,000 ewes and £91 from manure. The flocks of the prior of St Swithun's, Winchester, may have numbered as many as 20,000.

The Cistercian statutes forbade both meat-eating and trading in wool or hides, and before the middle of the twelfth century Cistercian farming was still geared primarily to subsistence. By the later twelfth century, however,

Cistercian abbeys were beginning to follow the Benedictine example. Only rarely did their flocks rival those of the greatest Benedictine monasteries in size, but they achieved even greater commercial success through targeting production more towards the export market. Meaux Abbey pastured 11,000 sheep in Holderness in the 1270s and perhaps another 3,000 elsewhere, though in later years its flocks dwindled to under a couple of thousand. Beaulieu Abbey's flock amounted to over 5,000 in the 1280s. Kirkstall seems to have had few sheep in 1284, but by 1301 its flock numbered between 4,500 and 5,400. Pope Nicholas' Taxation of around 1291 provides somewhat haphazard livestock figures, which show that Fountains Abbey then had some 18,000 sheep, Rievaulx 14,000 and Jervaulx 12,000. The figures are more complete for Wales, where Margam emerges as the most important producer, with 5,285 sheep, followed by Tintern (3,264 sheep), Abbey Dore (2,740 sheep) and Basingwerk (2,000 sheep). The flocks of the smaller houses of mid-Wales rarely exceeded 300, and Cymmer could muster only 25 sheep that year.

Some houses of canons also built up considerable flocks, particularly in Lincolnshire and Yorkshire. Bolton Priory rapidly expanded its flocks from 1,215 head in 1296-7 to 3,578 in 1310-11. In 1313 Thornton Abbey had 7,934 sheep which produced over 86 sacks of wool, yielding an income of nearly £700. Grants to the Premonstratensians of Newhouse gave them grazing for 700 sheep at Cabourn, 300 at Barnetby-le-Wold, 300 at Norton Disney, 300 at Habrough, 200 at Killingholme and 200 at Binbrook, mostly marshland, but including some land on the wolds. Grants to many Gilbertine houses included particularly extensive pasturage. The foundation endowment of North Ormsby included pasture for 200 sheep in Walcot and 200 sheep in Billinghay. The cartulary of Malton Priory records grants of pasture for up to 6,000 sheep, including grazing for 1,000 on Levisham Moor in north Yorkshire. In 1308 Malton had 160 ewes and 200 sheep at Ryton, 600 at Middleton, nearly 500 at Brompton and 200 at Kirby Misperton. By 1337 Haverholme Priory had received pasture grants for at least 3,680 sheep. Alvingham Priory received pasture for 1,200 sheep in North Conesby, along with pasture for 900 sheep on its grange at Cabourn and at least 600 at Swinhop; in 1283 it had 941 ewes, 1,005 wethers (castrated rams) and 503 lambs. Bullington Priory acquired pasture for 1,100 sheep at Faldingworth, 660 at Hackthorn, over 600 in Huttoft and 500 in Redbourne. Despite their access to extensive pastures, the Gilbertines normally ran their flocks as part of a mixed farming system, and few of their granges were devoted primarily to sheep. Alvingham Priory concentrated wool production on the barren heaths of North Conesby, while Bullington Priory's grange at Huttoft also seems to have operated as a specialised pastoral unit.

The management of sheep flocks

Sheep were normally housed in sheepcotes and fed with hay through the winter from Martinmas (11 November) to Easter, especially in the harsher climate of the north. During summer and autumn they grazed on commons or on the unploughed fallow, where they were commonly folded in wattle or hurdle pens which were moved around to distribute the manure effectively. The making of hurdles and the moving of folds was often a duty of monastic tenants; it is recorded on the Templars' property of Temple Ewell in Kent around 1185. Folds were also used to contain sheep during milking and shearing. Washing and shearing took place soon after midsummer. Sheep from all the manors on the estate were normally brought together at a central shearing place in June. The Cistercians of Merevale brought their flocks from Leicestershire and the Peak down to the abbey for shearing, and payments are recorded for hurdles, for penning and washing the sheep, and for bread and ale for the shearers. On the Cotswolds Westminster Abbey's shearing centre was Bourton-on-the-Hill, while Winchcombe Abbey concentrated its sheep at Sherborne, and Llanthony Priory at Barrington. Glastonbury's Hampshire manor of Damerham served the same function. One of the earliest grants to Warden Abbey included pasture for 200 sheep in West Warden, and in 1205 the abbey acquired an allowance for a further 600 over the eight days of shearing during the early summer. Old and weak sheep were selected for fattening and slaughter before Lammas (1 August), and there was normally a further cull around Michaelmas (29 September) to get rid of diseased stock. Around mid-September the rams were put to the ewes for lambing in mid-February.

During the early Middle Ages monastic houses often kept small flocks on a number of their manors, each with its own shepherd, who was answerable to the manorial reeve or bailiff. However, during the twelfth century, as wool production expanded as a source of income, significant changes took place in the composition of flocks. Ewes were always retained in some numbers for milking and breeding, but wethers (castrated rams), which produced more wool, came to account for more than half the flock. On one of Glastonbury Abbey's Dorset manors in 1300 there were seven rams, 338 ewes, 293 wethers, 234 hoggasters or hoggets (young sheep not yet shorn) and 192 lambs. In 1388 the Owston Abbey flock consisted of 158 wethers, 131 ewes, 76 hoggasters and 66 maiden ewes. Increasingly monastic houses reduced costs by placing all their sheep in the care of a master shepherd or sheepreeve, who then divided them into one or more breeding flocks and one or more wool-producing flocks made up solely of wethers. Crowland Abbey maintained a central flock after 1300 which received up to 1,800 sheep a year from individual manorial flocks, and in exchange sent out rams and replaced lost manorial stock. The greater mobility of flocks managed outside the manorial framework optimised the use of grazing land and helped to reduce the build-up of disease.

As monastic sheep farming became increasingly specialised, so it became more concentrated in those regions offering the best summer pastures – the coastal marshes, the chalk downs, the Cotswolds, Mendip, the Pennines and other northern upland moors. Crowland Abbey concentrated its flocks around the Fenland margins of Holland, Pershore on its Cotswold manor of Broadway, Winchcombe on its Cotswold manor of Sherborne, while Merevale pastured sheep in the Derbyshire Peak District. Rationalisation can be seen on Glastonbury Abbey's Wiltshire estates, where strip lynchets on the chalk downs of Monkton Deverill show that the manor had been cultivated before its conversion to a sheep-walk, whereas Longbridge Deverill, only a couple of miles away, where the Wylye Valley opened out into the clay vale, retained its arable fields.

Intercommoning agreements were arranged. In Staffordshire in 1246 the Augustinians of Trentham allowed the Cistercians of Hulton pasture for 400 sheep in Blurton and Cocknage in return for a similar concession on Hulton's pastures at Normacot. Much of the Mendip upland remained common pasture, and surrounding monastic houses acquired extensive rights there. Glastonbury Abbey had access through its various manors on both sides of the hills, and in 1517 was claiming grazing rights from Burrington eastwards to Downhead and Doulting. Witham Priory's foundation endowment had included extensive upland pastures which were farmed from its grange at Charterhouse-on-Mendip. St Augustine's Abbey in Bristol had a farm at Ellick near the head of Burrington Combe and another at Rowberrow. In 1233 the Knights Templars acquired 20 acres in a projecting part of West Harptree parish which became known as Temple Hydon, along with the much more valuable right to pasture 1,000 sheep on the hills. Grazing rights were also held by more distant monasteries, such as Bruern Abbey in Oxfordshire, which held property in Priddy and East Harptree.

Despite this tendency, considerable flocks still remained in the open-field areas of the midlands. In about 1280 Oseney Abbey kept about 3,000 sheep scattered around at least 17 of its manors (**14**), but the canons were beginning to concentrate their sheep-farming operation at Water Eaton which, because of its central position within the Abbey estates as a whole, was already developing as the central collecting point for fleeces.

By the later thirteenth century the flocks of lay lords and peasants were exceeding the numbers of sheep on monastic estates, and the monastic share of wool production fell still further after the middle of the fourteenth century. Nevertheless, the continuing demand for wool through the later Middle Ages encouraged many monastic houses to maintain sheep farming on some scale, even when their arable demesnes were being leased out. When Bristol Abbey leased its manor of Rowberrow in 1407, the tenant was required to pay the shepherd's salary and to provide hurdles for the sheepfolds, while making half the hay crop available for the abbey's sheep, and the abbot was to organise the

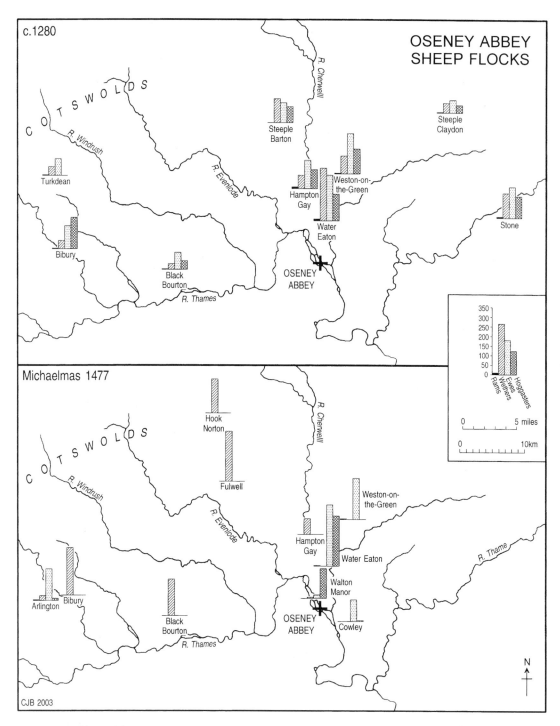

14 *Oseney Abbey (Oxfordshire): changes in the management of sheep flocks between c.1280 and 1477, showing the segregation of breeding ewes and wethers kept for wool production by the later Middle Ages.* Based upon figures from David Postles, 1984

washing and shearing of the sheep. Oseney Abbey's accounts in 1477 show breeding flocks of ewes on four manors (Water Eaton, Weston-on-the-Green, Arlington and Cowley), with a large number of hoggasters, probably for restocking the ewes, at Water Eaton, while five other manors (Fulwell, Bibury, Black Bourton, Hook Norton and Hampton Gay) kept only wethers for wool production. Water Eaton had, by then, become the hub of the whole operation, supporting a quarter of the abbey's entire flock – twice as many sheep as any other property (**14**). Even the small priory of Jarrow normally kept between 200 and 380 sheep throughout the fifteenth century, its sales of wool rising significantly after 1440, bringing in £5 to £8 a year. Merevale Abbey had reduced its flocks by the end of the fifteenth century, but was still moving several hundred sheep between its Leicestershire granges of Seal and Pinwall, and it still had a small flock of 80 head pastured at Croxden in the Peak District in 1538. Rievaulx Abbey retained Newlass Grange as a demesne sheep farm up until the Dissolution.

Transhumance of sheep

During the thirteenth and fourteenth centuries, as monastic flocks became more centrally managed, systems of transhumance were developed, whereby flocks were moved in summer onto upland pastures, where the mature, hardy wethers might be left to overwinter while the ewes and younger animals were brought down onto lower ground. Westminster Abbey had several hundred sheep grazing on its Cotswold manors of Todenham and Bourton-on-the-Hill, but some were regularly brought down to the lowland manors of Moreton-in-Marsh and Elmstone Hardwick for the winter. During the period 1213-23 Salley Abbey's flock at Marton in the Aire valley numbered around 480 in summer, but increased to 720 in winter, as sheep were brought down from the surrounding hills. Fountains Abbey had a number of sheep farms over the uplands of Malham Moor with sheepcotes, folds and small areas of enclosed meadow and pasture, each staffed by three or four shepherds and accommo-dating several hundred sheep, but in 1268 it also had winter pastures for 500 sheep at Kettlewell in the upper Wharfe Valley, for 400 sheep at Aldburgh in Uredale, and for 200 sheep at its Nidderdale granges of Bewerley and Heyshaw. On the Gloucester Abbey estate in the early sixteenth century 360 wethers were maintained in a sheepcote at Aldsworth on the Cotswolds, while 240 ewes spent the summer on the hills, but were brought down to Maisemore in the Severn Valley for winter.

Marshlands could be used in the same way. By the late thirteenth century Canterbury Cathedral Priory was moving up to 500 sheep down to the low-lying pastures of Ebony on Romney Marsh as soon as the winter flooding had receded, but at the end of each summer large numbers of year-old lambs and some ewes were moved to the higher pastures around Appledore, their place on the marsh being taken next spring by the new generation of lambs.

Wool production and the domestic market

The mobility of stock counted against the development of any very distinct breeds of sheep in the Middle Ages. Nevertheless, wool from the north, from the south-east and from Dorset and Wiltshire was generally coarse, and fetched relatively low prices. By contrast, sheep from the Welsh borders, the Cotswolds and the Lincolnshire uplands became noted for the length and fineness of their wool.

Wherever sheep were kept in quantity, wool yields would exceed immediate local needs, and so provided commercial opportunities from an early date. In 1193 the chronicler William of Newburgh described the wool of the English Cistercian monasteries as 'the chiefest part of their substance'. Indeed, it was so valuable that, in the same year, the entire clip from the English Cistercian and Gilbertine flocks was seized as a contribution towards Richard I's ransom. In 1253 Westminster Abbey sold 311 fleeces from its manors of Todenham and Sutton-under-Brailes, while in 1308, 200 fleeces were sold from its manor of Pershore. In 1297-8 Leicester Abbey's cash receipts from wool amounted to £220 3s 10d, more than one-third of its entire income. Wool sales provided over a third of Bolton Priory's total income between 1287 and 1305.

Fleeces from Benedictine and Augustinian flocks were normally sold as they came off the sheep's back, unsorted and unwashed, and they found greatest favour in the home market. By the early fourteenth century Gloucester Abbey was producing around 46 sacks of wool a year for home sale, compared to only five sacks for export. The cellarer's accounts of Worcester Priory show that a large part of the priory's income came from wool sales, yet little of it was exported. Even so, between 1287 and 1305 wool exports accounted for one-third of the entire income of Bolton Priory.

The export of wool

English wool acquired an excellent reputation, and was much in demand from continental merchants. Monastic production undoubtedly stimulated the growth of this trade, and during the early thirteenth century export licences were granted to a number of Cistercian monasteries permitting them to ship wool to Flanders and northern France. In 1212 Abbey Dore, Kingswood, Fountains and Furness already had contacts with merchants in St Omer. Despite the fact that the Cistercian statutes of 1237 had forbidden their members to trade in wool or hides, the export of wool came to play a major part in the economy of the English houses during the late thirteenth and early fourteenth centuries. By this time, Italian merchants from Genoa, Lucca and, above all, Florence had taken over the trade, entering into contracts with at least 57 Cistercian abbeys in England and Wales.

Around 1315 Francesco Balducci Pegolotti, agent in England of the Bardi company of Florence, compiled a guide for merchants, into which he incorporated a Flemish list drawn up some 20 or 30 years earlier, showing the minimum quantities of wool which could be bought for export from the English monasteries, and the price at each. Cistercian houses made up 85 per cent of his total (1,468 sacks, each sack being made up of about 200 fleeces), with the Benedictines the second largest exporters (460 sacks), followed by the Augustinians (424 sacks), Gilbertines (293 sacks) and Premonstratensians (231 sacks). Most Cistercian, Gilbertine and Premonstratensian monasteries graded their wool into three qualities ready for export, and it fetched good prices. Of the Cistercian abbeys, Fountains was the largest single exporter, expected to sell 76 sacks a year, the produce of over 15,000 sheep, but it was rivalled by Rievaulx (60 sacks) and Jervaulx (50 sacks). Among the Gilbertine monasteries, the Yorkshire houses of Malton and Watton headed the export table, producing respectively 45 and 40 sacks a year. Barlings and Croxton headed the Premonstratensian exporters, each with 25 sacks. The unwashed and unsorted Benedictine and Augustinian fleeces commanded lower prices. Bridlington Priory, which had good chalkland pasture on the Yorkshire wolds, was by far the largest Augustinian trader, exporting 50 sacks a year, no other Augustinian house managing more than 20. Peterborough and Winchcombe exported 40 sacks a year, but some of the wool sold through Benedictine houses may have come from tithes or from tenant farmers rather than from the abbey's demesne flocks.

Fleeces intended for export had to be carried to a port, or some other place convenient to the buyer. Packhorses were normally used to bring fleeces from the shearing centres to the woolhouses where they were cleaned, sorted and packed. Carts, or occasionally boats, then carried the large quantities of woolsacks on to the ports. Temporary storage might be arranged at granges and woolhouses en route. Holm Cultram Abbey acquired free rights of passage for its wagons, carts and packhorses to carry wool and other goods from Cumberland to the port of Newcastle-upon-Tyne. In the early thirteenth century the abbeys of Byland and Rievaulx were sending their wool to Clifton on the outskirts of York, whence it could be shipped down the Ouse and Humber to Hull. Boston and London were, however, the most important delivery ports.

Exports declined in the later Middle Ages. The chronicler of Croxden Abbey complained of difficulties in selling the abbey's wool due to the outbreak of war with the French, though it was still engaged in trade with Florentine merchants in the 1420s. Sales from Fountains were greatly reduced in the fifteenth century, only seven sacks being sold in 1457–8 and only four in the following year. With the decline of the export trade, wool from the northern abbeys more often found its way to local markets like Thirsk, York, Leeds and Beverley.

Goats

Goats were recorded on some manors in the Domesday drafts for East Anglia and the south-west. Glastonbury Abbey had 50 goats on its home demesne and smaller numbers on its manors of Wrington, Pilton, Baltonsborough, Winscombe, Walton, Ditcheat, Batcombe, Cranmore and Ashcott. Muchelney Abbey had 30 goats on its home manor. Goat numbers generally declined through the Middle Ages, but they were still kept in places where the feed was of inferior quality. In 1291 the canons of St Augustine's Abbey, Bristol, kept 40 nanny-goats on the island of Flatholm.

Pigs

Pigs were especially common in woodland manors, where they could be turned out to graze on acorns and beechmast. Ramsey Abbey's estates included extensive woodlands, from which flitches of bacon were provided as food rents, while 15 or 20 hogs were regularly sent to market from each manor. Peterborough Abbey developed something of a speciality in pig farming, with several of its manors carrying herds of a hundred swine or more. Production seems to have been geared primarily towards consumption within the abbey rather than sales in the market. However, pork normally made only a minor contribution to the monastic diet.

Horses

Walter of Henley believed that horses rarely justified the high costs of their keep, but horses were always preferred for harrowing, and were increasingly employed for ploughing and transport. By the thirteenth century horses already substantially outnumbered oxen on Canterbury Cathedral Priory's Romney Marsh manors. Extra feed was given at time of ploughing and when horses were set to other work, such as hauling timber for building works or maintenance of sea defences. A number of northern monasteries bred horses, mostly for their own use as pack and draft animals. Jervaulx Abbey gained a particularly high reputation for the quality of its horses. Bolton Priory maintained a stud of 50 to 90 head, grazing summer pastures at Malham and overwintering in the home grange. Kirkstall Abbey reared horses at Riston in the Trough of Bowland. Holm Cultram had a horse-pen in Inglewood in 1218-19. Even such a small priory as Jarrow normally kept a couple of horses for the monks' own use, and often two or three cart-horses as well. In the south of England, Quarr Abbey bred horses on the open moorland around the abbey.

Poultry and doves

Consumption of the eggs and flesh of birds was not prohibited by the Benedictine rule. There is plentiful evidence of geese, hens and ducks being kept by many abbeys from the thirteenth century onwards. Despite this, enormous numbers of eggs still had to be bought in – over a period of 32 weeks in 1491-2 Westminster Abbey purchased no fewer than 82,000 eggs. Squabs, the young of the domesticated rock-dove, taken before they learned to fly, provided occasional fare through the summer and autumn. More exotic fowl are occasionally recorded, such as the peacocks kept by Prior More of Worcester on his manors at Hallow and Grimley.

5
Assarting, reclamation and enclosure

Woodland clearance

Another way in which the agricultural productivity of monastic estates could be improved was by *assarting*, the permanent clearance of woodland in order to convert the land to arable, pasture or meadow. Rights to assart and conveyances of assarted land are frequently recorded in monastic cartularies. Some assarts were enclosed from the outset and held in severalty; others were parcelled into strips, added to existing open fields and farmed communally. They varied considerably in size – on the lands of Salley Abbey and Fountains Abbey they ranged from a quarter of an acre up to 100 acres. The work of clearing a large assart might extend over several seasons.

Monastic assarting in the royal forests

Special restrictions applied in those areas designated as forests, where royal hunting rights had legal priority over other uses. Many monasteries held lands within the royal forests, and assarts and purprestures there frequently brought them into conflict with the king's officials. In Berkshire in 1189-90 the Pipe Rolls record payments owing for over 50 acres of assarts belonging to Reading Abbey, 10 acres at Kintbury belonging to the nuns of Nuneaton, and 5 acres at Hartley belonging to Battle Abbey. Cistercian abbeys within or near royal forests were especially frequent offenders: between 1155 and 1212 Cistercian houses were fined on 40 separate occasions, and in 1282 Tintern Abbey was fined for clearing 200 acres of royal forest without royal licence.

Benedictine assarts

As we have seen, the older Benedictine monasteries were usually in fertile areas surrounded by arable fields, so opportunities for woodland clearance were, in general, confined to their more distant estates. Here the work was often under-taken by free tenants, to the benefit of both abbey and tenant.

Most of the larger Benedictine houses had some involvement in assarting. In 1102 Henry I granted waste land at Welford in the Lambourn Valley to Abbot Faricius of Abingdon so that he might cultivate it, with the proviso that improvements there and at Chieveley should not damage the king's forest. In 1109 Abingdon was making assarts in Bagley and Cumnor woods. At Bury St Edmunds Abbot Samson 'cleared many lands and brought them back into cultivation'. Burton Abbey held assarted land at Callingwood by the later thir-teenth century.

Westminster Abbey had extensive woodlands on some of its outlying estates at the time of the Domesday survey, especially at Hendon in Middlesex, Aldenham and Wheathampstead in Hertfordshire, Longdon in Worcestershire and Deerhurst in Gloucestershire. On all these properties the woodland had been much reduced by the early fourteenth century, and the proportion of tenanted land held by freemen extended from about 30 per cent at Aldenham and Pyrford to 87 per cent in Wheathampstead. A more direct part was played by Abbot Richard Barking, who took some of the newly-cleared land at Islip and Castlemorton into his own demesne.

Even where woodland lay outside the royal forests, it was often subject to common rights. The chronicle of Evesham Abbey describes how Abbot Randulf (1214-29) 'destroyed the wood at Sambourne called Langabey, an enormous loss to the abbey, for it was exempt from Forest Law; and also half the wood at Badby, and the large wood at Ombersley which is called Chatley, wishing to plough up these areas, but he was unable to do so because of the common pasture of our tenants and their neighbours.' His successor, Abbot Thomas Marlborough (1229-36) 'ploughed up 2 carucates of land at Chatley in Ombersley in his second year, having obtained the permission of Walter de Beauchamp, who had always obstructed this ploughing-up in the past because of the common pasture which he had there'.

Potential conflicts of interest were often resolved by compromises. In the second quarter of the thirteenth century the abbot of Pershore reached an agreement with Richard Burden, whereby the monks retained all the newly-cultivated lands which they had made in the manor of Hawkesbury, and could assart and bring under tillage land near Swangrove (a wood by the north-west corner of Badminton Park), as well as enclosing land in the field nearer the village. In exchange, the abbey gave Richard 50s and widened the way for him and his men towards Swangrove; and Richard was allowed to enclose two groves and to retain rights of common in all places where his ancestors had them.

A whole series of agreements concerning assarts appear in the register of Malmesbury Abbey. Abbot William Colerne (1260-96) gave the burgesses of the town's merchant guild an assart which they had made at Burntheath on the town edge of Malmesbury Common, in return for which the burgesses gave the abbot a portion of their heath called Portmansheath. Agreements were also made over assarts, breaches and intakes around Allington, Sheldon, Bolehide and Yatton Spinney on the Cotswolds west of Chippenham.

The fullest evidence of assarting on a Benedictine estate comes from Peterborough Abbey, which held extensive woodlands in the east midlands. Much clearance must have taken place before the Norman Conquest. Nevertheless, the low densities of plough-teams and population recorded by the Domesday survey in the Forest of Rockingham and Soke of Peterborough show that much under-developed land remained. Woods on the abbey's manor of Oundle made up the biggest single extent of wood recorded in Northamptonshire.

In June 1143 the monks received confirmation of their right to all assarts created up to that date. However, the extension of forest law under Henry II found the abbey paying fines for assarting in Werrington, Cottingham, Oundle and Great Easton in 1162-3. In 1189 Richard I gave the abbey almost complete exemption from forest jurisdiction within the Soke and in its neighbouring woodland manors, allowed it to enclose its assarts, and granted it 200 acres of assarts in the Soke and 400 acres at Oundle free of all forest dues.

Within the Soke numerous charters show Peterborough Abbey clearing land itself. The abbot appears to have assarted part of Eastwood before the end of the twelfth century in order to provide holdings of 4-5 acres each for the descendants of monastic servants. The abbey was also acquiring and engrossing some of the much larger acreages of clearances made by local freeholders during the second half of the twelfth century, including those in the manor of Paston, which it consolidated after the 1260s to provide an endowment for the sacrist's office. The Northamptonshire forest eyre of 1209 listed 145 acres of assarts then used for growing oats and wheat, of which 42 acres had been made by the abbot, the sacrist and the almoner, and most of the remainder by freeholders. The abbot himself had 21 acres of oats at Longthorpe on assarts he had made out of Westwood, as well as 3 acres of wheat and 6 acres of oats at Walton; the almoner had 2 acres of wheat at Dogsthorpe and 1 acre of oats at Walton; and the sacrist had 7 acres of wheat at Cathwaite and 2 acres of wheat at Dogsthorpe. The cellarer's grange of Belsize at the north end of Castor was developed from a core of 50 acres of woodland, legally disafforested in 1215 and bought up for assarting by the abbey over the next ten years. This was supplemented by other woodland acquired from freeholders and tenants.

Further west in Rockingham Forest Peterborough Abbey was assarting land around Oundle in the 1160s. Here the 400 acres confirmed to the abbey in 1189 became the nucleus of the grange of New Place, later called Biggin. Biggin became Peterborough's largest manor, already comprising some 1,150 acres of arable land by 1294. On the further side of the forest the abbey had licence in 1215 to clear 100 acres at Cottingham and Great Easton, and the survey of 1221 showed that 107 acres had been cleared. However, the declining rate of assarting through the later thirteenth century, both in the Soke and in Rockingham Forest, perhaps suggests that woodland was no longer so abundant, and that the abbey was increasingly concerned to conserve what remained.

read
to.

Augustinian assarting

The smaller landed endowments of the Augustinian canons generally gave them less opportunity for extensive assarting. Nevertheless, Merton Priory was fined the massive sum of 286s for assarts and purprestures in Surrey in 1176-7, St Augustine's Abbey in Bristol was fined 45s for assarts and other forest offences in Worcestershire in 1169-70, while Maiden Bradley Priory suffered a fine of 43s for assarts and waste in the Wiltshire forests in 1174-5.

Augustinian houses were particularly active in some of the under-developed parts of the north midlands. The canons of Wombridge and Lilleshall were clearing woodlands in Shropshire. The foundation charter of Ranton Priory in north Staffordshire refers to the house as 'St Mary of the Assarts'. The canons of Trentham acquired from Hulton Abbey in 1242 the right to take new land into cultivation and to make assarts at Normacot in Stone. Darley Abbey was fined for assarting in 1159-60, acquired three assarts near Derby later in the century, established its right to assarts in Ripley Wood around 1230, and was clearing land in Pentrich Wood in the 1260s.

Most Augustinian assarts were relatively small, but Waltham Abbey owed a fine of 140s for 100 acres cultivated or improved without consent in 1203-4. An inquisition into the grievances against the canons of Cirencester by the men of the town recorded a complaint that the abbot had destroyed much of Oakley Wood by assarting 100 acres there. A confirmation of an earlier charter to St Osyth's Priory by Edward I recorded the canons' right to assart and clear a total of 202 acres in various places, including 140 acres at Tolleshunt.

Cistercian assarting

Of all monastic orders, the Cistercians were most strongly associated with settlements in waste and wooded places. Often they were, indeed, faced with clearance operations immediately around the abbey site from the outset. The monks of Kirkstall found dense thorn scrub when they arrived there in 1125. Evidence of assarting from the time of the first settlement also occurs at Byland, Combermere, Tintern and Stoneleigh.

Nevertheless, while some new estate farms were carved entirely out of previously uncultivated land, such as Rievaulx's grange at Pickering, the role of the Cistercians as pioneer settlers should not be exaggerated. In reality, England had little virgin wilderness left by the twelfth century, and much of the Cistercian effort was directed towards resuming cultivation on previously-abandoned land. Some 40 per cent of twelfth-century granges occupied lands described as 'wasted' in 1086. The Vale of York, in particular, had suffered severely from the punitive measures undertaken by William the Conqueror's army in 1069 after the northern revolt. In Airedale and Wensleydale the monks were recolonising lands depopulated only since the late eleventh century. The importance of the Cistercian contribution lies less in the acreages of new land won than in the opportunities which piecemeal additions provided for extending and reorganising existing holdings into granges.

The progress of Cistercian assarting can most clearly be traced in Yorkshire. Along the northern edge of the Vale of Pickering, against the Hambleton Hills, Byland Abbey was clearing woods around Coxwold by 1177, and Rievaulx was moving into waste land in Skiplam. In the northern part of the Vale of York Fountains Abbey's granges of Wheldrake and Long Marston were largely made up of recently-assarted land. Byland was also clearing in this area. Further south Kirkstall received confirmation of rights to clear and cultivate woodland at its grange of Bessacarr in 1183-1200. Many abbeys also had interests in the Pennine dales. Rievaulx acquired 21 acres of woods and uncultivated land at Bolton in Wensleydale to be assarted in 1173-4. Fountains Abbey was assarting around its early granges of Brimham and Bradley, later extending its operations to Kettlewell in Wharfedale, to Littondale and around Malham. Kirkstall had many assarts in Bramley and in Airedale, and before 1190 was bringing new land into cultivation at Riddlesden, between its granges of Micklethwaite and Elam. As late as 1333 Jervaulx was assarting woods at Askrigg in Wensleydale. Most abbeys were also acquiring lands previously cleared by laymen – Fountains acquired 12 acres of assarts at Kirkheaton and a 36-acre woodland clearing at Markenfield towards the end of the twelfth century, while Byland acquired assarted lands in Denby overlooking the Calder.

In the Welsh borders Abbey Dore was linked with the Hospitallers of Dinmore in 1198-9 as being responsible for assarts in Treville Wood and in the hay of Hereford. Treville Wood, comprising some 1000 acres, was a former royal forest, of which the abbey purchased 300 acres from Richard I in 1198. Giraldus Cambrensis described how the monks had converted the oak wood into a wheat field, also that they had recouped the costs of the purchase three times over by selling the timber in Hereford for building. Half a dozen new granges were established through the former forest, several of which still survive as isolated farms. Morehampton Grange and Blackmoor Grange retain traces of moats.

Flaxley Abbey's foundation grant included 'all the land under the old Castle of Dean which remains to be assarted and that which is already assarted'. Henry II's confirmation charter quoted the extent of this land as 100 acres, and added a further 200 acres of assart land at Wallmore with pastures and meadows, and further assarts called Vincents Land.

Stoneleigh Abbey was settled in 1153-4 within the Forest of Arden on a former royal manor, surrounded by old-established agricultural communities, but close to extensive woodland, where assarting continued into the early fourteenth century. Combe Abbey, also in Arden, acquired many areas of wood which could be cleared, and assarted land which the donor had already enclosed.

Warden Abbey in Bedfordshire was alternatively known as St Mary de Sartis, and its first endowments were of all the previously-assarted land in Warden and Southill, and the wood between those two places, with permission to cut what wood was needed for the community's use. Henry II confirmed to the monks the wood of Ravenshoe, which they assarted and converted to arable. Ramsey Abbey granted Warden the wood of Middlehoe in Huntingdonshire, and Henry III gave the monks licence to assart or enclose it. Elsewhere it was recorded in 1303 that Stanley Abbey had assarted 88 acres of land at Pewsham, clearly the continuation of a prolonged campaign.

Occasionally the Cistercians appear to have undertaken the preliminary clearing of land which was only later conveyed to them by charter: for example, in the 1150s Rievaulx Abbey was given 10 acres in Pilley near Barnsley, and soon afterwards Fountains Abbey received land in South Stainley which, in both cases, had been assarted by the monks. In the same period Warden Abbey was granted land which it had cleared at Paxton.

The impact of monastic clearance upon local vegetation has been detected in some palynological studies. Analysis of pollens from a site north of Merebrook near Dieulacresse Abbey has demonstrated a change from oak and alder woodland to cereal cultivation and pasture. Similar changes in Upper Nidderdale can be related to assarting undertaken by Fountains Abbey.

Who did the actual work of clearance? The Cistercian statutes required the monks to spend part of each day in manual labour, but the bulk of the work, at least up to the fourteenth century, fell on the lay brothers, who were also responsible for the cultivation of the granges. Fountains Abbey seems to have arranged to share the work with local laymen in Long Marston, Wheldrake and Hawkswick. Kingwood Abbey's accounts in 1262-3 include payments to the assarters, implying that hired labour was used. Elsewhere, as on Benedictine estates, monastic tenants played a major role. In 1326 Stoneleigh Abbey was licensed 'to grant wastes which are . . . to be brought into cultivation in the manor of Stoneleigh . . . to tenants willing to receive them for life'.

The settlement and utilisation of marshland

Desolate marshland attracted ascetics at all periods. Hermits settled on the margins of the Fens in the sixth and seventh centuries, their sites later reoccupied by the Benedictine communities of Thorney and Crowland. The scanty remains of the late twelfth-century Premonstratensian abbey of Cockersand stand on a bleak, windswept saltmarsh on the shores of Morecambe Bay. Nunneries, in particular, often seem to have preferred the seclusion offered by marshes to the profits which might derive from reclamation.

However, marshland sites, especially on the coast, could be uncomfortable, even dangerous. During the winter of 1287-8 an incursion of the sea in Norfolk cut off all the outbuildings of the abbey of St Benet of Hulme so that they could only be reached by boat, and the abbey's horses were saved only by bringing them into the nave of the church. The Cistercian monks of Stanlaw, on the shore of the Wirral, endured repeated inundations from the Mersey, particularly in 1279, 1289 and 1292, and were finally driven to request a move to a new site elsewhere on their estates (to Whalley in Lancashire). Their petition stated that the very land on which the abbey stood was being eroded by the spring tides, and that the monastic buildings stood under 3-5ft of water. Margam also suffered from flooding and the encroachment of sand, while gales damaged its buildings in 1384. The lands of Goldcliff Priory were inundated in 1324, and the parochial nave of the priory church was so badly damaged by a great storm in 1424 that it was rebuilt on a safer location further inland. Thorney Abbey received licence in 1440 to acquire land up to £40 in value in compensation for damage caused by recent incursions of the sea. Even more sheltered inland marshlands sometimes proved intractable. An attempted Cistercian settlement at Otley on the edge of Otmoor in Oxfordshire was soon abandoned when the site proved, in the words of a later commentator, 'fitter for an ark than a monastery'.

Unreclaimed wetlands could be of considerable value, providing fish, wildfowl, summer pasture, fuel, reed for thatching and many other commodities. The obedientiaries at Ely included an official called the *roscarius*, whose task was to manage the rush and sedge. Lewes Priory in 1351 agreed to share the cygnets from two swans' nests with a co-proprietor on its Norfolk manor of Heacham. Turbaries where turves or peat could be dug for fuel were another valuable resource, especially in areas where wood was in short supply. The abbot of Byland was involved in two separate court cases in 1371 and 1372 with men who had illicitly cut turves in his turbaries at Cams Head and at Deepdale near Scarborough, and the abbot of Fountains was engaged in a similar dispute in 1423 over his turbaries at Malham and Kilnsey. Hexham Abbey's land in 1415 included 2 acres of meadow at Dotland used for drying peats. Turbaries in the Marshland district of west Norfolk were the subject of an agreement between the prior of Lewes, the abbot of Bury and the bishop of Ely in 1207. The account rolls and registers of Norwich Cathedral Priory and St Benet's Abbey show that both had important turf-cutting rights in east Norfolk between the twelfth and fifteenth centuries, and it was this activity which produced the distinctive landscape of the Broads, when the turbaries were abandoned and flooded. Turbaries were less important in the Somerset Levels, but Athelney Abbey retained rights to take fuel from the extensive alder beds in North Moor and Stathe Moor, while Glastonbury Abbey enjoyed similar rights in the Sowy moors. The Lanercost cartulary contains a couple of thirteenth-century grants of turbaries to the canons, illustrated by thumbnail sketches of figures with turf-cutting spades.

However, reclamation for permanent pasture, meadow or even arable land could offer rich rewards to those prepared to undertake it. On Battle Abbey's property at Barnhorne in 1305 arable land reclaimed from the marsh yielded twice the income of the upland arable, and reclaimed meadow three times as much. The pasture on Tintern Abbey's Moor Grange, on the Gwent Levels, was worth double what could be raised from their other holdings.

In general, coastal marshlands underlain by marine or riverine alluvium were more likely to undergo early and extensive colonisation than peat moors further inland, where reclamation began later. On the deeper peat moors grassland was usually the best option. However, a surprising amount of reclaimed land was converted to arable. Barley, much more salt-tolerant than wheat, could be grown on reclaimed coastal marshes, and oats, beans, peas and vetches are also recorded.

Reclamation was a complex and delicate process, involving the construction of embankments to keep water away from areas where it was not wanted and drains to remove surplus water. Often it was a piecemeal operation, nibbling out from the margins of higher ground, but sometimes more ambitious schemes were organised, involving substantial watercourse diversions. Not infrequently successful reclamation in one area simply caused extra problems somewhere else, so disputes were common. Also, as land dried out after drainage, the ground level itself could become lowered by several feet, thereby rendering the land more vulnerable to flooding than before. In coastal regions much of the reclamation undertaken optimistically during the marine regression of the eleventh and twelfth centuries was undone by a rise in relative sea level in the later Middle Ages, accompanied by severe storms.

Reclamation in the Fens

Around the margins of the Fenland was a string of Benedictine houses of pre-Conquest origin: Ely, Ramsey, Peterborough, Thorney, Crowland and Spalding. Later monastic foundations, the Benedictines of Bardney, the Cistercians of Revesby and Kirkstead, the Augustinians of Kyme, the Premonstratensians of Barlings and Tupholme, and the nuns of Stixwould, overlooked the wetlands of the Witham Valley. On the opposite side of the Wash, Lewes Priory had marshland estates in west Norfolk. It is, therefore, not surprising that monastic houses played a significant role in the reclamation of the Fens.

One of the earliest documented works occurs in the time of Abbot Brihtnoth of Ely (970-96), when Leo, the monk placed in charge of the abbey's temporalities, undertook the digging of a great ditch called the Abbot's Delf, which marked the boundary of the abbey's property in addition to aiding the drainage.

Peterborough Abbey lay on the western edge of the peat fens, which were valued for their pasture even though subject to occasional flooding. Here, fen reclamation became more important at just the time when woodland assarting was beginning to decline. The growth of settlements of small tenants, herdsmen and cottagers can be documented at Eye in the twelfth century and at Glinton by the early thirteenth century. The abbey developed two granges in this area. One was based upon the island of Oxney, where 25 acres on the island itself and a further 60 pieces of land amounting to 30 acres in the surrounding fen were purchased for the abbey by Bishop Aethelwold of Winchester. By 1125 a single cowherd lived there with 23 cattle, and it was regarded as part of the vaccary of Eye. Traces of a moat still surround the house there. Early in the fourteenth century Abbot Godfrey created a new grange on reclaimed pasture at Northolm, at the same time enclosing over 200 acres of meadow at Cranmore.

Quarrels over boundaries, over the raising and lowering of dykes and over rights of way over land and water involved all the fenland abbeys in prolonged legal disputes with each other and with other neighbours. The bounds of Kingsdelf were in dispute between Ramsey and Thorney in 1345, while in 1481 it was reported that an unknown malefactor had broken down the dyke of Knareditch, thereby drowning the land and destroying the crops of the abbey of Thorney.

Reclamation in the Somerset Moors (15)

The recurring inundations of the Somerset moors derived from a high rainfall on the surrounding hills and an obstructed outfall to the sea, complicated further by the high tidal range within the Bristol Channel. Piecemeal reclamation here can be documented at least from the twelfth century. At this period Glastonbury Abbey's control over its lands was weak, and the initiative lay mainly with its tenants until Abbot Henry of Blois (1126-71) began returning to a policy of direct management. Later abbots concerned themselves not just with new works, but also attempted to regain control of intakes made by others. By 1234 Abbot Michael Amesbury's survey records 722 acres of meadow reclaimed from the low land around the Sowy Island. Abbot Michael also began the process of reclaiming the moors around Brent, building the first sea-wall at Brent Marsh. From the middle of the thirteenth century the abbey stepped up its efforts, undertaking several major river diversions and

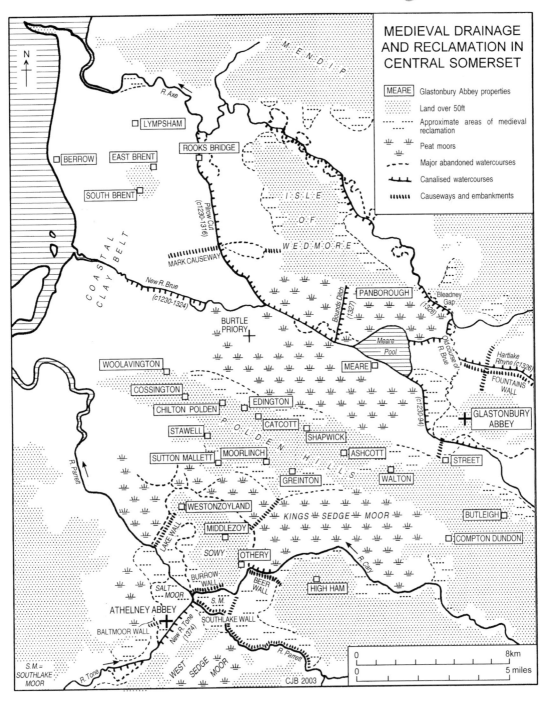

15 *Monastic drainage and reclamation in the Somerset Levels, showing causeways, embankments and canalised watercourses.*
Adapted from Michael Williams, 1970

constructing a series of floodbanks and causeways. The Rivers Brue, Hartlake and Sheppey, which all originally flowed north through the Panborough-Bleadney gap, were diverted westwards into Meare Pool, and the causeways of Beer Wall and Greylake Fosse were built. Further extensions and repairs to the sea walls at Brent were carried out during the fourteenth century under Abbots Adam Sodbury and Walter Monington. The extents of Glastonbury manors between 1309 and 1324 studied by Michael Williams have demonstrated the high value of meadowland in the Levels – at Shapwick only 17 per cent of the land consisted of meadow, but this contributed 55 per cent of the income from the manor, while at Glastonbury itself 34 per cent of the land lay under meadow, accounting for 64 per cent of the income.

One of the first well-documented reclamation episodes concerns the 485 acres of Southlake Moor, one of the lowest-lying moors, at the confluence of the River Cary with the Parrett. Although this was owned by Glastonbury Abbey, various other proprietors and tenants shared rights of common pasture through the summer. Around 1255 a series of embankments, up to 12ft high and 30ft wide, was constructed to surround the moor and exclude the flood-waters. Abbot Michael Amesbury and his successor, Roger Ford, prompted by the abbey's needs for more winter fodder and increased rent income, then embarked upon a policy of extinguishing rights of common pasture held by others in order to be able to extend the reclamation process further, and they achieved a degree of success in this.

Glastonbury Abbey's exploitation of the moors often brought it into conflict with adjacent proprietors. In 1311 a neighbouring landowner breached the Southlake Wall and the abbey complained that a thousand acres of barley, beans, oats and peas had been drowned (almost certainly an exaggeration), along with 50 acres of meadow and 300 acres of pasture. The bishops of Wells also had extensive pastures and fisheries there, and their tenants often retained common grazing rights on Glastonbury land and vice versa. During the 1320s the Hartlake Rhyne was realigned and the Bounds Ditch was constructed between the bishop's manor of Wedmore and the abbot's manor of Meare to mark the boundary between the two estates.

Athelney Abbey had extensive interests in the south-western portion of the Somerset moors. In 1374 it embarked upon an ambitious scheme to divert the River Tone, building the Baltmoor Wall to block its original northward outfall through the gap between Athelney and Lyng, and colluded with other owners to turn the flow eastwards into a new, straight, embanked channel, three-quarters of a mile long, joining the River Parrett near Burrow Bridge (**15**). This carried floodwater away from the abbey's own land on Salt Moor, but worsened the problems in the moors to the south and east. Athelney was never as powerful as Glastonbury, and its actions attracted much opposition from the dean of Wells and other proprietors.

Reclamation on Romney Marsh and the Sussex coast

Several monastic houses were involved in reclamation on Romney Marsh, an area vulnerable to occasional severe storms. Gervase of Canterbury describes the great floods of 1287-8, when the old Appledore Wall and other sea defences were breached, the River Rother turned into a new course, and the towns of Broomhill and Old Winchelsea were overwhelmed.

The Cathedral Priory of Christ Church, Canterbury, had extensive marshland holdings at Ebony, Appledore, Agney and Orgarswick, where it tried alternative policies to minimise the effects of flooding and to increase yields. From the beginning of the twelfth century Appledore was mostly held by tenants, whose leases required them to maintain the sea walls and drains against both salt and fresh water. These measures proved ineffective against the storms of 1287-8, and the abbey resorted to hired labour, spending over £128 on walling and ditching in 1293-4, nearly twice the annual revenue from the manor. By contrast, Ebony, on the Isle of Oxney, had no rent-paying tenants, but was worked entirely by hired labour, growing oats on reclaimed land and deriving most of its revenue from sales of corn, stock and dairy produce. Nearly half the sheep had drowned here in 1287-8, yet recovery was rapid. The priory invested considerable sums in new floodbanks in the ensuing years.

No further reclamation of marsh seems to have been attempted at Ebony after 1305, but efforts to keep the dykes in repair redoubled, suggesting that the process had been pushed to the very limits of what was possible. Timber poles and rails, hurdles, clay, straw, peat-moss, sand and stones were all used in the construction and reinforcement of sea defences at Appledore and Ebony, and hedges were planted on top to reinforce them. In the long term, however, the expense and effort counted for little, producing negligible increases in cultivated area or numbers of stock pastured. Canterbury's small manor of Orgarswick, on the eastern side of Romney Marsh, was primarily used for dairying and sheep farming, although in the time of Prior Henry Eastry the area under oats, legumes and wheat briefly rose to over 160 acres. A field-walking survey by Anne Reeves has contrasted the lack of medieval pottery in Orgarswick's fields with the extensive scatters on many of the neighbouring manors produced by manuring for cultivation.

The Augustinian priory of Bilsington was endowed in 1253 with land at Belgar in Lydd, where reclamation had received a setback from the storms of 1250 and 1252. In 1307 the canons established a claim to 250 acres of tidal marshland beyond the older enclosures, which opened the way for a new campaign of embanking and draining. In 1327 the prior secured the king's consent to enclose 60 acres of salt marsh with banks, to drain it and to bring it into cultivation. However, the cost proved too great, and in 1337 a revised licence permitted 40 of the 60 acres to be granted on perpetual leases to tenants, who were expected to carry out the reclamation works themselves, the canons withdrawing from any further direct involvement.

Further west on the Pevensey Levels Abbot Ralph of Battle (1107-24) began the reclamation of part of Hooe Level below Barnhorne, making large new fields which yielded good crops. The new lands were protected by the construction of the Crooked Ditch, with an embankment alongside it (**16**). Work continued into the middle of the thirteenth century, with the cutting of new watercourses in 1210-24 and 1235-48. The great storms of 1287-8 flooded the whole of the Pevensey Levels, but most of the damage was recovered. By 1305 even the manorial buildings had been moved further west to have easier access to the new land. Rising sea level caused renewed problems with flooding through the later fourteenth century, though the construction of new defences and raising of existing banks in 1356-7, 1374, 1385-6 and

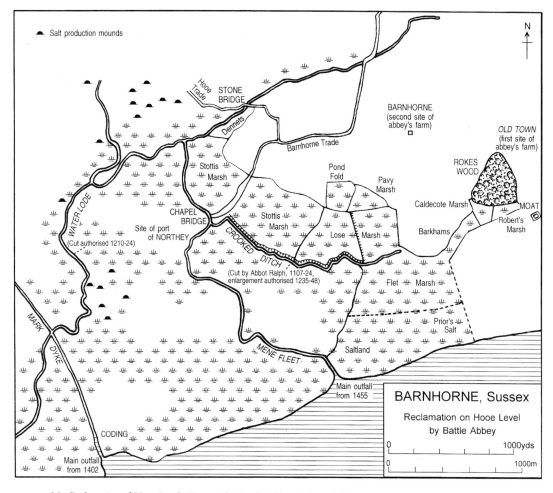

16 *Reclamation of Hooe Levels (Sussex) by Battle Abbey.* Adapted from Peter Brandon, 1971

1402 still permitted substantial acreages of the marsh to be ploughed. Eventually, however, further flooding in 1409, and particularly in 1420-1, caused cultivation to be abandoned in favour of permanent cattle pasture.

Reclamation in Essex and Kent

Much of Barking Abbey's property lay in the coastal marshes north of the Thames. The losses suffered by the nuns through the disastrous floods of 1377 and their subsequent expenditure in repairing the sea wall was acknowledged by the king, who released them from much of their obligation to maintain his park boundary at Havering in 1380. In 1384 the nuns were allowed to impress labourers for emergency works on Barking Marsh, which was in danger of being entirely lost to the sea. In 1409 they received tax relief in recognition of their efforts to preserve their lands at a cost of over £2,000, despite which they had lost 600 acres of meadow in Dagenham Marsh and another 120 acres of wheat elsewhere.

A little further upriver, the Cistercians of Stratford Langthorn had unwillingly taken on the burden of maintaining the sea wall around the marshes of West Ham. The abbot twice complained – in 1280 and 1292 – that other local proprietors had failed to contribute towards the cost. A later abbot in 1339 tried unsuccessfully to foist the responsibility for upkeep of one of the dykes at West Ham onto the nuns of St Leonard at Stratford-by-Bow.

On the southern side of the Thames estuary the priors of Christ Church, Canterbury, adopted a policy of leasing the marshes to freehold tenants and encouraging them to undertake the improvements. Parts of the Cliffe Marshes below Gravesend were enclosed by this means in the 1290s, as was the Seasalter Level near Whitstable in the 1320s, and similar works continued into the fifteenth century.

By contrast, in the East Kent marshes the priory itself took a much more active role. Its manor of Monkton on Thanet in 1288 included over 250 acres of marsh, of which 61 acres was leased to manorial tenants. By 1302 the priory demesne in the marsh had increased through a prolonged campaign of embanking and draining to 366 acres, while the holdings of the tenants had decreased to 53 acres. The earthen wall along the Stour estuary was reinforced with hurdles and piles and thatched with straw, groynes of poles and faggots were made along the estuary side to break the force of the waves, and ditches and gutters made for removing floodwater from the marsh. Here the new land was used entirely for sheep pasture and dairy farming. Further south, the prior held over 400 acres on the coastal marsh of Lydden, some of which was leased to tenants in the late thirteenth century, but much was kept in hand. Here we have detailed records of reclamation works in 1317-18, including the making of a new sea wall with a triple crest, the widening and deepening of ditches, and the conducting of watercourses through wooden gutters to the sea. As a result, the arable acreage was increased, while the numbers of agisted sheep more than doubled between 1291 and 1330.

St Augustine's Abbey in Canterbury also had two important manors with marshland holdings in east Kent, Chislet on the west side of the Wantsum channel, and Minster-in-Thanet. Here, too, reclamation works were undertaken during the twelfth and thirteenth centuries, including the Sarre Wall carrying the main road from Canterbury to Thanet over the Wantsum marshes. Canterbury Cathedral Priory's works at Monkton could not have worked without the co-operation of St Augustine's on the neighbouring manor of Minster-in-Thanet. Here the names of the 'Abbot's Wall' on Minster Marshes and 'Monks' Wall' in the loop of the Stour near Great Stonar tell their own story (**17**). St Gregory's Priory in Canterbury was also reclaiming land in Thanet.

Reclamation in Yorkshire

The Cistercian monks of Meaux were especially active in the wetlands of east Yorkshire. Meaux Abbey was founded on a low island in the wide marshy valley of the River Hull in 1150, and within a decade the monks had begun modifying the local watercourses. The first cut, the *Eschedike*, made between 1160 and 1182, may have been primarily a canal enabling supplies to be brought up to the abbey from the river. Part of the flow of the Lambwath

17 *The 'Monks' Wall' in the loop of the River Stour at Great Stonar (Kent), on the lands of St Augustine's Abbey, Canterbury*

stream was diverted into this during the second decade of the thirteenth century by a 20ft-wide channel called the *Monkdike*. The remainder of the Lambwath stream was then canalised between 1221 and 1235 into a 16ft-wide channel called the *Forthdike*. The newly-drained land was farmed from North Grange and the granges of Wawne and Heigholme. The mouth of the Hull was diverted and widened to improve its outfall to the Humber, the old course being reduced to a mere drain. The grange of Myton or Wyke was left marooned between the old and new branches of the river, and by the end of the fourteenth century had fallen into ruin, its lands being farmed from the abbey's manor of Tupcotes.

Along the Humber coast the monks of Meaux established further farms on reclaimed land at Keyingham, Salthaugh, Tharlesthorpe and Ottringham by the construction of the Sands Drain and its tributaries. Reclamation may have been made easier at this time by a slight fall in the relative sea level, but this was soon to be reversed. Most of the lands of the Humberside granges were no more than a few feet above sea level, and renewed flooding after 1250 caused extensive losses. The buildings of Salthaugh Grange were replaced on slightly higher ground a little further inland, but a survey of 1396 records 176 acres of Salthaugh Grange and 276 acres of Tharlesthorpe Grange being under water. Although some of the lands of Salthaugh were later recovered, Tharlesthorpe Grange lost well over half its total acreage, and its buildings were permanently abandoned.

Higher up the Hull Valley Bridlington Priory enclosed marshland north-west of Brandesburton to create new areas of meadow at Hempholme and Hallytreeholme. Bridlington was also active in the carrs of the Derwent Valley, in Flotmanby and Willerby. The mouth of the Yorkshire Ouse was protected by a series of embankments constructed before 1200, including Thornton Dam below Blacktoft, built by Thornton Abbey, and Temple Dam built by the Knights Templars of Faxfleet. Further up the Ouse, the Benedictine monks of Selby were also draining and embanking.

In the Vale of Pickering the monks of Rievaulx were reclaiming wetlands after 1158, establishing arable granges at Kekmarish by 1206 and at Loftmarish by 1307 and livestock farms at Lund Grange and elsewhere. The Gilbertine canons of Malton Priory founded a marshland grange at Ryton. In 1342, the abbot of Byland embanked the River Derwent to protect his pastures at Rillington Low Moor, but neighbouring villagers opposed this project and broke down the levees so that the pastures were again flooded.

Other marshland holdings

On a smaller scale, similar processes were taking place in many other wetlands. The Cistercian abbeys of Tintern and Llantarnam, the Victorine abbeys of

Keynsham and Bristol and the Benedictine priory of Goldcliff all had holdings in the Gwent levels. The Warwickshire abbey of Merevale was involved in drainage operations in its distant Lancashire estate of Altcar, which brought it into conflict with the Cistercians of Stanlaw. Yet another Cistercian house, Holm Cultram, obtained consent to reclaim land along the shores of the Solway Firth in 1292.

Records of medieval reclamation tend to be dominated by monastic sources, and it would be easy, therefore, to overestimate the monastic role. In fact, the real initiative often lay with secular lords, freeholders and local communities. Even on monastic estates, the first improvements were often made by tenants; for example, the reclamation, marling and cultivation of a marsh on the Glastonbury manor of Buckland Newton before 1178 was initiated by one Alfred of Lincoln, acting under a concession of abbot Robert. In many parts of the country extensive reclamation had been undertaken before the monasteries began taking their demesnes back in hand; often they simply acquired through grants or purchases lands which had already been reclaimed in order to consolidate them into granges.

End

Irrigated meadows and pastures

Natural winter flooding of marshland encouraged a good growth of early spring grass and, recognising this, monastic proprietors occasionally dammed streams to flood meadows artificially. A custumal of the abbot of Westminster lists services on his manor of Pyrford on the River Wey which include 'damming the water to overflow the lord's meadow'. Maurice Barley has suggested that the dams recorded on Rufford Abbey's grange of Inkersall in 1279, and at Rufford itself in 1335, may have been built by the abbey, not for millponds or fishponds, but to water the sandstone pastures, which were otherwise prone to parching.

Enclosure

Enclosed fields take many different forms and date from many different periods. Landscapes of ancient enclosure, which never passed through an open-field phase, survive in many parts of western Britain, East Anglia and the south-east. In these regions monastic proprietors might inherit and adapt systems of considerable antiquity. A detailed survey by Martin Wildgoose and Richard Hodges of Garendon Abbey's grange at Roystone in the Peak District has shown how the monastic enclosures were fitted around patterns of prehistoric and Roman fields, the different periods being distinguished by different types of wall construction.

During the early Middle Ages new enclosed fields were often a product of assarting or marshland reclamation. Coventry Priory's manor of Packwood in the Forest of Arden was entirely enclosed, with no element of communal husbandry. However, enclosure from waste did often conflict with common rights. The canons of Chetwode Priory complained of crop damage because deer from the king's Forest of Brill could not be kept out of their cornfields, and in 1256 Henry III allowed them to enclose their ploughlands. However, this enclosure was contested by various local men in 1313, who claimed rights of common over the land, broke down the enclosure and pastured their beasts there. Conversely, other proprietors might also wish to enclose lands over which monastic houses or their tenants claimed common grazing. In 1297 Abbot John Kent of Glastonbury reached agreement with William Knight of Lovecote concerning land at South Damerham, whereby the common pasture of the heath at The Howe was to be shared, William being allowed to enclose and hold in severalty 18 acres of the heath called Oldland which lay beneath the Howe, while the rest of Oldland was to be held in severalty by William from 2 February to 25 June and then in common by the abbot's tenants for the rest of the year.

Temporary enclosures could be made out of open fields. At Brokenborough, on the downs just north of Malmesbury, the productivity of the manor was increased by enclosing and cultivating part of the fallow field; the men of Corston and Rodbourn who owed ploughing services to the abbot of Malmesbury were permitted to make a breach in the dyke of Richard of Bremilham's land, wherever Richard decided, so that they could get in and out until they had completed ploughing, as had been the arrangement in Richard's father's time; they were to mend the dyke after ploughing and common rights were to continue.

During the later Middle Ages declining crop yields, reduced markets and high costs of labour had begun to tilt the balance away from arable farming, and monastic and lay lords alike began to look towards alternative forms of land use, in particular the relative profitability of sheep. John Rous, writing towards the end of the fifteenth century, castigated the monks of Pipewell who had converted the former village of Cawston-on-Dunsmore to an enclosed grange: "the monks are delighted with the profits of enclosure, but the local people who have been despoiled by it are grieved at the robbery committed". The extent to which open-field arable land was being enclosed for conversion to pasture during the fifteenth century eventually became a matter of national concern, and in 1517 a commission of inquiry was set up by Cardinal Wolsey to investigate the matter. The returns of this inquiry are geographically incomplete, and do not document enclosure before 1488, but they record accusations against the heads of over 40 monastic houses, mostly in the midlands. Despite the reputation of the Cistercians for their ruthless approach to enclosure, Benedictine and Augustinian houses figure equally prominently.

The prior of Daventry was said to have enclosed the fields of Thrupp in Norton (Northamptonshire) in 1489, converting 400 acres to pasture. The abbot of Peterborough had carried out smaller enclosures in nine different places, and at Southorpe the new closes are named: 24 acres in 'Moche Bette', 5 acres in 'Little Bette' and 6 acres in 'Sowbridgeclose'. The prior of Malvern had enclosed 262 acres at Shuttington. John Penny, abbot of Leicester, had enclosed and converted to pasture 216 acres in Baggrave and 124 acres in Kirkby Mallory. The abbot of Pipewell had enclosed and converted 200 acres in Rushton, and the abbot of Eynsham and prior of Bicester had done likewise at Little Rollright and Wretchwick respectively. Substantial enclosures were especially prevalent on home manors: the abbot of Stoneleigh, the prior of Bradwell and the prioress of Catesby had all enclosed 300 acres or more. At Water Eaton in Oxfordshire the abbot of Oseney was accused of enclosing 107 acres, and in 1511 he enclosed the whole of the South Field there by agreement with his tenants, granting them alternative lands which concentrated their holdings in the west and north of the township. Monastic lessees also appear amongst those charged, including John Arden, who had converted 200 acres of arable land on Rewley Abbey's manor of Willaston to pasture and enclosed 60 acres of pasture; William Counser, who had converted 30 acres at Fulwell where he kept 400 sheep for Oseney Abbey; and two lessees of Eynsham Abbey who had converted 200 more acres at Little Rollright. Smaller enclosures down to three acres are recorded.

Other substantial monastic enclosures escaped the notice of Wolsey's commissioners. Luffield Priory's township of Charlock in Abthorpe was wholly enclosed shortly before 1410. A survey of 1540 shows Pipewell Abbey's manor of Elkington as being wholly enclosed, but sufficiently recently for the names of the former open fields to be remembered. Sulby had been an openfield village in 1377, but by the Dissolution the Premonstratensian canons there held 1,180 acres of pasture in eight closes.

In the midlands the new enclosures were commonly bounded by hedges and ditches, often noted by Wolsey's commissioners. Some of the hedges can still be recognised today, gently curved in outline and generally richer in shrub species than hedges inserted later to subdivide the great closes. Where stone was readily available, walls might be built instead. Bailiff's accounts of 1387-8 record a number of stone field walls on Tintern's grange of Merthyrgeryn needing repair, and the remains of some of these can still be traced. The Roystone Grange survey was able to distinguish the thirteenth- and fourteenth-century monastic field walls from walls of earlier or later date by their use of massive boulders along the base and smaller stones laid in single thickness above. A particular feature noted here was the occurrence of L-shaped lengths of wall, now usually incorporated within later boundaries, originally used as funnels for collecting and penning sheep.

6
Monastic woodlands

Introduction

Not too long ago, historians and archaeologists tended to regard woodlands in a rather negative sense, as wild remnants of primeval forests which only became valuable when cleared and settled. Thanks very largely to the work of Oliver Rackham, this view has been completely overturned, and we can now recognise medieval woodland as a valued resource, carefully managed to serve a wide variety of needs. Woods provided building material, fuel, grazing and many other resources, often itemised in grants to monastic houses. Around 1219, for example, Snelshall Priory in Buckinghamshire acquired rights in the woods of Tattenhoe, allowing the monks sufficient timber for building, underwood to provide fuel for baking and brewing, and free pasturage for pigs.

The location of monastic woods

The Cistercians often found the isolation they sought by settling within wooded locations. Robin Donkin has noted that one third of all English houses founded before 1250 lay within or very near lands designated as royal forest. It has to be made clear that the idea of 'forest' in the Middle Ages was primarily a legal concept, implying an area subject to the special code of Forest Law, and that 'forests' frequently included large extents of open, unwooded countryside. Nevertheless, Flaxley Abbey, in the Forest of Dean, was hemmed in by dense woods to the west and north, Vale Royal was founded in a place called Monks Wood, described as 'an empty solitude . . . formerly the dwelling-place of bandits', while Leland emphasised the wooded setting of Grace Dieu, Llantarnam and Whitland. Houses of other orders developed from hermitages, such as the Benedictine nunnery of 'Holy Trinity in the Wood' at Markyate, sometimes occupied similar situations.

Some monasteries were endowed with compact blocks of woodland on the margins of their home manor. Remnants of Peterborough's home woods,

Westwood and Eastwood, survived on either side of the town long into the Middle Ages. Monks Wood, a mile south of Sawtry Abbey, covers almost exactly the same area today as the manorial wood recorded in the Domesday survey which was granted to the Cistercians in 1147 (**colour plate 5**). Worcester Cathedral Priory's principal demesne wood was Monk Wood in Grimley, 4 miles north-west of the city. By 1300 the monks were buying up pasturage rights held there by others in order to empark it. However, Monk Wood always seems to have been used primarily as a source of timber and fuel. It provided pales for Hallow Park in 1517; and at the Dissolution, when the manor was granted to the retired prior, William More, he petitioned the king for an annual grant of fuel from Monk Wood. Pershore Abbey lost its home wood of Tiddesley when part of its estate was granted to Westminster by Edward the Confessor, and was still trying in vain to recover its rights there in 1223 (**18**).

Where monastic houses lacked sufficient woodland nearby to meet their needs, one solution was to negotiate mutually beneficial exchanges of rights with other houses. The Domesday survey records a pre-Conquest agreement whereby, in exchange for a share of the fishery of Whittlesey Mere, the abbot of Peterborough was to provide the abbot of Thorney with pasture for 120 pigs, and if the pasture failed he was to feed and fatten 60 pigs with corn; he was also to find timber for one house of 60ft and poles for the enclosure around the house, and to repair the house and enclosure when they were decayed.

Another alternative was to seek to acquire woodland properties at a greater distance. St Peter's Abbey, Gloucester, had much land on the east side of the Forest of Dean. Evesham had a partly-wooded manor at Ombersley, 17 miles to the west in the Severn Valley. Eynsham Abbey's woodland was concentrated on its manor of South Stoke, which extended over the Chilterns to Woodcote, 22 miles away to the south-east. In 1109 Eynsham acquired what came to be known as Abbots Wood in Woodcote, comprising 348 acres. Its smaller woods in South Stoke were leased out to tenants, but the abbey retained Abbots Wood in demesne until the Dissolution. Ely Abbey drew its timber from a large block of woodland 50 miles away at Hatfield in Hertfordshire. Westminster Abbey had several hundred acres of woods in Essex (in Feering, Kelvedon and South Benfleet) and Hertfordshire (mostly in Stevenage), and further woodland nearly a hundred miles away in the Forest of Arden at Knowle, whence it sold 414 oaks for £90 in 1302-3. The Cistercians of Basingwerk held woods in the Peak Forest, while Warden Abbey had woodland in the Forest of Huntingdon.

Abingdon Abbey lay in open country in the Thames Valley, but its estates included woodland in four main locations. The most extensive, but most distant, woods lay 30 miles to the south-east, where Domesday Book records four hides of the abbey's land in Winkfield lying within the royal Forest of Windsor. The neighbouring manor of Whistley returned woodland for 50

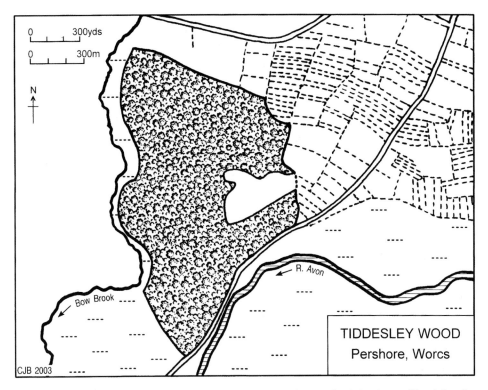

18 *Tiddesley Wood (Worcestershire): Pershore Abbey's home wood, granted to Westminster Abbey before the Norman Conquest, retains its medieval bounds*

swine in 1086, and receipts from pannage (fees for allowing pigs to forage for acorns and beechmast at certain seasons) and sale of pigs there appear in the kitchener's account of *c*.1377. The Domesday survey records a second block of woodland 15 miles to the south on the dip-slope of the Berkshire Downs, at Chieveley and Welford, which together provided pannage for 80 swine, and at Farnborough, which provided wood for fencing. Tithes from Farnborough in the eleventh century were paid in timber for building works at the abbey, and Abingdon still held a 30-acre wood there called Gungrove at the Dissolution. In 1428-9, eight cartloads of planks, joists and boards were taken from Welford to repair the abbey laundry. Closest to the abbey were the wooded hills of Cumnor and Wytham, within the great bend of the Thames to the north. Curiously the Domesday survey reveals very little wood in this area, but characteristic woodland place-names and charter evidence leave little doubt of its character. Bagley Wood, which still exists, is well documented from the twelfth century onwards. In 1408 the abbey acquired Upwood in Marcham, which it still held at the Dissolution. Finally, east of the Thames the abbey held some woodland in Cuddesdon, and in 1267 it proposed to enclose Coombe Wood to protect it from deer straying from the royal forest of Shotover.

Woodland management

Medieval woods were far from uniform, and surviving examples today reflect something of their ancient variety. Oliver Rackham's examination of the woods formerly belonging to Bury St Edmunds Abbey has shown that, while mixed woods of ash, hazel and maple are particularly common, Groton Wood is dominated by small-leaved lime, Westhall Wood in Rickinghall by hornbeam, Lineage and Spelthorne Woods in Long Melford by coppiced elm, while Felshamhall Wood in Bradfield St George is a plateau alderwood.

Woodland was managed in a variety of ways: high forest, where standard trees growing close together and competing for light produced tall straight trunks; wood-pasture, characteristic of deer parks and open forest glades, where trees were pollarded to allow them to produce crops of wood out of reach of browsing deer; coppices, where trees were cut to ground level at regular intervals, the wood then being fenced to exclude grazing livestock while the stools regenerated and produced a new crop of pole-wood; and coppice-with-standards, where a limited number of standard trees were left within a coppice in order to retain some supply of larger timber. All four management systems can be recognised on monastic properties (wood-pasture will be discussed in chapter 10).

The high forest system was relatively rare in the Middle Ages. Nevertheless, 8 acres of woodland in Nettlebed held by Dorchester Abbey in 1338 was said to be worth only 4s a year because there was no underwood, and this was presumably exclusively of timber standards. High forest also appears to be indicated by some of the surveys of monastic woodlands made at the Dissolution. Gilbert's Wood near Abbey Dore, valued at £80, was enclosed with a hedge and contained 120 acres, of which 13 acres was of 50 years' growth and the remainder of 100 years' growth or more. Here the age structure of the trees indicates past management by clear felling. A 1554 survey of another wood which had belonged to the Premonstratensians of Talley recorded over 120 great oaks of 80 years' growth and 60 oaks of 50 years' growth. The surviving roof of the Blackfriars in Gloucester shows that each tree had to be 50ft in usable length and over 2ft in diameter, which suggests a similar form of management, and it is known that this timber came from the Forest of Dean.

Coppicing, which produced fenceposts, wattling for the infill of timber-framed walls, faggots for monastic ovens and fireplaces, and fuel for industrial purposes, was the most widespread method of woodland management. One of the earliest detailed records of coppice management occurs in the Beaulieu Abbey account book for 1269-70. Beaulieu's estates were concentrated in the New Forest, and the account book includes a 'forester's table' giving production figures from the abbey's own woods – one acre of coppice cut every 20 years was expected to yield 4,800 bundles of firewood, 500 bushels of vine-stakes or fencing-rods and 4,000 oven faggots, with any wood left over going for charcoal, making a total of 2 tons of wood per acre per year. Sales from the coppices produced a regular annual income of a little over 2s per acre. A survey of the woods of the abbot of Bury St Edmunds in Long Melford in 1386 noted that in the 90 acres of Lineage Wood 15 acres could be cut each year, and that a similar six-year coppicing cycle was operating in the 80-acre Spelthorne Wood and in the 60-acre Little Park.

At the Dissolution the Abbey Cwmhir estate included a coppice-wood of 30 acres divided into 15 blocks, each of 2 acres, each block containing trees of uniform age from one year up to 20 years. A detailed survey of the 94 acres of demesne woods of the recently-dissolved Leicestershire nunnery of Langley purchased by Thomas Grey in 1543 describes six woods or closes plus the hedgerows about the demesne, including 10 acres thin set of 30 years' growth worth £3 5s 8d; 20 acres of 22 years' growth worth £40; 3 acres of 15 years' growth worth £5; 3 acres of 10 years' growth worth £15; and 30 acres of one year's growth worth £30, in addition to 16 acres of 10-11 years' growth retained for the lord's own use for building, fencing and fuel, 8 acres used as common waste and 4 acres destroyed by cattle.

In many former monastic woods coppicing continued into the nineteenth century. The north part of Leigh Woods, just west of Bristol, which had belonged to the canons of St Augustine's Abbey, was managed in this way throughout the Middle Ages, and remains today a characteristic ancient woodland landscape with many old coppice stools, dominated by small-leaved lime, with ash, oak, hazel and occasional wild service (**colour plate 6**). By contrast, the southern part of the wood, on a different manor, was used as a wood-pasture common from the Middle Ages to the mid-nineteenth century, and still has many old pollard oaks within more recent secondary woodland. Bury St Edmunds Abbey's Felshamhall Wood in Bradfield St George survives substantially intact within its ancient boundary bank; coppicing is documented here since 1252, and still continues today.

Coppice-with-standards may have become more common after 1543, when a statute required the retention of a minimum of 12 standard trees per acre. However, when Thame Abbey sold a crop of coppice wood and timber from 'Notepotegrove' in its Chiltern manor of Wyfold in 1355, the purchasers agreed to fell the wood by 'reasonable pieces' (possibly meaning separate coppices), but were allowed to fell the 'great trees' (standards) when they pleased during the term granted. The abbot and convent reserved the right to enclose those parts of the wood cleared after the underwood crop was taken away, to prevent animals from entering. At the Dissolution the Abbey Cwmhir estate included 10 acres of 10-year-old coppice which also contained short shredded 60-year-old oak standards, and another 20 acres of 20-year-old coppice with a few oak standards of 60 years' growth. The Bury St Edmunds woods of Groton and Howe, 37 acres and 4 acres respectively, together contained 200 30- and 40-year-old timber oaks in addition to 10 acres of coppice of 3 years' growth, 10 acres of 7 years' growth, 15 acres of 10 years' growth and 6 acres of 14 years' growth.

After coppices had been cut they needed to be enclosed in order to stop livestock from nibbling new shoots from the stools. Merevale Abbey's woods at Grendon were hedged, and the abbey paid Thomas Hegger for 22 days' work hedging and ditching around the coppices of Bentley Park in 1499. Shortly before the middle of the thirteenth century the monks of Meaux were permitted to widen the ditch around Routh Wood and to make ditches alongside the road from the wood to the abbey. This wood has gone, but the oval outline of the ditch around it still survives in part.

Monasteries and the royal forests

The extent of land under Forest Law fluctuated through the Middle Ages but, at its greatest extent in the later twelfth century, it may have covered up to one-third of the whole of England. Designation as forest did not force a monastery to surrender woods which it already owned there, nor did it prevent the king from granting rights and privileges within the forests to monastic corporations. Most forests were a patchwork of royal and private woods and pastures. Bordesley Abbey gave 100 marks for confirmation of possession of its woods of Holloway, Tutnall and Tardebigge within the Forest of Feckenham in 1230. In 1238 it paid a further £20 for the right to enclose its woods. By 1362 woodland made up the largest and most profitable part of Bordesley's grange of Knotteshull, amounting to 185 acres worth 92s, compared with 120 acres of arable worth 40s, 10 acres of meadow worth 10s and 24 acres of waste held in common. In 1252 Simon de Montfort, earl of Leicester, gave to the canons of St Mary-in-the-Meadows on the outskirts of Leicester 320 acres of land and wood in his chase of Leicester Forest, with all things growing there. The bounds of the grant were recited in detail, and the canons were permitted to enclose the land with a dyke and to cultivate it or make whatever profit from it they chose, free of all obligations, with the grantor retaining only his right to venison.

The confirmation charter granted by Henry II to Flaxley Abbey included rights to timber and wood for repair of their buildings, so long as they did not commit waste in the forest. The general terms of this grant were clearly susceptible to abuse, and the monks found it necessary to make frequent appeals to the king through the thirteenth century to reassert their rights.

Building timber

Monastic building programmes had a particular need for massive trees for spanning the roofs of great churches and other major claustral buildings. This need was usually greatest during the first half-century after the foundation, though later moves of site, rebuilding programmes or accidental fire damage might generate a fresh demand. Thirty oaks were used in the rebuilding of Thame Abbey's chancel in 1236.

Sometimes the timber could be supplied from the abbey's own woods, but the king often contributed by grants from the royal forests. Beaulieu Abbey received at least 128 trunks between 1204 and 1251, while Netley Abbey received 86 trunks between 1239 and 1291. In 1235 20 oaks went to Grace Dieu Abbey, 40 oaks went to Stoneleigh Abbey in 1241, and in 1298 80 oaks from Pamber Forest were granted to Westminster Abbey, all for repairs after fires. A total of 70 oaks from the royal park of North Petherton in Somerset were sent to the sisters of the Order of St John at Minchin Buckland between 1234 and 1236 for the rebuilding of their house after its destruction by fire.

In 1229 Flaxley Abbey was allowed two oaks in the hays of the Forest of Dean for the roof of an aisle in the church. Two years later the abbey was granted 10 oaks in St Briavels for repairs to its buildings, but it was only able to obtain four, and a second grant awarding the remaining six had to be repeated the following year. In 1233 four further oaks were granted for repairs, and the following year the constable of St Briavels was again ordered not to hinder the abbot in having the timber. Grace Dieu Abbey acquired 20 trees from the Forest of Dean in 1235, with further grants from Grosmont in 1240 and from Seinfrenny Wood near Skenfrith in 1253, involving journeys of 4 to 8 miles.

Many grants from the Forest of Dean were made to monastic houses at a greater distance, where building timber was more difficult to obtain. The Abbot of Pershore was allowed 100 oaks in 1233, and ten more oaks with their strippings went to Pershore in 1288. Between 1241 and 1265 a total of 61 oaks went to the Gloucester Blackfriars. In 1245 and 1246 100 oaks were supplied to Hailes Abbey, 20 miles away on the Cotswolds. Between 1251 and 1253 45 oaks went from the Forest of Dean to Halesowen Abbey, 20 of which were intended for the dormitory.

Elsewhere, Clarendon Forest provided five oaks to the Greyfriars in Salisbury in 1230, four oaks to Mottisfont Priory in 1275 and 30 oaks for the church of Wilton Abbey in 1276. Shirlet Forest supplied 30 oaks to Buildwas Abbey, 4 miles away, in 1232. The canons of St Thomas' Priory east of Stafford received six timber oaks from Teddesley Hay in Cannock Forest in 1255 and 1269, and in 1272 they received ten more oaks from Kinver Forest. Further grants for the church roof were made in 1275 and 1290. Stanley Abbey received 65 oaks from Pewsham Forest between 1214 and 1224, and grants from Pewsham and Melksham Forests continued in later years, including timber for the church tower in 1237. The prioress of Amesbury received 20 oaks from Chute Forest for the repair of the cloisters in 1231, and 16 rafters for the church roof three years later. The abbess of Romsey received five good oaks from Melchet Forest for planks for the dormitory in 1231.

Church furnishings also required quality timber. In 1230-1 the prioress of Amesbury had five oaks from Clarendon Forest for making and repairing stalls. The Cistercians of Cleeve Abbey had two oaks from the royal park of North Petherton in 1232 for their choir stalls. The abbot of Halesowen had five oaks from the Forest of Dean in 1251 for stalls and other works. The Oxford Blackfriars received six oaks from Pamber Forest for repairs to their stalls in 1291. Glastonbury Abbey had three oaks from North Petherton Park in 1250 for making images for the abbey church. Timber grants were also made for a wide variety of miscellaneous purposes: Stratford Langthorn Abbey received six 'batons' for a mill in 1225, while Fountains Abbey received eight oaks from Knaresborough for repair of a bridge in 1227.

Timber was often transported over considerable distances. Blackmoor Forest supplied 50 oaks for the church of Bindon Abbey, 12 miles away, in 1233. Biddlesden Abbey in Buckinghamshire in 1234 received 50 oaks from Henley Park, a distance of 36 miles. Ten oaks from Sherwood Forest were granted in 1255 to Salley Abbey, 75 miles away in Yorkshire. As early as 1177 Godstow Nunnery, just outside Oxford, was taking timber from the Wyre Forest, over 60 miles away. Perhaps the most impressive achievement of all is the carriage of 30 oaks to Bury St Edmunds from the Forest of Inglewood in Cumberland, a minimum journey of 250 miles. Such effort seems curious, almost perverse, for even where the recipient houses were in open country, there must always have been woodland much closer to hand. One reason may be that by the middle of the thirteenth century, the great oaks needed for major roofing works were getting in increasingly short supply, and could not be obtained from local woods which were regularly cropped. Even some of the royal forests were becoming so depleted by the 1250s that the king felt obliged to suspend benefactions. Another factor may be the local availability of skilled sawyers which, as Rackham has pointed out, may have been more critical than the location of trees at a time when transport was relatively cheap. Merevale Abbey employed two sawyers from Tamworth for 18s from Trinity Sunday to Christmas in 1498 to saw 18,000 boards.

Occasionally we find glimpses of the work involved in hauling timber. At the beginning of the twelfth century Abingdon Abbey was drawing timber from the Welsh Marches 'with great cost and heavy labour', using six wains with twelve oxen to each of them. It took six or seven weeks for the great waggons to get to Shrewsbury and back. Vale Royal Abbey was more fortunate in having timber supplies closer to hand in Delamere and Mondrem Forests, but the building accounts of 1278-81 vividly depict the hundreds of journeys made with horses bringing timber and boards to the site.

Fuel resources

Fuel for domestic warmth, cooking and industrial purposes was a never-ending demand. Glastonbury Abbey's final account roll of 1538-9 records the consumption of 27,000 bundles of fuel in this one year. The nuns of Wilton had a customary right to 80 loads of firewood a year from Melchet Forest. Henry II allowed the Cistercians of Quarr two loads of dead wood a year from the New Forest. In 1229 the sisters of Minchin Buckland received the first of a series of grants of dead wood, cablish (windfallen wood), thorn, buckthorn and maple from North Petherton Park for fuel. The alien priory of Monk Sherborne was allowed two cartloads of dead wood a week from Pamber Forest in 1246 'so that they take no greenwood'. In 1276 the Blackfriars of Wilton received 10 cartloads of brushwood from Clarendon Forest. In 1277 the prior of Cold Norton received 30 cartloads of brushwood from the royal park of Woodstock. Additional grants might be made in severe winters. Bruern Abbey had an allowance of two cartloads of wood a day from Wychwood Forest since its foundation, but in 1216 this was supplemented by a third load of dead wood, branches and underwood. In 1231 the nuns of Amesbury were allowed six dead trees from Buckholt, six from Chute Forest and three from Grovely Forest for their fire; two years later they received five loads of firewood from Clarendon Forest in addition to their customary privilege of estover there. Vale Royal Abbey was given all the dead wood in the Forest of the Peak, 30 miles away, in 1302, for a five-year term. Richard I granted the woods around Flaxley Abbey to the monks for firewood. The bounds of these woods are described in detail, and can be traced on the ground today. Nevertheless, asserting these rights again brought the abbey into conflict with the royal forest officials. In 1222 the constable of Bristol Castle was ordered to allow the abbot and monks to have reasonable estover (the right to collect firewood) in their woods of *Ermegrave* and *Ruggemore*, as they had been accustomed to have in the time of King John. Three years later the monks were again driven to petition the king to assign some spot in the forest near the abbey from which they could take firewood, and the king ordered such a plot to be measured off.

Allowances of fuel were regularly made to tenants. The Hundred Rolls of 1279 record that Eynsham Abbey allowed 23 villeins one cartload of wood each for 'cooking of their meat' from Abbot's Wood in South Stoke. The vicar of South Stoke was entitled to eight cartloads of firewood from the same wood in 1399, to be pulled by three horses, while in 1536 the lessee of the manor was entitled to 30 loads of hardwood for fuel, with 'sufficient hedgebote, cartbote and plowbote'. Firewood was also sold – in 1448 the woodward recorded sales of underwood called 'bechenwood' from Abbot's Wood for 60s 6d.

Industrial activities consumed considerable quantities of fuel in some areas. It has been estimated that 1 acre of wood converted to charcoal would barely make 2 tons of malleable iron. Flaxley Abbey's ancient right to two oaks a week from the Forest of Dean for the maintenance of its iron forge inevitably led to accusations of waste and damage. In 1229 the monks were allowed dead wood, underwood and old trunks, while being required to restrict their forging operations to the thorn spinneys on the edge of the forest. Finally, in 1258, Henry III gave the monks 968 acres of his demesne south of Cinderford, still called Abbot's Wood, in lieu of their ancient rights. The abbey had this wood free of all forest dues and restrictions, save only the hunting, herbage, eyries of hawks and any mineral works which might occur there. The terms of the grant permitted the abbot to enclose at any one time a tenth of the wood with a hedge to keep out deer and cattle so that it could be coppiced on rotation, which hedge was permitted to stand for four years. This arrangement did not end clashes with the forest officials, however. At the 1282 Dean Forest eyre the abbot of Flaxley was accused of damaging a hedge by burning it to make charcoal, while the abbot of Gloucester was also presented for making charcoal at Hope Mansell. Complaints were again laid against the abbot of Flaxley in 1331 for cutting his woods and making charcoal without view of the forest officials.

In the north midlands charcoal-burning is recorded several times in the woods of Croxden Abbey. Croxden seems to have been supplying forges worked by laymen rather than making iron on its own account (**114**). Sales of charcoal from the Newhay, a wood at Cheadle, fetched £11 5s in 1316, while sales of underwood from Oaken Park fetched £24 in 1329. In 1369 Abbot William Gunston raised 119 marks from charcoal sales. Further north the master smith of Fountains Abbey was granted the right in 1195 to collect as much dead wood within the Forest of Knaresborough, standing or lying, as he needed for making charcoal, in exchange for an annual rent of 10s and 60 horseshoes. Around 1200 two further benefactors gave Fountains Abbey 24 acres in Kirkheaton Wood and dead wood for charcoal for their smithies.

Monasteries possessing saltworks in Droitwich also had an insatiable need for fuel, and woodland to supply the demand was sometimes attached to their properties. In 956 five salt furnaces were granted to Worcester Priory, along with land in the woodland manor of Phepson. In 1086 Westminster Abbey's manor of Hussingtree rendered 100 cartloads of wood for the saltpans each year. Later commentators blamed the salt-workers for destroying woods in the area, though this may reflect their lack of understanding of the coppicing process. Leland similarly records the opinion of some local men that lead smelting at Strata Florida's grange of Cwmystwyth had ceased because the 'wood is sore wasted'.

Miscellaneous woodland products

Oak bark was in demand for leather tanning. Before 1182 Robert de Vaux granted the bark from timber felled in his woods in Gilsland to the canons of

Lanercost for their tannery. In 1199 Holm Cultram Abbey was permitted to take bark in the Forest of Inglewood. Around 1240 Gilbert Marshall, sixth Earl of Pembroke, gave to Tintern Abbey all the bark from wood felled in the lower forest of Went, for 2d a load.

The old name of the site of Flaxley Abbey, *Castiard*, means 'chestnut wood'. The sweet chestnut, introduced in the Roman period, had become naturalised in the Forest of Dean. The Crown reserved all chestnut timber to itself, but Flaxley Abbey's foundation grant included tithes of chestnuts from the forest, which produced a considerable income.

Common pasture rights in forests and woods

The designation of a tract of land as royal forest did not automatically extinguish all common rights, which were often of considerable antiquity. The pasturage of domestic cattle and horses and the pannage of swine were not incompatible with the maintenance of a wood-pasture regime suitable for deer. Henry III allowed the nuns of Ivinghoe to run 60 pigs every year in the forest of Windsor without paying herbage or pannage fees. Nevertheless, the practice of grazing, both for those with customary rights and for outsiders who purchased agistments, was at first strictly regulated by forest officials. In 1280 for example, it was reported that the Abbot of Beaulieu and the priors of Christchurch and Breamore had an excess of livestock grazing in the New Forest, damaging the pasture of the king's deer. Henry II's confirmation charter to Flaxley had spelled out the abbey's rights to pasture in the Forest of Dean for their young cattle and hogs and for all other beasts. However, repeated correspondence with the royal officials suggests that, once again, there were conflicts. In 1235 some of the abbot's cattle were impounded for trespass during the fence month (the fawning season in the 15 days before and after midsummer).

Common pasture rights were equally closely regulated outside the royal forests. In 1366 Eynsham Abbey allowed grazing in Abbots Wood in Woodcote to its own tenants from South Stoke and Woodcote, but no outsiders were admitted except for the canons of Notley, who paid 2lb of wax a year for using the common.

Conflicts over woodland

The resources of monastic woods were occasionally plundered by laymen. During Prince Edward's campaign against the remnants of Simon de Montfort's army, which had taken refuge on the Isle of Axholme in 1265-6, he felled Worksop Priory's wood of Grove for timber to make siege engines.

Henry III compensated the canons with a grant of two cartloads of heather from Sherwood Forest, not to exceed 60s in value. In 1303 Abbot Geoffrey of Buckland petitioned Edward, now king, for compensation for the quantity of wood taken for props, ladders and fuel by miners from the royal silver mines of Bere Alston, but he was awarded only £400, less than two-thirds of the assessed damage.

Assertion of common rights sometimes provoked outright violence. Flisteridge Wood in Crudwell, which Malmesbury Abbey claimed to have held since the seventh century, was taken within the Forest of Braden by King John. Despite this, the abbey retained all its traditional rights there, particularly the exclusion of outsiders' pigs between Michaelmas and Martinmas in order to preserve the mast. The cartulary records an incident in 1278 when the Earl of Hereford sent the pigs from his nearby manor of Oaksey to forage in the abbot's wood. The abbot's men had the intrusive pigs impounded at Crudwell, but the earl sent a large armed force from Oaksey to break down the gates of the pound, wounding a number of the abbot's men, and returning the pigs to Flisteridge Wood for 15 days until all the mast was consumed. Another dispute in the early 1220s between Warden Abbey and the thuggish castellan of Bedford, Fawkes de Bréauté, over the ownership of a certain grove, resulted in Fawkes killing one of the monks, wounding others, and dragging 30 of the community through the mud to imprisonment in his castle.

Conflicts arose not only with laymen, but also with other monasteries. In 1291 Robert, abbot of Buckland, sent his men into one of Tavistock Abbey's woods to cut timber for the repair of his salmon weir at Hatch Mill. They were apprehended there by Thomas Gyreband, the Tavistock woodward, but wounded him with an arrow so that he fled, leaving behind his coat, axe and bow. Later, in court, Thomas accused the Buckland monks of assault and theft of timber, but the jury confirmed the abbot of Buckland's right to take timber for his weir, and Thomas found himself in gaol for making a false claim.

Woodland conservation

During the early Middle Ages pressure to bring new land into cultivation to feed a growing population had resulted in extensive woodland clearances. As woodland declined in extent, however, much higher value was placed upon that which remained, and a concern for conservation can be detected on many monastic estates. Bury St Edmunds Abbey, while permitting many woods on its more distant holdings to be grubbed up during the twelfth and thirteenth centuries, took care to safeguard its more limited woodlands in west Suffolk and to manage them more intensively through coppicing. As early as 1248 Abbot William Hotot of Peterborough agreed not to sell woodland without the convent's consent, and 50 years later the chronicler commended Abbot

William Woodford, who would only sell woods at the highest rate, 'for he dared not use up the treasure of his church'. In 1251 Fountains Abbey was permitted to assart in Marston only 'outside the wood', and in 1279 the monks of Fountains and Salley agreed not to assart the wood called 'Rys' in Littondale. Early in the fourteenth century the chronicler of Pipewell Abbey castigated recent abbots who had attempted to reduce the abbey's debts by selling off their woods.

The famines and plagues of the early fourteenth century slowed the reduction of woodland by assarting almost to a standstill, but the result may have been to permit laxer forms of management. Later visitation records often include complaints of woodland resources being squandered. In 1438 it was said that the prior of Ulverscroft had cut down 500 good oaks and sold them for only 2d or 3d each, and that when the cowhouses needed repair he made do with ash because he had given away the oak he should have used. The prioress of Langley had sold the timber, had not harvested the underwood for fuel, and had left the woods unfenced after felling so that cattle had got in and trampled down the saplings. In 1446-7 the abbot of Peterborough was said to have wasted the East and West Woods of Peterborough and the wood of Fiskerton in Lincolnshire.

Woodland plantations

It is widely believed that the deliberate planting of woodland, whether for commercial forestry or amenity, was an innovation of the late sixteenth century. However, John Harvey has documented a number of medieval examples, and further instances have since come to light. Monastic estates furnish clear evidence of such plantations; and, although the extent of new woods fell far short of the acreages lost to assarting, it does again demonstrate a concern for the future.

The earliest case found so far is at Alton Priors in Wiltshire, where the Prior of St Swithun's, Winchester, planted a new wood of at least 12 acres in 1260, buying for the purpose 19 quarters of nuts for £1 5s 4d and 8.5 quarters of acorns for 8s 6d. A ditch 323 perches in length was dug around the wood and hedgerow shrubs gathered and planted to shelter the young trees as they grew. Another nutwood called Beauforest was planted in 1276 by the prior of St Swithun's adjoining the garden of his manor house at Silkstead, about 4 miles south-west of Winchester. Before 1287 Henry Newton, a canon of Dunstable Priory, had planted a wood of ash and other trees at Bradbourne in Derbyshire.

Further examples are recorded in the early fourteenth century. Godfrey Crowland, Abbot of Peterborough, planted a wood called Childholm east of Cranmore in Lincolnshire in 1304. The following year he planted another new wood at Northolm in Northamptonshire; and in 1318 he planted a wood called Nabwood at Werrington, north-west of Peterborough, 'where no wood was before', surrounding it with a ditch and a row of willows. Nabwood was felled in the nineteenth century, but aerial photographs still reveal its site as a crop mark, about 3 acres in extent. Elsewhere, John Rutherwyke, abbot of Chertsey, sowed acorns and planted young oaks in his hedgerows and groves east of Hardwyck Grange, Chertsey, in 1307, making further plantations in 1331 and 1339. William Chiriton, Abbot of Evesham (1317-44) enclosed Shrawnell Park at Badsey and had oaks, ashes and other trees planted there. Finally, the prior of Durham had acorns sown in the park of Beaurepaire (now known as Bearpark) in 1429-30.

7

Domestic buildings of monastic manors and granges

Estate domestic buildings and their functions

The Benedictine rule required monks to live within the precinct, where every monastery had its communal dormitory and refectory along with separate dwellings for the abbot or prior. However, the management of extensive estates could not be achieved without bases on outlying properties, and both Benedictine manors and Cistercian granges were provided with suitable dwellings. Similar arrangements were to be found on estates of regular canons and on the commanderies, preceptories and camerae of the military orders. Primarily these served as administrative centres for the demesne farms. Normally on Benedictine estates they were occupied by the abbey's stewards, bailiffs or reeves, while Cistercian granges provided accommodation for lay brothers. Such houses could be made available for the abbot and his retinue during tours of inspection. Sometimes important guests were entertained in them – King Edward I stayed for three days at Evesham Abbey's manor of Offenham in 1289.

Subsequently, as strict observance of the monastic rule relaxed, choir monks themselves occasionally resided outside the precinct. Some dwellings were used as rest-houses after blood-letting, a process recommended by contemporary medical opinion as a cure for the sick and as a therapy for the healthy. Each monk would be bled between three and eight times a year, usually in a room near the infirmary. He would then retire to some pleasant dwelling on the estates for several days of recuperation, before returning to his normal duties. Houses used for this purpose were called 'seyne' or 'seyney' houses. The site of the rest house at Badsey acquired by Abbot Chiriton of Evesham is known, though it was substantially rebuilt after the Dissolution. In the early fifteenth century Walter Langton, prior of Bardney, built a new rest house with a moat and bridge at Southrey. Monks from Westminster regularly retired to houses at Belsize, Hampstead, Hendon and Wandsworth. Other monastic rest-houses included Oxney, belonging to the monks of Peterborough, and Wickham, belonging to the monks of Spalding. Corndean Grange, a mile south of

Winchcombe Abbey, was acquired in 1299 by Abbot Walter de Wickewane from the abbot of Bruern in payment of a debt, and was used for the same purpose. The dependent cell of St Albans Abbey at Redbourn and Norwich Priory's cell at Kings Lynn both developed as places of recreation for monks from the parent house. The domestic buildings of Durham's dependent priory at Finchale were enlarged in more comfortable form in the fifteenth century, in order better to serve this function. The temporary release from monastic discipline must have presented some temptations. Bishop Orleton of Worcester forbade the Winchcombe monks to recuperate at Corndean after his visitation in 1329. Bishop Alnwick of Lincoln (1436-49) was scandalised to find Bardney Abbey's rest house at Southrey staffed by an unmarried woman, and ordered her immediate replacement with a male warden.

In wealthier monasteries, where portions of the estates were allocated amongst the monastic officials, the prior and other obedientiaries built houses of their own. Around 1214 the prior of Evesham was assigned his own house at Bengeworth with a garden and fishpond. The prior of Westminster similarly had his own country house at Belsize Park. Other properties, such as those within Glastonbury's parks at Sharpham and Norwood, and Evesham Abbey's house at Offenham, originated as hunting lodges.

By the later Middle Ages, as many manors and granges were leased out, their houses passed from direct monastic control. At the same time, however, abbots often retained selected houses on the estates, embellishing them with extra chambers, servants' quarters, chapels and stables till they equalled or exceeded the quality of their houses within the precinct. Here from time to time they escaped from the responsibilities of their office to lead the life of a country gentleman. Abbot Selwood of Glastonbury (1456-92) built a 'noble mansion' at East Brent, described as having a magnificent porch, hall, chapel and other sumptuous apartments. His successor, Abbot Richard Beere, refurbished the house at Meare (24), and had at Sharpham Park a house 'of his own new and sumptuous construction', with a chapel, parlour, private rooms, storehouses and kitchen. The porch at Sharpham bears the arms of the abbey and the pelican badge of Abbot Beere, along with the Tudor portcullis. William Parker, last abbot of Gloucester (1514-39), rebuilt and enlarged the manor house of Prinknash, where the south wing has an ornate first-floor oriel with a pendant-vaulted ceiling.

Some abbots lived on in their favourite properties after the Dissolution. Thomas Stephens, last abbot of Beaulieu, clung on to the former grange house of St Leonards. Abbot Pentecost of Abingdon retired to Cumnor (21). Abbot Lichfield of Evesham saw out the rest of his life in comfort at Offenham, dying there in October 1546. William More, last prior of Worcester, was still living at Crowle in 1558 (**colour plate 7**), and was buried in the parish church there.

The arrangement of buildings

At one time it was thought that many monastic granges were essentially small-scale versions of the abbey itself, with a church, refectory and dormitory surrounding a cloister. A few sites do, indeed, resemble this model. At Gorefields Grange in Buckinghamshire the Cluniac nuns of Delapré Abbey had added domestic ranges around a small cloister to the south of the earlier chapel by the end of the thirteenth century. Here we may be looking at buildings initially planned for regular conventual life. Pipewell Abbey's major grange at Cawston-on-Dunsmore was damaged in 1307 by a fire which swept through the cloister, chapel, dormitories, reredorter, refectory, kitchen and private rooms, including the abbot's own chamber. On most monastic manors and granges, however, the arrangement of buildings was not very different from those found on secular demesnes. The central component of the domestic range was the hall, a great communal room used for a variety of purposes. A dais at the upper end carried a high table, while the main body of the room accommodated trestle tables at mealtimes, which could then be removed to create space for entertainment or sleeping. Beyond the dais, a doorway gave access to one or more private chambers at first-floor level. The lower end of the hall was normally separated by a spere-truss and screen from a cross-passage, linking opposed doorways on either face of the building, and beyond this were the service rooms, the buttery, where the butts of ale, wine or cider were stored, and the pantry (from the French, *pain*, bread), used for the storage of foodstuffs. The kitchen was normally accessible by a third door on the lower side of the cross-passage, but was often detached from the main house.

The domestic ranges were normally enclosed by a wall, ditch or moat and entered through an inner gateway which separated them from the outer court, containing the farm buildings, to be considered in the following chapter. Nowhere does the entire complex survive intact. However, surveys in Wales and the north of England have revealed earthworks of many granges made up of an inner and outer court. Examples include the Neath Abbey granges of Monknash, Marcross (**19**) and Gelligarn; Abbots Llantwit, a grange of Tewkesbury; Burton-on-the-Wolds, a grange of Garendon; Kirkstead's grange of Gayton-le-Wold; Meaux Abbey's grange of Octon; Malton Priory's grange of Rillington; Bridlington Priory's grange of Willerby; the Fountains granges of Morker and Sutton; the Rievaulx granges of Newlass and Skiplam; and the Jervaulx granges of Kilgram, Newstead and Melsonby.

Documentary descriptions

Monastic chronicles often document new buildings and repairs to houses on the outlying estates. Evesham Abbey's manor of Offenham was destroyed by

19 *Marcross Grange (Glamorgan): aerial view of earthworks of a grange of Neath Abbey, looking westwards. The ruins of the abbey barn are casting a shadow to the right of the road*

fire during the time of Abbot Randulf in the early thirteenth century, and he rebuilt only the farm buildings. Abbot Brookhampton (1282-1316) built two apartments and a barn there. Abbot Ombersley (1367-79) added an outer gateway with a chamber above it and a stable adjoining. His successor, Abbot Yatton, rebuilt the hall in magnificent style, and added a splendid parlour. In 1422 Abbot Bromsgrove built a new room with a window of painted glass, and undertook major repairs to the chapel. Although this substantial house survived long after the Dissolution, only stone foundations remained in the 1900s. Abbot Brookhampton also built a vaulted room at Ombersley manor, where a new hall with chambers to north and south, a stable outside the lower gate and a small barn in the outer court were built in the 1370s, and a kitchen and chapel rebuilt around 1400. A survey of Ombersley in 1584 describes the hall, built of timber and roofed with tiles, rooms at its northern, southern and eastern ends, the old chapel built of stone with a tiled timber porch and with vaulted rooms beneath, and further rooms to the south and east of the chapel. The outer court lay to the east, and a pentice on posts led across it from the hall to a further building, then ruined past repair.

Elsewhere, Abbot William Yaxley (1261-93) improved many of the outlying manors of Thorney Abbey, building halls at Enfield and Charwelton, and reroofing the hall and chamber at Stanground. Richard Wallingford, abbot of St Albans (1328-36) built a manor house at Tyttenhanger on the manor of Ridge. However, this lay close to the main London road, and Richard's successor, Michael Mentmore (1336-49) finding the demands of hospitality there becoming too costly, demolished the house and sold the building materials. Abbot Mentmore preferred the more secluded manor house at Bradway in Abbots Walden, where he carried out repairs and built a chapel. Bradway, in its turn, was found to be inconveniently remote from St Albans, and Abbot John de la Moot (1396-1401), attracted by the fertile soil, beautiful woods and good water supply of Tyttenhanger, planned its rehabilitation. He began a new house and built two barns, but incurred criticism over the cost and for neglecting his other responsibilities during prolonged absences to supervise the building works; he died before its completion. His successor, William Heyworth, completed the house in 1411, and it remained a favourite residence of later abbots. Nothing survives today of either Tyttenhanger or Bradley.

Some of the many houses at the disposal of the abbots of Glastonbury are described in surveys. In the time of the last abbot, Richard Whiting, the house at Pilton comprised a hall, ten chambers, a well-house, cellar, kitchen, pantry, buttery, larder, bakehouse and wash-house, with a long chapel and a stable for ten horses.

A memorandum bound with a fourteenth-century register of the Augustinian Priory of St Mary Overy at Southwark records the actual dimensions of the main rooms at several of its manors. At Banstead the hall was 34ft by 28ft, the chamber 40ft by 16ft. At Addington the hall was 35ft long by 28ft broad, with two chambers 32ft by 18ft and 32ft by 11ft. At Mitcham the hall was 34ft by 32ft. At Reigate the chamber was 28ft by 15ft and that at Stokes was 31ft by 17ft. None of these buildings remain, but their recorded dimensions are similar to those of surviving dwellings on other monastic estates.

The original house of Abingdon's grange of Barton Court was destroyed in a riot in 1327, and replaced by what is described in 1538 as a 'large mansion'. A late medieval map shows a four-gabled, three-storey, timber-framed building with a central stack and arched doorway (**20**). After the Dissolution the house was greatly enlarged by the Reade family, then ruined in the Civil War. A gable end survives from the post-Dissolution extension.

Evidence from the north of England is more fragmentary. The Meaux chronicle records Abbot Thomas Burton in the 1390s repairing halls and chambers along with farm buildings at the granges of Salthaugh and Wharram. In 1495 the abbot of Whitby obtained oaks for three pairs of crucks, beams and wall-plates for the repair of his house at Goathland in Yorkshire. Nothing survives of these houses.

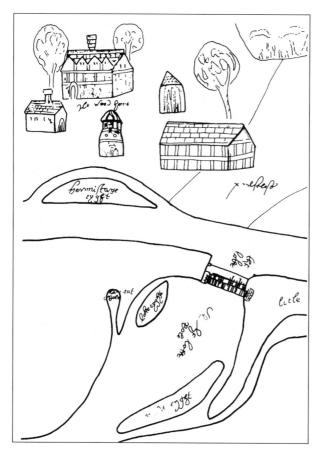

20 *Barton Court (Berkshire): Abingdon Abbey's estate farm, from a fifteenth-century map in the Abingdon Guildhall, showing the timbered house, possibly with a detached kitchen, timbered barn and dovecote. 'The loke', on the site of the present Abingdon Lock, may be the abbey's 'New Weir', which was under repair in 1375-6 and was a source of eels and other fish*

Post-medieval sources often provide a record of houses which have since vanished. Cumnor Place, maintained immediately after the Dissolution as a residence for Thomas Pentecost, last abbot of Abingdon, survived up to 1810. Something of its appearance can be deduced from early nineteenth-century descriptions and illustrations (**21**). It consisted of a fourteenth-century hall, 44ft by 22ft, lit by gabled two-light traceried windows, with a fine stone fireplace at the southern end, beyond which were two first-floor chambers. To the north a through passage separated the hall from a cross-wing containing the buttery and pantry with another large chamber above, lit by a reticulated-traceried window. In 1811-12 Lord Abingdon reused some of the architectural details in his reconstruction of Wytham church, a few miles away.

Surviving domestic buildings

Most surviving manorial dwellings on monastic estates date from the late thirteenth or early fourteenth centuries, but a few examples have a more ancient

21 *Cumnor Place (Berkshire): a property of Abingdon Abbey occupied by Thomas Pentecost, the last abbot, after the Dissolution, finally demolished in 1810*

core. St Augustine's Abbey in Canterbury, having acquired the derelict ancient nunnery of Minster-in-Thanet from King Cnut, began a major rebuilding operation there in the late eleventh or early twelfth century (**22**). The buildings were arranged around three sides of a small court. Herringbone masonry in the two-storey west range identifies this as the oldest part. Abutting against its southern end is the ruined tower of a chapel added before the mid-twelfth century, while the north range, added perhaps 30 years later, contained a hall. The hall was shortened and converted to a two-storey range and both north and west ranges were given new windows by Abbot Thomas Hundon (1405-20), whose initials appear in the north doorway. The Benedictine nuns of Yedingham had a house at Sinnington near Pickering, the hall of which survives, with a late twelfth-century window on the upper part of its east wall; all other windows were replaced in the fifteenth century, then blocked when the house was converted to a barn. The surviving hall of Lewes Priory's manor house at Swanborough retains a doorway and lancet from around 1200. Here too the hall was divided by an inserted floor and new windows were inserted around the beginning of the fifteenth century.

Halls were of two main types. Throughout the Middle Ages ground-floor halls predominated. In the east and south-east of England aisled examples occur, while in the west many were spanned by some variant of cruck

22 *Minster Court, Minster-in-Thanet (Kent): the late eleventh-century west range of the house of St Augustine's, Canterbury, with windows inserted by Abbot Thomas Hundon (1405-20). To the left is the ruined tower of the twelfth-century chapel*

construction. The early fourteenth-century great hall of Abingdon Abbey's manor house at Sutton Courtenay is spanned by a massive central cruck-truss carrying a crown-post with four-way struts, while the lower end of the hall has an aisled spere-truss separating it from the cross-passage (**23a**). Evidence for another base-cruck hall with an aisled spere-truss of similar date has been recognised at Wasperton, a manor which had been obtained by Coventry Priory some 50 years before.

Another group of halls at first-floor level above a storage undercroft has been defined. John Blair has recently suggested that some of these may actually be chamber-blocks attached to vanished ground-floor halls. However, some monastic examples retain enough of their original plan to demonstrate that genuine first-floor halls were constructed at least from the fourteenth century. Glastonbury Abbey's house at Meare was rebuilt by Abbot Adam Sodbury (1323-34), who also enclosed its courtyard with a stone wall. The existing house is predominantly of that date, and traces of three large pointed windows, later blocked and replaced with rectangular openings, indicate an important room at first-floor level (**24**). There were ground- and first-floor chambers at either end. A second dwelling there had a small hall, parlour and chamber. At Shapwick, the remains of the abbot's house are concealed behind a seventeenth-century façade, but enough survives to indicate a first-floor hall with

23 *Abingdon Abbey's house at Sutton Courtenay (Berkshire). Left (a) the interior of the early fourteenth-century hall, looking towards the spere-truss and screens passage. Above (b) smoke-blackened crown-post from the earlier hall, now within the chamber range*

24 *Meare (Somerset): Glastonbury Abbey's manor house, rebuilt by Abbot Adam Sodbury (1323-34). The blocked arched windows of the first-floor hall are visible to the right of the porch*

service wing to the west and chamber wing to the east. The medieval roof survived the later alterations, and dendrochronological investigation has yielded a date of 1489. A third surviving Glastonbury house, on the distant manor of Ashbury in Berkshire, was rebuilt around 1488 by Abbot Selwood. This is of chalk and brown stone, and had important rooms at both ground-floor and first-floor level. The large transomed windows with ogee cinquefoil cusping are much more typical of Somerset than Berkshire, and stonemasons were probably brought up from the West Country to do the job. The original wind-braced roof survives.

Beyond the dais end of the hall there was normally a cross-wing containing a first-floor chamber. At the Abingdon manor of Charney Bassett, the chamber in the late thirteenth-century south wing retains a splendid crown-post roof. The three-bay north wing of the same abbey's house at Sutton Courtenay contains smoke-blackened crown-post timbers showing that it was first built around 1300 as an open hall (**23b**); but an upper floor was inserted some 20 or 30 years later to convert it to private rooms when the new hall was built abutting its southern face.

Parts of the fifteenth-century screen, panelled with blank arcading, survive at the service end of the Lewes Priory manor of Swanborough. Remains of another screen survive at Sinnington. The fifteenth-century west wing of Abingdon Abbey's manor house at Culham, comprising a timber-framed upper floor with an arch-braced king-post roof and a stone-built lower floor containing a large open fireplace, may have been the original service range with an integral kitchen.

The domestic buildings of Pershore Abbey's important grange at Broadway remain substantially intact, with a hall, chamber and oratory all dating from the fourteenth century. The hall is 25ft by 19ft, with two-light ogee-headed transomed windows and a roof with arch-braced collars and wind-braces. Opposing doors at the northern end mark the position of the screens passage, beyond which two doors gave access to the buttery and pantry. Early illustrations suggest that there was a detached kitchen north of the hall, linked to it by a short pentice. A small staircase leads up from the south-east corner of the hall past a landing giving access to a tiny private oratory and to a grand private chamber, 26ft by 13ft, with a squint looking down to the hall and a large lateral fireplace. The abbey still reserved certain rooms in this house for its own use when the manor was leased out in October 1535.

Place Farm at Tisbury incorporates the much-altered late fifteenth-century inner-court domestic range of the grange of the nuns of Shaftesbury Abbey. The hall, reduced to a third of its original length, and now with an inserted floor, retains an arch-braced collar-beam roof with curved struts and wind-braces. Over a massive fireplace at its north end is a polygonal stone chimney-stack surmounted by a spirelet. Upper and lower chambers beyond the fireplace were linked with a further chamber in a long-vanished cross-wing.

25 *Saighton Grange (Cheshire): the porch, built by Abbot Simon Ripley c.1489, is all that remains of the country house of the abbots of St Werburgh's, Chester*

The service rooms were at the southern end, adjoining the surviving inner gatehouse. Remains of another Shaftesbury residence, incorporated into Barton Farm at Bradford-on-Avon, include a late medieval porch and a projecting wing with a first-floor room spanning a gateway, containing an arch-braced collar-beam roof. At Saighton Grange, principal country seat of the abbots of St Werburgh's, Chester, the porch tower, built by Abbot Simon Ripley around 1489, has escaped the Victorian rebuilding of the house. It has three storeys, a stair-turret, an oriel window, and a niche with a much-mutilated stone image (25). At Ince, another Chester manor, a stone range of early sixteenth-century appearance, with four two-light transomed square-headed windows on either side, encases an earlier great hall, and there is a separate, longer, lower range of lodgings. Recent investigation has shown that the existing stone structures superseded earlier timber buildings.

Surviving medieval domestic structures often present problems of interpretation. Salmestone Grange, near Margate, was a property of St Augustine's, Canterbury. Here the building of a new hall by the sacrist, Thomas Ickham, is

111

recorded in the 1380s. Two linked medieval domestic ranges survive, but the dateable portions look earlier, and neither can convincingly be identified with the documented building.

Many houses survive only as ruins or earthworks. The country house of Beaurepaire (now called Bearpark), first built by Bertram de Middleton, prior of Durham, following his retirement in 1258, developed under his successors into a sprawling range of buildings and courtyards covering some 15 acres. It was ruined by the Scots during the 1640s. The gable end of one range survives, with a window and trefoiled doorway. Foundations and earthwork terraces indicate the outlines of the remainder.

So far we have concentrated on Benedictine properties, but elaborate houses were also to be found on Augustinian estates. Hyde Farm in Stoke Bliss, Worcestershire, a property of the Augustinian sisters of Limebrook, includes an early fourteenth-century base-cruck hall. Ashleworth Court in north Gloucestershire was the principal country house of St Augustine's Abbey, Bristol (26). Built of blue lias, it dates from the mid-fifteenth century. A four-bay hall, now subdivided by an inserted floor, was lit by tall two-light mullioned and transomed windows with quatrefoil tracery. Two of the windows have been lengthened at their base. A fine arch-braced collar-beam roof survives, with three tiers of wind-braced purlins and an embattled wall-plate. A cross-passage with arched doorways separates the hall from ground-floor service rooms lit by single-light windows, over which is a chamber lit by two-light windows. The principal chamber occupies a cross-wing extending

26 *Ashleworth Court (Gloucestershire): one of two substantial houses built in the village by the abbots of St Augustine's, Bristol, in the fifteenth century*

eastwards from the north end, also with a fine timber roof. Within the angle of the two ranges is an oriel and newel stair. A second house in Ashleworth, now called the Manor House, was built as a private summer residence around 1460 by Abbot Walter Newbury. In contrast to the Court, this is wholly timber-framed. A late fifteenth-century chamber range from a house belonging to Leicester Abbey survives at Ingarsby. Prior Vivian of Bodmin (1508-33) had his favourite country seat at Rialton in Cornwall, and here the old hall retains a decorated waggon roof and three triple-light windows; there is a first-floor chamber and a tunnel-vaulted porch. A well in the courtyard has an ornate image niche in its rear wall.

If survival is any guide, the greatest investment in residential buildings outside the abbey precinct occurs on Benedictine and Augustinian estates in the midlands and south. For the reformed orders, agricultural buildings ranked as a higher priority than domestic comfort. Although the early Cistercian granges required accommodation for their lay brothers, very little remains. Garendon Abbey's grange at Thorpe Acre near Loughborough included an early fourteenth-century base-cruck hall, but this was demolished in 1967. A fragment of a fifteenth-century stone range is embedded within later buildings at Flaxley Abbey's grange of Dymock, but this was more probably the work of the lessees of the property. Surveys by the Welsh Royal Commission of Cistercian granges in Glamorgan belonging to the abbeys of Neath and Margam have revealed only scanty remains of five domestic ranges on 44 granges. Descriptions of the Jervaulx grange of Lazenby, newly built in the fifteenth century, and the Beaulieu grange of Upton, rebuilt shortly before the Dissolution, record little more than the most basic arrangements of hall, chamber and services. Additional chambers appear only on the most important granges, and only towards the end of the monastic period. Contracts for leasing the granges during the later Middle Ages usually specify which parts were to be used by the lessee and which parts retained by the abbey. When Moor Grange was leased out by the abbey of Meaux in 1535, the abbot reserved a chamber with beds for himself and his page, another chamber with beds for two of his servants, a cellar, and a room over the stable for his groom, while the lessee had the hall, another chamber and the kitchen, along with most of the farm buildings.

Substantial houses on monastic property were sometimes built by tenants, rather than by the abbeys themselves. When the Prior of Lewes leased out his Yorkshire grange of Braithwell in 1427, his new tenant was required to rebuild the hall with a room at the west end to specified dimensions of 32ft by 18ft; despite this, the prior retained the right for himself or his servants to stay there for up to three weeks a year. In 1969 Peter Salway recognised the remains of a timber-framed hall-house within a weatherboarded barn at Lewknor in south Oxfordshire. Three bays survived, with an open arch-braced tie-beam truss over the centre of the hall and an aisled spere-truss at the lower end, both with ornate cusped braces. This house was never quite completed, and its domestic use was short-lived. Though one of the Lewknor manors belonged to Abingdon, the abbey's finances were at a low ebb in the second quarter of the fourteenth century when the house was built, and the tenant of the abbey's rectory farm, John de Lewknor, seems a more likely candidate. Evesham Abbey's manor at Bretforton was alienated in the thirteenth century and not recovered until 1365. During that interval the existing manor house was built, a first-floor hall of four bays over a tunnel-vaulted undercroft, constructed of local blue lias rubble with Cotswold stone dressings. The fifteenth-century buildings of Leigh Barton, in a remote south Devon valley, have been described as a grange of Buckfast, but records show a family named Leigh in occupation there as freeholders from the thirteenth century to the Dissolution.

Excavated sites

Relatively few monastic manor houses have yet been excavated. A couple of sites explored in the 1960s, Evesham Abbey's house at Badby and Fountains Abbey's house at Cowton, revealed somewhat contrasting fortunes. Both were leased out in the later Middle Ages, but whereas at Badby little new work was undertaken after the buildings passed from the abbey's direct control, at Cowton a comprehensive rebuilding was undertaken by one of the tenants, presumably because of the run-down condition of what was there before.

Evesham Abbey's manor house at Badby was built by Abbot Roger Norreys (1189-1213) who, according to the abbey chronicle, was a thoroughly bad character: 'He lived in a most courtly and sumptuous style, with a magnificent table overflowing with food and drink in plenty . . . . He was more drunken and excessive than any other English monk . . . and did not consider simple fornication to be a sin . . . unless adultery and incest were added, and it is said that he showed no moderation in either of these'. At Badby, Broadwell and Bourton he had built 'noble, almost regal houses', where he 'feasted on deli-cacies with some of the brethren . . . devoting his time to his stomach and body the whole time until he was deposed'. Margaret Gray's excavation of Badby showed that Abbot Norreys' stone-built hall was the first structure on the site, its longer axis aligned east-west, with a fireplace and projecting chimney-breast at the east end. It was roofed with Cotswold stone slates. Shortly afterwards a chapel was added at the east end of the hall and a chamber and other buildings to the west. The chronicle records Abbot Boys building two new bakehouses or ovens in the mid-fourteenth century, and these were located on the north-west side of the hall. The last documented works were the renovation of the hall and chapel by Abbot Yatton in the later fourteenth century, and at this time the hall was reduced in size, given opposed doors for a screens passage at the west end, and reroofed with red clay tiles, while the chapel was enlarged.

A large hearth and bake-oven were added on the east wall of the hall, an extended wing added to the north, which may have served as stables, and two new rooms added to the earlier bakehouse block, probably serving as brew-houses. Badby was leased out after 1451, and no further major works were undertaken before the Dissolution, when the hall was altered again and several of the older buildings dismantled.

The Fountains Abbey grange at Cowton was leased out in 1310, but was then ruined through a succession of disasters: the great famine of 1315-16, the Scottish raids of 1318 and 1322, and the pestilence of 1349. In 1363 Abbot Robert abandoned any thought of resuming demesne farming there, and partitioned its estate among 20 free tenants. Colin Platt's excavations in 1962 found only limited traces of the earliest buildings, which had been of timber with stone footings; but around 1400 one of the abbey's tenants had replaced them with a courtyard farm. This included a tile-roofed, timber-framed hall, 36ft by 20ft, with glazed windows, on the west side, and a chamber 20ft by 16ft with a lateral stone fireplace on the north, along with a kitchen and various outbuildings.

Selby Abbey's grange at Stainer Hall was also explored during the 1960s. A building 90ft by 45ft was excavated, with dry-stone walling on clay foundations. The principal room was paved with stone flags and brick. Remains of a hearth and bake-oven were found. Pottery pointed to occupation in the fourteenth century and later.

Abingdon Abbey's grange at Dean Court was excavated by Tim Allen and the Oxford Archaeological Unit in 1984-5. Here the first of two successive complexes of grange buildings had superseded an assart farmstead of late twelfth-century origin. The earlier grange included a substantial L-shaped stone longhouse built in the second quarter of the thirteenth century, with a byre at the northern end and a wing projecting westwards from the southern end. Subsequently the byre was converted to domestic use, its open front walled in, and further partition walls were inserted to make a hall with a central fireplace and a square room at the southern end. Buttresses at the south gable and the stone base of an internal stairway indicated the presence of a first-floor chamber. To the east, farm buildings surrounded a cobbled yard. This first group of buildings was abandoned around the end of the thirteenth century and replaced by a more spacious complex 230 yards to the south-east. Here the domestic and agricultural buildings were more firmly segregated. The extant farmhouse had appeared to be of early seventeenth-century date, but removal of ivy unexpectedly revealed the arched windows of a chamber block dating from around 1300. The main body of the farmhouse occupied the site of the medieval hall. The farmyard lay to the south, with a barn, byre or stable and a circular dovecote, while to both west and east were a couple of small fishponds. The whole complex was surrounded by a boundary wall and moat. There were several peasant crofts nearby, but these had very largely been abandoned by the later Middle Ages.

Kitchens

Since kitchens constituted a fire hazard, they were often detached from the main domestic buildings and linked with the service range by a covered pentice. Roof timbers in the detached kitchen at Shapwick have yielded a date of 1428. A nineteenth-century illustration of Broadway shows what may have been a detached kitchen, since removed, north of the hall.

Elsewhere they were incorporated into a wing. Excavation at the later Dean Court grange revealed the kitchen immediately to the north of the hall, with two circular bread-ovens later replaced by a square malting-kiln, a pit which may have contained a wooden brewing-vat and a water-supply system with stone-lined tanks, possibly used as a temporary store for fresh fish or for soaking grain to germinate it before malting, and drains. Debris on the floor included bones of marine fish and carbonised seeds of wheat, oats, barley and beans.

Occasionally the kitchen formed an integral part of the main house. At Ashbury it lay immediately beyond the buttery and pantry, with the steward's room above. The fireplace survives, with an arch cut out of a single block of stone. At Salmestone Grange, too, a large fireplace and oven identify the kitchen. At Cowton the excavations revealed a kitchen 20ft square, with a stone hearth in the south-west corner, directly abutting the south end of the hall, and another structure which may be a bakehouse.

Water supply and sanitation

Monasteries are noted for the sophisticated nature of their piped water supplies and latrines flushed by diverted watercourses controlled by sluice-gates. Arrangements on properties outside the precinct relied more upon wells and garderobes. Jocelin of Brakelond recounts an episode which occurred while Abbot Samson (1182-1211) was on a tour of inspection of the Bury St Edmunds estates. Staying overnight at his manor of Warkton, he was woken by a mysterious voice warning him of danger; and found a candle in the privy which was about to fall upon the straw. Jocelin adds that, had a fire taken hold, he and all others in the house would surely have perished, for the windows were barred and the door locked. At Ashbury a garderobe was built into a wing beyond the staircase to the rear of the house, and this retained its original wooden seat until the 1950s. Excavation of a garderobe pit at Badby produced an unlikely find, a fourteenth-century sword.

On rare occasions improved facilities were installed. Fountains Abbey was bringing water through lead pipes to its grange at Malham by 1257. Prior Middleton of Durham's country residence of Beaurepaire was initially served by a cesspit; but this was superseded by a new latrine flushed with water when the south wing was extended around the end of the thirteenth century.

Domestic oratories and grange chapels

Visiting abbots, monks and canons, and resident lay brothers, would have required some place of worship from the outset. A distinction must be made between oratories serving for private devotions, and larger chapels intended for communal use by lay brothers, servants and local tenants. Oratories were small and usually adjoined the principal chamber. At Charney Bassett the first-floor oratory dates from around 1280, and is roughly 12ft by 10ft. At Broadway the oratory occupies the first floor of an oriel 13ft by 7ft, approached off a landing on the stairway up to the chamber. At Ashbury there appears to have been an oratory over the porch. Lewes Priory's manor of Swanborough incorporated a small ground-floor oratory at the east end of the hall with a private chamber over.

Grange chapels sometimes antedated the grange itself, serving a pre-existing lay community. Denis Mynard's excavation of Gorefields Grange revealed a twelfth-century chapel built in part of re-used Roman material, which was already standing when the nuns of Delapré took over the site. When the Cistercians of Combe removed the Warwickshire village of Lower Smite, the ancient church of St Peter lost its parochial function but was retained as a grange chapel. Remains of its nave, chancel and south aisle, with work of fifteenth-century date, were later incorporated into a brick-built farmhouse called Peter Hall. In Wales a number of granges incorporated sites of earlier Celtic hermitages, including Theodoric's Grange on the Margam estate, Llanfair Grange which belonged to Abbey Dore, and Grace Dieu's grange of Stowe which incorporated the hermitage of St Briavel. Other pre-existing chapels were absorbed into Margam Abbey's granges of Meles, Hafodheulig, Eglwysnynydd and Tanglwst.

Purpose-built chapels were at first restricted to the more important Benedictine properties. At Minster-in-Thanet the massive square west tower of the twelfth-century chapel survives in ruins (22), and the walls of the nave and apsidal-ended chancel have been traced by excavation. With intensified use of outlying properties during the thirteenth century, chapels became more common. On Thorney Abbey's estates Abbot Yaxley (1261-93) built a chapel dedicated to St Botolph on his manor at Charwelton, and Abbot William Clopton (1305-23) replaced the wooden chapel at Eldernall in Whittlesey with one of stone and rebuilt the chapel at Enfield. On Selby Abbey's grange of Stainer Hall a chapel was built outside the moat by 1286; excavation in the 1960s recovered carved stones which may have come from it, though the building itself remained unlocated. At Ramsey Abbey's grange of Bodsey the fourteenth-century chapel contains a north doorway with the principal moulding on its south face and a bar socket on its outer side, indicating that the chapel was itself sometimes used as an entrance to the inner compound. Salmestone Grange has a sumptuous free-standing chapel, consecrated in 1326, built of knapped flint, with traceried windows, an ogee-headed piscina and a king-post roof; in the fifteenth century it was linked to the hall by a pentice. At Prinknash a free-standing chapel east of the north wing of the house dates from the early sixteenth century. Foundations of the chapel at Yedingham Nunnery's grange of Sinnington have been traced. In 1479 chapels are documented on the Hexham estates at Bingfield, Cheeseburn and Salton-in-Cleveland.

The Cistercian general chapter remained opposed to the consecration of altars at granges throughout the twelfth century, partly to prevent any diversion of devotion from the abbey church, partly to avoid infringement upon local parochial rights. However, acquisitions of properties distant both from the abbey and from existing parish churches, forced a change of policy. Each abbot had to negotiate with the diocesan bishop, who would wish to safeguard the privileges and revenues of parish churches. In 1235 Thame Abbey secured agreement from the Bishop of Lincoln to have a chapel at their grange of Otley on the margins of Otmoor. Monks and lay brothers at the grange were permitted to use this, but the people of Oddington, in which parish it lay, were firmly excluded, and servants employed at the grange were required to attend Sunday mass at the parish church rather than the grange chapel. Similarly, when Waverley Abbey applied to celebrate masses at their grange at Neatham in 1250, they had to agree neither to ring bells nor to administer the sacraments to lay people. In 1339 the bishop of St David's allowed tenants of Strata Florida to make oblations at the abbey or at two of its more distant chapels, but insisted that they receive the sacraments from their parish priests. By contrast, in 1257 Llantarnam Abbey received consent to administer the sacraments to its farmers and tenants in its several chapels within and outside the abbey.

In 1246 the Premonstratensians secured from the Pope a general consent to have their own grange chapels on the grounds that this would avoid the need for continuing contacts with laymen. In 1255 the Cistercians won similar concessions. However, the policy of leasing and the withdrawal of the lay brothers effectively restricted the building of chapels to those granges which the abbey kept in hand, or where there was a perceived duty to serve local tenants. Of 54 Glamorgan granges surveyed by the Welsh Royal Commission, only a third had their own chapel. Margam Abbey's total of 13 chapels on its 27 Glamorgan granges was unusual.

A few granges had more than one chapel, though their concurrent use was usually brief. When Margam Abbey rebuilt Resolfen Grange on a new site at the end of the twelfth century, a new chapel was provided. The old chapel of the vacated grange remained in intermittent use, but in the 1220s Bishop William of Llandaff insisted that masses there should only be celebrated on the anniversary of its dedication, while masses at the new chapel should be only for the monks and not for other local people. Around 1230 Bishop Elias of

Llandaff consecrated a new chapel within the court of Margam's grange at Llangewydd; but when the monks built a second chapel outside the grange precinct a few years later, he ordered its demolition, presumably in order to prevent its use by lay people to the detriment of the parish church.

Few early Cistercian grange chapels survive. Beaulieu Abbey's late thirteenth-century chapel at St Leonard's is unusually large, 60ft by 25ft. More date from the fourteenth century. Kingswood Abbey had a grange with a chapel a mile south of Tetbury, where the kitchen of the later house of Estcourt Park retains a piscina in its south wall. St Pancras' Chapel at Cleeve Abbey's Stout Grange has been converted to a cottage. Jervaulx's grange chapel at Thrintoft, long used as a barn, has also recently been converted to a house. Later Abbot Huby of Fountains (1494-1520) provided chapels at Bewerley and at Brimham. The Bewerley chapel, rebuilt in the seventeenth century, retains Abbot Huby's initials. Fragments of a similar inscription are incorporated into later buildings at Brimham, and part of a late medieval building with a tiled floor has been excavated here. In the sixteenth century a lavish chapel was built for the occasional use of the abbot of Meaux at Moor Grange, and in 1535 this contained a table serving as an altar, furnished with a cloth painted with an image of the Virgin.

Gatehouses

Granges were normally entered by a gatehouse with a wide cart entry and a narrow pedestrian door, spanned by an upper chamber, leading into the outer court. There was often also an inner gate linking the farmyard court with the domestic compound. The thirteenth-century inner gate of Tewkesbury's grange at Abbots Llantwit is perhaps the earliest surviving example. Only at Shaftesbury Abbey's manor of Tisbury do both outer and inner gates survive. At Furness Abbey's grange of Hawkshead the chamber above the gate was used as a court-room (**27**). Further examples are documented. In 1306 the Templars acquired a licence to make and crenellate a great gate at their Lincolnshire preceptory of Temple Bruer, while Abbot William Clopton (1305-23) built a gatehouse on Thorney Abbey's manor of Stanground.

Moats

At least 15 per cent of monastic granges were surrounded by moats (**28** and **colour plate 7**). Usually an acre or less in extent, these often enclosed only the domestic ranges, leaving the farm court and its buildings outside. Moated granges frequently occur in clayland areas, being especially common in the Vale of York and in Holderness. By contrast they are rare in Wales and the

27 *Hawkshead (Lancashire): the gatehouse of Furness Abbey's grange*

south-west of England. It is difficult to understand why some sites were moated and others not. As Jean le Patourel has pointed out, the Meaux Abbey granges of Salthaugh, Keyingham and Ottringham all remained unmoated despite their low-lying situation in a region where moats are generally common.

Evesham's house at Badby was moated from the outset, the upcast being used to level the site before the first buildings were erected. Other moats were inherited from former secular manor houses which only later came into monastic hands. Ingarsby Old Hall, surrounded by a pentagonal moat, was the manor house of the former village, taken over by Leicester Abbey and converted to a grange in 1469. Many more moats may have been added after monasteries relinquished houses to tenants. On the Abingdon Abbey estates, with the exception of the later grange at Dean Court, hardly any of the houses retained in hand had moats, whereas a number of properties which had passed to lay tenants were moated. However, this may simply be an accident of survival. Moats can easily be filled up to the point where they leave little or no surface trace; indeed, the Dean Court moat was not recognised until it was revealed by excavation. At Shapwick Abbot Beere's terrier describes the house as standing within a moat containing an acre and a half and half a perch. The northern arm of this moat was located by geophysical work in 1993, then recorded in a trench cut for an electricity cable. Only subsequently was it realised that three sides of the moat were still faintly visible under favourable conditions as a slight earthwork.

Moats around monastic manor houses and granges were rarely formidable enough to deter a determined military assault, but they provided some security against illicit entry, theft and thuggery. During the social unrest of the late thirteenth and early fourteenth centuries monastic landholders may have felt more need for protection. When the Gilbertine sisters of Catley in Lincolnshire ordered their lay brothers to dig a ditch around the grange buildings 24ft wide, this was to safeguard them from 'losses and dangers'. Unfortunately, however, moats could quickly degenerate into foul and unhealthy pools, and they also imposed constraints against expansion of the grange. Possibly this was why the buildings of Meaux Abbey's grange of Hayholme were dismantled during the abbacy of William of Scarborough (1372-96) and then rebuilt outside the moat. Excavation at the North Grange of Meaux showed that whatever buildings the moated area had originally contained, they had moved elsewhere in the thirteenth century, when the site was occupied by a tile kiln.

Castles and crenellations

Although the ideal of monastic serenity seems at odds with the concept of military defence, monastic houses and granges were as vulnerable to assault,

28 *Abbots Morton (Worcestershire): aerial view of moat. Thomas Marlborough, abbot of Evesham, purchased land here in c.1230, and built a house 'quite habitable for when the abbots were to go there'*

arson and plunder as any other wealthy residence. Orders like the Knights Templars and Hospitallers developed a very specific military role, and both built castles in the Holy Land and elsewhere in Europe, though not in Britain. Even the contemplative orders sometimes acknowledged a need for protection. The choice of offshore islands by some of the earliest monastic settlers may have had as much to do with security as asceticism. Tynemouth Priory's headland was fortified on several occasions through its history, twice by the monks themselves – a strong wall was built with towers and a gate after 1296, following Edward I's invasion of Scotland, for protection against retaliatory raids; and in the 1390s, Prior John Wheathampstead repaired the walls and rebuilt the gate following damage by the Scots.

The construction of small earthen castles by military tenants foisted upon English monasteries after the Norman Conquest was noted in chapter 2. Monasteries also occasionally acquired castles. Barnwell Castle in Northamptonshire had been built by Berengar le Moine in the 1260s during Simon de Montfort's war, and when Henry III returned to power, Berengar was forced to sell his new castle to the monks of Ramsey, who retained it up until the Dissolution.

Many of the first generation of Norman Benedictine foundations in Wales, like Chepstow Priory, were protected simply by proximity to the castles of their founders. Subsequent foundations were less able to take advantage of such locations, and Gilbert Foliot, abbot of Gloucester (1139-48), commended Prior Osbern, in charge of one of Gloucester's cells in Wales, for 'strengthening the locks of your doors and surrounding your house with an impregnable wall' against the 'shaggy and wild-eyed Welsh'. By way of comfort, Abbot Gilbert added that, if the Welsh made bad neighbours, the English were worse. The site referred to was either Ewenny Priory, where the church was built like a fortress and the perimeter surrounded by a battlemented curtain wall with towers and two gatehouses, or possibly Cardigan Priory, where no remains survive.

Between the late thirteenth and early fifteenth centuries over 30 monasteries acquired crenellation licences through letters patent from the royal chancery, permitting them to fortify their own precincts. The same procedure was sometimes used for granges and for the preceptories and commanderies of the military orders. In 1365 Selby Abbey acquired a licence to crenellate its grange at Stainer Hall. In 1399 the abbot and convent of St Werburgh's, Chester, received crenellation licences for their houses at Saighton, Ince and Sutton. The hall at Ince has defensive intra-mural stair passages, a boundary wall and moat, which may have been a product of this licence. The Knights Templars acquired a licence to fortify the great gate of their Lincolnshire preceptory of Temple Bruer in 1306, and the Hospitallers did the same on their manor of Eagle in 1449.

Abbeys in the north of England frequently suffered from Scottish raids. In 1235 Holm Cultram Abbey obtained royal consent to arm its servants in order to prevent any further plundering of their granges, and in 1348 it acquired a licence to build a castle at Wolsty, near the coast south of Silloth, comprising a strong tower with an adjoining hall, chambers, prison, chapel, barn, larder, cattle-shed and stable. These buildings were later demolished, but foundations surrounded by a strong rectangular moat remain. Lanercost Priory was sacked by the Scots several times, and there the prior's dwelling took the form of a typical border pele-tower beyond the southern end of the west claustral range. Piel Castle, on a small island off the south coast of Furness, was built by Furness Abbey under a crenellation licence of 1327 (**colour plate 8**). It was temporarily dismantled in 1403, but then repaired and maintained till the Dissolution; remains of a keep and barbican and inner and outer baileys can still be seen. On the other side of the Pennines, Newminster Abbey built a pele-tower at Nunnikirk and small bastles with attached courts or barmkins at Greenleighton and West Ritton, all first recorded around the time of the Dissolution.

8
Monastic farm buildings

The layout of monastic farms

Complexes of farm buildings occur in the outer courts of many abbeys, on manorial farms and granges elsewhere on the estates, and on the preceptories and commanderies of the military orders. In general they reflected the typical mixed farming economy, though an arable or pastoral bias may be revealed by the relative size of different buildings. The early provision and arrangement of farm buildings was somewhat extempore, but attempts were made to improve their quality and to rationalise the farmyard layout for greater efficiency as time went on. In particular, considerable investment in new farm buildings can be detected between the late twelfth and early fourteenth centuries, the most profitable period of monastic demesne farming. At Bradford-on-Avon, for example, in the early fourteenth century, Shaftesbury Abbey planned an entirely new rectangular farmyard, with house and chapel to the north, granary to the east, barn to the south and a second barn or byre to the west (**colour plate 9**).

Construction costs were, however, considerable, and even during the high farming period, the building programme was usually prolonged, and modified, over several centuries. At Waltham the enlargement of the abbey in 1177 to accommodate Augustinian canons seems to have been the occasion for planning a new home grange. Initially this consisted of a large rectangular enclosure containing a barn. An entrance gate was added in the thirteenth or early fourteenth century, controlling access from the public road. During the fifteenth century further timber buildings were erected east and south-east of the barn, widely-spaced, perhaps as a precaution against fire.

No complete group of monastic farm buildings remains intact today. Barns, because of their sheer scale and quality of construction, have the highest survival rate, followed by dovecotes, but the count of other extant agricultural buildings is small. Occasionally, as at Bradford-on-Avon and Temple Cressing, the setting of the surviving barns preserves some elements of the monastic farm layout. More frequently the other farm buildings have been replaced since the Dissolution and the barn or dovecote survives as an isolated relic.

The entire layout of some abandoned monastic granges is preserved in the form of earthworks. The simplest type consisted merely of two ranges, a domestic building accommodating lay brothers and a storage or processing building, with an intervening yard. Other examples are much more complex and extensive. The Welsh Royal Commission's surveys of the earthworks of Neath Abbey's granges at Marcross, Gelligarn and Monknash, Margam Abbey's grange at Hafod-y-porth and Tewkesbury's grange at Llantwit Major, all reveal the remains of farm buildings and yards set within extensive embanked enclosures. In several cases, notably Marcross (**19**) and Monknash, there seems to be an inner complex occupying 5 or 6 acres set within an outer enclosure of up to 20 acres. Other complex earthwork examples are known elsewhere in Wales, for example at Merthyrgeryn. The English Royal Commission has recently surveyed similar sites in Lincolnshire, including the earthworks of North Kelsey Grange belonging to the Gilbertine priory of North Ormsby and the Knights Templars' preceptory at Willoughton. Earthworks near Sysonby in Leicestershire may represent a former grange of Garendon Abbey (**29**).

29 *Sysonby (Leicestershire): aerial view of enclosures probably representing a grange of Garendon Abbey*

On cultivated land, colour and height differences in crops caused by the effect of levelled ditches, pits and wall foundations just below the ploughsoil can often be detected from the air. Aerial photography has located the site of Beaulieu Abbey's Wyke Grange near Faringdon, which included at least a dozen substantial buildings of at least three different periods arranged around a court, with a complex series of banks and ditches forming further enclosures beyond.

While surviving remains on any given site are usually limited to one or two buildings or earthworks, documentary records may fill in the gaps. Bailiffs' accounts at Tintern Abbey's Merthyrgeryn Grange in 1387-9 mention the old and new byre, cowhouse, sheepcote, stable, granary, henhouse, pigsty and garden. Inventories of monastic property at the Dissolution often list the contents of outer court and grange buildings in some detail, though buildings which contained no items of value were usually omitted. At Waltham Abbey the home grange occupied 18 acres immediately north of the claustral enclosure. In 1540 the granary contained 10 quarters of wheat, the oat barn 5 quarters of threshed oats and 15 quarters of unthreshed oats, the plough-house contained a plough, harrows, five carts of various types, ox yokes and other equipment, the dairy contained several brass pots, cauldrons, a kettle and other equipment and there were 12 oxen in a stall. An Elizabethan plan of Tynemouth Priory shows a farm court immediately north of the church, with a great barn, two stable ranges and a cowhouse arranged around a barn yard and poultry yard.

Few monastic farm complexes have yet been subjected to large-scale excavation. The earthworks of a preceptory of the Knights Templars at South Witham in Lincolnshire, covering 17 acres, were excavated by Philip Mayes in the mid-1960s prior to being bulldozed for agricultural purposes. A group of domestic and service buildings and workshops was revealed, with a large farmyard to the north and west, enclosed by a wall and ditch and entered through a gatehouse. Around the margins of the farmyard were two large aisled barns, a possible carthouse, and a granary, stable, cowhouse and pigsties. Rescue excavations carried out at Waltham Abbey in the early 1970s by Peter Huggins identified a dozen medieval farm and industrial buildings in the yard of the home grange and the adjoining close.

Barns

William Morris declared the monastic barn at Great Coxwell to be 'the finest piece of architecture in England . . . as beautiful as a cathedral, yet with no ostentation of the builder's art'. Barns were usually the first and the largest agricultural buildings to be erected when the abbeys took their demesnes in hand, the centrepiece, both functionally and aesthetically, of the whole farm.

Monastic chronicles often record their construction. Abbot Randulf of Evesham (1214-29) built five new barns on the estates which are described as 'much better ones than had been there before'. Later in the century Abbot John Brookhampton (1282-1316) built 'eight magnificent barns', six in the Vale of Evesham and two on the Cotswolds, and the chronicler singles out the barn at Littleton as a particularly fine one. On the Glastonbury estates five great barns were built by Abbot John Taunton (1274-90). Abbot Yaxley of Thorney (1261-93) built a 'long barn' at Sawbridge. The Gloucester cartulary ascribes the building of the great barn at Frocester (**colour plate 11**) to Abbot John Gamages (1284-1306). Prior Fossor of Durham (1341-74) provided barns at Estrington and Allerton. Interestingly, written sources indicate monastic barn construction continuing long after the decline of high farming. Abbot Newland of Bristol built two new barns at Ashleworth in 1496-7, in addition to the great barn which still stands there. The tithe barn at Carlisle is attributed to Prior Thomas Gondibour (c.1465-1507).

Mike Thompson has recently discovered a detailed set of accounts for the building of a barn at Street in 1341, carried out under the direction of the Glastonbury Abbey cellarer, Thomas Everard. For this project 34 demesne oxen hauled 1,700 wagon loads of stone from the abbey's quarries at Doulting, while timber was brought in from Pilton and Northwood Park. The total cost amounted to £54 4s 3d, the largest proportion of the wages going to Walter Michel, the mason. Much of the work was carried out by labourers recruited from nearby manors who took their payments in bread, cheese and ale. This superseded an older barn, which was demolished a couple of years later, its timbers and iron hinges being salvaged for reuse in an oxhouse and carthouse.

Surviving monastic barns represent only a tiny proportion of those which once existed. In 1538 Beaulieu Abbey owned 27 barns. Of these only three survive today, one at Great Coxwell intact, one at Beaulieu St Leonards ruined, and the reroofed shell of a third at Shilton in Oxfordshire, so drastically modified that it escaped recognition until the late 1960s. Of the 15 great barns mentioned in the Evesham Abbey chronicle, only that at Middle Littleton still stands. Even during the monastic period we hear of losses. In 1441 it was reported at the bishop's visitation that a barn at Ivinghoe Priory had recently burned down, while in 1514 two of the barns of Norwich Cathedral Priory had collapsed through neglect. The great barns were especially vulnerable in the period after the Dissolution when so many monastic estates were dismembered, and accidents of fire and redundancy have continued to reduce the numbers since. The vast barn of St Augustine's Abbey, Canterbury, at Chislet Court, was burned down in 1925. The greatest loss of all is Reading Abbey's stupendous aisled barn at Cholsey, at 303ft the longest barn known in medieval England, demolished in 1815 (**30**).

The function of barns determined their shape, size and character. Their primary purpose was the storage of sheaves of unthreshed grain brought under

30 *Cholsey (Berkshire): engraving of the great barn of Reading Abbey, demolished in 1815*

cover after the harvest. Barns were typically long rectangular buildings, pierced by one or two broad passageways which were often paved with flagstones and used as threshing-floors. Four of St Albans Abbey's barns, at Abbots Langley, Croxley, Kingsbury and St Julians, had a single centrally-placed entry, which necessitated backing out the carts after off-loading. This was inconvenient, and the preferred pattern was to place pairs of opposed double doors at either end of the threshing-floor. The doors were usually set in projecting porches, which extended the size of the threshing floor, gave some protection from the weather on occasions when the doors needed to be open and provided shelter at harvest-time for carts filled with sheaves waiting their turn to unload. Since waiting carts would block the entrance, separate pedestrian doors were often provided in the side wall of the porch. Coxwell's great west porch had an upper room used by the granger or steward, and space for stabling horses. As soon as the laden cart could move forward, the sheaves would be unloaded into the bays on either side, and the emptied cart would continue out through the opposite door. It is usually possible to tell from the height of the doorway and the depth of the porch which was the entrance side and which the exit.

Throughout the winter, whenever grain was required for bread-making, brewing, animal feed, seed-corn or sale, sheaves were taken down from the stacks and threshed in the passage. The hard floor provided a good base for using a flail, and the through draft, created by opening the doors outwards at 90 degrees, helped to winnow the chaff from the grain. The porches often have small recesses to contain grease horns for softening the leather of the flails. The slope of the ground and the accumulation of manure in the farmyard sometimes made it difficult to open the doors fully, and to overcome this the base of each door was raised a foot or two above ground level. When the doors were shut, the gap at the bottom was filled by planks dropped into a slot in the door-jambs. The planks could also be left in place during threshing in order to save grain spilling out into the farmyard and to prevent pigs and hens from entering. Many of the greater barns had two pairs of opposed porches, but smaller barns rarely had more than one pair. Glastonbury Abbey's eight-bay barn at Doulting, measuring about 96ft by 27ft internally, is unusual in having two pairs of porches, which limits its storage capacity to only 75 per cent of its actual volume. Midway along the barn it is divided by an inserted wall, and this may imply some division of use which required independent entrances, one half perhaps housing the produce of the abbey's demesne, the other half that of its tenants. The smallest barns, such as Glastonbury's barn at West Bradley, often have no porches at all (**35b**).

Good ventilation was essential to prevent the stored crops from turning mouldy through residual damp. This was sometimes achieved by leaving open the putlog-holes, the small square openings accommodating the wooden scaffolding during the barn's construction (**35**). There would usually also be a number of vertical or cruciform slit-vents, deeply splayed inside, resembling the embrasures in a castle.

Two distinct structural traditions can be seen in medieval English barns. Aisled barns are generally found in eastern and south-eastern England, rarely occurring west of the Cotswolds. Amongst the finest surviving examples is Beaulieu Abbey's barn at Great Coxwell in western Berkshire, so admired by William Morris. The side and gable walls of this barn are built of local limestone, but internally the roof is carried by six pairs of aisle-posts, each over 22ft high, standing on stone bases themselves 7ft high, carrying three-way braces supporting the purlins and tie-beams. The two barns at Temple Cressing are both of aisled form, the Wheat Barn preserving its original scissor-braced roof, though the roof of the Barley Barn was converted to a crown-post structure in the fifteenth century (**31**). Five new aisled barns were built on the St Albans estates in the late fourteenth century, those at Croxley, Kingsbury and St Julians with crown-post roofs. Crown-posts also appear in the aisled barns of St Augustine's, Canterbury, at Littlebourne, Christ Church, Canterbury, at Brook, and of Rochester Cathedral Priory at Frindsbury. Other surviving aisled barns include those of Battle Abbey at Alciston and of Peterborough Abbey at Boroughbury. Peter Huggins' excavations at Waltham Abbey's home grange identified a five-bay timber-framed aisled barn built around 1200, extended westwards during the thirteenth century by seven extra bays to a length of 210ft, then reduced in size again after the Dissolution. Possibly this building was divided into two parts for the storage of different crops: it may be the wheat garner and oat barn of the 1540 inventory.

31 *An aisled monastic barn in the east of England: interior of the Barley Barn at Temple Cressing (Essex). When first built in c.1220, the roof was probably of scissor-braced form, but it was reconstructed using crown-posts during the first half of the fifteenth century*

Unaisled barns, commonly employing some form of cruck-truss, are more characteristic of the west and north of England. Raised base-crucks set high into the stone wall with some form of upper crucks or upper principals above the collar appear in the south-west. There are many variations on this theme, including magnificent examples at Bradford-on-Avon (**colour plate 10**) and Glastonbury (**35a**). Pershore Abbey's barn at Leigh Court is wholly timber-framed, consisting of 11 massive full crucks, resting on dwarf sandstone walls, spanning over 33ft internally, quite probably the largest extant cruck building in the world (**32**). Another magnificent full-cruck barn, at Wigmore Abbey's home grange, is known from a nineteenth-century sketch, and may have been even larger than Leigh; although this barn survived the great fire which destroyed the rest of the grange in 1875, it has been lost since. Cruck barns are limited in width (rarely more than 32ft), but can compensate for this in length, while the absence of aisle-posts permits greater flexibility of use.

Hybrid types are sometimes found. The eight central trusses of Evesham Abbey's barn at Middle Littleton are of raised-cruck form, but the slender scantling of the timbers and the wide span stretched the ingenuity of the carpenters, and in order to overcome some of the constructional difficulties, the two end bays are aisled. The Knights Hospitallers' barn at Siddington in Gloucestershire has a scissor-braced roof with central trusses of base-cruck form and two end-frames with aisle-posts.

The timber used in monastic barns was almost invariably oak. Dr Richard Pocock, passing by Boxley Abbey in Kent in 1754, thought that the roof of the abbey barn there was of chestnut, and he adds the cautionary note that 'it looks fair without when it becomes rotten within, and goes all at once'. However, no authentic chestnut building is known from medieval England, and Pocock's identification was almost certainly erroneous.

The size of monastic barns varied considerably (**33**). Since the destruction of the gigantic barns of Cholsey and Chislet, Beaulieu Abbey's barn at St Leonards, 224ft long by 67ft wide, is the largest upstanding example, though itself now ruined. Only slightly below the size of these monsters, we have a whole host of great barns over 130ft in length and usually more than 30ft wide, including Abbotsbury (now half in ruin, but originally 272ft by 31ft) (**34**), Tisbury, Leigh (**32**), Middle Littleton, Frocester (**colour plate 11**), Bradford-on-Avon (**colour plates 9** and **10**), Great Coxwell and Frindsbury. Then there is a group of medium-sized barns such as Glastonbury (**35a**), Pilton, and the five aisled barns of St Albans Abbey, which are generally between 80ft and 130ft in length and between 25ft and 30ft wide. Finally there is a group of relatively small barns, less than 80ft by 25ft, such as Shippon, Church Enstone and West Bradley (**35b**). The extreme range of

32 *A cruck-framed barn in the west Midlands: Pershore Abbey's barn at Leigh Court (Worcestershire)*

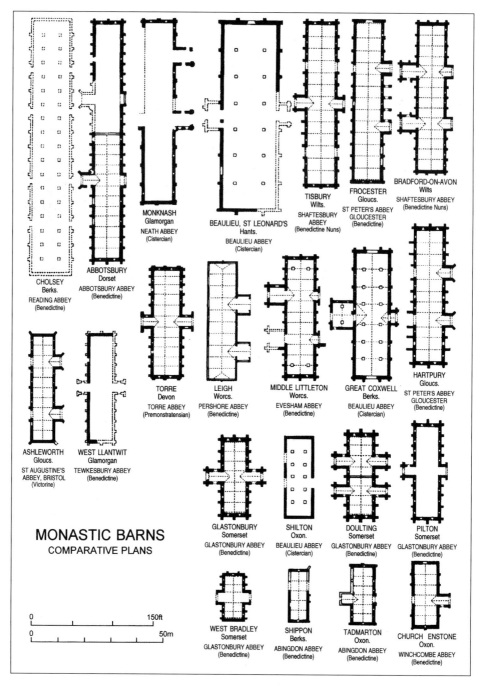

CHOLSEY
Berks.

READING ABBEY
(Benedictine)

ABBOTSBURY
Dorset

ABBOTSBURY ABBEY
(Benedictine)

MONKNASH
Glamorgan

NEATH ABBEY
(Cistercian)

BEAULIEU, ST LEONARD'S
Hants.

BEAULIEU ABBEY
(Cistercian)

TISBURY
Wilts.

SHAFTESBURY
ABBEY
(Benedictine Nuns)

FROCESTER
Gloucs.

ST PETER'S ABBEY
GLOUCESTER
(Benedictine)

BRADFORD-ON-AVON
Wilts

SHAFTESBURY ABBEY
(Benedictine Nuns)

ASHLEWORTH
Gloucs.

ST AUGUSTINE'S
ABBEY, BRISTOL
(Victorine)

WEST LLANTWIT
Glamorgan

TEWKESBURY ABBEY
(Benedictine)

TORRE
Devon

TORRE ABBEY
(Premonstratensian)

LEIGH
Worcs.

PERSHORE ABBEY
(Benedictine)

MIDDLE LITTLETON
Worcs.

EVESHAM ABBEY
(Benedictine)

GREAT COXWELL
Berks.

BEAULIEU ABBEY
(Cistercian)

HARTPURY
Gloucs.

ST PETER'S ABBEY
GLOUCESTER
(Benedictine)

MONASTIC BARNS
COMPARATIVE PLANS

GLASTONBURY
Somerset

GLASTONBURY ABBEY
(Benedictine)

SHILTON
Oxon.

BEAULIEU ABBEY
(Cistercian)

DOULTING
Somerset

GLASTONBURY ABBEY
(Benedictine)

PILTON
Somerset

GLASTONBURY ABBEY
(Benedictine)

0   150ft

0   50m

WEST BRADLEY
Somerset

GLASTONBURY ABBEY
(Benedictine)

SHIPPON
Berks.

ABINGDON ABBEY
(Benedictine)

TADMARTON
Oxon.

ABINGDON ABBEY
(Benedictine)

CHURCH ENSTONE
Oxon.

WINCHCOMBE ABBEY
(Benedictine)

33 *Comparative plans of monastic barns: large barns (top and second rows), medium-sized manorial barns (third row) and small tithe barns (bottom row)*

34 Above *Abbotsbury Abbey barn (Dorset): the surviving gable end was designed to impress. The original length of the barn was almost twice that of the part of the building still roofed over, making this England's longest surviving monastic barn*

35 Right *Glastonbury Abbey barns: (a) the barn on the edge of the precinct at Glastonbury is particularly richly decorated; (b) the tithe barn at West Bradley (Somerset), while smaller and much simpler, is still a substantial construction*

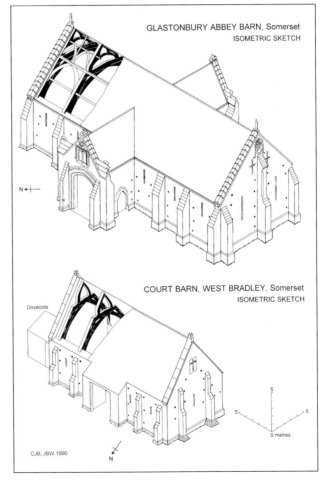

GLASTONBURY ABBEY BARN, Somerset
ISOMETRIC SKETCH

N

COURT BARN, WEST BRADLEY, Somerset
ISOMETRIC SKETCH

Dovecote

5

5   5

0 metres

CJB, JBW 1990

N

sizes raises a number of questions about how they were used, and their place in the estate organisation.

The greatest monastic barns seem to be without parallels on single manors held by secular lords. Clearly only wealthy estates would command the resources to build on this scale. While the immediate priority after harvest was to bring the corn under cover as quickly as possible, the centralisation of grain storage from several adjacent manors may have saved on building and maintenance costs without making an enormous difference to the distance the sheaves had to be carted. Monasteries whose lands were not particularly extensive might elect to concentrate all their grain storage in a single large barn in the outer court, as appears to have been the case at Abbotsbury.

The middle range of monastic barns is broadly similar in size to many barns found on lay estates, and it seems likely that these were built to serve the individual demesne manors. On the Glastonbury estates at least one, sometimes two, barns are recorded on most of the principal demesnes, and the surviving barns at Glastonbury itself, at Pilton and at Doulting all fall within this range.

Finally, the much-misused term 'tithe barn' is not to be equated, as it so often has been, with the great monastic barns. Tithes were one tenth of the produce of a manor payable to the abbey where it had appropriated the parish church. True tithe barns are, therefore, likely to be relatively small. Winchcombe Abbey's barn at Church Enstone, built for the rectorial estate some 75 years after the abbey appropriated the living, measures only 72ft by 26ft internally. Abingdon Abbey's barn at Shippon, designed to house the tithes destined for the kitchener's office, was even smaller.

On some manors there were two or more separate barns intended for storage of different crops. At least two barns are recorded in the home barton at Evesham, and the chronicle specifies that one built by Abbot Brookhampton was intended for barley. The two fine barns of the Knights Templars' preceptory at Cressing have traditionally been known as the 'Wheat Barn' and the 'Barley Barn'. Elsewhere, however, it is clear that a single barn housed several different crops. The arrangements within two of Glastonbury Abbey's barns are described in a survey of 1189: at Wrington the northern and central parts should be filled with wheat, the southern end with two stacks of oats, one of which was to be 2ft lower in order to leave room for three loads of beans; while at Winscombe the dimensions of the stacks of wheat at the west end and oats at the east end are quoted, with space also for barley and beans. An early fourteenth-century record from Oseney Abbey contains estimates of stacks of unthreshed grain in 11 of the abbey's manors in Oxfordshire, Gloucestershire and Buckinghamshire. At least six of those manors contained more than one barn, yet virtually every barn contained three or four different cereal crops plus peas or vetches. An inventory of Merevale Abbey's grange at Newhouse in Leicestershire in 1538 lists 20 quarters of wheat, 4 quarters of rye and 12 quarters of peas in the barn.

Barns represented a massive capital investment, and it seems likely that their volume was fairly carefully calculated to ensure that each one had sufficient storage and processing space. What proportion of the interior was actually used for grain storage? Obviously the size of the harvest varied from year to year, so some flexibility was essential. The bays between the cart porches would normally be left clear for threshing, but could provide overflow capacity in glut years. The 1189 description of Glastonbury's Wrington barn indicates that the northern bays between gable end and doorway were filled right up to roof-ridge level, the central bays between the doorways up to wall-plate level, and the southern bays up to collar-beam level. To enable estate stewards to estimate the size of the harvest from the space occupied by the stacks of unthreshed grain in a barn, a mid-fourteenth-century memorandum in Gloucester Cathedral Library states that one stack of wheat 30ft broad, 15ft long and 10ft high (i.e. 4,500 cubic feet), should contain 40 quarters. However, there are simply too many imponderables for us to determine from the capacity of any barn, the expected volume of the annual harvest or the arable acreage of the hinterland it served.

When were the barns built? Both documentary records and stylistic dating need to be used with caution. Although, as noted earlier, barn construction is often recorded in monastic chronicles, we cannot assume that documented buildings necessarily equate with those now standing. A number of writers have wrongly identified the Evesham chronicle description of a tithe barn at North Littleton built by Abbot Ombersley (1367-79) with the surviving great barn at Middle Littleton, which is over half a century earlier.

Like most functional buildings, barns can be very difficult to date by architectural style, and estimates on this basis are often highly suspect. The Barley Barn at Temple Cressing was traditionally dated to around 1450 and the Wheat Barn to around 1530, but the appearance of both barns was drastically altered in the late Middle Ages, and subsequent re-examination has pushed their origins back much earlier. A vent in the east gable of the Siddington barn in Gloucestershire is hooded with a triangular moulding curiously reminiscent of some Anglo-Saxon windows and, as Freddie Charles has pointed out, the barn projects into the churchyard almost as if it antedates the church itself. However, a pre-Conquest date seems so inherently unlikely that it must surely be discarded.

Two monastic barns have medieval datestones: an inscription in the much-altered barn of Kingswood Abbey at Calcot, high up on the Cotswolds, records its construction in 1300 by Abbot Henry (36a); while a reset inscription in Winchcombe Abbey's barn at Church Enstone states that it was built in 1382 by Abbot Walter Wynforton (36b). Datestones may record repairs rather than the original construction, and they can be transferred from one building to another, but in these cases the inscribed dates seem compatible with the buildings containing them.

36 *Date-stones in monastic barns.* Above (a) *Calcot (Gloucestershire): the reset stone records the building of a barn by Henry, abbot of Kingswood, in 1300. Parts of this structure may survive in the existing, much-altered barn.* Below (b) *Church Enstone (Oxfordshire): 'This barn was founded and built in the year 1382 by Walter de Wynforton, abbot of Winchcombe, at the request of Robert Mason, bailiff of this place'*

Technical advances in timber-framing provide another possible aid to dating. Over a period of 30 years Cecil Hewett undertook a detailed study of the typological development of medieval carpentry, based upon his own sound practical experience as a skilled woodworker. In the early 1960s this led him to propose that the two barns at Temple Cressing were both about three centuries earlier than the dates then generally accepted. At a time when most architectural historians were reluctant to believe that any extant timber building could be much older than the fifteenth century, this provoked a storm of controversy; but gradually the notion that timber buildings could survive from the early Middle Ages and that study of their carpentry could be a useful guide to dating gained ground. Hewett dated the Hospitallers' barn at Siddington to the first quarter of the thirteenth century because it still employed open notched-lap joints, a type superseded by secret joints during the building of the nave at Wells Cathedral between 1210 and 1220. However, even the richest monastic houses did not necessarily follow the latest carpentry fashions in their farm buildings. Valuable though Hewett's work is, it would be unwise to expect precision from this type of evidence.

37 *Coggeshall Abbey barn (Essex), possibly the oldest surviving monastic barn in England: though much altered in the late fourteenth century, radiocarbon dating of the principal posts has suggested a construction date close to that of the abbey's foundation in 1142*

Since the 1970s the dating of barns has been revolutionised by scientific techniques. Radiocarbon examination of the principal posts in the aisled barn of Coggeshall Abbey (**37**), traditionally ascribed to the fifteenth century, produced an unexpectedly early date-range centred close to the abbey's foundation in 1142. Although substantial reconstruction occurred in the late fourteenth century, when the original passing-braces were removed and crown-posts inserted, this has a good claim to be the oldest monastic barn surviving in England.

Dendrochronology, the science of dating timbers by analysing the pattern of annual growth rings, can give a precise felling date if the sapwood survives. The timbers of the Middle Littleton barn, previously attributed to Abbot Ombersley (1367-79), yielded earlier dates from dendrochronology, which make its identification with the 'very fine' barn built by Abbot Brookhampton (1282-1316) virtually certain. Timbers from the Doulting barn, previously dated no earlier than the mid-fourteenth century, were felled in 1288-90. Samples from Coxwell point to a construction date very shortly after 1300, which accords well with the general character of the carpentry. Although it had been assumed that the roof of the Frocester barn dated from the documented construction of Abbot John Gamages in the late thirteenth century, re-examination by Freddie Charles and Walter Horn cast doubts upon its authenticity, and dendrochronological work subsequently confirmed that, following a fire shortly before the Dissolution, the entire roof had been replaced over the thirteenth-century walls. Dendrochronological examination of the Temple Cressing barns has vindicated Hewett's contention that both barns were much older than previously supposed, confirming the Wheat Barn's construction at around 1270, and giving a date of around 1220 for the Barley Barn.

Even when several different strands of evidence are available, it can still prove difficult to reconcile them. Written records of a thatched barn at Glastonbury run from the early fourteenth century up to 1364-5, then, after a gap in the accounts, a record of a barn being roofed with stone tiles appears in 1389-90. The obituary of Abbot Walter Monington lists all the major building works carried out during his abbacy (1342-75), without mentioning the barn; yet dendrochronological investigation of its roof timbers indicate that the trees were felled between 1343 and 1361. Did Abbot Monington's obituary for some reason omit to mention this building, or was it built between his death and 1389-90 using timber which had been felled a couple of decades earlier? While medieval builders had no inhibitions about using green timber as a matter of course, occasional building contracts show that seasoned timber was used if it was available. Although there can be little doubt that the existing Glastonbury barn was completed within the second half of the fourteenth century, its precise date remains elusive.

Monastic barns can be awe-inspiring by reason of their size, yet many of them are purely functional structures without decorative frills. Externally, were it not for its scale, Pershore Abbey's Leigh Court barn would appear the most mundane of vernacular structures. Occasionally, however, a greater level of architectural flamboyance shows that the barn was designed to impress. The gable end of the Abbotsbury barn is given dignity by two tiers of moulded string-courses and by stepped central and angle buttresses continued upwards to terminate in embattled pedestals (**34**). Ornament is most conspicuous at Glastonbury (**35a**), where figures of angels and decorated trefoiled vents adorn the main gables, corbelled heads support the gable copings, the porches have *fleur-de-lys* finials and mullioned traceried windows with figures of animals over their side buttresses, and plaques depicting the symbols of the four evangelists are set near the apex of each gable. Some of the same decorative detail also appears at Glastonbury Abbey's barn at Pilton, but here the barn was clearly designed to be seen mainly from the northern side, which faced across the valley to the abbot's manor house. Significantly this is the entrance side with the larger porches, and the vents between the buttresses are of more ornamental cruciform shape, whereas on the south they are mere slits. Here the barn can be seen as the grand centrepiece of a designed landscape, including park, ponds, orchards, vineyard and gardens, all visible from the abbot's house.

Hay barns

Hay was not normally stored in the barn with other crops. Even more than cereals, it was liable to spontaneous combustion if stored warm and moist without ventilation. Often it was ricked in the open with a thatched covering. Separate hay barns were sometimes built in the abbey's outer court, Abbot Burton of Meaux constructing one adjacent to his own stable, and Prior Fossor of Durham building a great hay barn for the guesthouse. One of the buildings excavated at Waltham Abbey was timber-framed with a row of central posts to support a loft above, and this can probably be equated with the hay barn listed in the 1540 inventory.

Granaries

The purpose of granaries was to store the grain once it had been threshed. This presented special problems. Grain was much heavier in relation to its volume than unthreshed sheaves; it was equally liable to turn mouldy in damp conditions; it would germinate if it became too warm; and it was vulnerable to rats, birds and other predators. The granary floor had to be raised above ground level, yet able to carry a considerable weight, while good ventilation was needed without providing access for vermin. Granaries were built adjoining the bakehouse in the outer court at Thorney by Abbot David (1238-54), and at Durham by Prior Fossor.

The bursar's accounts of Durham Priory record granaries on about two-thirds of all its manors. The identification of granaries from written sources can be problematic, since the Latin words *grangia* (barn) and *horreum* (granary) tend to be used indiscriminately. An inventory of Jarrow Priory in 1338 distinguishes between a barn and a granary for malting, but the barn disappears from the records after 1379, and a 1417 inventory lists only the granary. Some were incorporated into barns, Torre Abbey's barn at Shiphay Collaton having an upper floor probably used for this purpose. Free-standing examples on posts or staddles are also recorded from the later Middle Ages.

Relatively few granaries remain, perhaps because they were so frequently timber-built. The granary at Meaux Abbey's Skerne Grange burned down in the mid-thirteenth century, causing the loss of over 400 quarters of grain. However, south-west of the main claustral buildings at Castle Acre, the ruins of a massive fourteenth-century granary can be seen, with six square stone piers along its centre supporting the now-vanished upper floor. Around the adjoining court are scantier remains of a second granary, maltkiln, bakehouse and brewhouse. The presence of a spine wall in a small building with an external stairway adjoining the barns excavated at South Witham suggests that this, too, was a granary. The most complete surviving example stands near the

38 *Bradford-on-Avon (Wiltshire): the cruck-framed granary adjoining the great barn on Shaftesbury Abbey's estate farm*

great barn at Bradford-on-Avon, a cruck-roofed building resting on massive stone pillars, probably originally entirely timber-framed above, though now clad in stone (**38**).

Livestock housing

Most manorial demesnes and granges contained some facilities for handling livestock. However, some monastic outstations fulfilled more specialised pastoral functions as vaccaries (cattle ranches or dairy farms) or bercaries (sheep farms). These differed from the general-purpose grange in lacking major cereal storage buildings and features such as dovecotes, while containing some distinctive structures of their own. They normally consisted of a house for the supervisor (often a lay-brother) and a rather more basic dwelling for the herdsmen or shepherds, along with cattle-byres or sheepcotes, and a range of stock pens and enclosures.

Bolton Priory, which nearly tripled the size of its sheep flocks between 1296 and 1311, established 13 new bercaries over the same period, in some cases by converting existing cattle farms or arable holdings. Fountains Abbey developed a string of cattle farms in Nidderdale, from Dacre almost up to the head of the valley. Jervaulx had a chain of cattle lodges over its Wensleydale pastures, controlled from its grange at Dale. Meaux Abbey had its principal cattle farm at Heigholme in the Hull Valley.

While many of these pastoral farms were permanently occupied settlements, others in upland areas served only as summer shielings. In 1256 Lanercost Priory acquired rights to build a cow-fold, sheep-fold and two shielings in Askerton in north-east Cumberland. Livestock shelters were also built at resting-places on regular transhumance routes.

Remains of abandoned monastic sheep and cattle farms survive in upland areas above the present margins of cultivation, especially in the north of England. Earthworks surveyed by Steve Moorhouse at Dundale on Levisham Moor, 650ft up in the North Yorkshire Moors above Pickering, include three separate yards enclosed by banks, containing at least half a dozen buildings, the remains of a stock farm of the Gilbertine canons of Malton (**39**). Another site on Malham Moor in the Pennines, probably identifiable with a holding of the Augustinians of Bolton Priory, included up to a dozen ruined buildings scattered amidst a series of pens and enclosures of varying size.

In the Peak District the site of a cattle lodge of Croxden Abbey can be recognised from the foundations of several buildings terraced into the flank of the Manifold Valley at Musden. Excavations at Garendon Abbey's Roystone Grange have demonstrated that the first buildings erected in the late twelfth century were of a vernacular nature, a three-bay aisled house containing a dairy with an adjoining yard and cattle-shed. A much grander two-storey hall was added in the early thirteenth century, but abandoned towards the end of the century as the site was affected by increasing waterlogging.

In 1956 Aileen Fox excavated a summer cattle lodge 1,100ft up on Dean Moor on Dartmoor, on land which had belonged to Buckfast Abbey. A house

39 *Levisham Moor (Yorkshire North Riding): the earthworks are the remains of the buildings of a bercary belonging to Old Malton Priory*

and large byre were set parallel with each other, terraced into the steep slope, flanking a central enclosed yard, with a stone-walled paddock to the south. The buildings lay within, and reused, a 4-acre late Bronze Age enclosure extending down to a stream.

Remains of such specialised farms are less likely to be found in the lowlands of southern England, mainly because they continued to be occupied and have been modernised and rebuilt. Nevertheless, there was a string of dairy farms belonging to Abingdon Abbey along the rich grasslands of the Vale of White Horse at Thrupp, Culham, Charney, Goosey and Shellingford, all of which rendered cheeses to the abbey. The memory of this function is preserved in the string of modern farms bearing the name 'Wick', which here has the specialised meaning of 'dairy farm'. Rye Farm on Andersey Island between two branches of the Thames appears to have supplied the bulk of the abbey's milk. Canterbury Cathedral Priory had dairies at Romney, where costs of purchase and repair of equipment, including presses, bowls, cloths, scoops, churns and cheese moulds, are recorded. No churns are listed on Tavistock Abbey's dairies at Hurdwick, Leigh and Werrington, and here clotted cream was probably raised by scalding and worked into butter by hand.

Cattle-sheds and byres

On some lowland manors cattle were kept out in the open throughout the winter. However, occasionally this caused problems, as in 1287-8, when Canterbury Cathedral Priory's farmers had to carry fodder by boat to beasts cut off by floodwaters on Romney Marsh. Cattle-sheds providing shelter, particularly for younger and more valuable beasts, became a regular part of monastic investment during the high farming period of the thirteenth century. Examples were built on the Peterborough estates by Abbot Walter of St Edmunds (1233-45) and Abbot Godfrey Crowland (1299-1320). The chronicle of Adam of Damerham records Abbot Robert Petherton of Glastonbury (1261-74) building new cattle-sheds at Glastonbury and Sowy in Somerset, at Damerham in Hampshire and Christian Malford in Wiltshire.

Late thirteenth-century management regulations at St Peter's Abbey, Gloucester, required that cords of fixed length be kept in each cowshed in order to measure and control the quantity of fodder given to the animals. On the Canterbury Cathedral Priory estates feeding from troughs and in stalls was common, with high-quality feed such as oats and vetches being reserved for calves and dairy cattle likely to repay the extra investment.

Details of cattle housing are recorded in various sources. In 1253 Canterbury Cathedral Priory spent 18s 4d on building a new cowhouse at Agney on Romney Marsh. A much larger cowshed, requiring 1,000 laths, built on the same manor in 1282-4, cost 75s. A cowshed on the Templars' preceptory of

Rothley accommodated one bull, 26 oxen, 11 cows, nine steers and four calves in 1309. Repairs to a cowshed on Battle Abbey's property at Dengemarsh are recorded in 1320-1. In 1304 a second cowshed was built on the Glastonbury manor of Baltonsborough, with a roof requiring 75 tiles. Building accounts for a new byre made at Street in 1343, completed at a cost of £11 5s 8d record its dimensions as 63ft by 20ft, and it required 600 wagonloads of stone from Doulting and 12 quarters 6 bushels of sand from Fenny Castle for tiling and pointing the walls. An oxhouse is listed on the Tewkesbury Abbey grange of Abbots Llantwit in the accounts of 1449-50. The inventory of Jarrow Priory mentions a cow-byre in 1348, and £15 9s 6d was spent on the repair of a byre there in 1472-3. A new cowhouse 80ft long was built by Abbot Thomas Burton of Meaux in the 1390s. A survey of the Jervaulx grange of Kilgram just after the Dissolution mentions an oxhouse and cowhouse.

Archaeological evidence for cattle housing remains limited. A possible byre in the outer court at Fountains has been identified by survey. At Tynemouth Priory the cowhouse depicted on the Elizabethan plan was partially excavated by George Jobey; it was 20ft wide with a paved central drain allowing room for two rows of stalls separated by wooden partitions, and could have accommodated up to 30 beasts. Cowsheds were amongst the preceptory buildings excavated at South Witham. A late twelfth-century byre just 15ft square on Rievaulx Abbey's land in Upper Eskdale probably belonged to a summer shieling. Near one of the entrances in the south-east corner of the yard of Waltham Abbey's home grange a buttressed brick structure was erected around the last quarter of the fifteenth century, 237ft long by 31ft wide. It included domestic accommodation with a fireplace at the southern end, while the northernmost bay contained an oven. The intervening range was subdivided by brick footings into seven bays each 15ft 6in (one perch) wide, with one wider bay. Each of the stalls would have had room for four oxen. The inventory of 1540 lists 12 oxen in the stalls, along with six carthorses and seven horses used in the malt mill.

Sheepcotes

Walter of Henley recommended that sheep should be housed through the winter months from Martinmas (11 November) up to Easter. Sheepcotes are frequently mentioned in thirteenth- and fourteenth-century chronicles and accounts. Abbot Walter of St Edmunds (1233-45) and Abbot Godfrey Crowland (1299-1320) both built sheepcotes on the Peterborough Abbey estates. They might occur within the outer court of the abbey, within manor farms or granges, or in more isolated locations on upland or marshland pastures. Three sheepcotes are recorded on Abingdon Abbey's manor of Shellingford Newbury in 1398-9. Winchcombe Abbey's Cotswold grange at

Cutsdean had a sheepcote 'near the great gate' in 1390. At Minchinhampton a sheepcote is recorded 'on the Down' in the fifteenth century. Often they were administratively linked with regular granges, but physically detached from them. Rievaulx Abbey's sheephouse at Sproxton was connected by a bridge over the River Rye to the grange at Griff, while its sheephouse at Wether Cote, 700ft up on Skiplam Moor, was worked from Skiplam Grange, over a mile to the south and 250ft lower on the edge of Kirkdale. A sheepcote at Moor House was linked with the Fountains grange of Bewerley on the lower ground to the east.

Building accounts and illustrations show that sheepcotes were often built of timber on low stone sill walls. In 1289 the earl of Gloucester allowed Neath Abbey timber from his Glamorgan woods for buildings at Tetburn Grange (Cwrt Herbert in Cadoxton) which included a sheepcote. Abbot Robert Petherton of Glastonbury (1261-74) is recorded as building a stone sheepcote at Winterborne in Wiltshire. Their most distinctive characteristic is their length. A sheepcote built in 1352 on Battle Abbey's manor of Appledram, 100ft long by 14ft wide, was at the lower end of the range, sufficient to accommodate around 165 sheep. Abbot Thomas Burton of Meaux built a new sheepcote at Wharram Grange, 160ft long, for breeding ewes. Fountains Abbey's sheepcote at Greenbury was probably L-shaped, being described as 260ft in either direction. There was often a hayloft above with storage for winter feed. The Templars' sheepcote at Rothley is said to have accommodated 342 sheep and 123 lambs. Sheepcotes were normally thatched, and when Bristol Abbey leased out its farm at Rowberrow in 1407, the abbey retained the sheephouse and responsibility for its repair, while requiring the tenant to provide straw for thatching it. When the monks of Fountains acquired pasture rights for 300 sheep at Sawley near Ripon, the donor also gave them the right to take fern for litter and roofing the sheepcote, and they were permitted to use the manure of the sheep as they wished.

Examples isolated on remote pastures were normally surrounded by a hedged or walled enclosure used for marshalling and sorting sheep. The close attached to Rievaulx Abbey's sheepcote at Willerby in 1152 occupied half an acre, Fountains Abbey's sheepcotes at Baldersby in the Vale of York and at Allerston in the Vale of Pickering each had 3 acres attached, while Combermere Abbey's sheepcote at 'le Cotes' had 4 acres.

The earthwork remains of former sheepcotes can often be identified from their length. Meaux Abbey's sheephouse at Wharram-le-Street was about 160ft long and 50ft wide. Another characteristic example has been discovered by Grenville Astill on Bordesley Abbey's Combe Grange near Chipping Campden. However, few have yet been explored by excavation. Arthur Raistrick recorded a timber-framed structure on dwarf stone walls, 48ft long by 18ft wide internally, at Priors Raikes on Malham Moor which may be the sheepcote recorded in the compotus rolls of Bolton Priory from 1290 onwards, later leased to Fountains Abbey. Nearby was also a small rectangular hut with a hearth at one corner, presumably used by the shepherd. The associated enclosure lay on the east side with massive walls and signs of post and wattle fencing. Paths of limestone flags were set down the middle of both sheephouse and yard. Uncharacteristically short, this building alone might have provided winter shelter for a small breeding flock of 50 or 60 ewes, but it was only one component of a much more extensive complex of stone-walled enclosures and other buildings.

Woolhouses

Most abbeys exporting wool had a single warehouse where the wool could be stored, washed, sorted, graded and packed, and be available for inspection by merchants. The Gilbertine statutes insisted on centralising wool storage at the priory, so their woolhouses were normally in the outer court. The Cistercians had more latitude to place their collecting points wherever it was most convenient, so they may occur either at the abbey or at one of the granges. Some of the larger Cistercian houses, such as Rievaulx, Byland and Meaux, also made their storage facilities available to smaller monastic houses and lay proprietors. The nuns of Arden regularly sent their wool to Byland Abbey's woolhouse at Thorpe Grange, 10 miles away. Security was an important consideration, so woolhouses are rarely in isolated locations, and they were usually strongly constructed. Meaux Abbey's woolhouse at Wawne Grange was stone-built and originally roofed with lead, though later re-roofed with tiles. Cleanliness of storage conditions was also important. Arbitration following a dispute between the Cistercians of Pipewell and a group of merchants from Cahors in 1291 required that boarding should be firmly attached to the floor and walls of the woolhouse during the term of storage, to prevent contamination by dirt or damp. A mid-twelfth-century aisled building south of the outer court at Fountains Abbey, originally believed to be the bakehouse, was reinterpreted as the woolhouse following further excavations by Glyn Coppack in 1977-9. The woolhouse built by Beaulieu Abbey in Southampton in the late fourteenth century still survives (**40**).

Stables

Stables were provided within the outer court to accommodate riding-horses for members of the community needing to travel on the abbey's business, and also to serve the guesthouse. A survey of the site of Reading Abbey in 1650 mentions a former stable, 135ft long by 30ft broad. In the south-west corner of the precinct flint walls of a building of about this width, but at least 230ft

40 *Beaulieu Abbey's woolhouse in Southampton (Hampshire)*

long, have been located by excavation. It had been gutted by fire and then rebuilt after the Dissolution. Little evidence of internal fittings survived.

   Where horses were employed on farm work they were usually housed with the cattle or oxen. At Waltham Abbey the six carthorses and seven malt-mill horses listed in 1540 were probably accommodated in some of the bays of the oxhouse in the grange yard, described earlier. Purpose-built stables for farm horses appear rarely, though a late medieval stable range survived in the outer court at Tisbury until the late nineteenth century.

Pigsties

The reduction of pannage through woodland clearance may have led to an increase in the practice of fattening pigs in sties during the Middle Ages. Little is known of the housing of pigs, either from documentation or from archaeological evidence. The manorial accounts of St Augustine's Abbey, Bristol, refer to pigs foraging in the hillside woods at Ashleworth, but there were also two pighouses there under one roof. Beaulieu Abbey's pigs were regularly fed with kitchen swill, malting dregs and granary rejects, which implies some form of sty. The Durham cellarers' accounts mention at least two swinehouses and sties. A pigsty at Battle Abbey was thatched with broom in 1478-9. Two possible pigsties were among the farm buildings excavated at the South Witham preceptory.

Cartsheds and equipment shelters

Carts were often stored within the barn, on the threshing-floor or in the porch. However, cartsheds are occasionally recorded on monastic properties. In 1343 a new cartshed was completed on Glastonbury's manor of Street. Measuring 30ft by 20ft, it was built end-on to the byre, and its construction used 300 wagonloads of stone from Doulting. The timber for the roof was partly salvaged from the demolition of an old barn, and payments are also recorded for felling and collecting 24 alder trees on the moors nearby for rafters. At Waltham a building named as the plough-house in the 1540 inventory contained in addition to a plough and harrows the bodies of two dung carts and a lime cart with one pair of wheels and two more carts with iron-bound wheels. This might be equated with an unaisled timber-framed building excavated in the centre of the grange yard, 100ft long and 27ft broad.

Poultry-houses

The construction of hen-houses by Godfrey Crowland, Abbot of Peterborough (1299-1320) is recorded. A small shed for poultry covered with straw thatch was made in the cellarer's garden at Battle Abbey in 1464-5. The Durham Priory cellarer's rolls mention a goose-house paved with flagstones in 1474-5, a capon-house, the walls of which were being pointed in 1502-3, and a hen-house, boarded in 1512-13. Clearly these were more than ephemeral structures, but such buildings have yet to be recognised archaeologically.

Dovecotes

Dovecotes occurred on monastic estates from the twelfth century onwards. Initially the high costs of building and stocking them limited their occurrence to a few manors on any estate. The flocks foraged freely for most of the year, supplementary feeding being required only in the depths of winter, and sometimes in June and July before the pea harvest.

Early writers believed that the function of dovecotes was to provide a supply of fresh meat through the winter as a relief from salt beef and mutton. However, even if this were required, doves do not breed between October and March, and the first brood hatched in March was often kept for breeding purposes. Each pair produces a couple of chicks eight to ten times a year over a period of about seven years. The cellarer's rolls of Durham Priory record pigeons being eaten particularly in September and October, but never through the winter months. Maxstoke Priory in Warwickshire had two dovecotes on its home manor in the 1340s with others at Fillongley and Shustoke, which together yielded about 640 doves a year. In 1416-17, four different dovecotes produced 731 pigeons for consumption at Selby Abbey.

The building of dovecotes is recorded in many monastic chronicles and account rolls. They appear most common on Benedictine estates in the south and midlands, where cereal surpluses might most readily be produced. At least ten examples are recorded on the estates of Evesham Abbey between the early thirteenth century and the Dissolution (**7**). Seven dovecotes were built on Dunstable Priory's land between 1248 and 1273. On the Glastonbury estates Abbot Petherton (1261-74) built a new dovecote at Ashbury, two more were built by Abbot John Taunton (1274-90), while Abbot Monington (1342-75) built a new dovecote at Pilton. At St Albans Matthew Paris tells us that Abbot John in 1396 'built a great and ingenious pigeon-house in his own garden, and excellently repaired the old pigeon-house there'. The treasurer's account of Abingdon Abbey records the large sum of £6 11s 10d spent on building a dovecote in the town of Abingdon in 1383-4, including 13s 9d for digging stone at Cumnor, 8s 9d for 4 quarters and 3 bushels of lime and 6d for wooden scaffolding, while the sacrist's account in 1396-7 mentions three dovecotes in Marcham, two on the rectory estate and one at Hyde Farm. The repair with lime of a dovecote in the West Orchard at Durham is mentioned in 1344, 1485-6 and 1502-3.

It is often difficult to match up the documentary records with surviving examples. Of the ten dovecotes mentioned in the Evesham sources, only two (those at Kinwarton and Wickhamford) seem likely to be equated with existing buildings, while at least four more dovecotes of medieval appearance survive on the abbey's estates but lack contemporary documentation. Some of these may have been built by tenants rather than by the abbey itself, though they include an especially large and well-built example at Hillborough. One heavily restored round dovecote at Marcham may be one of the three there mentioned in the Abingdon sacrist's account. The survey of the Hospitallers' estates carried out by Prior Philip Thame in 1338 mentions a dovecote at the Quenington commandery in Gloucestershire, which is probably the one which still stands there today.

Occasionally nestholes were incorporated within some other structure. At Evesham there were nestholes in the tower of the barton gate. At West Bradley a square dovecote, subsequently partly ruined, reduced in height and re-roofed, was attached to the gable end of Glastonbury Abbey's barn (**35b**). Nestholes occur within the east porch of Beaulieu's great barn at Coxwell.

More frequently dovecotes were free-standing buildings. A circular plan was preferred (**41, colour plates 12** and **13**), since the squabs could then be collected from the nest-holes by means of a potence (an Old French word meaning a crutch or gibbet), a device consisting of a ladder mounted to spars fixed at the top and bottom of a central post revolving on iron bearings. An example survives at Kinwarton (**42**). The size of dovecotes varied considerably:

41 *Shapwick (Somerset): interior of dovecote on the Almoner's Manor of Glastonbury Abbey (see also* **colour plate 12**). *The absence of perching-ledges and the irregular reconstruction of nestholes during subsequent repairs may reflect the limited funds available to one of the less important officers of the abbey*

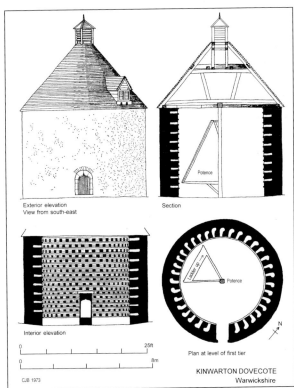

Exterior elevation
View from south-east

Section

Potence

Interior elevation

Potence

Ladder up

0   25ft

0   8m

CJB 1973

Plan at level of first tier

N

KINWARTON DOVECOTE
Warwickshire

42 *Kinwarton (Warwickshire): a midland-type dovecote with timbered roof and lantern, acquired from Robert Grene by Abbot William Boys of Evesham (1345-67)*

on monastic estates internal diameters ranging from 10ft 6in up to 26ft have been recorded. The nestholes were normally staggered diagonally, in order to reduce weakening of the wall, and elbowed within the thickness of the wall to provide extra security for nesting birds. Some dovecotes are equipped with internal perching ledges at every course, or every two or three courses, of nestholes. The number of nestholes can vary from a couple of hundred to a thousand or more. On rare occasions the nestholes were set vertically one above another – in a now collapsed example at Wick near Pershore, which may have belonged to Westminster Abbey, the nestholes were very closely set, and the intention seems to have been to cram in as many as possible, even to the extent of squeezing half-a-dozen below the relieving-arch of the doorway. Later texts counsel against overcrowding, recommending three or four nestholes for each two pairs of birds. The roof was commonly timber-framed and conical, with a louvered turret at the apex.

In the far west of England and in Wales medieval dovecotes commonly had a more archaic form of domed corbelled stone roof with a simple central aperture or oculus. Examples survive at Monkton Priory (**43b**) and on the Hospitallers' property at Rosemarket, both in Pembrokeshire, at Tewkesbury Abbey's grange at Llantwit Major and, in more ruinous condition, at Neath Abbey's granges of Monknash and Gelligarn. At Garway in Herefordshire the

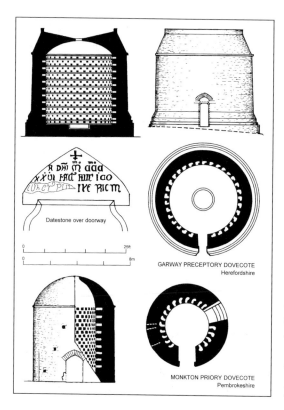

Datestone over doorway

0 _____ 25ft
0 _____ 8m

GARWAY PRECEPTORY DOVECOTE
Herefordshire

MONKTON PRIORY DOVECOTE
Pembrokeshire

43 *Western stone-roofed dovecotes.* Above and centre (a) *Knights Templars' and Hospitallers' preceptory at Garway (Herefordshire); the datestone over the doorway reads 'In the year of our Lord 1326 this dovecote was built by Richard'.* Below (b) *Monkton Priory (Pembrokeshire)*

44 *Bretforton (Worcestershire): a rectangular medieval dovecote on an Evesham Abbey manor. The original doorway, now blocked, is faintly visible to the right of the ranging-pole*

upper part of the roof was dished in the centre to feed rainwater through the opening into a round cistern for drinking and washing, which was also replenished and drained by a channel at ground level. Over the door of the Garway dovecote is a datestone recording its erection by one Richard in 1326, after the preceptory had been passed from the Templars to the Hospitallers (**43a**).

Experiments were also made with square and rectangular dovecotes during the Middle Ages (**44**). Excavations at Waltham Abbey have shown a round dovecote being replaced by a square timber-framed one on the same site in the fifteenth or early sixteenth century. Conversely, however, Glyn Coppack's work at Thornholme Priory has revealed a square stone-built dovecote in the outer court apparently as early as *c*.1170. Partly rebuilt in the early fourteenth century, it was abandoned a little over a century later, perhaps because of an epidemic, since the floor was littered with the bones of dead birds. A circular earthwork elsewhere in the precinct probably represents its successor. Notley Abbey's square dovecote at Long Crendon contains over 1000 nestholes, of which about 400 are carried in four tall spur-walls projecting from the centre of each internal wall. About half of a large double rectangular dovecote survives at Frocester Court. This is first documented in 1508-9, but analysis of its mortar and its reuse of Norman sculptural fragments probably salvaged from the rebuilding of the parish church both point to it being contemporary with the great barn nearby. A square clunch-walled dovecote at Canons in Mitcham, which belonged to the Augustinian canons of Southwark, has the date 1511 incised on one wall. Illustrations survive of a remarkable cruciform dovecote within the precinct of Lewes Priory, sadly demolished around 1800, which is said to have contained 3,328 nestholes; if this was medieval, it would have been the largest example known.

Dovecotes produced several important by-products. The feathers were used for mattresses. The cartulary of Gloucester Abbey includes a set of rules for its manors, probably from the later thirteenth century, which includes an instruction for the dovecotes to be swept out twice a year, the dung to be used as manure for the kitchen-gardens. It was also used for softening leather and preparing parchment.

9
Monastic gardens, orchards and vineyards

Introduction

Gardening has been a feature of monastic life since the late third century, when St Anthony created an irrigated subsistence plot in the Egyptian desert. Several of the earliest monastic codes, including the Rule of St Benedict, required gardens to be enclosed within the precinct for the solace and sustenance of the monks. The famous plan made in the early ninth century for Abbot Gosbert of St Gallen in Switzerland, depicts a kitchen garden and physic garden with named herbs and vegetables laid out in parallel beds and an orchard and shrubbery in the cemetery. Kitchen gardens, infirmary gardens and ornamental grounds are all authenticated from English records in the later Middle Ages. Gardens played an especially important part in the life of the hermit orders, and in that of the urban friars who held little other landed property. A memory of the long-vanished gardens of the Greyfriars in Oxford lingers on in the place-name 'Paradise Square', located incongruously in the city's dingy inner suburbs.

Much of the herbal and horticultural knowledge of the Middle Ages came from the classical world. Bede had access to a copy of Pliny the Elder's encyclopaedia. The herbal of Apuleius Platonicus, originally compiled around 400, was translated into Old English around 1000, and an illustrated copy made shortly before 1100 survives from Canterbury. Another herbal, compiled at the Abbey of Bury St Edmunds before 1120, derives its text from both Pliny and Apuleius, but includes some especially beautiful original illustrations of plants drawn from life.

Gardens within the monastic precinct

Records of gardens in English monasteries become increasingly frequent after the tenth century. The biography of Abbot Eadfrith of St Albans (939-46) recounts his earlier life as a hermit tending his herbs and vegetables. In the time

153

of Abbot Brihtnoth of Ely (970-96) one of the monks, named Leo, was responsible for planting gardens and orchards on the island, the chronicler commending his skill with fruit trees and shrubs. The Latin-Old English vocabulary compiled by Aelfric of Cerne in 995 gives the names of over 200 herbs and trees, most of which could have been cultivated in England. The plan of Canterbury Cathedral Priory made around 1170 to show the course of the water pipes and drains installed by Prior Wibert depicts a vineyard and orchard outside the precinct, and a *herbarium* with rows of plants and a trellis fence within the infirmary cloister (often translated as 'herb garden', this term appears to mean a small enclosed plot with turf and flowers). Towards the end of the twelfth century Giraldus Cambrensis praised the setting of Llanthony Priory on the outskirts of Gloucester, 'a place so beautiful and peaceful, provided with...fruitful vines and set about with gardens and orchards'. On several occasions monarchs visiting the nearby castle arranged access by bridge over the moat so that they could enjoy the priory gardens.

Under the obedientiary system the gardener's office often kept separate accounts. The fullest collection comes from Norwich Cathedral Priory, which has some 30 rolls surviving from between 1340 and 1419. Gardeners' accounts from Abingdon have been published for four years, 1369-70, 1388-9, 1412-13 and 1450-1, and others are available from Glastonbury Abbey and Maxstoke Priory. Often the gardener's responsibilities involved income and expenditure beyond the garden itself, but the accounts invariably throw some light upon the nature of the gardens and their produce.

Monastic gardens could cover up to 10 or a dozen acres. Within the precinct at Glastonbury there were at least two separate gardens, the Great Garden and Little Garden, as well as an orchard producing cider apples and pears and a vineyard. Originally all gardens were used by the whole community, but often by the late Middle Ages separate plots were assigned to the abbot and to various obedientiaries. At Abingdon the kitchener, precentor, sacrist and keeper of works all had their own gardens. In 1450 a new garden was laid out on the west side of the guesthouse, while a survey made after the Dissolution mentions the 'privy garden' which was probably attached to the abbot's house. The precinct of Norwich Cathedral Priory included a separate physic garden and a small garden for the sacrist. The Battle Abbey accounts identify the kitchen garden, cellarer's garden and infirmary garden. The precinct of Maxstoke priory included at least two walled gardens belonging to the sacrist and the infirmarer. In 1299 the abbot of Winchcombe obtained royal leave to block up a public road called Pettigrew's Lane partly in order to extend and link up two of the abbey's gardens; he was also required to provide an alternative route over his own land.

Monastic gardens were enclosed with walls, hedges or wicker fences (**45**). Abbot Thomas Burton of Meaux repaired a wall between the orchard and the garden of the abbot's chamber, which extended from the corner of the prior's

45 *Wicker-fenced garden depicted in stained glass in the cloister of St Augustine's Abbey, Bristol (now Bristol Cathedral)*

garden to the abbey precinct wall. Repairs to the garden walls at Abingdon cost 20d in 1414-15, and in 1428-9 a key was bought for the main garden gate. There was regular expenditure on hedging and cleaning out ditches around the cellarer's garden at Battle, and similarly at Maxstoke Priory. Soil fertility was carefully maintained. At Beaulieu manure from the guesthouse and stables was reserved for the gardens. Investigation of the garden area of Denny Abbey has shown that domestic refuse was dug in as a fertiliser, and a water cistern provided irrigation. At the Austin Friars in Hull deep bedding trenches cut into the clay subsoil were filled with compost and domestic debris.

Not all of the land, however, was intensively cultivated. Large parts of both Glastonbury gardens were grazed by horses, at other times being mown for hay or providing winter pasture for sheep. Nettles were cut in the pasture and used as fodder, in pottage, in cheese-making, or dried for their fibre. Similarly at Battle Abbey both the infirmarer's and the cellarer's gardens included some pasture. The gardens at Maxstoke in the fifteenth century included grass mown for hay, and the infirmary garden at Westminster also sometimes produced a hay crop. In 1465-6 a man was paid for rooting up brambles and thorns in the cellarer's garden at Battle. Material from a well in the garden of the London Greyfriars suggested a varied habitat including grassland, scrub and water-filled ditches or ponds.

Cloister garths have often been planted out as small formal gardens in later times, but there seems little evidence of this practice in the Middle Ages. The bishop of Lincoln's visitation of Bardney Abbey in 1414 received a complaint from the sacrist that Brother Thomas Southwell had made a garden in the cloister, where there had previously presumably only been grass. Gardens were sometimes inserted into cloister garths after the Dissolution, as at Haughmond Abbey, when parts of the monastic buildings were converted to domestic use.

Kitchen gardens

The St Gallen plan shows 18 beds of vegetables and potherbs, containing onions, garlic, leeks, shallots, celery, parsley, coriander, chervil, beet, dill, lettuce, poppy, savory, radishes, parsnips, coleworts, black cumin and something partly illegible which may be carrots. Apart from the root crops, which were slow to appear in England, most of these plants could have been cultivated by monasteries in this country.

Gardener's accounts identify the most commonly grown plants. The records of Anglesey Abbey in 1326 record the sowing of mustard and pot-herbs. Thomas Keynsham, gardener of Glastonbury Abbey in 1333-4, details receipts from sales of garden produce and purchases of seeds. The Glastonbury vegetable plots produced onions, beans, leeks and garlic (in that year the gardener provided 3 quarters of onions and 2,000 heads of garlic to the abbey kitchen and 6,000 heads of garlic to the larderer, with a further 3,000 heads being kept for seed). In 1345-6, 1,300 heads of garlic from the gardens of Maxstoke Priory were consumed by the canons and their household. Beans, coleworts and leeks are mentioned in a description of the Eynsham Abbey garden in about 1360. The cellarer's account of 1416-17 at Peterborough records a purchase of leeks for his garden, with two women being paid 2d a day for 11 days to plant them. The cellarer of Battle also regularly bought seedlings of leeks and onions. The gardens of St Augustine's Abbey in Bristol produced onions, garlic, leeks and beans, while green peas of an early ripening variety called 'hastyngez' were grown in the great garden there in 1491-2 and 1511-12.

At Beaulieu the account book of 1269-70 shows the gardens in charge of an officer called the 'keeper of the curtilage'. Here it appears that there was no single large kitchen garden; instead, small cultivated plots were fitted into odd spaces between the outer precinct buildings and workshops. Five men were employed in the gardens who were also required to dig graves when necessary. Various vegetables were supplied for the kitchen, but only leeks and beans were produced in sufficient quantity to be sold.

Incidental mentions of gardens or garden produce appear in many other sources. The Barnwell Observances, a set of instructions issued to the Augustinian canons of Barnwell, require the infirmarian to tend canons who had been bled with sage and parsley washed with salt water; the fraterer had to provide flowers, mint and fennel to scent the refectory, and the almoner had to provide peas and beans for the poor.

Produce from the kitchen garden often went directly to the table, thereby escaping notice in the accounts, so it is easy to underestimate the importance of garden vegetables in the monastic diet. Pottage often provided the first dish at dinner. Its basic ingredients were some combination of leeks, coleworts, peas, beans and oatmeal, boiled up in stock, and enriched with onions, shallots, garlic, parsley or other herbs. Evidence from Westminster Abbey suggests that green vegetables constituted a major portion of the diet in the early Middle Ages, but declined in popularity with the increase of meat-eating during the fifteenth century.

Although herbs were widely used for flavouring, specific mentions in monastic accounts are not common. A fifteenth-century dietary from Muchelney mentions sage, borage, langue-de-boeuf (a culinary variety of bugloss), parsley, marigold, rosemary, thyme, hyssop, summer savory and Good King Henry as flavourings for pottage. Parsley was used at Durham, while bay and rosemary were grown at the London Charterhouse. Saffron and other herbs were grown at Bristol and Norwich. The waterlogged fills of two fifteenth-century drains at the Oxford Blackfriars have provided evidence of mustard and marigold.

To what extent monastic kitchen gardens succeeded in supplying the need for vegetables and potherbs is difficult to assess. Obviously yields varied from season to season. The gardens of Norwich Cathedral Priory often produced more than the community needed itself: receipts are recorded in 1400 from sales of onions, leeks, garlic, and mustard seed, while surpluses of peas, beans, beets and carrots were sold in other years. However, the accounts reveal a sharp decline in income from the garden during the early sixteenth century. The bishop's visitation in 1514 records a complaint from two monks that John Sybbys, the gardener, had brought the office almost to ruin through his care-lessness in allowing sheep and other livestock the free run of the grounds.

Elsewhere, kitchener's accounts sometimes record purchases to make up shortfalls in production. In the late thirteenth and early fourteenth century, the bursar at Durham was buying in herbs like fennel and saffron. On one occasion in the late fourteenth century the kitchener at Abingdon had to purchase garlic and onions, along with more exotic foodstuffs, though in 1440-1 onions were sold from the garden. The Sibton Abbey kitchener bought in onions, garlic and mustard in 1363-4, while the Selby kitchener purchased cabbages, leeks, onions and garlic in 1416-17. The kitchener of Bristol and the cellarer of Battle both made regular purchases of mustard.

Apart from food crops, a variety of miscellaneous plants were grown. The Glastonbury account records flax and hemp, and gallium, which may be either madder or bedstraw, used for dying cloth. Hemp and flax were also grown at

Eynsham. The gardener's accounts of Anglesey Abbey in Cambridgeshire in 1326 record the cultivation of hemp, flax, madder and teasels. Teasels also appear in one of the gardens of St Augustine's Abbey in Bristol. Sales of osiers and faggots are recorded from the gardens of Norwich Priory in 1400.

Physic gardens

None of the early monastic rules suggest that the cultivation of herbs for medicinal purposes formed any part of the monks' duties. Indeed, Cassiodorus advised those who looked after the sick to put their trust in God rather than in herbal potions. However, the expansion of monastic life within the Carolingian empire saw a growing interest in healing, and the St Gallen plan shows beds with 16 different medicinal herbs – kidney bean, savory, rose, horse mint, cumin, lovage, fennel, tansy or costmary, lily, sage, rue, flag iris, penny-royal, fenugreek, mint and rosemary. Experiments with herbs became an important function of many monasteries during the early Middle Ages before the emergence of professional medical schools at Salerno and Montpellier. Glastonbury Abbey's library contained an Anglo-Saxon leech book compiled at Winchester towards the end of the ninth century which is remarkable for the range of exotic drug plants which it lists.

Plants grown as medicinal herbs in the infirmarer's garden at Norwich included rhubarb, peony, fennel and squills or sea-onion. Accounts of seed purchases include opium poppy on one occasion. Peony was noted in the Glastonbury leech-book as a cure for sciatica; the infirmarer at Durham bought 3lb of peony seeds in 1299, and peony seed is reported to have been found at Winchcombe Abbey. The plant referred to is probably the Mediterranean single pink peony, *paeonia mascula*, which still grows on the island of Steep Holm, where it is unreliably claimed to be a survivor from the gardens of the small community of Augustinian canons there. The walled infirmary garden at Maxstoke appears to have been of some size, though the records of seed purchases in the later fifteenth century (garlic, leeks, onions, cabbages, flax and hemp) and proceeds from sales of apples, pears, garlic, hemp, linseed, cabbages, eggs and honey suggest that it may by then have lost its special purpose. Poisonous plants with a potential anaesthetic or analgesic use were grown in enclosed gardens where there was no risk to livestock – a large proportion of the seeds from a waterlogged pit at Waltham Abbey were identified as henbane and hemlock.

Ornamental gardens

We should not suppose that all monastic gardens were solely utilitarian. In 1092 William Rufus is said to have arrived unexpectedly at the gates of

Romsey Abbey, which housed the 12-year-old Edith, last legitimate heiress of the Anglo-Saxon royal line. The abbess, suspicious of his motives, hastily had Edith disguised as a nun while diverting the king towards the gardens 'to admire the roses and other flowering herbs'. Certainly nothing in Rufus' record suggests that he had any great passion for horticulture! Though the story may be apocryphal, it probably preserves a genuine tradition about a famous garden there. Desiccated plant remains found in a wall at Romsey included not only a species of *allium*, possibly garlic, but also box leaves, which point to the existence of ornamental formal gardens. Evidence of box has also come from a fifteenth-century context at the Oxford Blackfriars. Lavender was grown in one of the gardens of St Augustine's Abbey in Bristol.

At St Albans the management of a *virgultum* or little garden, which had been enclosed within a wattle fence by Abbot William Trumpington (1214-35), was assigned to the guesthouse-master, perhaps implying that it was intended for the enjoyment of visitors. At Peterborough in 1302 Abbot Godfrey Crowland made a new *herbarium*, 2 acres in extent, enclosed within a double moat spanned by bridges, and planted it out with pear trees and other ornamental plants. To provide recreation and enjoyment for the monks of Evesham, Abbot William Boys (1345-67) fenced off part of a garden and orchard by the River Avon to exclude the cattle which had formerly grazed there. Shortly before the Dissolution the Glastonbury sacrist's account of 1538-9 provides a passing reference to a flower garden, which may have provided flowers for decorating the shrines and altars in the church. The abbot had his own private walled garden, about 54ft square, and we find Richard Whiting, the last abbot, receiving payment of a debt from a local gentleman in his bay arbour there.

Garden buildings and equipment

Most monastic gardens would have contained some outbuildings. At Abingdon repairs to buildings in the garden are documented in 1369-70; by the Dissolution the kitchener's garden and orchard included a separate dwelling with a gatehouse, courtyard and dovecote. Shelters for garden labourers and sheds for storage of tools and equipment must have been common features. The Battle cellarer's accounts mention a thatched, timber-framed structure called the 'garden house' on several occasions between 1319 and 1513, and in 1478-9 a timber fireplace was made in this building. One of the gardens of Maxstoke priory included a thatched 'lodge' in the 1460s.

An inventory survives of the goods in the store of Brother Thomas Eynsham, gardener at Abingdon Abbey in 1389. It provides an interesting glimpse of the miscellaneous contents of a medieval garden shed: vine-props, four ladders, an axe, a saw, three augurs, a sieve and riddle, rope, two harrows with iron teeth, two pitchforks, a seed-basket, a bushel measure, a mallet, a trowel, two pairs of shears, a scythe for the grass and two harvest sickles, three spades, three shovels, two rakes for gathering moss, a dungpot, and miscellaneous fishing and wine- and cider-making equipment. Purchases of equipment are recorded elsewhere, including a shovel for the garden at Peterborough Abbey in 1416-17, and two earthen pots for watering plants in the cellarer's garden and kitchen garden of Battle Abbey in 1464-5.

Gardens of the Carthusians

Gardens played a particularly significant part in the daily lives of the hermit monks of the Carthusian order, providing a place both for manual labour and for contemplation.   Several of the gardens enclosing the cells at Mount Grace have been excavated. Each was about 50ft square, with a geometrical arrangement of beds and paths edged in stone, with trenches and pits marking the position of plants. Unfortunately soil conditions have not favoured the preservation of plant material here.

Gardens on outlying monastic estates

Monastic manor-houses on outlying estates would also normally have had some sort of gardens attached to them. A survey of Hexham Abbey's estates in 1479 notes two walled gardens totalling 3 acres on its grange across the Tyne at Anick and five gardens totalling 6 acres at Bingfield. Abbot William Colerne of Malmesbury (1260-96) had a garden with two pools made on his manor of Purton, and another at Crudwell. John Harvey has documented the improvements carried out by successive priors of Winchester at their rural retreat at Silkstead, about 4 miles south-west of the city. By 1276 there was a vineyard and a *herbarium* surrounded by a tile-capped wall. A kitchen garden and apple orchard appeared soon after. In the time of Prior Richard Enford (1309-26) Gilot the gardener was tending the vines and walks in the gardens and adjoining woodland plantation; another *herbarium* was made next to the chapel in 1311-12, turf was dug for laying lawns, and a new stone wall, over 100ft long, 9ft high and 2ft thick, capped with 3000 flat tiles and 80 ridge-tiles, was built alongside the vineyard. The garden of another Winchester Priory manor, Michelmersh, appears to have been of a more utilitarian nature: in 1283 half a bushel of peas was bought for planting there.

On the Glastonbury estates a garden 5 acres in extent attached to the court at Shapwick is mentioned in a survey of 1327. The 1333-34 gardener's account notes quantities of leeks from the gardens of Meare and Pilton for the abbot's use when he visited those manors. Remains of the garden walls built by Abbot Adam, enclosing 3 acres and 1 perch at Meare, still survive. By 1516 there was an outer garden and orchard at Meare east of the walled enclosure, occupying a further 2½ acres, adjoining the vineyard and fishponds. The manor-house of Mells, itself rebuilt after the Dissolution, sits within a rectangular enclosure surrounded by a high stone wall, which may date from the time of Abbot Beere or Abbot Whiting.

In 1310 Godfrey Crowland, abbot of Peterborough, began the enlargement of an existing garden on his Northamptonshire manor of Eye, enclosing it with a new wall and making four pools within it. The following year he took in a further piece of ground to make an orchard beyond the new wall, planting it with varieties of fruit trees and surrounding the whole with hedges and ditches.

Experiments with more exotic crops were carried out after the fourteenth century. Most of the saffron used in medieval English kitchens was imported, but it was extremely expensive because it was so laborious to harvest. Prior More of Worcester managed to obtain 3½oz of saffron from his garden at Worcester and 2¼oz from his manor at Grimley in 1519, but it was always an uncertain crop in the English climate, and in 1532 we find him buying saffron in Hereford.

The fullest monastic list of garden herbs comes from a record of purchases of seed for the Abbot of Westminster's private garden at Eye in 1327, which included borage, chervil, coriander, cress, fennel, hyssop, langue-de-boeuf, parsley and savory as well as other vegetables. Generally root and tuber crops made little significant contribution to the English diet before the end of the Middle Ages, but there is an unusually early reference to skirrets sold from the garden at Eye manor in 1275-6; while in 1327 beet seed was bought for the same garden.

Archaeological evidence of garden produce from outlying estates remains limited, but peas, beans and lentils were identified at the Abingdon grange of Dean Court, along with seeds of fennel.

Bee-keeping

Privileges granted to the Cistercians of Vale Royal in 1276 included the right to keep bees in Delamere Forest. Early bee-skeps were also kept in bee-boles, recesses in sheltered garden walls. Bee-boles have been recorded on 11 monastic sites in England. They are difficult to date, but a group at Buckfast Abbey may go back to the twelfth century. At Beaulieu Abbey the account book of 1269-70 reveals at least a dozen of the workshop departments having their own beehives, producing over 60 gallons of honey, of which half was sold; honey was also produced on many of the granges. Other communities acquired honey through the market: in 1416-17 the kitchener of Selby purchased over 20 gallons, all of which was consumed within the abbey by the monks and their guests. Until imports of sugar began, honey was the only sweetening agent available. It was also used to make mead which, before the Norman Conquest, was often drunk on feast days in place of ale. Occasional records of mead consumption continue through to the thirteenth century, though it declined in popularity as wine became more readily available.

Orchards

The St Gallen map of the early ninth century shows apples, pears, plums, service, medlar, peach, quince, mulberry, fig and cherry in the cemetery garden. The consumption of fresh fruit in monasteries is generally poorly documented, however, as fruit produced in a monastery's own orchards and gardens often reached the table without ever finding mention in the accounts. On occasions the archaeological evidence is much fuller. The Oxford Blackfriars are known to have had extensive gardens outside the city walls to the south, and deposits from a drain there indicated consumption of a wide range of fruits, including apple, pear, plum, sweet cherry, raspberry, alpine strawberry, grape and fig.

Like other crops, yields would have varied considerably from year to year. The orchards of Maxstoke produced only 1½ quarters of apples in 1458, less than one apple a week for the priory's occupants; five years later, a yield of 10 quarters is recorded, sufficient to provide every canon, servant and guest with an apple a day throughout the year. References to 'old apples' in the accounts suggest that they were sometimes stored through to the following year. Sales of apples and pears are recorded from the Westminster infirmarer's garden throughout the fourteenth century, from Abingdon in 1388-9 and 1412-13, and from Norwich after 1400.

Walled orchards several acres in extent were found within many monastic precincts, especially in the south, the west and the west Midlands. Twelve acres of orchards formerly belonging to the royal castle of Gloucester were granted to the canons of Llanthony by King John in 1199. The extent of orchards increased during the thirteenth century, as individual abbots and priors improved their own private grounds. Henry Eye, for many years gardener of Barnwell Priory before his election as prior in 1251, was commended for his great care in planting and tending apple-trees with his own hands, and various kinds of pears. New orchards were planted at Spalding by Prior John (1253-74). At Malmesbury Abbot William Colerne (1260-96) had apples planted in his own garden, and there were further orchards for the enjoyment of the monks.

Apples were the most important orchard crop. Sweeter cultivated varieties had already supplemented the native wild crab-apple during the Roman period, and monastic houses may have played an important part in bringing further new strains of apple from France after the Norman Conquest. By the thirteenth century varieties such as the pearmain and costard are recorded by name, and there was a thriving trade in rootstocks and grafts.

Orchards were also appearing on the estates beyond the precinct walls. Considerable quantities of apples were being sent to Glastonbury Abbey from some of its outlying manors in 1333-4, over 43 quarters from Pilton alone, and between 8 and 12 quarters from Batcombe, Ditcheat, Meare, Shapwick, Godney and Marksbury. Abbot Selwood (1456-92) planted on the manor of East Brent an orchard of over 3 acres with the finest varieties of apples and pears, and the terrier of Abbot Beere (1493-1524) records an outer garden and orchard 2½ acres in extent at Meare. The rural retreat of the priors of Winchester at Silkstead was adorned with apple trees. On the Peterborough manor of Eye Abbot Godfrey Crowland in 1311 extended the existing gardens, planting a new orchard with many sorts of fruit and surrounding it by hedges and ditches. Orchards are recorded as far north as Hexham Abbey's grange of Anick in 1479.

Cider-making may have been introduced by the Normans, becoming especially important in certain southern and western counties. An early fourteenth-century writer estimated that 10 quarters of apples ought to yield 1 tun (252 gallons) of cider. In about 1235, tenants working for Glastonbury Abbey at Damerham were to receive an allowance of 2 gallons of cider each day. The apples from Glastonbury's orchards at Sowy were apparently all made into cider on the spot in 1333-4 rather than sent in to the abbey. Some monastic houses regularly produced surpluses for sale. Beaulieu Abbey produced 18 tuns of cider (4,536 gallons) in 1269-70, of which 10 tuns were sold, while sales of 1 or 2 tuns from several of its granges are also recorded. In 1369-70 3 tuns of cider were sold from Battle Abbey for 55s, of which 12s was deducted for expenses and 20s for buying barrels and collecting apples. The Battle cellarer's garden produced 7 pipes of cider in 1435-6 (one pipe being 126 gallons), and in 1438-9 10 tuns were sold for 22s 4d. The Augustinian sisters of Aconbury in Herefordshire in 1344 produced 34 gallons of cider from their manor of Bonshill, of which 24 gallons were sold; eight years later they sold twice that quantity from their grange at Malmshill. Sales of cider are also recorded from Anglesey Abbey in 1326 and from Abingdon in 1388-9. Occasionally, as at Winchester in 1352 and Battle in 1369, the apple crop was inadequate and no cider was made. Payments were recorded at Maxstoke Priory in 1460 for washing crab-apples gathered in the park, but these may have been destined for verjuice; improved varieties such as pearmain were generally preferred for cider.

Buildings, equipment and storage vessels for apples and cider-making are often recorded in monastic accounts. There was an apple-house at Durham in 1484-5, and another is recorded at Abingdon just after the Dissolution. The most substantial item of equipment was the cider mill, a circular stone trough within which apples were crushed by a millstone drawn round by a horse or donkey. No certain medieval examples are known to survive, but the Battle Abbey accounts of 1440-41 record 3s 4d spent on two spindles for the cider mill, while in 1512-13 repairs to the mill cost 8d and a lock and key for its door 6d. The Abbot of Tavistock had a cider press at Plymstock, and in 1475, 504 gallons of cider were produced from the abbey's orchard there; another 378 gallons made in the previous year and now ready for drinking were shipped up the Tamar to be offloaded at Morwellham and carted to the abbey. The abbey's tenants contributed a toll of 378 gallons in exchange for using the equipment themselves. Similar receipts and expenses continue to be recorded in the abbey's accounts until 1489, after which both orchard and press were leased out for an annual rent. The gardener's store at Abingdon Abbey in 1389 included three mallets for crushing apples. Barrels were often purchased to store cider. Beaulieu Abbey bought 15 empty tuns in 1269-70 for 13s 5d. Worcester Priory purchased 4 empty tuns for cider in 1294-5 which, including necessary repairs, cost 5s 6d, while the Abingdon gardener paid 3s 4d for 2 tuns in 1388-9.

Pears were less widely grown than apples, though both trees often appeared in the same orchard. Abbot Neckham of Cirencester (1213-16) mentions a highly-prized French variety called the 'Rewel', commonly grown around La Rochelle, named after St Rule, Bishop of Arles. The Warden pear, first raised by the Cistercians of Warden Abbey in Bedfordshire, and perhaps brought there from Burgundy, was widely cultivated by the thirteenth century. Wardens were amongst the orchard produce sold by the Abingdon gardener in 1388-9, and they were also grown in the gardens at Bristol. They were used especially for baking in pies. Abbot Godfrey Crowland was planting pear-trees in a garden at Peterborough in 1302. Other varieties may have been used for perry. The orchards of Maxstoke Priory in Warwickshire contained at least two varieties of pears in the fifteenth century, one of which *(volemus)* is probably Warden.

Cultivated cherries had been grown in Britain by the Romans, and were enjoyed throughout the Middle Ages. Norwich Cathedral Priory had a separate cherry orchard, and we are reminded that these were not solely a subsistence and cash crop when we find the gardener in 1484 making a window seat from which the blossom could be admired. Cherry trees were growing in the vineyard at Ely in 1302. Evidence for other fruits is limited. The gardens of Bristol Abbey produced plums. The Westminster Abbey customary compiled in around 1270 required the gardener to supply plums, cherries and medlars to the abbey as well as the commoner orchard fruits. Peaches are often said to be a Tudor introduction, though John Lydgate, a Benedictine monk of Bury St Edmunds (1330-1400), writing on the street cries of hawkers in London, recorded that they were readily available in the fourteenth century. Giraldus Cambrensis commented on the use of mulberries for making wine by the monks of Canterbury after a visit there. The gardens at Abingdon contained a fig tree, though in some years it failed to produce ripe fruit.

Hazel and walnut trees often seem to have been grown in monastic orchards. Hazel nuts were commonly recorded under the name 'filberts', because they ripened around the feast of St Philibert (22 August). The Abingdon gardener's accounts record both expenses for collecting nuts from the orchard and income from sales of filberts. Filberts were also produced from the sacrist's garden at Norwich and the gardens of St Augustine's Abbey, Bristol. Hazel was growing in the infirmarer's garden at Westminster, but not walnut. The nut plantations at Alton Priors and Silkstead on the lands of St Swithun's Priory, Winchester, were noted in chapter 6. The culinary use of almonds is frequently recorded in monastic accounts. These were mostly imported from southern Europe; Winchester Priory was, for example, buying almonds from a Lombard spice merchant in 1334-5. Some varieties will fruit in southern England, however, and the possibility that some almonds were locally-grown cannot be ruled out.

There are some indications of a decline in fruit production in the later Middle Ages. Several possible reasons can be suggested, including worsening climatic conditions, increasing neglect as more monastic orchards were leased out, and the degeneration of fruit stocks introduced from Normandy 300 years earlier. Nevertheless, Pershore Abbey still retained valuable orchards at the Dissolution, some being acquired by the royal commissioner, Anthony Southwell, while John Stonywell, the last abbot, received a garden and two apple orchards as part of his retirement settlement. Abingdon Abbey's precinct still contained at least 7 acres of orchards at the Dissolution, and as late as 1537 the last abbot was still attempting to ensure the improvement of lands leased out at Radley by imposing a condition that the tenant should plant two apple or two pear trees there every year. Ironically a major boost to fruit culture was just beginning in the 1530s when Henry VIII sent his gardeners abroad to acquire the best available varieties for the royal orchards, but this came too late to benefit the monasteries.

Vineyards

Whether vine cultivation in Britain survived the end of the Roman administration long enough to influence the first monastic founders is uncertain. Bede, writing in Jarrow, but perhaps with a knowledge of monastic practices further south, asserts that vines were commonly grown in the eighth century, and King Alfred's laws make provision for compensation for damage to vineyards. The minster of SS Peter & Paul at Canterbury, predecessor of St Augustine's Abbey, claimed to have been granted land at Chislet containing a vineyard in 605, and though the charter is a forgery, the abbey certainly grew vines there later on.

More reliable references occur from the tenth century. In 956 King Edwy confirmed a vineyard at Panborough to Glastonbury Abbey, and the same vineyard was recorded in the Domesday survey, then covering 3 arpents (an arpent is a French measure equivalent to an acre, used particularly for vineyards). The site of this vineyard is almost certainly on the 3 acres of shelving round below the steepest slopes of the hill, the only suitable land on this largely marshland property. A few years later, in 962, a vineyard at *Waecet* (usually identified as Watchet in Somerset, though Watchfield in Berkshire is a more likely site) was granted to Abingdon Abbey, 'with the vine-dressers on the estate'.

The Domesday survey records vineyards on monastic property on a dozen localities in the midlands and south of England (**46**). Glastonbury Abbey by then had further vineyards, 3 arpents in Glastonbury itself (probably on Wirrall Hill) and 2 arpents at Meare, in addition to that at Panborough. 1 arpent of vines belonged to Muchelney Abbey. Evesham Abbey's chronicle records that Walter, the first Norman abbot, caused vines to be planted on the further side of the river opposite the abbey, and the Domesday Book confirms the existence of a newly-planted vineyard there, on the manor of Hampton (**47**). Shaftesbury Abbey had one arpent of vines at Bradford-on-Avon. On the eastern side of England, Westminster Abbey had 2 arpents at Staines and 4 more newly planted near the monastery. The abbot of St Augustine's, Canterbury, now had 3 arpents of vines at Chislet. Ely Abbey had 3 arpents at Ely itself (the northernmost vineyard then recorded) and 2 arpents at Barking in Suffolk. The abbey of Ste Trinité du Mont at Rouen had a dependent priory at Harmondsworth, where there was 1 arpent of vines. Other records follow soon after. The chronicle of Malmesbury Abbey records a vineyard being planted on the southern slopes adjoining the abbey by a Greek monk who had joined the community in about 1084.

Vine cultivation in England probably reached its greatest extent between about 1100 and 1220, when the climate was at its most favourable. Average summer temperatures were a degree or two warmer than today, frosts very rare after the beginning of May, and Septembers usually warm and dry. William of Malmesbury described how the country around Gloucester was planted more thickly with vineyards than any other region in England, its fertility producing grapes which cropped more plentifully and were more pleasant in flavour, 'yielding nothing to the French in sweetness'.

In 1108, when the estates of Ely were divided between the monastery and the new bishop, the monks retained the old vineyard, and a new one was made for the bishop. The locality became known to the Normans as *l'Isle des Vignes*. Ely Abbey also owned several other vineyards, including one of about 4 acres at Vine Hill off Holborn in London where, in 1299, 35s 3½d was spent on the erection of a thorn hedge 121 perches long, and 69s 1½d on digging and weeding. One of the last entries in the Peterborough text of the Anglo-Saxon

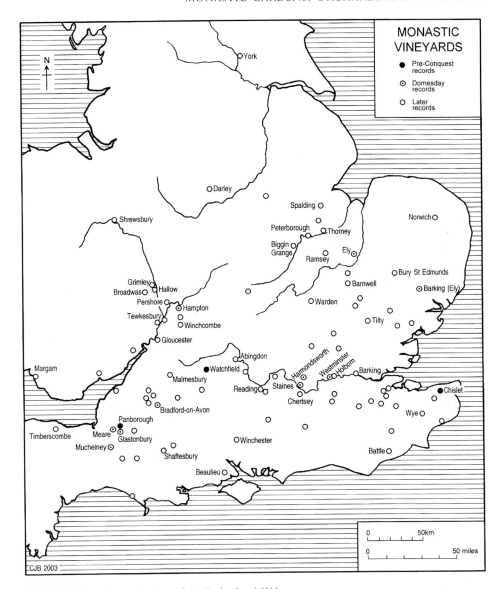

46 *Distribution of monastic vineyards in England and Wales*

Chronicle records Abbot Martin of Bec planting a new vineyard there in 1137. The Cistercians of Margam had a vineyard by 1186. More records of new vineyards appear in the thirteenth century. Henry Eye, gardener at Barnwell Priory, who became prior in 1251, successfully established vines there. At Bury St Edmunds the abbot had a vineyard enclosed for the enjoyment of monks who were sick or who had recently been bled. Vines at Spalding were planted by Prior John (1253-74). Norwich Cathedral Priory's vineyard was replanted in 1297, 1300 and 1323. Peterborough Abbey established a new vineyard on its grange of Biggin in 1307-8.

47 *Hampton (Worcestershire): site of the vineyard planted between 1074 and 1086 by Walter, first Norman abbot of Evesham*

Vines were a labour-intensive crop, requiring pruning in January or February and again in summer, hoeing and weeding throughout the summer and harvesting in October. Many of Glastonbury Abbey's tenants from scattered manors up to a dozen miles away owed services of several days' work in the vineyards at Glastonbury and Panborough, while the inhabitants of Meare had to contribute the considerable sum of 12d each towards the expenses of digging the vineyard there. Similar peasant labour services are recorded at Reading and Ramsey in the twelfth century and in the Worcester Cathedral Priory vineyards in the thirteenth century.

William of Malmesbury describes the vines at Thorney Abbey being cultivated in two ways, some trailing over the ground, others supported on poles or stakes. The Italian system of 'high culture', not favoured in England today because it takes vines several years longer to begin cropping, and produces good crops only in exceptionally warm summers, seems to have been employed widely in the Middle Ages. In 1388-9 the propping of vines in Abingdon Abbey's vineyard cost 4s 6d. The forester of Beaulieu Abbey accounted for the production of 775 vine stakes in 1269-70, of which 375 were used in the abbey itself.

The sites of former vineyards may be remembered in local tradition or commemorated by later field-names. South- or southwest-facing slopes were preferred, and some examples, such as Pershore Abbey's vineyard on Allesborough Hill, meet this expectation. Others occupied less obviously attractive sites. Those of Evesham (**47**) and Ely stood on east-facing slopes. Thorney Abbey's vineyard was exposed to northerly winds across the Fens. Tewkesbury Abbey's vineyard, first recorded around 1195, faced north over a frost-hollow. So long as the slopes were not so steep as to be in shade for prolonged periods of the day, this did not greatly matter. At Beaulieu Abbey, instead of a single vineyard, several hundred vines seem to have been planted out in warm sheltered corners wherever there was a bit of spare space within the precinct.

An acre of vineyard might be expected to produce on average 400 gallons a year. It is difficult to estimate how much of the wine consumed in English monasteries was home-produced. Some wine from northern France, the Rhineland and Burgundy was being imported well before the Norman Conquest, a trade mentioned by the merchant portrayed in Aelfric's Colloquy. Henry Plantagenet's marriage with Eleanor of Aquitaine brought the vineyards of the Garonne region under English control after 1154, and much greater quantities of Gascon wine were then shipped from Bordeaux to the ports of Bristol and Southampton.

Even during the climatic optimum of the early Middle Ages there were occasional years when the grapes did not ripen sufficiently to be made into wine. An alternative was to ferment them for verjuice, a kind of sharp vinegar used in cooking and pickling. In 1296, Ely Cathedral Priory received £10 from sale of 9½ butts of wine produced in the previous year (a butt was 126 gallons), but it also sold 21 gallons of verjuice. In 1412-13, the gardener's account at Abingdon recorded that nothing had been received from grapes that year because they remained in the infirmary for making verjuice. Must, newly-pressed grape juice not yet fermented, was provided for the Abbot of Battle and his guests in 1278-9, and in 1319-20 Battle's manor of Wye provided 22 gallons of must.

After 1220 the beginnings of a contraction in vine cultivation can be discerned. Christ Church, Canterbury, seems to have abandoned its vines by about 1230. A rental of the Worcester priory estates in 1240 records two vineyards at Broadwas and Grimley then surviving, and the prior continued to extract payments in lieu of services in the vineyard from his villeins at Hallow, though the latter had ceased to exist. The prior of Bath disposed of his vineyard at Timberscombe to a layman in 1245. The former vineyard of Battle Abbey was producing only hay by 1275, and the site was later culti-vated for oats and peas.

The decline of English vineyards becomes more marked during the four-teenth century. Bulk imports of cheap and better-quality Gascon wine had increasingly eroded the market for the local product, despite some disruption in trade during the Hundred Years War and the eventual loss of Bordeaux to the French in 1453. Severe labour shortages after the Black Death made the cultivation of finicky crops like vines increasingly difficult. Climatic change, resulting in the onset of duller and wetter summers, harder winters and, most significantly, late spring frosts, was also a factor. During the first half of the fifteenth century a succession of unusually severe winters and cold springs ruined many vines, not just in Britain but also in northern France. Two-thirds of Glastonbury Abbey's former vineyard at Meare had been converted to arable land and one-third to meadow by 1355. The decline in production of the Abingdon Abbey vineyard is evident in the accounts after 1369, and the last gardener's account of 1450-1 records no receipts from grapes or wine. The last recorded sales from the Ely Abbey vineyard occurred in 1469. Glastonbury Abbey's Panborough vineyard was still producing some grapes in the mid-fourteenth century, but by 1517, its site was under arable cultivation. The vineyards of Evesham Abbey at Hampton and Pershore Abbey at Allesborough had gone down to pasture by the Dissolution.

Despite the general picture of decline, however, some monasteries did struggle on with their vineyards throughout the later Middle Ages. Peterborough Abbey was still hiring labourers to stake its vines and weed its vineyard in 1404-5. The Ely vineyard was still maintained in 1469, though little wine had been produced over the previous 150 years. As late as 1509 at least 50 monastic and episcopal vineyards still survived in England. Richard Layton, one of Cromwell's commissioners, ever-alert for scandal, reported in 1535 that the sub-prior of Warden Abbey had been apprehended in the vineyard with a whore. Even in 1540 Barking Abbey still had a vineyard of 5 acres, fenced in with elms, well stored with vines, yielding a rent of 20s while a map of Tilty Abbey in the same county shows two vineyards managed by post-Dissolution owners in 1593.

10
Monastic deer parks and rabbit warrens

Monks and Hunting

A monk there was, one of the finest sort
Who rode the country; hunting was his sport.
A manly man, to be an abbot able;
Many a dainty horse he had in stable...

The Rule of good St Benet or St Maur
As old and strict he tended to ignore:...
He did not rate that text as a plucked hen
Which says that hunters are not holy men...

This monk was therefore a good man to horse;
Greyhounds he had, as swift as birds, to course
Hunting a hare, or riding at a fence
Was all his fun, he spared for no expense.

Thus Geoffrey Chaucer introduces one of his characters in the Prologue to the Canterbury Tales. Does his caricature give a fair picture of contemporary reality, or is it merely another scurrilous libel upon monastic life?

Certainly hunting was frowned upon by the ecclesiastical authorities, and repeated attempts were made to curb it. Pope Innocent III's ecumenical council of 1215 forbade the clergy to hunt or to keep hawks or hounds. In England the austere Archbishop Peckham of Canterbury (1279-92) declared that monks who hunted defrauded the monastic founders who had provided endowments for them to pray and sing masses, not to disport themselves in worldly enjoyments. Archbishop Melton of York forbade the monks of Whitby from keeping their own or other peoples' hunting dogs in the abbey in 1320.

Records of bishops' visitations nevertheless noted numerous transgressions through the later Middle Ages. Following the visitations of St Werburgh's at Chester in 1315 and 1323, the prior was forbidden to hunt, and it was suggested that leftover food from the refectory should be given to the poor rather than fed to the greyhounds and hunting dogs. In 1338 the prioress of White Ladies near Brewood was reprimanded for hunting and keeping hounds. In 1345 Bishop Grandisson of Exeter found that Abbot John Courtenay, along with the prior and another monk of Tavistock, had been keeping hounds and forbade it, repeating the prohibition three years later. In 1355 the canons of Haughmond incurred disapproval for keeping special horses for hunting. In 1347 three canons of St Thomas' Priory outside Stafford had kept hounds in the priory and had gone hunting in the company of laymen. A later visitation of the same house in 1518 found that the number of hunting dogs had increased since the previous visitation despite their prohibition, and it was again ordered that all hunting dogs must be removed. In that same year, the prior of Ranton complained that the canons often left the priory without his permission in order to hunt. In 1435 the monks of Muchelney were forbidden to leave the abbey for pleasure trips or hunting expeditions. A similar picture emerges from the records of those orders exempted from episcopal visitation. In 1478 Abbot Redman of Shap was appointed Visitor of all the English houses of Premonstratensian canons, and over the next dozen years or so, he issued a string of prohibitions against hunting and keeping dogs.

Despite official disapproval, many exceptions were acknowledged. When Abbot Henry of Cluny prohibited all members of his order from keeping hawks, falcons or hunting dogs in about 1310, he excepted 'those who, in their particular monasteries, have the right, custom and usage of hunting. In these cases we permit them to have hunting-dogs, enjoining that they should keep within the bounds of moderation and decency in this exercise of theirs'. In 1458 the Cluniac code again attempted to legislate against the 'dogs and puppies which defile the monasteries, and oftentimes trouble the service of God by their barking, and sometimes tear the church books'. Archbishop Winchelsey permitted the Abbot of Gloucester to retain 12 hunting dogs in 1301, and Archbishop Arundel agreed in 1407-8 that the abbot of Glastonbury should keep a 'reasonable number' of hounds for use in the abbey's parks and warrens.

The heads of the greater monastic houses, operating as feudal lords with responsibilities for entertaining important visitors, could, in fact, hardly avoid some involvement in this most popular of all aristocratic pastimes. Jocelin of Brakelond describes how in the late twelfth century, Abbot Samson of Bury St Edmunds 'made a number of parks which he filled with beasts, and kept a huntsman and hounds; and when any distinguished guest came to him, he would sit at times with his monks in some woodland glade and watch the hounds run; but...[Jocelin adds, somewhat sanctimoniously]...I never saw him taste venison'. Henry Knighton, chronicler of the Augustinian abbey of St Mary-in-the-Meadows in Leicester, describes how Abbot William Clown

(1345-78) 'in the coursing of hares...was considered the most celebrated and renowned master among all the lords of the kingdom', his reputation being such that King Edward III and the Black Prince had an annual engagement of coursing with him; yet, Knighton continues, 'he himself often used to assert in council that he would not have taken delight in the frivolity of hunting if it had not been solely for displaying civility to the lords of the kingdom and to gain their goodwill and to obtain their favour in the business affairs of the abbey'. In the last generation before the Dissolution the abbot of Merevale was a frequent hunting companion of Sir Henry Willoughby in the 1520s, while Prior William More of Worcester was another noted huntsman and falconer.

Acknowledgements of the rights of monks to hunt in specified areas are numerous. According to the cartulary of St Werburgh's, Earl Ranulph II of Chester had permitted Abbot Ralph and his successors to hunt stags and other wild animals throughout the Palatinate. In later years attempts were made to impose some restrictions. In 1285 Abbot Simon accepted a reduction of his hunting rights in exchange for an endorsement of his claims to tithes of all venison taken in Cheshire. In 1351 a later abbot was persuaded to reduce his allowance of game from Delamere Forest, and in 1354 the abbey's hunting rights in Cheshire were relinquished entirely; in 1425 the entitlement to game and coursing rights was once more confirmed. The Abbot of Abingdon was permitted to hunt roebuck in his woods of Cumnor and Bagley.

Poaching offences are frequently recorded. Abbot Bonus of Tavistock was accused of trespass in the royal park of Kerrybullock near Stoke Climsland in 1329, and his successor John Courtenay, along with the abbots of Buckfast and Buckland, was reported for deer-hunting on Dartmoor in 1335 and 1341. Monks of even the strictest monastic orders were not immune from temptation. In the Somerset Forest Pleas of 1270 a case was brought against Brother William and others of the Carthusian priory of Witham, that they had taken a hart in an enclosure in Mendip Forest, and that they had also hunted another hart with mastiffs in Cheddar Wood. It was added, moreover, that Brother William was accustomed to fix wooden stakes, pointed and hardened by burning in a fire, into gaps in the enclosure where the deer were accustomed to pass, and by such engines secure their capture.

Monastic houses were also often accused of harbouring lay poachers and receiving stolen deer. Poachers in the Forest of Dean seem regularly to have received shelter from the monks and lay brothers of Tintern, the canons of Llanthony and the Knights Templars of Garway. The Abbot of St Augustine's, Bristol, appears as a major receiver of stolen deer in 1270. Presentments were made in the Rockingham Forest eyres of 1272 and 1286 against Ramsey Abbey for harbouring deer poachers. The abbots of Beaulieu and Titchfield and the priors of St Denys and St Mary's Hospital in Southampton were similarly accused in the New Forest Pleas of c.1257. Witnesses were not always unbiased. A charge of trespass and poaching in the royal park of Kings Cliffe in Rockingham Forest laid against Abbot Kirkton of Peterborough in 1503 was apparently a reprisal for his attempt to extract rents and services from another manor tenanted by the park's keeper.

Monastic Deer Parks

Deer parks were a familiar feature of the medieval English landscape. Leonard Cantor's pioneer survey collected evidence for about 1900 examples, while Oliver Rackham's extrapolation from a more detailed survey of five eastern counties suggests that there may have been as many as 3,200 parks, occupying an estimated 640,000 acres, or two per cent of the entire land surface of England. In the south-west of England nearly nine per cent of all known medieval parks were in monastic ownership. Glastonbury Abbey held at least seven parks on its estates, the prior of Winchester six parks in Hampshire alone. The Benedictine abbots of Abbotsbury, Cerne, Sherborne, Hyde, Malmesbury and Muchelney, the abbesses of Wilton and Shaftesbury, the priors of Bath and Frampton and the Premonstratensian abbot of Titchfield all had at least one park (**48**).

Medieval parks were far removed from the modern concept of the park with its neat ornamental plantings and public recreational facilities. They were equally unlike the Georgian idea of the park as a landscaped setting for a great house. That is not to say that there was no consideration of aesthetic pleasure in their creation. Abbot Chiriton of Evesham beautified his newly-enclosed park of Shrawnell with oak and ash plantations in the early fourteenth century. Their principal purpose, however, was to preserve areas of semi-wild wood-pasture to provide a habitat where fallow deer could be kept until required for the table.

Records of 'hays' and 'leapgates' in Anglo-Saxon charters show that some forms of hedges or enclosures connected with the management and trapping of red and roe deer existed well before the Norman Conquest, and it is possible that a few deer parks may be of pre-Conquest origin. King Edgar's charter to Pershore Abbey in AD 972 mentions a 'leapgate' near Wadborough Park Farm, where the Domesday survey also names a deer park. The Domesday Book also records woodland at Churcham where St Peter's Abbey, Gloucester, 'had its hunting in three *haias* before and after 1066'. The vast majority appear to have been created between the twelfth and mid-fourteenth centuries, following the introduction of fallow deer from the continent. The number of new parks tailed off during the later Middle Ages, though occasional examples were still being created into the early sixteenth century. Robert Kirkton, penultimate abbot of Peterborough, made a new deer park near the abbey in the area later known as St John's Close. Its battlemented stone gateway still stands, adorned with emblems of the new Tudor dynasty (**49**).

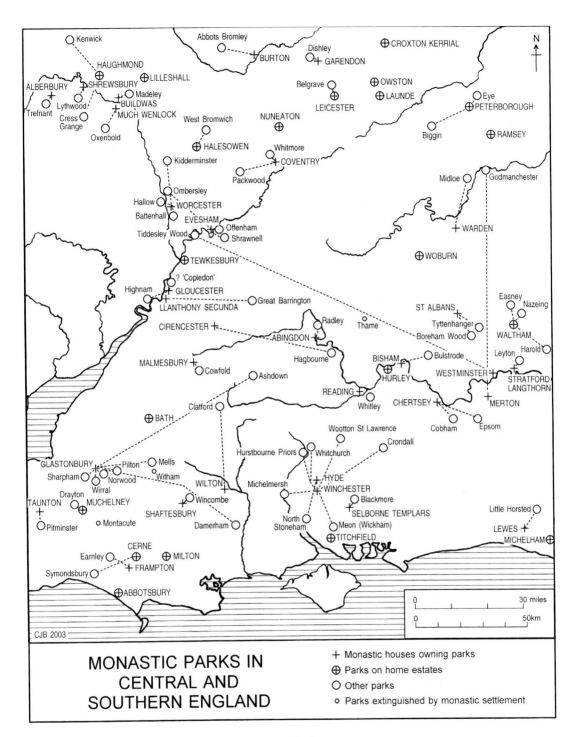

48 *Distribution of monastic parks in central and southern England*

49 *Peterborough (Northamptonshire): Prior's Gate built by Abbot Robert Kirkton, c.1510, as the entrance to his deer park*

It was, in theory, necessary to obtain royal permission to enclose a deer park, since all deer were deemed to be the property of the king. It was particularly advisable to do this if the land lay within or near one of the king's forests, for the penalties for transgressing could be severe. In 1251 the prior of Much Wenlock paid a considerable fine of £200 to retain his unlicensed park at Oxenbold in Corvedale. Emparking licences were normally enrolled in the Pipe Rolls or Close Rolls, although licences are recorded for only a small proportion of known medieval parks. Moreover, they cannot always be accepted as reliable dating evidence. Sometimes emparking licences were taken out retrospectively as a safeguard. On other occasions multiple licences were acquired simultaneously for many separate properties on an estate. In 1332, for example, the prior of St Swithun's, Winchester, acquired a licence to empark woods in Michelmersh, Hurstbourne Priors, Whitchurch, Wootton, Meon and Crondall, while in 1338, the abbot of Furness was permitted to empark his woods of Rampside, Sowerby, Greenscoe, Hagg, Millwood, Claife and Furness Fell. In such cases it seems unlikely that the emparkment of all these localities can immediately have been put into effect, and it is more probable that the purpose was a declaration of intent, simply to keep emparking options open.

Deer are capable of leaping a considerable obstacle, and in order to contain them parks required formidable boundaries, often consisting of an internal ditch with a high external bank carrying a cleft-oak paling. The maintenance of such boundaries could be costly, but the older Benedictine abbeys were sometimes able to impose this as a labour service upon their tenants. In the early thirteenth century various tenants of Glastonbury Abbey were required to put in several days' work each year to repair the ditch and palings of the abbot's park at Pilton, while others had to maintain specific parts of the circuit, 32ft or 64ft in length. These services were owed not just by those living nearby, but by tenants in widely scattered villages up to 18 miles away. The remains of such boundaries can still be impressive today: the southern bank of the abbot's park at Cerne Abbas still stands up to 9ft high and 18ft wide in places. Occasionally stone walls were used. The prior of Durham's park of Beaurepaire was enclosed by palings after the emparking licence of 1267, but in 1311 these were replaced by a stone wall. The abbot of Glastonbury's park at Pilton had a wall 3 miles in circuit, entered through a gatehouse. At Bath John Leland saw the ruined stone wall of the bishop's and prior's parks side by side, then without any surviving deer. Access to palings or walls for maintenance sometimes caused difficulties. In 1275 a dispute arose between Bishop Burnell of Bath, owner of the park of Huish Episcopi, and the Abbot of Muchelney, owner of Drayton Park, over an intervening strip of ground just 7½ft wide. This was resolved by an agreement that the strip was owned by the bishop and that he had full rights of access to maintain his park wall, but the abbot's beasts could continue to graze there.

Attempts to reconcile needs for the maximum extent of pasture with the minimum length of paling or walling resulted in many of the earlier parks acquiring a circular or oval outline (**50**). Later examples tended to be less distinctive as they were more often converted from former agricultural plots with rectilinear outlines, and created at a time when it was more difficult to build massive boundary earthworks due to increasing labour costs.

Monastic parks were frequently stocked with deer given by the king or other benefactors. Edward I gave the prior of Much Wenlock 12 does from the park of Willey in 1291 and six bucks and six does from Feckenham Forest in 1294 to restock his park at Madeley. The Duke of Lancaster gave Leicester Abbey permission to enclose and empark its wood beside the road to Anstey, opposite his own park, and Henry Knighton describes how he permitted the temporary breaking down of the facing sections of the two pales, the blocking of the road by nets and the strewing of hay and oats across its course in order to encourage some of his own deer to enter the abbot's new park.

Conversely, the passing of a pre-existing park into monastic ownership sometimes resulted in the cessation of its original function. This was particularly likely to happen where, as at Louth or Thame, a new abbey was actually

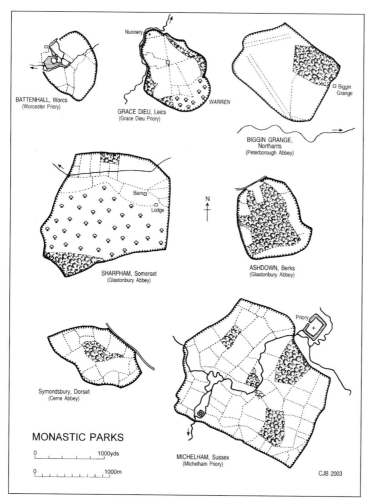

BATTENHALL, Worcs
(Worcester Priory)

Nunnery

GRACE DIEU, Leics
(Grace Dieu Priory)

WARREN

Biggin
Grange

BIGGIN GRANGE,
Northants
(Peterborough Abbey)

Barn

Lodge

N

SHARPHAM, Somerset
(Glastonbury Abbey)

ASHDOWN, Berks
(Glastonbury Abbey)

Priory

Symondsbury, Dorset
(Cerne Abbey)

MONASTIC PARKS

0   1000yds

0   1000m

MICHELHAM, Sussex
(Michelham Priory)

CJB 2003

50 *Monastic parks: comparative plans*

built within its bounds. By the thirteenth century the monks of Thame were keeping sheep in the old park. At Montacute the deer park became part of the endowments of the new Cluniac priory in 1192, and a century later it had faded from the record. The park of Belton in Leicestershire similarly disappeared from the records of Grace Dieu Abbey at an early date.

Elsewhere, even where some deer were still kept, other functions such as wood and timber production and grazing of farm livestock became increasingly important. Abbot Anselm of Bury St Edmunds had granted parks at Chelsworth, Semer and Bradfield to the infirmarer's department of the abbey in about 1130. Monks Park at Bradfield was re-enclosed in 1269 by the tenant, John de St Clare, and the park became compartmented with some coppice-woods, although the abbot retained the right to take a couple of does there each winter. In around 1250 the abbot of Abingdon reserved all timber oaks in Radley Park for his own use, but allowed his keeper, John le Parker, any branches blown down by the wind. The keeper was allowed to put five pigs, five oxen and one horse into the park only after the abbot's own pigs had been pastured at Michaelmas. The main gate of the park was to be opened only twice a week in the presence of the abbey bailiff as a precaution against the illicit removal of timber or venison by cart. The abbot of Bury St Edmunds had a park of 260 acres at Long Melford, formed out of Elmesete Great Wood, an uncompartmented wood-pasture which in 1386 yielded £2 per annum in grazing rents, but only 8s from wood sufficient for 600 faggots. A herd of wild fawn cattle which survived up to 1806 in the park of Abbots Leigh, perhaps similar to the famous white cattle of Chillingham or Chartley, was reputedly descended from the herd of St Augustine's Abbey, Bristol.

The famines and plagues of the fourteenth century resulted in labour shortages and high wages. Maintenance of parks solely for deer became an increasingly expensive luxury, and many could no longer be afforded and were abandoned. Cerne Abbey was receiving an annual income of 6s 8d from the herbage of Symondsbury Park in 1356, but it then contained no deer.

Others were maintained by more flexible styles of management, retaining some deer, while having compartments set aside for cattle or sheep pasture, temporary arable, rabbit warrens or coppice wood. The canons of Maxstoke in Warwickshire acquired the old hunting park of the Clintons some time after 1343; by the 1430s this provided grazing for the priory's farm livestock, and in 1460 was a source of crab apples for verjuice. In 1479 Hexham Abbey permitted the prioress of Lambley to keep cattle in Byres Park in the barony of Langley in exchange for a new tablecloth each year. Surveys of several of Glastonbury Abbey's parks at the Dissolution clearly show that these were then compartmented. Northwood Park still had 800 deer, but also contained 172 acres of coppice-wood felled and sold on a 16-year rotation. Sharpham Park included 160 deer, but was also used as horse pasture and was said to contain 200 timber oaks in addition to 80 acres of oak, ash and maple coppice felled on a 14-year rotation.

Despite the overall decline in the number of deer parks, other forms of farming were affected by the same labour problems, and the easing of pressure on land resources encouraged some landowners to resort to emparkment as a means of salvaging something from their properties. In 1412 the prior of Llanthony enclosed a new park out of the open fields of Barrington. Surviving copyholders in the parish continued to protest about this right up to the Dissolution.

Rights of free warren: hares and small game

Many monastic houses claimed rights of free warren, which permitted them to hunt small game (particularly hares and wildfowl) and vermin not protected by Forest Law on their estates. In 1252 the prior and convent of Ely held rights of free warren in their demesne lands throughout Suffolk and Cambridgeshire, wherever they lay outside the royal forest. The limitation on hunting rights accepted by Abbot Simon of St Werburgh's, Chester, in 1285 still permitted him free warren on most of his demesnes.

Hares and vermin were usually hunted using dogs. The monks of Chertsey were permitted to keep hounds and to hunt foxes, hares and cats in their own woodlands in Surrey. The nuns of Wix kept a small pack of harriers in the Forest of Essex to hunt hares for the benefit of their sick. In 1221 Henry III allowed the Abbess of Barking to hunt foxes and hares in Havering Park. The monks of Merevale retained rights to hunt small game in Bentley Park and the outwoods. Abbot Clown of Leicester's prowess in hare coursing has already been noted.

The use of hawks to pursue wildfowl and small mammals was equally popular. The Regard of the Forest of Dean in 1282 recorded that the abbot of Gloucester had eyries of hawks in his wood at Birdwood. In the early fourteenth century services due to Vale Royal Abbey from one Cheshire manor included the feeding of the abbot's puppies, and rents were sometimes paid in sparrowhawks, bows and arrows. In 1368 Abbot Litlington of Westminster offered a waxen image of a falcon at the altar for the recovery of his own sick hawk.

Rabbits and coneygres

Rabbits are not a native species, but were introduced to Britain in the twelfth century. They were valued for both their flesh and their fur, and although they needed careful tending to keep them alive through the winter and to protect them from predators and poachers, they could be raised on poor soils which were fit for little else.

Rabbits make their first appearance on the offshore islands of the south-west. The earliest known documentary record is in 1176, when the abbot of Tavistock claimed a tithe of rabbits from the Scilly Isles. The Isle of Wight, which had no foxes before 1845, also contained a number of valuable coneygres or rabbit warrens: Christchurch Priory obtained the tithe of rabbits from the island manor of Thorley in 1292, while Quarr Abbey had rabbit warrens on its lands at Arreton, Combley, Newnham, Shalcombe, Redway and Claybrook. By the middle of the thirteenth century inland rabbit warrens were becoming increasingly common. The abbot of Bury St Edmunds and the priors of Ely and Thetford all established coneygres in the otherwise unproductive sandy soils of the Brecklands. Medieval illustrations show that rabbits were caught and killed in a variety of ways. The canons of Maxstoke bought a ferret for use in their warren in 1490. Prior More of Worcester reserved the right to hunt in his own warrens with bows, greyhounds, ferrets and nets.

Attempts were made to enclose coneygres to prevent escapes. In 1280 the abbot of Keynsham acquired a licence to enclose with a stone wall a pasture called 'Wynterleye' within Filwood Chase and to convert it to a rabbit warren. Also in the thirteenth century the abbot of Cirencester enclosed the former common pasture known as the Querns on the outskirts of the town for use as a rabbit warren, and a 'keper of the game of conyes' was still there in 1538.

Although escaped rabbits rarely survived for long in the wild, there were occasional complaints of their destructiveness. In 1378 an annual allowance of four dozen coneys from Aldbourne Warren was confirmed to the abbess of Lacock in compensation for the damage they did to her adjoining lands. In the same year nearly a fifth of the Bury St Edmunds demesne crop at Elmswell was destroyed by the abbot's own rabbits, and in 1391 they consumed his entire oat crop at Mildenhall.

Lodges were often built to provide accommodation for warreners tending the rabbits. Tavistock Abbey maintained a coneygre in Dolvin Wood with 'a little house within it called "le lodge" '. Rievaulx Abbey's warren at Newlass was also equipped with a house. Because rabbit warrens were often in isolated locations, some protection against poachers was required. On Thetford Warren, in the southern Breckland, a small tower-house was built for the prior of Thetford's warrener soon after 1400 (**51**). The building is rectangular in plan, about 20ft by 32ft, and of two storeys. Its walls are mainly of flint, with some brick and fragments of reused stone perhaps salvaged from earlier buildings in the priory itself. The ground-floor is lit only by narrow loops, the

51 *Thetford Warren (Norfolk): the fortified fifteenth-century warrener's lodge of the prior of Thetford*

entrance is protected by a murder-hole above, access to the upper floor is by an internal spiral staircase, and the roof, formerly protected by a parapet, offered a wide view. A partial intermediate floor with sluices front and rear suggests that the lower portion was used as a game larder, while remains of a garderobe and a large fireplace show that the warrener lived in the upper storey.

Monastic consumption of game

Venison was rarely available for purchase through the market, so its consumption may be under-represented in monastic accounts; bones of fallow deer were recorded in some number at the Austin Friars in Leicester. Hare intermittently figures amongst purchases for the Battle Abbey kitchen. Rabbit was eaten in small quantities at Peterborough Abbey throughout the winter of 1370-1. The cellarer of Durham regularly bought 20-30 coneys a week in 1390-1. The kitchener of Selby in 1416-17 accounted for 41 coneys from Crowle Warren and four from Thorpe Willoughby, of which 39 were eaten in the abbey and six given away. Even in the late Middle Ages when Quarr Abbey's warrens on the Isle of Wight were leased out, the monks reserved eight brace of rabbits from the Combley warren. Prior More of Worcester had between 100 and 300 brace of rabbits from Henwick Warren in most years through the 1520s and 1530s, plus smaller numbers from his deer parks at Hallow and Battenhall. Hare and rabbit bones are, however, usually sparsely represented in monastic middens.

The consumption of partridges, swans, wild geese, herons, teals, woodcocks and fieldfares all receive occasional mention in the kitchen accounts of Battle, Peterborough and Selby. The pheasant, a native of the Caucasus region, was introduced into England around the time of the Norman Conquest, and retrospective quotes in later medieval sources suggest that it may have been available on the estates of Waltham, Rochester and Malmesbury before 1100; more secure mentions of purchases of pheasant occur in the Durham accounts in the late thirteenth century and in the Selby accounts in 1416-17.

On the whole, game appears to have made only a small contribution to the monastic diet, being reserved mainly for special feast days and the entertainment of important visitors. The nuns of Wilton nevertheless consumed three deer carcasses, 16 swans, 13 partridges, 13 peacocks, and an unspecified number of larks alongside more regular fare at the installation of a new abbess in 1299, and the feast went on for several days.

11

Monastic fisheries
and fishponds

Fish in the monastic diet

> I am a fisherman...I lay down nets in the stream from my boat, and I set baited hooks and creels...I sell my fish in the city, and I would be able to sell more if my catch was greater...I catch eels, pike, minnows, burbots, trout and lampreys, and whatever swims in the flowing stream.... Sometimes I go to sea, and there I catch herring, salmon, porpoise, sturgeon, oyster, crab, mussels, winkles, cockles, plaice, soles and lobster; but I do so rarely, because a large ship is needed on the sea...and I do not join the whalers because it is too dangerous, though many receive a high price for whales.

The fisherman's responses, among the dialogues with men of familiar trades written around 998 by Aelfric of Cerne as an aid to teaching Latin in the monastic school, confirm the existence of a well-organised fishing industry. Because of the Benedictine prohibition on consuming the flesh of four-footed beasts, fish played an important part in the monastic diet. The first Norman prior of Winchester, shocked to find the monks there eating meat, weaned them off it by having the cook serve up exquisite dishes of fish. Although the restrictions on meat-eating were later relaxed, abstinence was still maintained three days a week and throughout the fast seasons of Advent and Lent. Also meat was expensive, and economic necessity often dictated what strict religious observance had failed to enforce.

Around 1300 the daily allowance for one monk at Christ Church, Canterbury, was set at one plaice, two soles, four herring or eight mackerel. Dinners at Westminster included fish on about 215 days each year, the allowance per head being about 1¼-2lb. At Bolton Priory, purchases of fish accounted for two-thirds of the total kitchen expenses between 1287 and 1305. The Sibton Abbey kitchener spent a total of £13 15s 8d on fish in 1363-4, compared with £2 6s 7d on eggs and dairy produce and £1 18s 3d on meat. At St Swithun's Priory, Winchester, as late as 1514-15, fish still constituted the

main course of the main meal on 59 per cent of the days for which information is available.

Sea fish were far more important in the monastic diet than freshwater fish.
The cellarer's accounts of Durham priory record the consumption of no less
than 65 different kinds of marine life. Herring and varieties of cod, including
ling, haburden, keeling and milwell, commonly formed the bulk of purchases.
Oily fish like herring were unsuitable for drying, but could be salted down and
sold as 'white herring'. After the late thirteenth century an alternative method
of preserving herrings was devised; stringing them up in specially-built
chimneys and smoking them over slow wood fires produced 'red herrings',
which had excellent keeping properties. Cod were more frequently dried as
'stockfish' or 'hardfish', or pickled as 'greenfish'. Dehydrated stockfish would
keep almost indefinitely, and was amongst the cheapest varieties of fish
available. To make it edible it had to be beaten, soaked and stewed: a kitchen
inventory of Durham Priory in 1459-60 lists amongst the equipment 'two
beating-hammers for the stockfish'. At Westminster about 50 per cent of the
fish consumed was salted, smoked, dried or pickled, with cod becoming significantly more popular in the later Middle Ages than the cheaper herring.

More expensive varieties were occasionally consumed as luxuries. At
Westminster turbot, thornback ray, sole and conger eel appeared at the abbot's
table and on feast days. At Winchester the monks ate thornback ray, conger
and red mullet on rare occasions, usually as pittances rather than as the main
meal. The abbot of Selby acquired three-quarters of a barrel of sturgeon for his
own table in 1398-9, but this was a rare treat. The abbess of Syon reserved
rights to half of any porpoise taken on her Devon manor of Sidmouth in the
fifteenth century.

Freshwater fish purchased in the market were also expensive. Barbara Harvey
has estimated that roach and dace, though served frequently through the
winter, made up no more than 7 per cent of the overall weight of fish
consumed at Westminster Abbey during the first quarter of the sixteenth
century. Pike and fresh salmon appeared there only on feast days. The
kitchener of Selby accounted for 1,221 eels, 104 salmon, 12 pike, 67 pickerel
and 4,400 roach and perch and 1 tench in 1416-17, but this compares with a
total of 40,030 red herrings, 1,440 white herrings, 869 dried fish and 477 salt
fish used in the same year.

Sea fisheries

During the colder period of the eighth and ninth centuries, cod and herring
extended their range southwards, while improvements in the design of sea-
going ships and the introduction of the drift-net increased catches. Dried
Norwegian cod were being imported well before the Norman Conquest.

Herring were available from the North Sea. Plaice, whiting, mackerel and salmon could also be obtained around the British coasts. Quantities of herring, smelt, flatfish and whiting bones at Westminster Abbey point to a considerable increase in fish consumption in the late Saxon period. By the later Middle Ages more distant waters were being exploited. The Durham cellarer's rolls in the early fifteenth century frequently mention purchases of 'Iceland fish', probably cod. Some monastic houses had their own ships and coastal depots, others purchased their fish at the ports.

The herring fair at Great Yarmouth was famed throughout western Europe, and many monastic houses bought fish there. The cellarer of Durham purchased 20 lasts of herring in 1307-8 (well over 200,000 fish, a last being a boatload or 12 barrels). Beaulieu Abbey acquired land with quayside access at Northtown by Yarmouth in the mid-thirteenth century to establish its own fish-drying and kippering depot, and its own ship, the *Salvata*, regularly plied between the port and the abbey. Several other Cistercian monasteries, including Waverley, Boxley and Robertsbridge also acquired property in the town.

Other east coast ports were also important markets. In 1225 Boxley Abbey sent a ship all the way from Kent to Berwick-on-Tweed to bring back herring. Fountains Abbey was buying herring in Redcar in 1267. In 1416-17, the kitchener of Selby purchased 39,960 red and white herring in York, along with smaller quantities of salt ling, dried fish and salmon, also 30 lobbes (pollack) at Scarborough and 120 dried fish at Hull. Meaux Abbey acquired a plot in the ill-fated port of Ravenserodd around 1240 for the erection of a herring store. The destruction of this port by the sea a century later is vividly documented in the abbey's chronicle. At the Cluniac priory of Broomholm, 17 per cent of the total expenditure on food recorded in 1415-16 was on fresh, red or white herring, with occasional purchases of cod, ling, halibut, salmon and sturgeon. Broomholm Priory bought its cod, herring and ling at Cromer, while Thetford Priory purchased herring in Southwold in 1499-50. Sibton Abbey bought herring at Dunwich and Yarmouth in 1363-4, and keeling at Cley-next-the-Sea in 1367. The monks of Ely took an annual render of 30,000 herring from Dunwich after 1108.

South coast ports were also of some importance. In 1451 the cellarer of Canterbury Cathedral Priory bought in Folkestone 10,000 fresh herring for the monks and 5,600 salt herring for the servants, along with 400 greenfish from Dover and a cask of salmon and a cask of sturgeon. The Winchester kitchen bill of 1334-5 included payments for 42,000 red and 11,300 white herring and quantities of salt salmon, cod, ling, hake, mackerel and conger bought at Portsmouth and Southampton. The Southampton brokage book for 1440 records twelve casks of red herring being carted from Southampton to St Swithun's at Winchester, and five casks of red herring and three barrels of white herring carted to Romsey Abbey. King John had granted all fishing rights in the Beaulieu estuary to his Cistercian foundation there, and in 1278 two Southampton men fishing in the river were attacked by the monks and lay brothers with swords, axes, bows and arrows. The following year the same two fishermen were apprehended while attempting to re-establish their rights and this time their boat was confiscated. Glastonbury Abbey frequently purchased fish in Lyme Regis.

In addition to its Yarmouth depot, Beaulieu Abbey also had fishing interests in Cornwall. Around 1240 the abbey purchased a building at Porthoustock in St Keverne for drying fish, with an open yard adjoining, 10ft by 20ft. In 1269-70, it spent 52s 6d on two new boats and 14s 6d on mending nets there. In 1317 a second plot was acquired nearby at Porthallow with a slipway where the abbot's men could draw up their boats. Elsewhere in the west country the foundation charter of Torre Abbey gave the canons the right to trawl for fish in Tor Bay, and in 1327-8 they were permitted to spread and dry their nets below the cliff on land belonging to the neighbouring manor of Cockington.

In Wales, Rhys ap Gruffydd granted Strata Florida Abbey the right to fish in Cardigan Bay between Aberarth and Aberaeron. Vale Royal and Strata Marcella both had rights in the herring fishery of Aberystwyth. The Cistercians of Aberconwy had fishing rights in the Conwy estuary, and in 1258 their abbot was buying nets in Chester. The 1093 foundation endowment of St Werburgh's, Chester, included a right to one ship with 10 nets for fishing in Anglesey.

Fish could also be supplied at inland fairs. Kingswood Abbey bought herring, mackerel, salmon, eels and oysters at Priddy Fair on Mendip in 1241. Stourbridge Fair, held in a field outside Cambridge, was the source of the salt ling, organ ling, haburden, hardfish, salt salmon, red herring and sprats purchased by the cellarer of Newnham Priory in Bedfordshire in 1519-20.

Royal gifts to religious houses sometimes included fish. In March 1260 Henry III purchased 4 lasts of herring (about 13,200 fish) for distribution among 'poor houses of religion'. Between July 1238 and February 1244 the Cistercian nuns of Tarrant Crawford received five separate gifts of a last of herrings. In 1239, the canons of St Bartholomew's in London received 4 lasts of herring for Lent; and in 1260 the king gave the purchase price of 1000 herrings to the Austin Friars of Clayhanger near Tottenham. Herrings were also sometimes passed on by the monasteries to their peasant tenants for harvest and plough-boon meals. As late as 1573, former tenants of Holm Cultram Abbey were bemoaning the loss of the 17 white herring, six red herring and quarters of cod and salmon which the abbey had allowed them for three days' work at plough boons.

Sea fish were being marketed deep into the midlands by the thirteenth century. The small Augustinian priory of Bicester purchased 200 herring in 1296, and from then on red, white, half-salted and even fresh herring, mullet, plaice, whiting, mackerel, milwell, ling, stockfish and oysters regularly feature in the bursar's accounts. On one occasion, in 1302, no less than 10,000 herring were delivered to the priory kitchen. Bicester bought its fish from local markets at Bicester, Oxford and Wantage, and also at Stourbridge Fair. The account of the kitchener of Abingdon Abbey in about 1377 lists purchases of herring, cod, milwell, haddock, stockfish, whiting, ling, smelt, red mullet, sturgeon, mackerel and oysters. Winchcombe Abbey was able to provide a corrody in 1317 which included 1000 herring and 100 stockfish a year. In 1381-82, Pershore Abbey was buying fresh sea fish not only in Gloucester and Bristol, but also in Coventry, of all unlikely places.

The preponderance of sea fish consumption even far inland is borne out by the archaeological evidence. At the Austin Friars in Leicester, freshwater fish bones were conspicuously absent from the kitchen midden, whereas cod, haddock, ling and plaice were represented in quantity. Cod was the principal species recovered from the midden of Castle Acre Priory, and cod remains have also been found on many other sites, including Kirkstall Abbey, Pontefract Priory and Valle Crucis Abbey. At the Oxford Blackfriars, herring were the dominant species, followed by cod and haddock, while freshwater fish were represented only by small quantities of the unpalatable chub and the meagre gudgeon. Disconcertingly, marine fish bone deposits have even come from the excavation of freshwater fishponds at Taunton Priory and Southwick Priory, derived from the dumping of waste material.

The east-coast fisheries were in decline by the late fourteenth century, the herring industries of Yarmouth and Scarborough suffering especially through foreign competition and loss of markets during the Hundred Years War. When Beaulieu Abbey's depot at Northtown was lost to coastal erosion, no effort was made to re-establish it. By contrast, the western hake and pilchard fisheries, slower to develop, but less dependent upon continental markets, prospered in the later Middle Ages. Syon Abbey, having acquired control of the former alien priory of St Michael's Mount in 1461, built up a considerable business in Cornwall, investing in new fish-houses with preserving facilities and leasing them out, collecting dues in salt and tolls from fishermen drying their nets on shore, and selling cured fish.

Foreshore weirs

Estuarine fisheries are recorded in Saxon charters. As early as 679 Abbot Brihtwold acquired fisheries in Thanet. Some foreshore fisheries consisted of a V-shaped arrangement of hurdles, brushwood fences or stone walls pointing out to sea, with a trap at the apex. Bury St Edmunds Abbey's 'sea-hedge' at Southwold, noted in the Domesday survey, was probably of this type. An alternative form consisted of a series of conical basketwork traps set in a wooden framework.

Between 956 and about 1060 Bath Abbey held an estate at Tidenham at the confluence of the Wye and Severn, which drew much of its income from estuarine fisheries. One of the Tidenham charters distinguishes two types of contrivance, the *haecweras*, of which there were four examples on the Wye, and the much more numerous *cytweras*, of which there were 64 on the Severn and 36 on the Wye. The meaning of these terms is not known, but it is possible that the *haecweras* were sea-hedges and the *cytweras* frames with basketwork traps. The tenant of the estate had either to supply 40 large rods or a fother of small rods and net twine for building the weirs or build eight yokes for three ebb tides himself. Every alternate fish and every rare or valuable fish, particularly sturgeon, porpoise and herring, belonged to the abbey. By the time of the Domesday survey the number of fisheries at Tidenham had greatly been reduced and the property had passed into the hands of the king.

Tintern Abbey had fishery rights in the Severn estuary at Woolaston and made weirs at Alvredeston just upstream. In 1411-12 Tintern paid 11s to have a new foreshore weir called 'Erlisgout' made at Moor Grange. Margam Abbey had a salmon fishery in the mouth of the Afan. Holm Cultram Abbey had fisheries along the shores of the Solway Firth by the 1190s.

Shellfish

Bede notes that Britain produced many kinds of shellfish and Aelfric's description of the fisherman's catch confirms that their collection was a well-organised trade. On monastic tables they generally appeared at supper rather than at the main midday meal. At Westminster, mussels were consumed regularly on Sundays through Advent and Lent, while cockles were eaten occasionally in late spring, following the end of the Lenten fast. Oysters were commonly eaten at Winchester, mussels and shrimps rather less so, while periwinkles and whelks were available on only a few days each year.

Like sea fish, shellfish could be transported over considerable distances. Oysters figure several times in the accounts of Bicester Priory, while Fountains Abbey was purchasing oysters at York, Hull and Scarborough in the fifteenth century. Kept cool and moist in barrels of brine, oysters can survive dormant for months.

Excavations at Kirkstall Abbey produced numerous oyster and mussel shells, as well as a few cockles and whelks. The small size of the oyster shells suggests that they were eaten young. They seem to have been more popular in the early Middle Ages, when prohibitions on meat-eating were more strictly observed, but were comparatively poorly represented in a midden by the new fifteenth-century kitchen. Oysters have been reported from many other monastic sites, including Pontefract, Castle Acre, Llanthony and the Leicester Austin Friars, along with smaller quantities of other shellfish.

Lake and marshland fisheries

Natural freshwater lakes and marshes were important sources of fish, and the rights of monastic houses to exploit them were carefully defined. In the north of England the monks of Furness were allowed to fish with one small boat and to have 20 nets in both Windermere and Coniston Water, Fountains Abbey had fishing rights in Derwentwater and in Malham Tarn, while Meaux Abbey fished in Hornsea Mere. In Wales the Cistercians of Basingwerk had fishing rights in Lake Bala, Margam Abbey in Kenfig Pool and Neath Abbey in Crumlyn Bog.

Fisheries were an especially valuable resource in the eastern Fenlands. Most of the great Benedictine houses around the Fens claimed to have had fishing rights there from the time of their first foundation; although some of the charters reciting those rights are highly suspect, some probably do reflect interests of genuine antiquity. Peterborough, Ely, Thorney, Ramsey and Bury St Edmunds all received tens of thousands of eels and other fish in annual rents. Eleventh-century assignments of property to Thorney Abbey included 2 *ores* spent on a fishing-boat and net, while a further five boats were bought for 2 *ores* apiece (the *ore* being a Danish accounting unit equivalent to 20 English pence).

Whittlesey Mere, midway between Peterborough and Ramsey, was a focal point of monastic fishing interests. Peterborough Abbey's forged foundation charter of 664 claimed ownership of 'all the meres and fens in Huntingdonshire', and in 972 it claimed 'two-thirds of Whittlesey Mere with its waters, weirs and fens'. Thorney Abbey's 973 foundation endowment included 'the island called Whittlesey' and 'a quarter of the lake called Whittlesey Mere and two fisheries'. Early in the eleventh century, Ely Abbey acquired one-third of Whittlesey with other fisheries at Upstave on Starnea Dyke, Undley and Little Thetford. In around 1020 Abbot Aelfsige of Peterborough purchased a quarter of Whittlesey Mere in exchange for land elsewhere, and in around 1054 Ramsey Abbey also acquired a fishery there. The Huntingdonshire folios of the Domesday survey record the abbots of Ramsey and Peterborough each having one boat on Whittlesey Mere, while the abbot of Thorney had two boats there, one of which was held of him by the abbot of Peterborough, along with two fisheries and two fishermen. In the Cambridgeshire part of the same mere, the abbot of Ely received 2s from a weir, while the abbot of Thorney received 4s from a weir and 20s more from fish.

Other important early monastic fisheries were located 20 miles to the east, beyond Wisbech. Thorney Abbey's foundation charter records that fisheries around Upwell, Outwell and Elm were bought for £21 by Bishop Aethelwold of Winchester, who re-established the abbey as a Benedictine house in 972–3. A catch of 16,000 eels was expected there each year, of which the bishop decreed that half were to go to Thorney and half to his other foundation at Peterborough. The charter confirming King Edgar's foundation of Ely Abbey a couple of years before included an annual gift of 10,000 eels from Upwell and Outwell which had previously been owed to the king. Ramsey Abbey's largely fabricated charter of 974 claimed that its original endowments had included the services of 20 fishermen at Upwell and Outwell, together with 60,000 eels a year. Early in the twelfth century Ramsey acquired two more fisheries at Upwell. Bury St Edmunds acquired a fishery in the same locality in 1022-2, along with a render of fish formerly due to the king, while at the same time the queen's annual gift to the monks of 4,000 eels from the fishery of Eriswell near Lakenheath was confirmed. So valuable did Upwell become that, by the late thirteenth century, no fewer than 16 different religious houses held lands, rents and fisheries there.

At Wisbech itself the Domesday Book records the abbot of Ely receiving 1,500 eels from the fishery, while two fishermen paid him 14,000 eels and 13s 4d by way of tribute. The abbot of Bury St Edmunds had a fisherman there rendering 5,000 eels, the abbot of Ramsey had eight fishermen paying 5,260 eels, and the abbot of Crowland had three fishermen rendering 4,000 eels.

Some 25 miles south of Wisbech, Crowland Abbey received 500 eels from the fen at Cottenham in 1086, along with 12d from tribute of fish. The abbot of Ely had a boat which fished in Soham Mere nearby, while the abbot of Bury St Edmunds had a fisherman with a draw-net operating there. Ely Abbey was also receiving 6s from fishing tolls at Swaffham in Norfolk. When the new see of Ely was created in 1108, an annual render of 23,000 eels from Stuntney was reserved to the monks. Many other renders of eels to monastic houses are recorded from the Fenland though it is not always clear whether they were from natural meres, from river-fisheries or from mills.

Subsequently, fisheries were often made out of abandoned turbaries. In 1327 the Augustinian canons of Bourne Abbey in Lincolnshire received confirmation of their rights to cut and dig turf in Bourne Fen and of 'all the fisheries made, or to be made...as well in turbaries, dykes and cuts as in running water'. The same was happening in the Norfolk Broads, where the Abbey of St Benet of Hulme's former turbaries in Hoveton, Irstead, Barton and Neatishead all became valuable fisheries.

When the Cistercians appeared on the scene they too were eager to have access to the fishery resources of the Fens. Sawtry Abbey's foundation grant included marshland and fisheries in Whittlesey Mere, while Kirkstead Abbey acquired fishing rights in Wildmore Fen.

After the Fens the most important area of marshland fisheries was the Somerset Levels, where Glastonbury Abbey had particularly extensive holdings. The inquisition made for Abbot Henry Sully in 1189 catalogues a string of fisheries along the River Axe, one at Clewer yielding 7,000 eels, one at Nyland yielding 2,000 eels and one at Marchey yielding 7000 eels. A total of 30 salmon from Northload were owed at the feast of the Assumption, along with ten small salmon from Hunstreet at the Nativity. Further south, Glastonbury had a fishery at Middlezoy, two-thirds of which belonged to the abbey and the remainder to the abbot himself. Two more fisheries at Othery, on the edge of King's Sedgemoor, were leased out, one yielding a rent of 3,000 eels and 17d. The tendency of fishweirs to obstruct the flow of water and to cause flooding provoked many conflicts after the late twelfth century, when increasing values were placed upon marshland pasture. It was reported that the bishop of Bath and Wells had destroyed seven of Glastonbury Abbey's fisheries on the Axe, and in 1242 the abbot retaliated by breaking down three of the bishop's fisheries with his boats on the same river.

The most important of all Glastonbury's fisheries was at Meare Pool, which in earlier sources is usually called 'Ferramere' or 'Ferlingmere'. A charter purported to be of *c*.670, surviving only in a later copy, but probably having some authentic basis, records a grant by King Cenwalh of Wessex to Abbot Beorhtwald of land at Ferramere with two small islands in the fishery in part of the pond. In 1189 there were two fisheries at Meare paying 30d. Bishop Savaric's short-lived union of Glastonbury Abbey with the see of Bath in 1200 assigned the island of Meare to the bishop, but the water of Ferramere was to be held in common by the bishop and monks. In 1327 Abbot Adam Sodbury reached an agreement with Dean Godleigh of Wells which defined the boundary between the abbot's manor of Meare and the dean's manor of Mudgeley, and allowed the abbot access to two weirs in Meare and one in Westhay. The abbot was to have the entire pool of Ferlingmere, with the Rhyne down to the dyke called 'Lichelake' and the sole right to fish there. The dean and his successors could water their cattle at the pool, but were permitted to cross it by boat only between the hours of sunrise and sunset, presumably a safeguard against poaching. In 1351-2 a similar agreement was reached between Abbot Walter and Bishop Ralph whereby the bounds of their estates in Queen's Sedgemoor were fixed along the Hartlake Rhyne, with the abbot to hold the land to the south with half of the fishery, both parties being permitted to raise a fish weir. The value of the Meare fishery declined later in the Middle Ages through the silting of the lake and the encroachment of reed-beds; nevertheless, the assessment of Glastonbury's possessions in 1535 described Meare Pool as a fishery 5 miles in circuit and 1½ miles across, 'wherein are great abundance of pike, tench, roach and eels and of divers other kinds of fishes'. By 1638 it had been drained, and was described as 'lately a fish pool'.

Elsewhere in the Somerset moors, Muchelney Abbey held two fisheries on its home manor, which yielded 6,000 eels in 1086. Athelney Abbey's fisheries were more concentrated towards the western margins of the levels. In the late twelfth century it acquired three fisheries in the lower Tone valley, two of which it retained in demesne, leasing the other to a tenant; it was also owed

30 sticks of eels (a stick comprised 25 eels) from another fishery. Around 1180 the fishery of Moorcock Eastweir was yielding 5,000 eels a year, while another important Athelney fishery on the River Parrett at Statheweir yielded 1,000 eels. The weir at Burrow Bridge on the Parrett was said to be causing much damage through flooding, and in 1249 the abbot of Athelney was complaining about the seizure of his nets there by the moorward of the dean and chapter of Wells. In 1250 Abbot Robert relinquished to the dean Athelney's right to 80 acres of alders on Stathe Moor, but reserved to the bishop's decision the question of where the abbot and monks ought to fish. By 1270 the Statheweir fishery seems to have come into the hands of Glastonbury Abbey.

Several minor monastic houses also had interests in the Somerset moors. In 1261 the small priory of Burtle acquired half the fishery there and half the island of Talham. In 1247 the Hospital of St Mark at Billeswick in Bristol was involved in a dispute over its fishery at Hamweir in Weare. In 1327 a further dispute over the mills and watercourses at Lower Weare produced an agreement whereby the bishop and dean and chapter of Wells were forbidden to fish in the new channel of the River Axe, while the master and brethren of the hospital were excluded from fishing in the old course. The old and new courses of the river are still evident today.

Millstreams

From the eighth century, there are records of watermills yielding renders of eels from traps set in millstreams. Numerous instances appear in Domesday Book. Evesham Abbey's manors of Norton and Lenchwick included two mills rendering 2,000 eels a year in 1086, which can almost certainly be identified with Chadbury and Twyford mills, the lessees of which each still had to provide 40 sticks of eels to the abbey in the early thirteenth century. Beaulieu Abbey had an eeltrap in its mill at Kindleweir near Radcot, where the yield of 8½ sticks of eels accounted for 12 per cent of the total receipts from the mill.

River fisheries (52)

References to river fisheries sometimes imply merely a general right to fish from the bank, or from boats, along a certain stretch of river, using nets or rod and line. Fishing rights in the Thames between Wallingford Bridge and Mongewell were confirmed to Reading Abbey in 1220-1, while further downstream Chertsey Abbey had similar rights between Egham Pool and Langham Pool. An affray on the River Lune in 1314 between the boatmen of Furness Abbey and Lancaster Priory centred on how many catches each could take.

1 *Eynsham Abbey (Oxfordshire): the 'Way' marking the western boundary of the home estate granted by Aethelmaer and confirmed by charter of King Aethelred the Unready in 1005*

2 *A Benedictine abbey in its setting: Tewkesbury Abbey in the Severn valley, looking towards the Cotswolds*

3 *A Cistercian abbey in its setting: Tintern Abbey in the Wye valley*

4 *Brotherilkeld in Eskdale (Cumberland): enclosed valley meadows and fellside grazing around the site of a vaccary of Furness Abbey*

5 *Monks Wood (Huntingdonshire), acquired by the Cistercian abbey of Sawtry in 1147*

6 *Leigh Woods, Abbots Leigh (Somerset): ancient coppice wood formerly belonging to St Augustine's Abbey, Bristol*

7 *Crowle Court (Worcestershire): earthworks of a moat surrounding the place of retirement of William More, last prior of Worcester*

8 *Piel Castle (Lancashire), built by Furness Abbey under a crenellation licence of 1327*

9 *Bradford-on-Avon (Wiltshire): aerial view of estate farm of Shaftesbury Abbey showing the great barn, granary and domestic range*

10 *Bradford-on-Avon (Wiltshire): interior of Shaftesbury Abbey's barn showing the raised base-cruck roof*

11 *Frocester Court (Gloucestershire): aerial view of estate farm of St Peter's Abbey, Gloucester, showing the great barn (left) built by Abbot John Gamages (1284-1306)*

12 *Shapwick (Somerset): dovecote on the Glastonbury Abbey Almoner's Manor*

13 *Wickhamford (Worcestershire): dovecote built by Abbot Randulf of Evesham (1214-29), reconstructed since partial collapse in 1904*

14 *Buildwas Abbey (Shropshire): aerial view showing fishpond to south-west of the claustral buildings (left margin of photograph)*

15 *Westonzoyland (Somerset): roof of church nave; similar carved wooden angels appear in several other churches on the Glastonbury Abbey estates*

16 Above *Newton Arlosh (Cumberland): the fortified church of an unsuccessful new town promoted by Holm Cultram Abbey in 1305*

17 Below *Callington (Cornwall): chapel over holy well at Dupath, acquired by the Augustinian canons of St Germans in 1432*

18 *Muchelney (Somerset): new house provided by Muchelney Abbey for the parish priest under the terms of an agreement made in 1308*

19 *Old Byland (Yorkshire North Riding): the green, centrepiece of the planned village laid out by the Savignac community of Old Byland in 1143*

20 *Norton St Philip (Somerset): the George Inn, built in about 1375 by the Carthusian community of Hinton Charterhouse to accommodate merchants attending its fairs and markets*

21 *Northleach (Gloucestershire): aerial view showing the church, market place and main street of the new town developed in the early thirteenth century by St Peter's Abbey, Gloucester*

22 *Stow-on-the-Wold (Gloucestershire): a corner of the market-place of the new town developed by Evesham Abbey following the acquisition of a market charter in 1107-8*

23 *Abbots Bromley (Staffordshire): the former market-place of a failed borough promoted by Abbot Richard de Lisle of Burton in 1222*

24 *Barton Bridge, built by Shaftesbury Abbey to link its estate farm with the town of Bradford-on-Avon (Wiltshire)*

25 Left *Irthlingborough Bridge (Northamptonshire): the crossed-keys symbol of Peterborough Abbey on one of the cutwaters*

26 Right *Waltham Abbey (Essex): the new millstream cut by Abbot Walter in 1190, also used by boats bringing produce to the abbey's wharf*

27 Below *The Pilrow Cut near Mark (Somerset), looking northwards towards the Mendip Hills: a canal cut by Glastonbury Abbey in the thirteenth century*

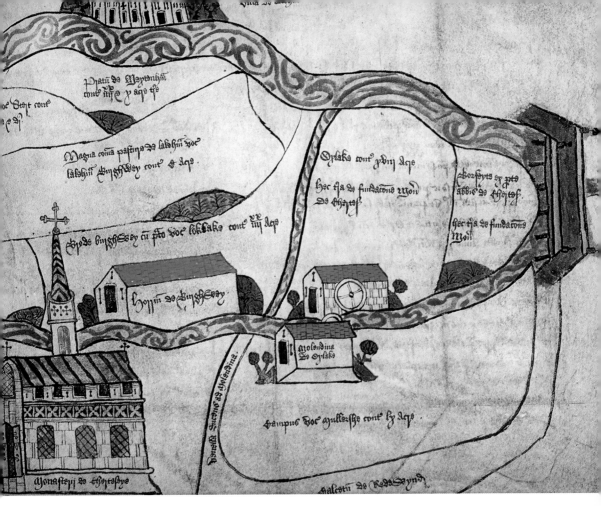

28 Opposite above *Castle Acre Priory (Norfolk):
the ruined granary and terminus of the monastic
canal from the River Nar*

29 Opposite below *Earthworks of the watermill
of Hailes Abbey (Gloucestershire): the hedge bisects
the former millpond*

30 Above *Chertsey Abbey (Surrey): fifteenth-
century plan from the cartulary made to illustrate a
dispute over pasture rights, showing the abbey
church, the barn at Burway built by Abbot
Rutherwyke in 1313-14, the Oxlake mills with
two undershot wheels, the village of Laleham on the
main stream of the Thames (top), and the timber
bridge (right)*

31 Right *Post mill depicted in the background of a
fifteenth-century wall painting of St Christopher in
the church of Ditcheat (Somerset), on the estates of
Glastonbury Abbey*

32 Left *East Pennard (Somerset): aerial view showing windmill mound in the middle foreground; this may be the site of the windmill from which the granger of Glastonbury Abbey received tolls in 1361-2*

33 Below *Dunkeswell Abbey (Devon): remains of fishponds*

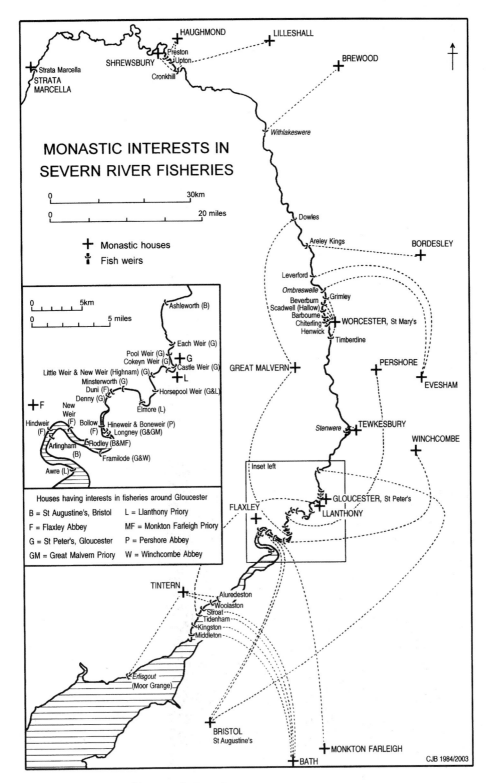

MONASTIC INTERESTS IN SEVERN RIVER FISHERIES

0   30km

0   20 miles

✝   Monastic houses

   Fish weirs

0   5km

0   5 miles

HAUGHMOND   LILLESHALL

Preston

Upton

SHREWSBURY

BREWOOD

Cronkhill

Strata Marcella

STRATA MARCELLA

Withlakeswere

Dowles

Areley Kings

BORDESLEY

Leverford

Ombreswelle   Grimley

Beverburn

Scadwell (Hallow)

Barbourne

Chiterling

Henwick   WORCESTER, St Mary's

Timberdine

Ashleworth (B)

Each Weir (G)

Pool Weir (G)

Cokeyn Weir (G)

Little Weir & New Weir (Highnam) (G)

Minsterworth (G)

Duni (F)

Denny (G)

New Weir

Hindweir (F)

Bollow (F)

Artingham

Rodley (B&MF)

Awre (L)

Castle Weir (G)

Horsepool Weir (G&L)

Elmore (L)

Hineweir & Boneweir (P)

Longney (G&GM)

Framilode (G&W)

G

L

F

GREAT MALVERN

PERSHORE

EVESHAM

Stenwere   TEWKESBURY

WINCHCOMBE

Inset left

FLAXLEY

GLOUCESTER, St Peter's

LLANTHONY

Houses having interests in fisheries around Gloucester

B = St Augustine's, Bristol   L = Llanthony Priory

F = Flaxley Abbey   MF = Monkton Farleigh Priory

G = St Peter's, Gloucester   P = Pershore Abbey

GM = Great Malvern Priory   W = Winchcombe Abbey

TINTERN

Aluredeston

Woolaston

Stroat

Tidenham

Kingston

Middleton

Erlisgout (Moor Grange)

BRISTOL St Augustine's

MONKTON FARLEIGH

BATH

CJB 1984/2003

52 *Monastic interests in fisheries in the River Severn*

Nets were widely used. Fountains Abbey had the services of two fishermen in the River Ure with two boats and a fishing net. Hexham Abbey had two fisheries on the Tyne in 1298 with places for drying nets at 'Dripintell' and 'Foul'. In 1388-9, equipment in custody of Abingdon Abbey's gardener included two different sorts of net, a 'wade' and a 'chanenet', while 6d was spent on repairing the nets that year. In 1491 Tintern Abbey was leasing a fishery and a 'corrock net' on the Wye. The Lanercost cartulary includes a late fourteenth-century sketch of a fishing net alongside a record of a late twelfth-century grant of fishery rights in the rivers Eden and Esk. The first known treatise on angling, published in Wynkyn de Worde's *Book of St Albans* in 1496 and attributed to Juliana Berners, Prioress of Sopwell, lists fish commonly caught by rod and line – trout, salmon, grayling, barbel, chub, bream, tench, perch, roach, dace, bleak, ruff, flounder, minnow, eel and pike.

A river fishery could also consist of basketwork traps set in a wooden framework similar to the estuarine fish-weirs described earlier. Multiple examples, such as the five fisheries held by Abingdon Abbey on its Thamesside manor of Barton in 1086, were probably of this type. Furness Abbey was permitted to take oxcarts into Lancaster Forest for timber for its fish-weirs on the River Lune. When Tintern Abbey acquired half of Ashweir on the Wye around 1246, the grant included timber for its upkeep, but when it acquired a share of Bigsweir in 1326, no corresponding claim to timber from the royal forest was allowed. Beaulieu Abbey used thorn hedging in repairing Kindleweir near Faringdon in 1269-70. Tewkesbury Abbey had a stone weir in the late thirteenth century, while Abingdon Abbey became involved in a dispute over the digging of turves for repair of a fishery at Culham. The late medieval map of the Thames at Abingdon shows a weir with five sluices and paddles just below Barton Court on the site of the modern Abingdon Lock (**20**). This may be the 'New Weir', for the repair of which the abbey accounts record purchases of planks, piles, ropes, nails and stone through the late fourteenth and fifteenth centuries.

The fish-traps set in the weir were made out of green willow or osier which would survive immersion throughout the season. In 1336 Battle Abbey paid 3d for the planting of willow in an area called 'le causey' by the Thames at Preston Crowmarsh. A lease of Bristol Abbey's weir at Ashleworth on the Severn in 1491 included land called the Neyte and the loppings of willows from Withygrove and Calcroft, the burden of repair and maintenance of the weir and traps falling upon the tenant. Terms used in contemporary sources for different types of fish-traps included *kiddle* (hence the expression 'kettle of fish'), *wele* and *putt*. In 1376-7, Worcester Priory's cellarer recorded expenditure of £6 6s 10d on making and laying down 76,000 kiddles for the prior's fish-weirs. Ten years later, the kitchener's account recorded profits from sales of 4,000 surplus kiddles. Beaulieu Abbey spent 12d on making weles and putts for its weir at Inglesham on the Thames in 1269-70. The Abingdon accounts refer to frequent purchases of weles through the fifteenth century. In 1460

Bicester Priory paid 12d to John Willis for four days' work in making weles. The accounts of Eynsham Abbey include expenditure on *clereweles*, *eseweles* and a *drystewele* for its fisheries on the Thames and Evenlode, but the precise meaning of these terms is unknown.

Like estuarine and marsh fisheries, river fisheries receive mention in charters with nominal dates from the late seventh century onwards. Malmesbury Abbey claimed that in 688 King Caedwalla of Wessex had granted to Abbot Aldhelm land at the confluence of the Wiltshire Avon and Wylye for a fishery. Lands at Henbury and Aust acquired around 690 by the ancient monastery of St Peter's in Worcester also included a fishery. Evesham Abbey claimed to have received a grant of fisheries with two weirs at Ombersley on the Severn in 706. A charter of King Athelstan to the minster which was the predecessor of Milton Abbey mentions a weir on the Avon at Twyneham (now Christchurch). These early charters may in part be fabrications, and do not provide secure proof of the existence of fish-weirs in the seventh century. Weirs are mentioned with increasing frequency, however, in genuine charters after the tenth century. When Edward the Confessor endowed Westminster Abbey with large parts of the former estates of Pershore Abbey and Deerhurst Priory in the 1060s, the grant included their weirs on the Severn and Avon. Hemming's Cartulary notes the villeins of Ribbesford on the Severn owing services to Worcester Cathedral Priory of making 'hedges' or 'hatches' for catching fish.

The Domesday record of fisheries is inconsistent, being very full in some counties and non-existent in others. In Worcestershire two-thirds of all fisheries recorded were held by monastic or ecclesiastical lords or their tenants. Most of them produced only a few hundred eels or a few shillings in annual income, though Evesham Abbey's fisheries at Ombersley yielded 2,000 eels. Other fish are rarely mentioned, though St Peter's Abbey in Gloucester was owed an annual due of 16 salmon from its burgesses in the city. A few fisheries had already been abandoned; on Milton Abbey's land at Twyneham 'there was a fishery, but now there is none'.

Fixed weirs could obstruct the passage of boats, and David Pannett has shown that the sites of many medieval fisheries on the upper Severn can be located from the presence of small eyots (locally known as bylets) separating the barge channel from the weir. The monks of Tintern were permitted to build half a weir and to 'make backwaters' on the River Usk on their grange of Monkswood, where the island still remains. At Fiskerton (a name which itself implies a settlement of fishermen) a length of stone revetment along the bank of the River Witham, where stone net-sinkers and fish remains have been found, may be the remains of a fishery called 'Barlingmouth' acquired by the Benedictine nuns of Stainfield shortly before 1200. The Westminster Abbey archives include a diagrammatic sketch plan made in the 1460s or 1470s recording fishing rights in the River Colne between Harefield and Denham, showing two diagonal bars or weirs linked to either bank (**53**).

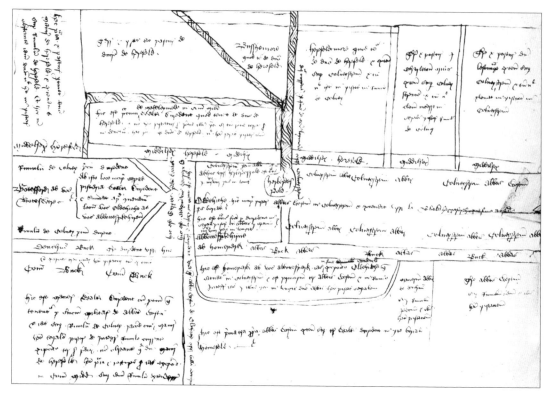

53 *Map made for Westminster Abbey in c.1478 to support the abbey's case in a dispute over fishery rights in the River Colne between Denham (Buckinghamshire) and Harefield (Middlesex). The river is shown diagrammatically as a broad band through the middle of the sketch, and the angled lines resembling lock gates represent fish-weirs*

Some fish-weirs were shared by more than one proprietor (**52**). Abingdon Abbey's fishery at Culham was shared with the royal manor of Sutton Courtenay on the opposite bank. A weir on the Severn at Framilode had been shared between the abbeys of Gloucester and Winchcombe since the time of Edward the Confessor, under an agreement whereby Gloucester supplied the large timber for its maintenance and Winchcombe the small timber. Perhaps because it was inconveniently distant from Winchcombe, the abbot and convent there exchanged their share in the weir in 1320 for a lump sum and annual payment from Gloucester. A few miles upriver the prior of Llanthony and the abbot of Gloucester held 'Horsepoolswere' jointly.

From the early thirteenth century attempts were made to control the number of fish-weirs through legislation. One concern was the risk to stocks through indiscriminate capture of young fish. In 1395 accusations of illegal fishing were made against the abbots of Tewkesbury, Gloucester and Bristol and the prior of Llanthony-by-Gloucester who, between them, had a dozen weirs on the Severn (**52**). It was said that the abbot of Gloucester and the prior of Llanthony had been selling fish which were legally too small to be eaten, and to prove it six buckets of such fish were confiscated and given to the poor. The accused were brought to trial in May 1396, but all managed to evade punishment on various technicalities. In 1397 it was said that the weles in one of Tintern abbey's weirs caught young salmon in defiance of the royal statutes.

A greater concern was the conflict between fisheries and water traffic. In 1280 Sibton Abbey extended its stakes at Orford into deeper water, thereby impeding navigation. In 1292 an order was made for the destruction of the abbot of Tewkesbury's stone weir in the Severn because it obstructed the passage of boats, but clearly nothing was done, since the weir was still a subject of complaint in 1395. In 1330 Abbot de Camme of Tintern was said to have raised several of the abbey's weirs on the Wye by 5 or 6ft, thereby obstructing the passage of boats carrying supplies to the earl of Lancaster's castle at Monmouth. The earl complained to the king, but men sent to lower the weirs were assaulted by several of the monks. In 1351 the abbot of Fountains was accused of obstructing the River Derwent by putting new piles to his weir at Wheldrake, where there had previously been a channel 50ft wide at the top and 20ft wide at the bottom of the river sufficient for all boats.

Fishponds

Supplies of freshwater fish from lakes and rivers were not always reliable, and some means of sorting and storing live fish and breeding them was needed. Artificial fishponds are referred to by Roman authors such as Varro, Pliny and Seneca, and they make an early appearance in monastic settings. The name of *Vivarium*, the great Calabrian monastery founded by Cassiodorus in the sixth century, literally means 'fishpond', and the foreground of a stylised drawing of the church there made in the eighth century (now in the state library at Bamberg) shows fish in a rectangular stone-lined pond.

Given their dietary requirements, it might have been expected that the monasteries would continue to lead the field in fishpond construction. We have no reference to monastic ponds in England before the Domesday survey, however, and that locates only two 'stews or fishponds' *(vivaria vel piscinae)* at Bury St Edmunds. Chris Currie has argued persuasively that the introduction of fishponds into England was a secular aristocratic initiative and that the monasteries were considerably less innovative in this area than many earlier writers had supposed.

It was only after the middle of the twelfth century that fishponds began to proliferate, both within monastic precincts and on demesne estates and granges. Even then, many of the early records are of pre-existing ponds given to monasteries by lay benefactors. William Ferrers, earl of Derby, gave the monks of Tutbury a fishpond at Stanford in Needwood around 1170, while the canons of Mottisfont received a pond at Timsbury from William Brewer in 1227. The first known records of monastic construction are the fishponds made by Abbot Adam (1160-89) on the lands of Evesham Abbey, though unfortunately the chronicler does not tell us exactly where they were. Abbot Simon of Pershore (1175-98) had a fishpond at a place called 'Lokebrig', which was probably at Ufnell Bridge just north-west of the town. At about the same period the Fountains cartulary records a fishpond in the park south-west of the abbey at Sawley Hall, and a second pond, constructed before 1185, at Cayton Grange. Robert Burnell, Bishop of Bath and Wells (1275-92) gave the monks of Bath £10 to build two fishponds.

The construction of fishponds could only be achieved by sacrificing some meadow or pasture, and this did not please everyone, even within the monastic community. At Bury St Edmunds Jocelin of Brakelond records how Abbot Samson 'raised the level of the fishpond at Babwell...to such an extent that...there is no man, rich or poor, having lands by the waterside...but has lost his garden and orchards. The cellarer's pasture on the other side of the bank is destroyed, the arable land of the neighbours is spoiled, the cellarer's meadow is ruined, the infirmarer's orchard is drowned through the overflow of water, and all the neighbours complain of it. Once the cellarer spoke to him in full Chapter concerning the magnitude of the loss, but the abbot at once angrily replied that he was not going to give up his fishpond for the sake of our meadow'.

Disputes also occurred between monastic neighbours. In the 1270s the Augustinian canons of Cirencester began enclosing land at Duntisbourne Nutbeam in the Cotswolds in order to make a new mill and fishponds, thereby encroaching over land where the Benedictine monks of Gloucester claimed common pasture rights. This conflict was finally resolved in 1275, when the monks relinquished their claim.

A few monastic fishponds still contain water today, many more survive in the form of banks and depressions (**colour plate 14**), while others are known only from the evidence of documents and early maps. Functionally, a distinction can be made between *vivaria,* larger ponds where fish were allowed to breed and grow, and *servatoria*, smaller ponds where live fish ready for the table were stored near the point of consumption. Some small, single, rectangular store ponds, such as those at Valle Crucis and Thetford, were filled only by ground water seepage. Other single ponds, including those at Great Malvern and Cirencester, were fed by leats diverted off local streams. Chains of two, three or more ponds, which would allow storage and management of a wider range of fish, are very common. At Dunkeswell a stream from the north-west fed two fishponds a couple of acres in extent (**colour plate 33**), the outflow then dividing into two watercourses, one flowing along the northern boundary of the precinct, the other passing beneath the west front of the church before turning east to serve the southern claustral buildings as a drain before entering the river. Fred Hartley has recorded a flight of four ponds at the Augustinian abbey of Owston, while four even larger ponds once existed at the Cluniac priory of Daventry. Ponds in a chain were not necessarily all constructed at the same time. At Evesham two small linked store ponds survive as ornamental pools in the Abbey Park, while the site of a larger pond immediately to the south has been infilled as a rubbish dump. The three ponds accord well with the chronicle record that Abbot Randulf, early in the thirteenth century, made 'a second and third fish pool at Evesham, for there was already one'.

The number and extent of ponds bears little relation to the wealth or status of the monastery. The twelfth-century plan of Canterbury Cathedral Priory shows only one fishpond within the precinct. Ian Burrow's survey within the Glastonbury precinct has also revealed only one small medieval pond. Yet Maxstoke Priory, a comparatively modest Augustinian house, had up to eight fishponds of various sizes within its precinct, with a moated enclosure and two further ponds just outside the wall. There appears to be a broad tendency for ponds around houses of the Cistercians, Premonstratensians and other reformed orders to be larger and more complex than those of the older Benedictine abbeys. This is probably simply because the former generally settled in remote locations with more space, whereas the latter were more often in congested urban settings.

The claustral buildings of the Premonstratensian abbey of Halesowen stand on a low, flat spur of land between two headstreams of the River Stour. They are enclosed within a perched, three-sided moat fed by a contour leat along the valley to the north. Both valleys are blocked by a series of impressive clay dams, making six or seven ponds to the north and three to the south (**54**). It is not known exactly when these were built, but the court rolls contain references to thefts of nets and stakes and illicit fishing in the ponds from the 1270s. Several other Premonstratensian sites have complex pond systems. At Sulby a massive dam spanned the valley to hold back one enormous pond, with the River Avon diverted into a high-level leat to the south. Beyond this, several seepage-fed ponds were cut into the valley side, while below the main dam to the west there was a series of smaller ponds and tanks. Croxton Abbey had a chain of ten large ponds and three small ones extending for over a mile along the bottom of a narrow valley.

Above the Cistercian abbey of Quarr, by Newnham Grange, a spring fed a pond, the overflow from which was diverted into a leat along the western side of the valley, with two more large ponds occupying the old valley bottom. There was a further pond by the south wall of the abbey precinct, while still further downstream the same watercourse powered the abbey mill.

The Cistercian abbey of Byland had a particularly extensive system of ponds. John McDonnell has shown that some major alterations to the local watercourses were carried out when the abbey was first founded. Several of the streams rising on the Hambleton Hills which formerly drained eastwards

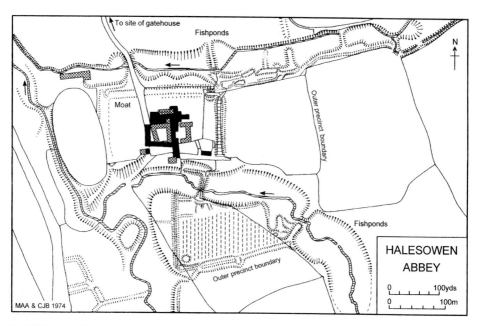

54 *Halesowen Abbey (Worcestershire): plan of the precinct earthworks showing the fishponds*

towards the North Sea were intercepted by an artificial cut, the Long Beck, which diverted them towards the Irish Sea. The original headstream of the Holbeck fed a chain of small ponds just west of the precinct, extending upstream almost to the abbey's earlier site at Stocking. Within the precinct the whole valley north of the abbey was flooded. Part of the overflow from this lake filled a cistern which flushed the drains, while two further ponds to the west and south of the abbey draining towards the Long Beck powered mills. All the ponds would probably also have contained fish. In the parallel valley to the south a much larger pond, covering 50 acres above High Kilburn, was lost to the abbey before 1190 during a dispute, though the monks may have recovered it by 1319. In 1234-5 they negotiated to build a further fishpond on their grange of Oldstead, nearly a mile downstream below the modern Cams Head Farm, with rights of access for maintenance, fishing and drawing nets. This lower pond was 45 acres in extent, but deeper than the earlier pond, and retained by a massive earth and clay dam with a stone core. This dam survives, 450 yards long, nearly 30ft high in the middle, and resembles a railway embankment in its impact upon the landscape. The terms of the grant obliged the monks to remake the road from the abbey to Kilburn if the upper end of the pond flooded it, but this provision proved unnecessary since the surveyor had made his calculations correctly. The area of ponds controlled by the Byland monks may have approached 160 acres at its maximum extent.

While some ponds impress by their scale, others do so by their complexity. At Kirkstead the system includes a series of seven long parallel ponds of varying width, all linked by a single channel at one end (**55**). Chertsey Abbey had a rather similar series of six parallel ponds west of the outer court, within a rectangular area enclosed by further watercourses. The Abbey of St Benet of Hulme has a remarkable group of five small ponds enclosed within a moat and three or four parallel ponds immediately outside it (**56**), with six or seven other small ponds scattered through the remainder of the precinct. At Waltham Abbey Peter Huggins has mapped two nearly square and two longer rectangular ponds, with cropmarks of several associated buildings, some 400 yards north of the church, and a moat-like enclosure, which may also have contained fish, surrounding an orchard east of the church. Peterborough Abbey had a complex of four square and rectangular ponds immediately south of its moated garden. Maps made by Ralph Agas in 1578 and by Loggan in 1675 show two or three small tanks within the gardens of Rewley Abbey on the outskirts of Oxford, with a couple of slightly larger ponds on the further side of the

55 *Kirkstead Abbey (Lincolnshire): an unusual arrangement of long, narrow, parallel fishponds on the edge of the abbey precinct*

56 *Complex fishponds within the precinct of the Abbey of St Benet of Hulme (Norfolk)*

precinct ditch to the north. Such ponds may also have served as ornamental garden features.

Many monastic precincts, including Chertsey, Cleeve, Stanley, Revesby, Ulverscroft, Michelham, Pinley, Halesowen and Calendar, were surrounded in part or in whole by moats, some of which also served as fishponds. At Abingdon the moat is shown on the late medieval map, and the gardener's account of 1450-1 records expenditure upon basketwork fish-traps to be placed in it.

Fishponds are also found on outlying manors and granges. According to the chronicle of Evesham Abbey, Abbot Randulf (1214-29) made new fishponds at Broadwell on the Cotswolds, at Honeybourne and Lenchwick in the Vale of Evesham and at Ombersley and Lineholt in the Severn Valley. A fishpond was amongst the appurtenances of Bengeworth manor assigned to the prior in 1214-16. Abbot Boys (1345-67) acquired various properties in Kinwarton from Robert Grene, including two fishponds (now reflooded). Abbot Yatton (1379-1418) 'magnificently made anew with stone the head of the fishpond called Trylpool at Ombersley', while the fishpond at Wickhamford was also in existence in his time.

Even single outlying ponds could be quite large. A dam at Daisy Banks, a mile north-east of Abingdon Abbey, would have retained a pond of up to 10 acres, and a perforated quartzite net-sinker has been found here. In 1250-1,

Waverley Abbey made a pond near Tilford, 14 acres in extent, on land given by the bishop of Winchester. Beaulieu Abbey's pond at Sowley, first recorded in 1269 when stone was brought to construct a causeway there, was probably even larger, though the 90-acre extent of the present pond may result from its adaptation to power a blast furnace in the seventeenth century. One of two ponds at Fleet which belonged to St Swithun's Priory at Winchester still covers 130 acres, and was fished with nets from boats; when it was leased out towards the end of the fifteenth century, the prior had to provide timber to keep the causeway separating the two ponds in repair.

Occasionally more complex layouts are found on Cistercian granges. Bordesley Abbey's Sheltwood Grange had a flight of three fishponds with the stream diverted along the side of the valley, while at New Grange a stream was dammed to form a large millpond, with smaller fishponds below the dam and in a tributary valley to the west. On the estates of Stoneleigh Abbey Bockendon Grange has a chain of four ponds, alternately large and small, the lowest including an island, while at Cryfield Grange the valley is spanned by three dams with side leats; further ponds are documented at the home grange and the granges of Hurst and Stareton. Fountains Abbey's grange of Haddockstanes included four ponds covering 40 acres.

The construction of the larger and more elaborate ponds clearly required much labour and considerable water-engineering skill. Natural watercourses had to be diverted out of the valley bottom, dams had to be built, sluicegates made and feeder and overflow leats constructed. Small ponds were sometimes constructed immediately above larger ones to serve as silt-traps. At Bordesley Abbey the River Arrow was canalised into a straightened course for more than half a mile along the northern flank of its valley in order to accommodate two parallel sets of fishponds and a separate millpond. Part of the original river course can still be followed as a sinuous depression along the valley floor. When this site was first surveyed in the 1960s, several smaller ponds were noted close to the claustral buildings, and it was plausibly suggested that the river diversion and the construction of the larger ponds took place during a subsequent expansion of the precinct. More recent excavation by Grenville Astill has demonstrated, however, that this impressive undertaking was completed within a few decades of the first monastic settlement.

Fishpond construction might cause other changes to the landscape. At the Benedictine abbey of Eynsham in 1217 Abbot Adam acquired a licence which permitted him to block off part of the old road from Eynsham to Stanton Harcourt in order to enlarge the precinct, to accommodate new farm buildings and apparently also to provide space for a new set of ponds. Land had to be acquired by purchase or exchange from several other occupiers, including one Harvey, son of Peter, whose house stood beyond the Chil Brook towards Stanton. The results of Abbot Adam's intervention can still be seen (**94c**). The road now called Abbey Street terminates in a cul-de-sac, but its former course across the valley can still be traced on aerial photographs, linking up with the present Stanton Harcourt road beyond the further side of the Chil Brook. Immediately west of this road was a small embanked and moated enclosure, precisely where the cartulary locates Harvey's house. Excavation of this site by Graham Keevill in 1991 showed that it had been occupied up to the middle of the thirteenth century, but was then abandoned following its acquisition by the abbey. Having stopped up the old Stanton Harcourt road, Abbot Adam was obliged to provide an alternative route, and this is the modern Station Road, known before the nineteenth century significantly as 'New Bridge Street'. Once the precinct had been extended westwards, the brook was itself then diverted out of its old course and a chain of five rectangular fishponds constructed along the old valley floor. Four of these ponds lay within the new precinct extension, west of the old road. There is also a group of five much smaller store ponds on the north side of the valley a hundred yards down-stream, and it seems likely that these are the ponds within the abbey garden described in a survey of about 1360 as 'recently made'. A description of the abbey site by the antiquarian Thomas Hearne, who visited it in 1706, is of some interest:

> 'I am told by some of the seniors at Eynsham that the monastery there had 52 fishponds belonging to it, according to the number of weeks in a year, which seems to be true from divers holes near to the place where the monastery stood, which without doubt were once fishponds'.

A total of 52 fishponds would be quite without precedent on any monastic or secular site in Britain, and one suspects that Hearne was having his leg gently pulled by the old men of the town.

Fishponds were often enclosed in order to prevent livestock from damaging the banks and dams. The sacrist of Ely spent 1s 6d on repairing the wall around the fishpond in 1291-2. The dangers of inadequate maintenance are well illus-trated by an episode which occurred at Hailes Abbey in 1337. Here the natural slope of the ground was cut back to accommodate the lower stage of the dormitory range and the refectory, which were built in part over the old stream course. Immediately above, on the rising ground to the south-east, the outline of one rectangular pond can still be seen. During Vespers on the Vigil of Corpus Christi the sluice-gates of this pond gave way, and a torrent of mud and water swept through the east range into the cloister. Monastic ponds which survived the Dissolution were equally likely to give trouble in later years. A pond at Frensham, made for Waverley Abbey before the middle of the thirteenth century, contained water until 1841, when the dam burst and the pond drained away.

What types of fish were kept in the ponds? When Richard de Wych, Bishop of Chichester, was entertained at Selborne Priory in about 1250, the prior is said to have been unhappy with the provisions available, and invited him to the fishpond where a net was drawn, initially without success. The bishop was then asked to give his blessing to the operation, whereupon 'behold a pike, three feet in length or more, lay stretched out above the cords of the net, not constrained by the mesh of the net or by the strands of the rope, but as if enticed from the water by the holy man's blessing'. Although this sounds like a classic fisherman's story, it is clear from other sources that pike were particularly favoured. The sacrist of Ely spent 10s on live pike for the fishpond in 1291-2. The ponds of Tewkesbury Abbey were stocked with bream in 1204, and in 1245 Henry III granted Byland Abbey ten prime female bream from the Foss Pond in York to stock the Cams Head pond. In 1301 the prior of Bicester stocked his pond with pike, perch and roach. In 1350 the prior of Worcester was complaining of the theft of pike, bream, perch and roach from his ponds at Hallow and Bedwardine. Stoneleigh Abbey's ponds at Cryfield Grange were producing perch, roach, bream, tench and pickerel in the 1380s. Environmental sampling of the fishponds at Owston Abbey produced scales and bones of pike, bream, roach and perch, all of which are good to eat, along with rudd and chub, which are rather less so.

Popular accounts and traditions often speak of carp, but these are of oriental origin, reaching north-western Europe from the Danube basin, and not appearing in England before the 1460s. Although carp do not breed prolifically here, in other respects they are ideal for small, still-water ponds, requiring little attention and foraging in the depths out of the reach of herons. The ponds in the garden of the London Charterhouse are said to have yielded 300 carp a year.

Left alone, ponds would in due course become silted and fouled, and fish would become prey to fungal diseases. Regular cleansing was, therefore, normal practice. Partial draining every five years or so also provided an opportunity for netting and transferring mature fish to the store ponds. In 1294-5, Westminster Abbey's ponds at Knowle in Warwickshire were cleaned out at a cost of £17 4s 11d. This seems an extraordinarily expensive operation compared with the 8d spent on cleaning out the Abingdon fishpond in about 1377. One of the ponds of Bicester Priory was cleaned out in 1452 and again five years later, when one Geoffrey Dyger and his mate were paid 2s 8d for four days' work. In chains of ponds complex systems of leats and sluicegates were installed to ensure that each pond was capable of being emptied independently of the others. When Croxden Abbey's fishpond was emptied in 1300, few fish were found apart from 500 eels; on this occasion a mysterious 40ft timber called 'the bolt' was removed. The dam of this pond was restored in 1346 with 'pipes and rings'.

The fullest evidence for the stocking and management of ponds comes from the journal of William More, last prior of Worcester. From 1518 to 1535 he documented operations on four sets of ponds, at Battenhall, Crowle, Grimley and Hallow, describing their enlargement and cleansing, the construction of leats, and the carriage of timber for making sluice-gates, thorns and stakes for reinforcing the banks and dams and clay for puddling the pond beds. In summer the ponds were normally restocked with eels, bought cheaply at 50 for a penny, in quantities of up to 1,400 at a time; between 1518 and 1524, the prior put in some 6,486 store eels, but no more were stocked after the latter year. Over the same period, some 2,254 tench, along with smaller quantities of pickerel (young pike), bream, perch and roach, were placed in the ponds through the winter and early spring. More acquired his first carp in 1531. Fishing normally took place in late March, and at intervals of four to ten years each pond was drained or bailed for stock-taking and repairs prior to restocking. The remains of the moats and ponds at Battenhall and Crowle are still visible today (**57** and **colour plate 7**).

Where did the fish come from, and how were they transported to the ponds? Prior More on several occasions ordered live fish from a private supplier at Ripple on the Severn, between 10 and 14 miles away from his four ponds. Earlier, in 1240, we find Henry III allowing Abbot Richard le Gras to stock his ponds at Evesham with live bream from the royal ponds at Feckenham, 13 miles away, while the abbot of Pershore received a similar gift from the same source for his ponds at Broadway, 18 miles away. In 1229 the king gave the abbot of Fountains 60 bream for his pond from the Foss Pool, involving carriage over 23 miles. In 1301-2, four bream were carried 40 miles from Turweston in Buckinghamshire to Westminster Abbey's ponds at Knowle.

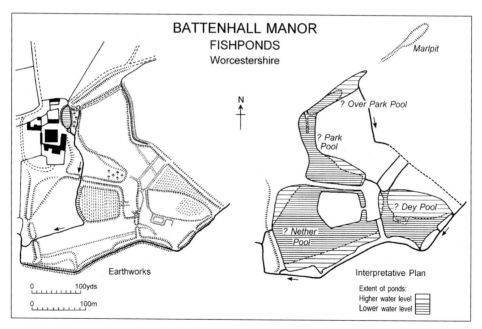

57 *Battenhall (Worcestershire), plan of fishponds: the earthworks suggest that the ponds could have been flooded and operated at two alternative levels regulated by sluice gates; several of the ponds are named in the journal of Prior More of Worcester (1518-35)*

58 *Meare (Somerset): the fourteenth-century fish-house of the abbots of Glastonbury*

Occasionally monasteries supplied the king, as in 1299 when Stanley Abbey sent bream and pike to the royal fishponds at Marlborough Castle. Carriage of live fish by road over journeys lasting up to 12 hours was by no means uncommon. Packed in wet grass or straw, and perhaps revived at intervals by being dunked in streams along the route, live fish were quite capable of surviving this form of transport.

Fishhouses were often built near ponds to provide storage for boats, hooks, nets, fishtraps, bait and other equipment, and perhaps to provide facilities for salting, drying or smoking fish. They may also have provided accommodation for fishermen in the Abbey's employment. The sole survivor of this type of building is the Abbot of Glastonbury's two-storey stone-built fishhouse at Meare, which dates from the second quarter of the fourteenth century (**58**). The upper floor appears to have been used for domestic occupation, while the lower floor may have been used for storage and for smoking fish. This stood near the natural lake of Meare Pool, and a survey has also revealed three small store ponds close by (**59**). The Meare fishhouse was perhaps unusually substantial and elaborate, and other examples which have not survived may have been little more than sheds or huts. Furness Abbey's acquisition of the fishery of Esholt Tarn in 1299 included the right to build a hut there. Various repairs to a fish-house at Durham are recorded, including the fitting of a glass window in 1490-1. A survey of the earthworks of a set of fishponds at Washford in Warwickshire, which appear to have belonged to the Knights Templars, revealed several buildings, and subsequent rescue excavation by Margaret Gray showed one of these to be a small timber and daub-walled structure containing

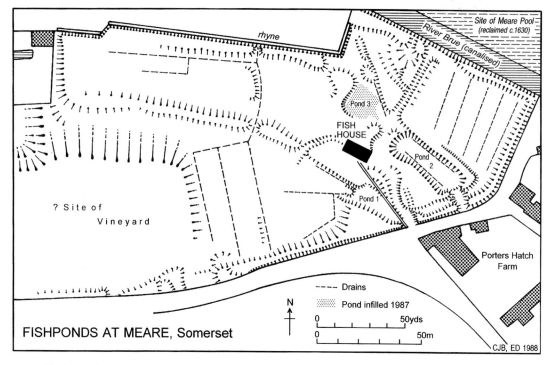

Map labels:
- rhyne
- Site of Meare Pool (reclaimed c.1630)
- River Brue (canalised)
- Pond 3
- FISH HOUSE
- Pond 2
- Pond 1
- ? Site of Vineyard
- Porters Hatch Farm
- N
- ---- Drains
- Pond infilled 1987
- 0   50yds
- 0   50m
- FISHPONDS AT MEARE, Somerset
- CJB, ED 1988

59 *Meare (Somerset): plan of store ponds and other earthworks east of Glastonbury Abbey's manor-house at Meare*

a furnace, perhaps for smoking or drying fish before storage. One of the ponds at Washford contained a circular skep with a woven rush base, which may have been used to transfer fish from one pond to another (**60**). A medieval stone building on the shore of Byland Abbey's Cams Head pond at Oldstead Grange had one end partitioned off with a large hearth to serve as a smoking chamber. Lead and baked clay net weights of various sizes have also been recovered from this site. The remains of several stone-built smokehouses have been recorded on Fountains Abbey's grange of Haddockstanes. Another stone building has been noted on a flat area of one of the dams at Titchfield Abbey. When invasion from France was threatened in 1365, Quarr Abbey fortified one of its fishhouses on the Isle of Wight.

How efficient were monastic ponds in producing fish? The sheer scale and complexity of some examples has prompted suggestions that they were not merely supplying monastic subsistence needs, but were conceived as commercial ventures. Certainly on occasions surplus fish were sold. Byland Abbey enjoyed freedom of tolls on fish it brought to market, while the Abingdon Abbey accounts twice record an income from sales of fish, 12s 8d in 1388-9 and 21s 4d in 1412-13. Such records are exceptional. Chris Currie has stated that, without supplementary feeding, a pond an acre in extent could hold about 200lb of bream, but since bream take five years to reach edible size, it would be capable of producing only about 40lb per annum. Assuming 175 fish days a year, at which each monk would receive a minimum of 6oz (or 8oz unprepared weight) per day, Currie calculates that in order to be self-sufficient in fish, a small house of ten monks would need to produce 850lb a year and would therefore require 21 acres under water, while a large house of 40 brethren would require 90 acres. The needs of monastic servants, guests and corrodians must also be supplied. Even taking into account catches from further fishponds and millponds on the outlying estates, few English monasteries had ponds this extensive. There are occasional records of supplementary feeding, for example at Abingdon in 1322-3, when 2d was spent on feeding the fish, and at Peterborough in 1416-17, when two sticks of small eels were bought to feed to the pike, but again such references appear very rare. Yields from most monastic fishponds were insufficient to satisfy even the regular domestic demands of the monks, let alone to produce a marketable surplus. It seems that their primary purpose was to supply occasional freshwater fish for feast days and the entertainment of important visitors.

Finally, it must be remembered that fishpond use and construction did not necessarily come to an end when the monastic communities were extinguished. Caution is needed in the interpretation of sites where there was continuing secular occupation. Did the small community of Fontevraultine nuns at Grove Priory really have the resources to divert the River Ouzel to

60 *Washford (Warwickshire), a fishpond of the Knights Templars: discovery of a fish-skep with a woven rush base during emergency excavation in 1968*

make room for the large fishponds occupying the former valley bottom, or was this carried out after the end of the thirteenth century when the site came into the hands of the king? The extraordinary serpentine watercourse known as the Crankles at Bury St Edmunds is pointed out as the abbey's fishpond, but its form is unique. The fishponds of the Premonstratensian abbey of Titchfield were first made in the thirteenth century, but were remodelled immediately after the suppression in 1538 by Thomas Wriothesley, who added four new ponds and stocked the whole complex with 500 carp. At Old Warden a substantial dam over 15ft high would have held back a considerable lake in the valley immediately south-east of the abbey, with a complex series of smaller rectangular ponds and ditches around its head; but many of these earthworks may be associated with the gardens of the great house built on the abbey site by Sir John Gostwick soon after he acquired the property in 1537.

12
Churches and chapels on monastic estates

Introduction

The purpose of this chapter is not to discuss the churches used by the monks themselves (monastery churches are already the subject of a vast literature), but rather to examine the churches and chapels under monastic control which served lay communities. The distinction is not, however, entirely clear-cut. Lay people often had access to part of the nave or aisles of Benedictine and Augustinian churches for worship; while a few churches designed for monastic communities passed into exclusively parochial use before the end of the Middle Ages, while remaining monastic possessions.

The origin of churches

Records of churches in Anglo-Saxon England exist from the time of Augustine's mission in 597 when, according to Bede, King Ethelbert of Kent allowed him the use of an ancient church of Roman origin at Canterbury dedicated to St Martin. This still survives as a parish church outside the city walls to the east. Its chancel incorporates coursed brickwork of Roman date and its nave has very early features which probably date from Augustine's enlargement of the Roman building.

Many of the earliest religious communities, before they became more strictly contemplative, had some involvement in missionary and pastoral work, establishing further churches within their own hinterland. The biography of Bishop Cuthbert of Lindisfarne records him consecrating a church in 686-7 built by Abbess Aelflaeda of Whitby at *Osingadun* (possibly Ovingham in Northumberland). Hugh Candidus, a twelfth-century chronicler, attributes the foundation of at least half a dozen subsidiary minsters to Abbot Cuthbald of Medeshamstead during the 670s. One was at Brixworth, where the nave of a great eighth-century basilican church survives; another was at Breedon-on-the-Hill, where much eighth-century sculpture was reused in the existing

Norman building. A slightly later grant of land at Breedon was made specifically to provide for a priest attached to the religious community, to baptise and preach to lay people living nearby. Medeshamstead was later refounded as the Benedictine abbey of Peterborough, and Breedon became an Augustinian priory in 1122, but Brixworth never regained its monastic character, serving as a parish church through the later Middle Ages. Aldhelm, abbot of Malmesbury and later bishop of Sherborne, is credited with the building of a number of churches, and the chancel at Somerford Keynes, a place granted to him in 685 for the support of the monks at Malmesbury, retains a seventh-century doorway.

Two more Canterbury churches, St Mildred's and a lost St Mary's, appear to have been granted in the early ninth century to the nuns of Minster-in-Thanet and Lyminge respectively, as refuges from the Danes. St Mildred's, which retains megalithic quoins of pre-Conquest date, subsequently passed with other properties of Minster-in-Thanet to the Benedictine abbey of St Augustine. The nuns of Shaftesbury similarly received land at Bradford-on-Avon in 1001 to serve as a place of refuge, and the well-known Anglo-Saxon church which stands there today seems likely to have been built by them soon afterwards (**61**).

Anglo-Saxon laws recognised a hierarchy of churches. The bishop's seat was in the 'chief minster' or cathedral. Each diocese also contained several 'ordinary minsters', large churches, often themselves dating from the conversion period, commonly on royal or episcopal estates, served by teams of clerics whose task was to spread the gospel in the surrounding countryside. The term *mynster* is simply the Anglo-Saxon rendering of the Latin *monasterium*, but the spread of the Benedictine rule in the tenth century created a much stronger distinction between the communal, contemplative way of life practised in 'monasteries' and the pastoral functions undertaken by priests in 'minsters'. Some minsters retained a distinctive character as ecclesiastical communities without ever adopting the stricter discipline of a monastic rule. The third tier consisted of private or proprietary churches, founded from the seventh century onwards by Anglo-Saxon thegns on their own property for the use of their own family and followers. Proprietary churches proliferated through the later Saxon period, and they could be sold, bequeathed or mortgaged, like any other property. Ownership could be fragmented, through joint foundation or by division amongst heirs, so Domesday Book occasionally records fractions as small as one-twelfth of a church. Revenues from such churches were usually small, and most of them remained in lay ownership at the time of the Norman Conquest. Finally the law recognised 'field chapels' with no graveyard, serving remote and isolated communities.

The reforms begun by Dunstan in the tenth century separated the monks from pastoral duties, so from then on they took no part in preaching or administering the sacraments to lay people. Nevertheless, by that time, most of the larger monasteries had already come to own at least a few private churches

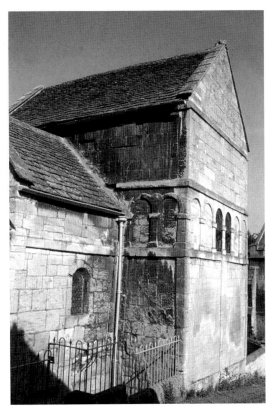

61 *St Laurence's church, Bradford-on-Avon (Wiltshire): hidden from view by surrounding dwellings, stables and sheds until its rediscovery in 1856, this has sometimes been identified with the minster founded before 705 by Aldhelm, abbot of Malmesbury; however, it is now generally attributed to a rebuilding by Shaftesbury Abbey following the nuns' acquisition of the ancient minster in the tenth century*

staffed by secular clergy. Some had been acquired as part of the original endowment, given with other land by the founder, or from subsequent bene-factors, or through exchange. Others had been provided by the monastery for the use of lay servants or local tenants. The Domesday Book records some 70 churches in Suffolk belonging to Bury St Edmunds Abbey and another 20 belonging to Ely Abbey.

Reform and reorganisation

The four-tier hierarchy of churches described above underwent several signif-icant organisational changes before the parochial system of the high Middle Ages emerged. Little more need be said here of the cathedrals, though in view of the distinction now made between 'minsters' and 'monasteries', it is of interest that the reformers had already ejected the secular clerics from the cathedrals of Winchester, Worcester, Sherborne and Canterbury before the end of the tenth century and replaced them with Benedictine monks, and that another half-dozen cathedrals would be staffed by Benedictine monks before 1110.

The territories, responsibilities and privileges of the 'ordinary minsters' had been eroded by the proliferation of private churches with graveyards. Some of them were reorganised as regular Benedictine monasteries in the tenth century, while others developed into collegiate churches, or were reformed as communities of Augustinian canons in the twelfth century. Most minsters lost their distinctive role after the Norman Conquest, however, and were reduced to ordinary parish churches. Even then, vestiges of their former status often remained, such as an unusually large parish, a large cruciform building, a number of dependent chapels, or rights to burial fees from a number of surrounding villages.

Another important change after the Norman Conquest was in the revenue of the church. Whereas in England, church-building by local lords had been a matter of personal convenience, in Normandy the proprietor was accustomed to receive part of the tithes, offerings and burial fees from the incumbent. The imposition of the Norman system in England resulted in churches becoming viewed as profitable assets. As their character changed from private to public use, from proprietary to parish churches, the local community was expected to support them by payment of various local customary dues, in particular by the payment of tithes.

During the century after the Norman Conquest, as the potential income from churches increased, their private ownership by laymen began to attract disapproval. Many of their new Norman owners were persuaded to grant them, with their income, to the monasteries. Abingdon Abbey had for some time before the Norman Conquest received two-thirds of the tithes of the royal estate of Sutton Courtenay. In exchange for a payment of £20, William Rufus gave the church to the abbey, reserving only that the priest should retain all his rights for the term of his life, after which the monks would have unencumbered ownership. In this case, the abbey agreed to allow the priest's son to succeed him, in exchange for a further grant of the chapelry of Milton with its revenues. It was 50 years before the abbey came into full possession, but the transition from the Anglo-Saxon to the Norman system had been achieved without disruption, to the benefit of all parties. Rufus gave a number of churches on his East Anglian estates to Battle Abbey on a similar basis, their incumbents retaining their position for their own lifetime in exchange for paying 10s per annum to the monastery and giving two night's hospitality to visiting abbots.

The recipient abbey sometimes used churches acquired in this way as the nucleus of a dependent priory or cell. Battle Abbey established colonies at St Olave's in Exeter, St John's in Brecon and St Peter's in Carmarthen, all given to it between 1087 and 1110. Norwich Cathedral Priory did likewise at its churches of Aldeby and Hoxne. All Saints church in Fishergate, just outside the walls of York, was granted to Whitby Abbey by William Rufus on condition that some monks should dwell there, and it was intermittently staffed by three or four monks. St Bartholomew's church at Sudbury and St Mary's at Hurley were granted to Westminster Abbey, St George's at Dunster to Bath Abbey, St Mary's at Cardiff to Tewkesbury Abbey and St Leonard's at Snaith to Selby Abbey on similar conditions. English churches were also given to abbeys in Normandy for the establishment of alien priories. Some of these developed a genuine conventual life, sharing their church with a parochial congregation, while others were little more than devices for managing distant estates (Ogbourne St George in Wiltshire became the administrative centre for 24 manors belonging to Bec Abbey, widely scattered between Devon and East Anglia). The Hundred Years War disrupted contacts with the parent houses, and most of the alien priories were suppressed between 1360 and 1450.

By 1170 perhaps a quarter of all churches in England were owned by religious houses. The majority of them did not become monastic cells but served the local community alone. How did the monasteries regard the parish churches on their estates, and what part did they play in their building and maintenance?

Income from churches

Records of taxations such as Pope Nicholas IV's ecclesiastical tax of 1291, the Nonarum Inquisitions of 1342 and the *Valor* of 1535 record income from both *spiritualities,* that is the taxable clerical income from each parish, and *temporalities,* income from landed properties. Assessments often show a significant proportion of the revenue of monastic houses coming from parish churches and chapels, in several different ways.

No church could be maintained solely from voluntary offerings. The laws of King Ine of Wessex (688-726) had required a due called *church-scot* to be paid each year by Martinmas, with stringent penalties for defaulters. This was levied upon all free householders in proportion to their holding, and was normally paid in grain. By the tenth century church-scot payments were reserved to the old minsters; later churches built within their territories had no automatic right to such dues from their own parishioners, except by special agreement. Church-scot payments were a substantial imposition upon the farmers paying them, and in bad harvest years could cause considerable hardship.

Other customary payments, probably of equally ancient origin, are recorded in the time of King Athelstan (925-39). These included *plough-alms,* a payment of one penny for every plough-team working in the parish, to be paid within a fortnight of Easter; and *soul-scot,* initially a voluntary offering of a portion of a dead man's goods made to the priest at his grave-side. Customary payments of soul-scot were eventually replaced by compulsory mortuary fees.

Glebe land was another potential source of income. From very early times, priests had been allocated their own lands within the fields, thereby entering into a sort of agricultural partnership with the community. Old minsters were often endowed with several hundred acres. Proprietary churches served by a single priest needed less, and records from Wessex and south-western Mercia suggest an average endowment of 30 or 40 acres of glebe for each church.

Tithe payments to parish churches ultimately superseded church-scot. Gifts of one-tenth of the value of harvested crops, new-born farm livestock and the profits of mills and fisheries had been encouraged from the earliest years. Initially tithes were not tied to local churches, but could be applied to any religious aims the donor chose. In the later seventh century, Archbishop Theodore of Canterbury ruled that tithes should be given only to pilgrims, to the poor, and by lay founders to their churches; yet while he wished to encourage thegns who built churches on their property to reserve at least a part of their tithe payments to maintain a priest, he did not want the multiplication of proprietary churches to consume the entirety. In the ensuing centuries what had begun as a voluntary offering was consolidated as a legal obligation and directed more firmly towards supporting individual churches. The laws of King Edgar (959-75) required tithes to be paid to the old minsters from their entire territory, and threatened severe penalties for non-payment. Men who had built proprietary churches could give one-third of their personal tithes for their support, the remainder being reserved to the minster within whose territorial bounds they had been built. Men wishing to support a priest at a field chapel without a graveyard were permitted to do so only out of what profits remained to them once the full tithe had been paid to the minster. Further income could come from altarage, oblations and offerings at shrines. When a monastery acquired an advowson (the right of presenting priests to the benefice), it also acquired a regular pension from the church.

Collecting pensions from scattered, distant churches could be difficult, however, and conflicting claims or refusal to pay could result in costly litigation. Monastic houses began to look for alternatives. One expedient was to invite a third party to take over the advowson for an agreed term of years in exchange for a fixed annual payment. The monastery was then assured of its portion of the income, while the intermediary hoped to profit from the difference between the receipts at the church and what he paid to the monastery.

Appropriation of churches

Usually the best option of all was the process of appropriation, whereby the monastery became, in effect, the rector, taking over the whole benefice as its own property, and retaining all the church's revenue from the *great tithes* (corn, hay and wood) and most of the glebeland. Its duties then included the maintenance of the chancel of the church and the appointment of a vicar to carry out pastoral care. In some cases, the *small tithes* (tithes of calves, lambs, poultry, milk and eggs), income from altarage, and perhaps a portion of the glebe, were set aside for the direct maintenance of the vicar. Alternatively the monastery might absorb the entire endowments of the church, or farm them out, using part of the income for the vicar's stipend.

The down side of appropriation was the temptation for the abbey to economise by leaving the vicar with an inadequate income and no guaranteed tenure. By the end of the twelfth century, diocesan bishops were beginning to assert the necessity for episcopal permission before appropriation, and to insist that the vicar should not be removable at will, should have sufficient income and should be responsible to the bishop for spiritual matters. These requirements were endorsed by the synod of Westminster in 1102 and by the Lateran Council in 1179. When Tewkesbury Abbey received confirmation of various churches from Bishop Nicholas of Llandaff (1148–83), it was on condition that, when their rectors died, vicars should be instituted with an adequate stipend.

Appropriation could be a costly process, requiring not only a licence for alienation in mortmain of the rectory, but often also a papal bull, and it placed a burden of responsibilities upon the abbey. Disputes could arise: the monks of Tewkesbury had acquired papal consent for the appropriation of Fairford after the death of its rector, but this was opposed by the bishop; several monks were sent to claim the church when the rector died in 1231, but were ejected with such force that they barely escaped alive. In 1283 Waverley Abbey became embroiled in a prolonged lawsuit with the Archdeacon of Surrey over the payment of small tithes, which dragged on for 15 years. Normally, however, the costs were more than offset by the advantages of controlling the whole of the church's income.

The value of appropriation may be illustrated from the finances of Norwich Cathedral Priory. In 1291 the prior received £46 8s from portions or pensions from 28 parish churches in Norfolk and Suffolk. Spiritualities then made up less than 10 per cent of its total revenues. By 1535 the priory's annual income had more than doubled to over £1,000, the increase arising very largely out of the numerous churches appropriated during the intervening period. In Norfolk it held the appropriations of 30 rectories and half of two more, yielding an income of over £207. The most valuable rectory, Bishops Lynn, was worth £38 13s 4d on its own. Within the city of Norwich ten rectories, together with tithes from the gardens of the Whitefriars, produced an income of £21 11s 8d, and the priory also held seven more city rectories where no claim had been made upon the parishioners for some years because of their poverty. In Suffolk the priory also held three small rectories producing £9 6s 6d.

Appropriation licences were often granted to tide a community over a period of financial embarrassment. In 1292 Little Malvern Priory appropriated the church of Stoke Gifford in compensation for damages suffered during the Barons' War, and in 1368 it appropriated Whatcote church in compensation for the recent loss of some of its Irish possessions. In 1360 the church of Llanbadwrn Fawr was appropriated by Vale Royal in order to help with rebuilding the nave of the abbey, which had collapsed during a violent storm. In 1382 the nuns of Barking were permitted to appropriate Hockley church because so much of their land had been reduced in value by recent floods. In 1499 the monks of Peterborough received consent for the appropriation of North Collingham on the grounds that recent droughts had dried up their fisheries.

Sometimes particular churches became attached to one of the obedientiaries' offices. The church of Warboys was given around the middle of the twelfth century to the almonry of Ramsey Abbey, with the agreement that the two priests who had a life interest in it should pay a pension to the almoner, and when they both died he was to have the rectory and all the income.

Despite the potential rewards, not every abbey pursued this option. When Abbot Samson of Bury St Edmunds regained the church of Woolpit, lost to the abbey for 60 years, he contemplated its appropriation but, to avoid conflict with the bishop of Norwich, settled for a pension of 10 marks from the incumbent. Bury St Edmunds had acquired the patronage of over 60 churches by 1200, and took considerable income from them in pensions and portions, but for the most part elected not to appropriate them.

Occasionally, if it was discovered that rectorial expenses persistently exceeded the income from tithes, the appropriation might be reversed. In 1455 Haverholme Abbey restored the tithes of the depopulated village of Thorpe-by-Newark to the vicar in exchange for a fixed pension. Four years later Oseney Abbey, despairing of any profit from its poverty-stricken parish of Chastleton, resigned the entire income and expenses of the rectory and its farm buildings to the vicar, retaining for itself only the right of patronage and an annual pension of 40s.

Expenditure on churches by monasteries

Monastic possession of churches inevitably involved some outgoings, such as costs of maintenance and payment of stipends for priests. Under canon law the founder of a proprietary church and his successors had theoretically been required to assume responsibility for repairs to the entire building. Communal use had, in effect, however, shifted part of the burden to the parishioners, and it became customary for the patron of the advowson to maintain the chancel, while the local congregation took responsibility for the nave. This arrangement was endorsed by statute in the 1220s.

During the thirteenth century many chancels were rebuilt and extended. The Cistercian movement had ushered in a new spirit which rejected the florid Romanesque style introduced by the Normans and promoted the more austere style of Early English architecture, while at the same time encouraging the clergy to observe greater separation from the lay congregation. Moreover, the promotion of the doctrine of the Holy Sacrament by the Fourth Lateran Council in 1215 and Pope Urban IV's institution of the Feast of Corpus Christi in 1264 both placed a new emphasis on the Eucharist and its setting. Monasteries of all orders responded to the new requirements. Peterborough Abbey acquired the church of Polebrook in Northamptonshire in 1232, and rebuilt its chancel and transepts very shortly after. The chronicle of Evesham Abbey attributes the rebuilding of the chancels of Church Honeybourne, Hampton and Willersey and the church at Norton to Abbot Brookhampton (1282-1316). Another source dates the reconsecrations after reconstruction of Badsey, Norton, Bretforton and Church Honeybourne to 1295. The chancels of Bretforton (**62**) and Church Honeybourne survive from this period and are very similar, each with a stepped group of three cusped lancets under a blank arch. Chancel rebuilding continued at a slower rate through the fourteenth century. The existing chancel at Cuddesdon in Oxfordshire was rebuilt by Abingdon Abbey in 1375-6 using stone from its quarries at Wheatley nearby (**63**).

The high costs and the division of responsibilities meant that it was relatively unusual for any church to undergo comprehensive rebuilding at one date. However, this occasionally took place under monastic patronage. Abingdon Abbey had held the advowson of Uffington since the twelfth century, and a

62 *St Leonard's, Bretforton (Worcestershire), one of Evesham Abbey's churches: the chancel was one of several in the Vale of Evesham rebuilt by Abbot Brookhampton, and a reconsecration is documented in 1295*

63 *The chancel of All Saints' church, Cuddesdon (Oxfordshire), rebuilt by Abingdon Abbey, using stone from its Wheatley quarries, in 1375-6*

church was reputedly built there by Abbot Faricius (1100-17), but an undocumented total rebuilding around the middle of the thirteenth century removed virtually all traces of his work.

The prosperity brought to some parts of England in the fifteenth and early sixteenth centuries by the wool and cloth trades resulted in extensive rebuilding of naves, porches and towers by parishioners, often on a lavish scale. By contrast, monastic patrons generally adopted a more parsimonious approach, so chancels often remained comparatively meagre structures. Pershore Abbey's small and unadorned chancel at Hawkesbury, Glastonbury's chancel at Westonzoyland, Lewes Priory's chancel at Melton Mowbray and the chancel of St Petroc's parish church in Bodmin, which belonged to Bodmin Priory, all contrast starkly with the grand naves built by the parishioners. In 1440 a complaint was made that the chancels of several churches appropriated to Launde priory were in ruin.

Despite this, some churches on the Glastonbury estate display clear evidence of a strong personal interest by individual abbots, extending beyond the chancel (**colour plate 15**). The church adjoining Abbot Adam Sodbury's favourite manor-house at Meare was rebuilt by him and rededicated in 1323, and the existing chancel, tower and south porch are all of this period. The south aisle was later rebuilt by Abbot John Selwood (1456-92), whose initials are prominently displayed on its parapet (**64a**). Abbot Selwood also

64 *Monograms of abbots of Glastonbury on four Somerset churches: Abbot John Selwood at* (a) *Meare,* (b) *Ashcott; Abbot Richard Beere at* (c) *Westonzoyland,* (d) *St Benignus, Glastonbury*

contributed to the rebuilding of the church of High Ham, and his initials also appear on the tower at Ashcott (**64b**) and on a bench-end at East Brent. The monogram of Selwood's successor, Richard Beere, appears on the porch and parapet of St Benignus at Glastonbury (**64d**), rebuilt in the 1520s, on a buttress of the south chapel (**64c**) and on a bench-end at Westonzoyland, on a bench-end at Othery, and on the south porch at Chedzoy. Similarly, John Cantlow, prior of Bath, took a particular interest in the church of Widcombe, contributing to its rebuilding, and electing to be buried there after his death in 1499. Both of the two parish churches at Evesham include splendid fan-vaulted chapels provided by Clement Lichfield, the last abbot.

The extent to which the monasteries influenced the design of parish churches in their care through the employment of masons and carpenters who may also have worked at the abbey itself, requires further study. In the Vale of Evesham, the late medieval gabled stone roofs of the porches at Hampton and Church

221

Honeybourne, supported internally by transverse arches, are locally idiosyncratic, and it may be significant that both churches belonged to Evesham Abbey.

Lastingham provides an example of a church designed for Benedictine worship, but used only briefly before passing into parochial use. In 1078 Abbot Stephen of Whitby, troubled by coastal raids, sought to move part of his community further inland. He was offered the site of the long-abandoned monastery of St Cedd, founded around 654, between the Vale of Pickering and the North York Moors. Here Stephen began constructing a grand new abbey church, with a crypt enclosing the site of St Cedd's shrine and an apsidal chancel above. The new site turned out to be as vulnerable to robbers as Whitby itself, however, so in 1081 the building was abandoned with only the east end complete, and Stephen's monks moved on to York. Lastingham's nave was completed on a more modest scale around 1228, when it was handed on for parochial use. It remained a possession of St Mary's Abbey, York.

Monasteries and town churches

One very good reason for religious communities building new churches for laymen was in order to reserve the monastic church more exclusively to their own use. Although lay people had often been allowed to worship in the west part of the nave or in one aisle of monastic churches, this arrangement was never wholly satisfactory. Attempts to separate monastic from parochial worship can be traced from the later eleventh century, when separate churches were first built on the margin of the precinct for the use of servants, guests, pilgrims, traders and craftsmen. The church of St Margaret by Westminster Abbey was constructed, according to a later source, by Edward the Confessor 'for the greater honour and peace of the monks as of the parishioners'. As the town of Bury St Edmunds grew and prospered, the monks became increasingly disturbed by its inhabitants holding services in the nave of the abbey church. Around 1107 they built St Mary's church on the south-eastern margins of the town, to be served by a priest appointed by the abbot. At Winchcombe an old church within the precinct dedicated to St Pancras had become ruined, and the existing town church of St Peter was built on or close to its site in the 1470s. The parish churches adjoining the Benedictine abbeys of Eynsham and Muchelney probably had similar origins.

Sometimes a new parish church abutted directly on to the abbey, an unsatisfactory solution which could remain a source of friction. At Sherborne the parochial nave of All Hallows was built as a western extension to the nave of the monastic church. The townspeople set up a new font in All Hallows to which the monks objected, and the resulting dispute culminated in a riot in 1437 during which the abbey church was severely damaged. At Romsey the townspeople had originally used the north aisle and transept of the nuns'

65 *The east end of Pershore Abbey (Worcestershire) and the parish church of St Andrew, built to serve that part of the town given to Westminster Abbey by Edward the Confessor in 1065*

church, but in 1403 they were permitted to add a new nave within the angle of the building. Some of the nuns found the parish church a convenient way out into the town, and it was ordered that the doors in the screen separating the two churches should be kept locked. At both Sherborne and Romsey the parochial naves were demolished after the Dissolution when the townspeople bought the monastic churches for their own use.

Proximity of a parish church to a monastery can arise in other ways. The small church of St Andrew which stands under the shadow of the east end of Pershore Abbey's church (**65**) was never a Pershore possession, being built instead by Westminster Abbey to serve the inhabitants of that part of the town granted to Westminster by Edward the Confessor in 1065.

Several monastic towns have two or more smaller churches in addition to the abbey itself. Abbot Wulsin, regarded by the chronicler Matthew Paris as the founder of the town of St Albans, built three new churches at its entrances in 948: St Michael's to the north-west, St Peter's to the north and St Stephen's to the south.

Glastonbury had two churches outside the Abbey precinct. The foundation of St Benedict's, at the west end of the old market-place, is recounted in the chronicle of John of Glastonbury. It was previously dedicated to St Benignus or Beonna, semi-legendary successor of St Patrick, who died at Meare around 470. His relics were translated to Glastonbury on 27 June 1091, the church reputedly being founded on the spot where the procession rested before progressing on to the abbey. St Benignus served the pastoral needs of the lower end of the town, but remained technically a chapel-of-ease to the abbey until the Dissolution. Glastonbury's second church, St John Baptist, is first recorded in 1175, and archaeological work has confirmed the existence of a twelfth-century church beneath the present building. Its revenues were appropriated by the abbey in 1203. The existing structure is largely of the later fifteenth century.

Evesham also has two town churches, but here we have the curious sight of both standing in the same churchyard within the monastic precinct wall (**66**). St Laurence's, the closer of the two to the site of the abbey church, is probably the older; it is always mentioned first in ecclesiastical documents, and its existence is recorded in the abbey's chronicle in 1195, though none of the visible fabric is older than the thirteenth century. This probably served the older part of the town, since its parish included the market-place of Merstow Green outside the west gate of the abbey. There is no documentary or archi-tectural evidence for the existence of the second church, All Saints, before the twelfth century, and it seems likely that this was built to serve a planned extension to the original town, which will be discussed further in chapter 14.

Towns founded by monastic houses after the Norman Conquest usually came as intruders into an established parochial pattern. By then it was difficult to create a new parish for them, so they were often served by chapels, distin-guished by their lack of a graveyard. Westminster Abbey's new town of Moreton-in-Marsh lay within the ancient parish of Bourton-on-the-Hill, and

66 *Two parish churches in the same churchyard at Evesham (Worcestershire): St Laurence's (left) served the old town around Merstow Green; All Saints (right) served the twelfth-century New Borough*

67 Newton Abbot (Devon): tower of the former St Leonard's chapel built by Torre Abbey to serve its new town founded within the ancient parish of Wolborough

its chapel remained without burial rights until 1512. The Premonstratensian canons of Torre established a chapel dedicated to St Leonard within the ancient parish of Wolborough, to serve their new town of Newton Abbot. Its tower survives in the centre of the town, the rest of the building being demolished in 1836 (**67**).

Churches on Benedictine estates

Benedictine estates sometimes retained archaic forms of ecclesiastical organisation, inherited from their minster predecessors and persisting into the later Middle Ages. Pershore Abbey provides an example. Domesday Book records that church-scot amounting to one horseload of grain was due to the abbey every year on St Martin's Day, not only from the hundred hides which it still held, but also from the 200 hides which then belonged to Westminster. An enquiry into the abbey's ancient privileges after its records had been destroyed by fire in the early thirteenth century confirmed its claim to the ancient right of sepulture for all landholders dwelling in 20 of the surrounding manors, many of which had since passed into the hands of Westminster Abbey or other lords. Many of the original chapelries within Pershore's ancient territory took a long time to acquire full parochial independence. Strensham acquired burial rights only in 1393, Martin Hussingtree in 1400, Upton Snodsbury in 1426, and even then those rights were achieved only by payment of compensation to the abbey, which retained a portion of the tithes. In Westminster Abbey's portion of Pershore the chapels of Besford, Defford, Wick and Bricklehampton remained dependencies throughout the Middle Ages.

A few Benedictine monasteries claimed not only financial and patronal rights over their churches, but also complete spiritual jurisdiction. Anglo-Saxon kings had sometimes conveyed immunity from all external interference over monastic endowments. This had the effect of restricting the bishop's abilities to try and punish offenders against church law in those monastic franchises. From there it was a short step to the monastery taking upon itself the right to fine offenders. Such jurisdictions were known as *peculiars*.

By the beginning of the twelfth century, four classes of monastic peculiar can be recognised. At the lowest level, the abbot's jurisdiction applied only within the monastic precinct. Though secular priests might minister to monastic servants and dependants in a public church there, its position might place it outside episcopal jurisdiction. The church of St Margaret's within the abbey cemetery at Westminster had originally been subject to the bishops of London; but when Bishop Foliot attempted to impose his rights in the 1170s, the monks appealed to the pope and secured a bull confirming its exemption in 1189.

The second level consisted of the whole town or village around the abbey. At Bury St Edmunds the bishop of Elmham expressly relinquished all rights in the town itself, the banlieu of which was defined by four crosses. The Conqueror's foundation of Battle was given supreme jurisdiction over a banlieu consisting of all lands lying within a league of the high altar. Around 1122 Bishop Ralph of Chichester recognised the townspeople's church of St Mary as free of all customary dues and fines, though later bishops seem to have regained some jurisdiction over it.

Glastonbury Abbey claimed a more extensive franchise covering churches on the adjoining islands, reputedly granted by King Ine and confirmed to Dunstan, with the right to hold ecclesiastical courts in place of the archdeacon and to receive the fines. Ely and possibly Ramsey had similar rights. In all these cases there were limits to the abbey's exemption, however, and the bishop was able to retain a degree of control. The monks of St Augustine's, Canterbury, claimed special rights over the Isle of Thanet and its churches, but were unable to re-establish these after the Norman Conquest and, despite an appeal to the pope, they were able to preserve a limited degree of immunity for just five of their churches.

In only two cases did a Benedictine house successfully establish complete jurisdiction over a whole group of churches. The initial endowment of Evesham Abbey at the beginning of the eighth century had consisted of a consolidated block of discrete estates at the east end of the Vale. From the start the tithes from these properties seem to have been absorbed within the general income of the abbey, which then appointed and paid secular priests to serve the local communities. This system lasted throughout the Middle Ages, the 12 churches of the Vale remaining technically dependent chapels of the abbey, and outside the bishop's jurisdiction. Evesham claimed to have held special rights over these churches going back to 1016, and its rights were confirmed after an appeal to the papal court in 1249. Similarly, St Albans Abbey had traditionally exerted archidiaconal rights over a group of 15 churches in and around the town, and in 1163 secured complete freedom from episcopal intervention in them. Both abbeys were free to invite any bishop they chose, not necessarily their own diocesan, to perform episcopal consecrations at their churches.

Churches on Cistercian estates

The Cistercian reforms included a rejection of all revenue from churches, altars and tithes. Occasionally, offers of gifts of churches were actually turned down. When Roger Mowbray offered the monks of Byland the advowsons of Thirsk, Kirby Moorside and a third church in about 1143, the scrupulous Abbot Roger refused the gift, and the churches went instead to the canons of Newburgh.

By 1170, however, Pope Alexander III was reprimanding the abbots of Furness and Swineshead for owning churches, and it is evident that many Cistercian houses had begun to accept gifts forbidden by earlier statutes. In 1178 Salley Abbey was on the verge of abandonment since its crops had all rotted in the ground and, in order to save it, Maud Percy, the daughter of its founder, gave it the church of St Mary at Tadcaster, the chapel of Hazlewood and an annual pension from another chapel at Newton. In the time of Abbot Thomas (1182-97) Meaux Abbey attempted to appropriate the church of Wawne, of which it already held half the advowson, in exchange for a pension to its co-patron, the Priory of Aumale in Normandy, but this came to nothing.

The pope had granted to the Cistercians exemption from payment of tithes on lands which they themselves cultivated. This privilege was intended to support poverty-stricken communities in their early years when they were actively clearing new land, since the uncleared waste had never paid tithes anyway. However, it caused considerable friction with diocesan bishops and clergy when, in later years, they began to acquire churches in old-settled areas. Numerous disputes over tithe payments are recorded. In 1215 the Fourth Lateran Council decreed that the Cistercian exemption should continue for all lands acquired before that date and for all lands afterwards brought into cultivation from the waste; but that tithes should be paid on all other lands acquired subsequently.

King John had endowed Beaulieu Abbey from the outset with the advowsons of Shilton and Inglesham and the chapel of Coxwell, and soon afterwards Faringdon, Little Faringdon and Langford came into its hands. Almost immediately the rector of Faringdon, one of the canons of Salisbury, complained to the pope that his church was unjustly impoverished by the refusal of the abbeys of Beaulieu and Stanley to pay tithes to the parish church, and a compromise was reached whereby the monks agreed to a token payment.

In 1232 Pope Gregory IX agreed that Beaulieu could appropriate the churches of Coxwell, Inglesham and Shilton, so long as divine services continued undiminished, vicars were appointed to serve them, and dues to bishops and archdeacons were maintained. The vicar's portion for Inglesham, as drawn up by the bishop of Salisbury in 1240, was to include a croft near the vicarage-house, all offerings at the church, all the small tithes plus the tithe of hay, and a generous livery of 2 quarters of wheat, of oats and of barley. A similar portion was provided at Coxwell, except that one-eighth of the tithe of sheaves, 40s a year and pasture for 20 sheep replaced the corn livery. At Shilton, where the vicar was instituted in 1252, the bishop of Lincoln required him to hold 3 virgates of land, to receive the altarage and the tithe of hay and 1 mark in cash from the monks, with the abbey also undertaking to provide hospitality for the archdeacon on his visitation and to pay for any necessary repairs to the chancel without demur.

By far the largest part of Beaulieu's ecclesiastical income came from the Cornish church of St Keverne, given by Richard, earl of Cornwall, in 1235. This had been a collegiate church of secular canons with considerable landed endowments, later becoming a prebendal church of Exeter Cathedral. When the bishop confirmed the church to the abbey, the latter agreed to allow the vicar a stipend of 15 marks a year. The former rector objected through the papal court, declaring that the monks intended to convert the church to a grange; although they claimed that they needed the extra income for works of hospitality and charity, Beaulieu was in reality in such a desolate location that little or no hospitality was ever asked of them. They had moreover failed to disclose an annual income of £1,000 in rents. Richard of Cornwall agreed a compromise whereby his grant to the abbey continued, while the rector received an annual pension of 20 marks until a suitable benefice could be found for him elsewhere. Beaulieu was still involved in expensive litigation over its right to claim tithes on other possessions of St Keverne nearly 30 years after Earl Richard's grant. The early arrangement for the vicar's portion was superseded by a new agreement in 1269, whereby he was to receive the vicar's house, the altarage income and the tithes of beans and peas from the gardens of the parish, while the abbey took the tithes of fish, and of beans and peas grown in the fields. Unusually, and probably because of the distance from Beaulieu, the vicar also undertook to maintain the chancel of the church.

A special feature of some Cistercian precincts was the *capella ad portam*. The naves of Cistercian monastic churches were reserved for the use of the lay brothers, and parochial use was not permitted. Where there was a small local population, however, services were provided for them in a chapel near the precinct gate. After the Dissolution some of these chapels themselves passed into parochial use, notably at Kirkstead (**68**) and Merevale, while others fell into ruin or were converted to other purposes.

Churches on Augustinian estates

As a clerical rather than a contemplative order, the Augustinian canons were equipped to undertake parochial responsibilities, and often did so, though not without occasional opposition. Churches figured prominently in the endowments of many Augustinian houses (**69**). Henry I granted the canons of Carlisle a group of churches, with the rather vague proviso that the clerks who served them should have whatever proportion of the income they needed, the canons taking the rest. Ralph Deincourt, founder of Thurgarton, endowed it with all 10 churches on his demesnes, while Norton Priory's foundation endowment included seven churches.

On the eve of the Dissolution some 36 per cent of the entire wealth of the Augustinian order in Britain was derived from spiritualities. In some cases the proportion was considerably higher. Tithes accounted for more than half of Norton Priory's revenue in 1535. Dorchester Abbey had comparatively little landed property, and around two-thirds of its income came from spiritualities.

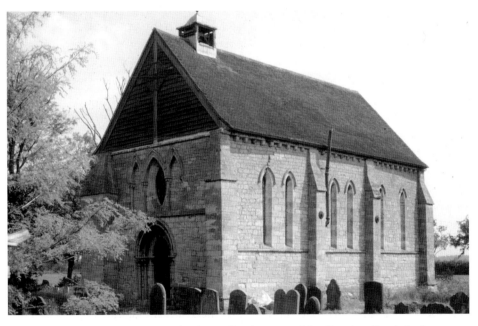

68 *Kirkstead (Lincolnshire): St Leonard's, the* capella ad portam *of the Cistercian abbey, built about 1230-40*

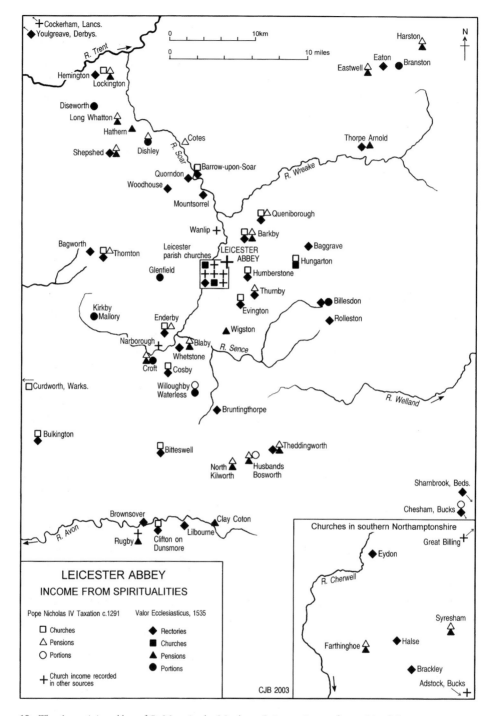

69 *The Augustinian abbey of St Mary-in-the-Meadows, Leicester: income from spiritualities*

As successor to a pre-Conquest cathedral, the nucleus of its ecclesiastical property was a group of five local chapels which had formerly been served by prebendaries. A further half-dozen churches with their dependent chapels had been granted to the canons before the end of the twelfth century. Most of the chapelries of Dorchester Abbey formed a peculiar which remained in the abbot's jurisdiction and outside that of the archdeacon. Its churches of Pishill and Shirburn were appropriated before 1220, and Bix Brand was also appropriated in 1275. In 1301, the bishop gave licence for the churches of Bix, Pishill and Nettlebed to be served by chaplains instead of vicars, because of their poverty.

Churches on Premonstratensian estates

Although the Premonstratensian statutes copied the Cistercian rejection of churches as sources of revenue, by the time the order reached England this restriction had effectively lapsed. From the outset most Premonstratensian houses acquired advowsons, income from glebe land, tithes and offerings. Hugh de Welles and Robert Grosseteste, two successive reforming bishops in the diocese of Lincoln where many of the order's houses were concentrated, took steps to limit the practice of installing removable curates. They insisted on vicars having security of tenure and an assured and adequate stipend.

The canons were then forced to find an alternative way of exploiting their spiritualities. Increasingly from the middle of the thirteenth century abbots adopted the practice of presenting their own canons to vicarages of which they were rectors. In this way the abbey acquired the tithes and oblations through one of their members which they could no longer claim as a corporate body. Such canons then lived on their benefices fulfilling all the functions of a parish priest. They were nevertheless expected to follow their rule as closely as could be achieved outside the confines of the abbey, early regulations insisting on two or three canons being resident in each benefice in order to retain the monastic discipline. They were moreover obliged to attend chapter on certain occasions, particularly at visitations and elections.

Declining numbers in the fourteenth century made it impossible to maintain more than one canon at each church, and something like a quarter of all churches in England held by the Premonstratensians between 1325 and 1400 were appropriated. Again, exceptional financial problems were often quoted as a reason. Not only had Croxton Abbey been destroyed by fire in 1326, but the Scots had also devastated the abbey's Yorkshire estates; the appropriation of Finedon in Northamptonshire brought in an annual income of £40, less the vicar's portion of 15 marks. Damage done by incursions of the sea were quoted in 1338 when the canons of Cockersand requested the appropriation of the rectory of Mitton, while floods and the burden of hospitality prompted the canons of Langley to request the appropriation of Thurton church in 1343.

Chapels-of-ease

Chapels-of-ease were the successors to the 'field chapels' of the Anglo-Saxon laws, serving lay communities who lived inconveniently distant from their parish church. Abbot Ethelelm of Abingdon (1071-84) built a wooden chapel in the forest hamlet of Whistley to save its inhabitants from the dangerous crossing of the Loddon fords on the way to their parish church at Sonning. Such chapels occasionally caused concerns about infringements against the mother church's rights and disputes over responsibility for their maintenance. A temporary chapel was built at Newbold in Leicestershire when the inhabitants of the hamlet expressed fears about travelling to their parish church at Owston during the civil strife of Stephen's reign. Owston Abbey complained in 1353 that Newbold's inhabitants had maintained this chapel ever since, to the prejudice of the mother church, but in 1361 they permitted masses to be celebrated there four days a week. Nicholas Frome, abbot of Glastonbury (1420-1455), refused to accept any responsibility for repairing the chancel at West Pennard, and when some of the inhabitants of the hamlet instituted legal proceedings against him he seized their holdings. West Pennard was a chapel of St John's, Glastonbury, of which the abbot was rector. He seems to have taken the line that since the chapel had been provided solely for the convenience of the local inhabitants, they should bear sole responsibility for its upkeep. The case rumbled on for years, and it was not until 1528 that Abbot Whiting finally secured freedom from any duty of repair through the Archbishop of Canterbury's court.

Pilgrimage chapels and holy wells

Chapels associated with holy wells form a special category. Although not restricted to monastic estates, they often came into monastic ownership and might then be promoted as places of healing and venues of pilgrimage. Many springs and wells had been venerated in pagan times before becoming sanctified by early Christian missionaries. In western Britain, where they are most common, they often bear dedications to local hermits and holy men of the Celtic church, such as St Seiriol's Well on the lands of Penmon Priory in Anglesey. Elsewhere they might be associated with Anglo-Saxon saints, such as St Aldhelm's Well on Glastonbury Abbey's manor of Doulting. St Margaret's Well and the adjoining chapel at Binsey near Oxford recall the legendary refuge of the eighth-century St Frideswide, and four centuries later both were under the care of the canons of St Frideswide's Priory.

To regulate access to a holy spring, the water was often conducted into a bath or dipping-tank enclosed within or beneath a chapel. The spring in the Clent Hills which miraculously arose on the site of St Kenelm's martyrdom

70 *St Kenelm's chapel in the Clent Hills (Worcestershire), reputed place of martyrdom of Prince Kenelm of Mercia in 821; the chapel was built by Halesowen Abbey, the holy well being enclosed within a crypt beneath the chancel*

in 821 lay on land given to Halesowen Abbey in 1215. There was already a chapel by the well, and during the fourteenth century its east end was rebuilt in two storeys, the spring being enclosed within a crypt below the chancel (**70**). Dupath Well near Callington in Cornwall was acquired by the canons of St Germans in 1432, and they built a small chapel over the basin (**colour plate 17**).

The most famous holy well chapel in Britain was St Winifred's Well at Holywell in Flintshire. According to legend, Winifred, the niece of the seventh-century holy man St Beuno, was decapitated by a thwarted suitor. Beuno's prayers restored her to life and she went on to become Abbess of Gwytherin. The spring which arose on the spot where her head fell belonged to St Werburgh's Abbey, Chester, from 1093 to 1203. The Welsh then regained control of the region and in 1240 Dafydd II of Gwynedd granted it to the Cistercians of Basingwerk. Towards the end of the fifteenth century, a large benefaction from Margaret Beaufort, Countess of Richmond, enabled Abbot Thomas Pennant to rebuild the structure, with a chapel in the upper storey and a vaulted well-chamber below. The water was conducted to a pool outside in which pilgrims could bathe (**71**). Another Cistercian abbey, Llantarnam, looked after the chapel and holy well at Pen-rhys Uchaf above the Rhondda Fach, which began to attract large numbers of pilgrims in the fifteenth century.

71 *Holywell (Flintshire): St Winifred's Well, reconstructed by Thomas Pennant, abbot of Basingwerk, in the late fifteenth century*

Even the greatest English pilgrimage centres, Canterbury and Walsingham, never rivalled Rome or Compostela. A few roadside chapels were nevertheless built for the use of those travelling to monastic shrines. Chapel Plaster at Box may have served as a place of hospitality for pilgrims heading for Glastonbury. The Slipper Chapel at Houghton St Giles in Norfolk is claimed to be where pilgrims to Walsingham paused to pray before undertaking the last part of their journey barefoot, though there is no authentic early record of this. The Red Mount Chapel on the east wall of Kings Lynn, built in 1456, also reputedly served as a wayside chapel on the road to Walsingham. St Edmund's Chapel at Hunstanton (**72**) stood over a landing-place believed to have been used by pilgrims to Bury St Edmunds. The best evidence comes from St Catherine's Chapel on the hill overlooking Milton Abbey, where a stone tablet promises an indulgence of 120 days to pilgrims who stopped there (**73**).

Resiting of churches by monastic houses

Because of the status of consecrated ground, ecclesiastical buildings were relatively stable features of the landscape, and it was unusual for them to be relocated. However, the gift of a church to a monastery occasionally resulted

72 *Hunstanton (Norfolk): ruins of St Edmund's chapel, traditionally visited by pilgrims to the shrine of St Edmund at Bury*

73 *St Catherine's chapel on the hill above Milton Abbey (Dorset): the stone tablet promises an indulgence of 120 days to pilgrims who stopped there*

in the erection of a new building. When William FitzErnis gave the Cluniac priory of Castle Acre his church at Sutton in the Holland district of Lincolnshire in the late twelfth century, he included 3 acres of land where he requested the monks to build a new stone church. The old wooden church was to be dismantled and the bodies buried by it to be taken to the new churchyard.

Monastic communities seeking isolation occasionally removed a parish church which stood inconveniently close to their own gates and rebuilt it elsewhere. Savignac monks pulled down the church of Byland in the Rye valley when they removed the village in 1143, but they rehoused the villagers a mile away and built a new church for them (chapter 13). Here the old church may have been dismantled first in order to reuse some of the stonework since the new building incorporates an early Norman chancel arch and other early Norman fragments in the porch.

Cistercian estates contain several examples of church removals. Barnoldswick in the West Riding was the first settlement of the Cistercians who moved to Kirkstall in 1152. Its church was pulled down when the site was converted to a grange, but was replaced by a new church at Coates later in the Middle Ages. Waverley Abbey dismantled the old church at Frensham and replaced it on a new site in 1239. If Beaulieu Abbey's church of St Keverne in Cornwall was ever converted to a grange, as the rector had complained in 1235, it had been rebuilt by the late fifteenth century using some of the old piers.

The occupants of a new village might themselves request a church to be provided in a more convenient location. At Shapwick on the Glastonbury estate, when the present village was laid out in the tenth century, the ancient church was left in isolation half a mile to the east. Having made do with it for over 350 years, in 1329 the villagers finally persuaded the abbey to petition for a replacement to be built within the village. The new church was consecrated in 1331. Here, in contrast to Old Byland, the original church was evidently maintained in use until the new building was ready, since no reused masonry can be seen. Shapwick church contains one curiosity, however: a central tower, built at a time when towers had almost universally gravitated towards the west end. This anachronistic plan, in fact, faithfully replicated that of the old church, which has been revealed by aerial photography, geophysical survey and excavation.

Lost churches

The number of churches on monastic estates fluctuated through the centuries, and some disappeared without replacement. As early as the tenth century the reorganisation of multiple estates into smaller units and the consolidation of parishes sometimes made churches left on territorial margins redundant. Boundary perambulations attached to Saxon charters rarely mention functioning churches, since these usually lay near the centre of the property. However, the bounds of the large estate confirmed to Pershore Abbey by King Edgar in 972 pass by a couple of lost churches on the Cotswold scarp, a 'church-stead' east of Dyrham and a site named as Cada's Minster, just outside the Willersey hill fort. Early timber churches, which represented less investment than a stone building, were perhaps more readily abandoned.

Churches which had served village communities might be removed without replacement if those settlements were superseded by Cistercian granges. The parish church of Treton was taken over by Bruern Abbey when Sandbrook Grange was established in place of the village, and was maintained as a grange chapel up to the Dissolution. Rufford Abbey bought out the rights of the last parson of Cratley, and the church subsequently disappeared from the landscape. The chapel of Myton near Hull, a village replaced by a grange of Meaux Abbey, was destroyed probably in the 1220s. Margam Abbey, intending to establish a grange at Llangewydd, acquired the patronage of its ancient church and by 1196 had paid off the last parson with 2 marks of silver in exchange for his promise not to trouble the monks with any further claims; by the middle of the following century Llangewydd church had ceased to exist. In 1234, the bishop of Llandaff confirmed to Margam Abbey five chapels, all of which had been withdrawn from any form of parochial use. Some of them were converted to grange chapels, some to farm buildings, others were pulled down. The former parish church of St Mary, Sawtry Judith, was absorbed after the foundation of the Cistercian abbey in 1147 as a *capella ad portam*, then fell into ruin after the Dissolution. Another occasional cause of abandonment in the thirteenth century was appropriation; in 1236 the canons of Cirencester persuaded the lord of Wiggold, a hamlet a couple of miles north-east of the town, to release them from their duty of serving its chapel, which has since disappeared.

The third period of church abandonment occurred during the later Middle Ages, reflecting reduced congregations after periods of famine and plague and in some cases the desertion of villages. By 1474 the abbot of Louth Park had ceased to provide a priest for the chapel at Brakenholme because no-one lived there any longer. Daventry Abbey's chapel at Thrupp in Norton was abandoned after the hamlet's depopulation and enclosure. Leicester Abbey's rental of 1477 records the disappearance of the abbey's former chapel at Hamilton. The chapel-of-ease at Newbold by Owston had also been abandoned after the hamlet had been reduced to a single farm. Dorchester Abbey's chapels at Fifield and Warpsgrove have vanished entirely, while its church at Bix Brand lies in ruins. About a dozen churches and chapels recorded on the Abingdon Abbey estates no longer survive, though only two, Tubney and Seacourt, are directly associated with deserted village sites.

There have been further redundancies since the Reformation. Villages consisting of more than one manor might be equipped with more than one church, particularly if one was in monastic ownership. In later years separate provision became superfluous. Ramsey Abbey's church of St Andrew at Barnwell remains in use, but only the chancel of All Saints on the crown manor survives. At Maidwell St Mary's church on the secular manor has survived, while that belonging to the abbey of Bury St Edmunds has disappeared.

Priests' houses

Medieval clergy houses varied greatly in character, reflecting the wide range of status of their occupants, from holders of wealthy benefices whose dwellings might rival the manor-house down to chaplains able to afford little more than a peasant cottage. Where the church was appropriated to a monastery, the monastery was often required to build and maintain a vicarage-house. In 1268, for example, Eynsham Abbey agreed to provide a timber-framed dwelling for the vicar of Histon in Cambridgeshire, comprising a hall 26ft by 20ft with a chamber and garderobe at one end and a buttery at the other, along with a kitchen, bakehouse and brewhouse, all under one roof.

In 1308 an agreement was reached between Bishop Haselshaw of Wells and the Benedictine abbey of Muchelney, which had appropriated the parish church. The abbey was to appoint the priest and to provide him with a new house in place of the older vicarage house. He was also to receive an allowance of bread, 2 gallons of best monastic ale a week and a meal each day from the monastic kitchen, meat on Sundays and Tuesdays and eggs or fish on the other days (**74**). The house, built of the local liassic stone, still survives (**colour plate 18**). Originally it was a two-bay open-roofed hall with a parlour and best chamber at the east end and the service rooms with an extra chamber over them beyond the cross-passage at the west end. The service rooms are small, possibly because the vicar continued to receive his food allowance from the abbey kitchen. There was also a narrow room over the passage itself, possibly for a servant. The original house was soon improved by the insertion of new windows in the best chamber. Shortly after 1470 the hall windows were replaced by the existing square-headed windows, each divided into eight lights by a transom and mullions of Ham stone. At the same time a panelled ceiling was placed in the parlour and the roof reconstructed. Soon after the Dissolution the hall itself was divided into two storeys by an inserted floor, which required further alterations to the windows and the insertion of a new chimney-stack, while later alterations included the demolition of a rear turret enclosing a staircase to the chamber and a garderobe.

Walton near Glastonbury was a mere chapelry of Street, but the old parsonage-house alongside the churchyard is a very grand two-storey building

74 *Sculpture from Muchelney (Somerset), probably depicting the parish priest collecting his allowance of bread and ale from the abbey kitchen following an agreement made in 1308 (see also* **colour plate 18***)*

in two staggered parallel blocks, linked at the angle by a newel stair, with a fine semi-octagonal bow window at one gable end spanning both storeys. Clearly this was much more than a chaplain's dwelling, and it was probably built for the rector of Street, perhaps by Abbot Selwood, who was both patron of the living and lord of the manor.

13
Monasteries and rural settlement

Introduction

The names of many English villages recall former monastic ownership. West Monkton in Somerset and Monkton Deverill in Wiltshire were both ancient possessions of Glastonbury Abbey, while Monkton in Durham belonged to Jarrow Priory. Further coinages occurred after the Norman Conquest, when bureaucratic requirements made it necessary to distinguish between places with similar names; Buckland Monachorum, Abbots Langley, Milton Abbas, Priors Marston and Nunthorpe all acquired their qualifying epithets between the twelfth and fourteenth centuries. Minchinhampton, from the Old English *mynecen*, meaning 'nun', belonged to the Abbaye-aux-Dames in Caen. Most places incorporating the name 'Temple' belonged to the Knights Templars.

Villages were never ubiquitous in Britain. Three contrasting zones of rural settlement are recognisable by the twelfth century. Only the central zone, extending from Northumberland through the Vale of York into the midlands and central southern England, was dominated by nucleated villages. Significantly, this was also the heartland of open-field farming. The zones to the west and east were characterised by more scattered hamlets and isolated farmsteads. Contrary to earlier beliefs that nucleated villages were established by the first generations of Anglo-Saxon settlers replicating a familiar form of settlement from their continental homelands, they are now interpreted as a product of reorganisation between the tenth and twelfth centuries. The earliest monastic foundations therefore generally took place within a context of dispersed settlement.

Monasteries interacted with lay agricultural settlements in various ways. During the economic expansion of the early Middle Ages they may have played an active part in the planning of new villages. Monasteries have also been blamed for the disappearance of many settlements, however, particularly during the twelfth-century Cistercian expansion, and again during the sheep-farming boom of the later Middle Ages.

Monasteries and the origins of the nucleated village

Some of the most ancient monastic properties were centred upon multiple estates in which dispersed but inter-dependent communities, each serving a specialised agrarian function, supplied produce both to each other and to the estate centre. By the later tenth century, however, many monasteries had embarked upon a policy of more intensive exploitation, fragmenting their holdings into discrete, more or less self-sufficient agricultural settlements. The foundation of nucleated villages may well have come about as a result of dismembering the large multiple estates into more compact and more productive holdings based upon communally-organised strip farming, which required a larger labour force.

The clearest evidence has come from Glastonbury. In 729, by a charter known only from fourteenth-century copies, the abbey claimed to have received from King Aethelheard of Wessex a large tract of land straddling the Polden Hills. The name of one of its constituent parts, Shapwick, still recalls its original function as the estate sheep farm. Cossington and Woolavington, towards the west end of the Poldens, were apparently added to the original grant later in the eighth century. At the time of the Domesday survey the abbey retained Shapwick as part of its own demesne. Catcott, Edington, Chilton Polden, Woolavington and Sutton Mallet, all recorded as attachments to Shapwick, were then held from the abbey by sundry thegns. Stawell, Moorlinch, Walton, Ashcott, Greinton and Pedwell, which may have been part of the original estate, were also held by abbey tenants, but were regarded as separate vills by 1086. In 1983 Nick Corcos suggested that the dismembering of the Polden estate into its separate components was begun in the wake of Dunstan's revival of the abbey in the 940s. He also pointed out the distinctive ladder-like street pattern of Shapwick, Edington, Cossington and Woolavington, suggesting that the planning of new villages and open fields might be a direct product of this reorganisation.

In 1989 Shapwick became the focus of a multi-disciplinary research project directed by Mick Aston and Chris Gerrard. Although the regulated layout of its streets provides persuasive evidence of a planned village (**75**), internal inconsistencies suggest either that it was not all laid out at the same time, or that separate plan units within it reflected some form of social differentiation. Pottery collection and test-pits dug in gardens throughout the village have now produced evidence of occupation from the tenth century onwards, and excavation in 1994-6 located a building containing tenth-century material aligned on one of the side lanes. Post-excavation work on this project is continuing, but nothing has so far emerged to contradict Corcos's original hypothesis that a planned village superseded an earlier, more dispersed pattern of settlement in the tenth century.

Elsewhere on Glastonbury's empire, Michael Costen has suggested that the villages of East and West Lydford were laid out after the subdivision of the

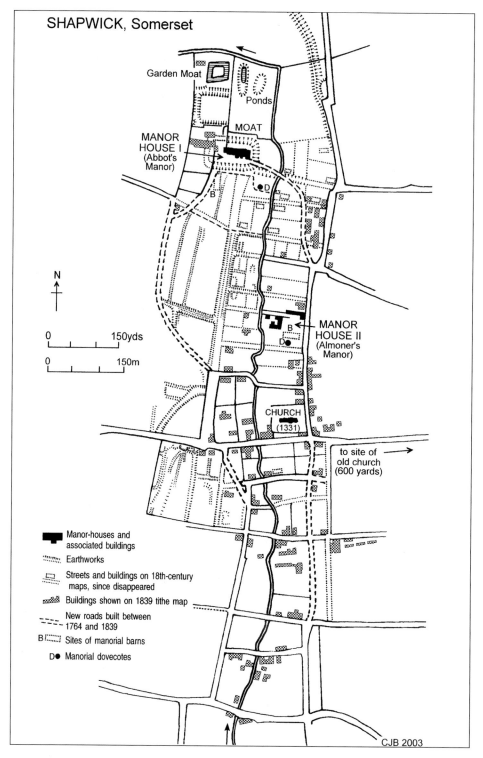

75 *Shapwick (Somerset): plan of village, based upon the tithe map of 1839, modified to show changes of plan since 1764-5 and earthworks of medieval features*

Lydford estate, while Shepton Mallet, Croscombe and Pylle emerged as separate settlements within the Pilton estate, all probably in the later tenth century. More recently Nick Corcos has proposed that Burrington too was laid down as a planned village, separated both from the nearby manorial hamlet of Bourne and the more distant estate centre of Wrington, after the abbey's acquisition of the property in around 957.

Teresa Hall has recognised several Dorset villages formerly in monastic ownership which contain regulated linear plan elements, including Sydling St Nicholas, a possession of Milton Abbey, and Sixpenny Handley, which belonged to the nuns of Shaftesbury. Tarrant Monkton has a similar plan and, if this was of monastic instigation, it must surely have been laid out before 1102, when the monks of nearby Cranborne, who held this manor, moved to Tewkesbury 75 miles away. Sherborne Abbey's manor of Corscombe contains two groups of planned crofts some distance both from the church, which seems to be the centre of an earlier nucleus, since deserted, and from the abbey's grange.

The extent to which village formation in the early Middle Ages was a product of seignurial intervention or peasant initiative remains a matter for debate. While in theory monastic lords had the power to impose their will, it is unlikely that changes of this magnitude could successfully have been achieved without the active co-operation of their tenants and the recognition that the changes would be mutually advantageous.

Settlement reorganisation after the Norman Conquest

New religious houses might attract peasant settlement outside their gates. The alien priory of Loders in Dorset, founded around 1107, probably instigated the linear village to the east. Roberta Gilchrist has commented on the number of rural nunneries located at the periphery of villages, a juxtaposition conveniently providing a labour force for the nuns and enabling the lay congregation to use the nunnery church. Often nunnery and village may have been planned together. Nun Monkton, in the valley of the Yorkshire Ouse, is a three-row village around a triangular green with the nunnery at its apex. The Royal Commission's earthwork survey of Orford has shown that the nunnery was planned in conjunction with a single-row peasant village. Elsewhere, as at Chatteris, the nunnery was initially isolated and the village added later. Susan Oosthuizen has suggested that the nuns of Chatteris may also have been responsible for a planned extension of the village of Barrington, where in 1086 they had 13 tenants.

A more widespread policy of village creation after the Norman Conquest has been demonstrated by Lucille Campey on the lands of Durham Cathedral Priory, where the bursar's rental of c.1400 records the tenurial status, rents and services of each croft sufficiently systematically to permit a reconstruction of contemporary village plans. The Durham estates had been devastated by William the Conqueror's scorched-earth policy after the northern rising of 1068, and their division between bishop and monks in the time of Bishop Ranulph Flambard (1099-1128) allowed both to develop their own programmes of reconstruction. The monastic holdings include a number of new villages with linear two-row plans, such as Wallsend and Newton Bewley, laid out to accommodate customary tenants each farming about 30 acres, some owing labour services, others paying a cash rent. Other two-row villages, including Ferryhill, West Rainton and Westoe, were attached to an earlier nucleus of freehold property, while villages with more complex plans, including Kirk Merrington, Billingham, Aycliffe and Wolviston, seem to have coalesced out of several pre-Conquest nuclei through a process of directed expansion.

By contrast, the Cistercian monks sometimes achieved the isolation they sought by removing villages which stood in their way. Their role in village depopulation will be examined further below. Rarely, however, was such a step taken without either their founder or the monks themselves providing alternative accommodation for the villagers. In the 1143 foundation charter of Revesby Abbey its founder lists by name 13 tenant families in the neighbouring village of Sythesby and 11 families at Thoresby whose lands were to be given to the abbey. All were offered land elsewhere, which they all accepted.

In the same year Henry Mowbray offered the Savignac monks temporarily settled at Hood new quarters in the Rye valley, at a village known as Byland. On their arrival they removed its occupants to a new planned village around a rectangular green, over a mile away and 400ft higher up on the moorland plateau (**colour plate 19**). The local road pattern still shows evidence of diversions up into the new village. In 1147, the year in which the Savignacs were merged with the Cistercians, the monks were persuaded by their neighbours at Rievaulx to move on again, and they took the name with them to their final permanent settlement at Byland Abbey. From that time on the new planned village, confusingly, became known as Old Byland. The abbey still had 19 tenants there at the Dissolution.

Similar reorganisations of local settlement patterns appear around other Cistercian monasteries. The foundation of Rufford Abbey in 1146 prompted the removal of the villages of Rufford, Cratley and Inkersall and their replacement with a new planned settlement at Wellow, surrounding a triangular green and enclosed within a large boundary ditch. The removal of the villages of Upper and Lower Smite by Combe Abbey coincides with an expansion of Brinklow, formerly a mere hamlet, while the absorption of Lower Smite's church into the grange resulted in the upgrading of Brinklow chapel to the status of a parish church. The ledger-book of Stoneleigh Abbey records the monks initially occupying a place called Cryfield, having first moved away its villagers to a new settlement called Hurst; soon afterwards, when the monks moved on to Stoneleigh, Cryfield became a grange. The foundation of Valle Crucis Abbey in 1201 resulted in the removal of some of the inhabitants of the hamlet of Llanegwestl and their resettlement elsewhere on the founder's lordship at Northcroft and Stansty. Local tradition relates that the inhabitants of Hailes were resettled at Didbrook, where a new church was built by 1257. When the monks of Aberconwy were moved to Maenan in 1284, five tenants were displaced and received lands elsewhere in compensation.

New villages were sometimes established in order to exploit donations of waste. The preceptory of Temple Bruer was founded on a wild tract of heathland in the middle of the twelfth century, and the Templars soon established a new village alongside it in order to accommodate labour to help them work their lands. The names of tenants listed in the survey of Templar property in 1185 show how successful the knights had been in attracting immigration from neighbouring settlements. The village was later abandoned, but aerial photographs still show traces of two regular rows of crofts on either side of a rectangular green.

Replanning of villages in the later Middle Ages

Although there remained scope both for expansion (over greens or open-field strips) and for contraction, the shape of most villages had become relatively stable by the twelfth century. Nevertheless, radical changes still sometimes occurred.

The disruptive effect of the Black Death may be indicated at Wawne, on Meaux Abbey's land. Here, from the twelfth century, the settlement was a loose-knit agglomeration of about a dozen timber buildings around a loop of lanes. Around the middle of the fourteenth century part of this area was abandoned. It was then replaced by a new single-row village further south, with 16 houses on stone foundations built along one side of a green. This settlement in turn fell into decay, to be superseded by two brick-built farms in the middle of the seventeenth century.

An unusual example of seignurial intervention in the 1470s transformed the Somerset village of Mells where, according to John Leland, Abbot Selwood of Glastonbury had a whim to rebuild the village 'to the figure of an Anthony Cross, whereof indeed he made but one streetlet'. The cross associated with St Anthony was T-shaped, so it was only necessary for the abbot to create one new street perpendicular to the old through road (**76**). Even this probably represented no more than the straightening-out of an older lane to the church, since it incorporated two earlier buildings. Other dwellings have been rebuilt at a much later date, but three of Abbot Selwood's distinctive stone-built terraced cottages survive, each with an asymmetrically-placed passage

76 *Mells (Somerset): aerial view showing the village replanned by Abbot John Selwood of Glastonbury in the form of a St Anthony cross; his monogram survives in the doorway of no.6, New Street (inset)*

separating the ground floor rooms and giving access from the street to the rear court, and each with a spiral staircase to the upper floor contained within a polygonal projection alongside the rear door. His monogram was also incorporated into the doorways of two of the older cottages.

Deserted villages on Cistercian estates

The evidence for deserted medieval villages was hardly recognised in England before 1945. Then the pioneer investigations of Maurice Beresford in Warwickshire and William Hoskins in Leicestershire opened the floodgates.

Within 30 years local fieldwork and documentary research had identified some 2,500 sites all over the country. From the start it was recognised that many examples lay on monastic estates, Hoskins listing 10 villages destroyed to make way for monastic granges in Leicestershire alone.

The Cistercians acquired a particular notoriety for their ruthless attitude to estate management, and their association with village depopulation was examined in another important pioneer study by Robin Donkin in 1960. Although the order's policy was to seek empty, remote and uncultivated places, by the twelfth century little land capable of being farmed remained wholly unused. Inevitably, therefore, Cistercian colonies gravitated towards the margins of occupied areas rather than positions of extreme isolation. The twelfth-century writer Walter Map, no friend of the order, declared that where no solitude existed, the Cistercians would create one themselves by razing churches and villages and evicting their inhabitants. In 1284 Archbishop Peckham acceded to Edward I's request to dedicate a new site at Maenan designated for the Cistercians of Aberconwy, while expressing some concern that, 'wherever they set foot they destroy villages, take away tithes and detract from the authority of bishops'.

The proximity of many Cistercian abbeys to deserted villages lends some weight to these accusations. Bordesley Abbey lay near the vanished Domesday vill of Osmerley, and the earthworks of two deserted hamlets lie within a mile of the precinct. Domesday Book records 32 families living at Hailes, and the parish church still stands close to the abbey, but little trace of any village remains. The Cistercian settlement at Barnoldswick in 1147 was immediately followed by evictions from the nearby villages of East and West Marton, Bracewell and Stock, all very shrunken settlements today, and when the monks moved on to Kirkstall in 1152 their earlier site was converted to a grange. Meaux Abbey's chronicle relates how the North Grange occupied the place where the village of Meaux once stood, and the abbey and grange earthworks are still surrounded by the ridge and furrow of the former arable strips of the displaced villagers. Donkin concluded that, where a new abbey was founded, the removal of nearby settlements was usually swift and decisive, though, as described above, their occupants were usually rehoused elsewhere.

Even when the abbey site itself lay on the waste, nearby villages were likely to suffer removal. Pipewell Abbey was settled on land cleared from woodland east of Pipewell village, which was then superseded by the abbey's West Grange. The very name of Bruern Abbey tells us that it was founded on heathland (Latin *brueria*), but soon after 1170 its founder made over to it the whole manor and church of Treton, a mile to the south-west, where the Domesday settlement of 23 families had soon given way to Sandbrook Grange (**9**).

Since the Cistercians' original design was not just to settle in isolation but also to exclude all contact with lay farmers, the creation of more distant granges might also result in evictions. Many Cistercian estate farms have the earthworks of deserted villages as neighbours, including the Rievaulx granges of Griff and Newton, the Jervaulx granges of Akebar and Braithwaite, and the

Meaux granges of Croo and Dringhoe. It should not be assumed that these villages were all removed when the granges were first created. Practicality often diverged from ideology. When the abbey received only part of a vill, it had to work its way towards exclusive control by opportunistic exchanges and purchases of demesne, open-field-strips, assarts and waste, and this might take many years. The process was sometimes reversed, since large arable demesnes could not be managed by just a few lay brothers. Hired peasant labour became increasingly necessary as the numbers of lay brethren declined. A second phase of depopulation might follow in the later Middle Ages, when conversion to sheep farming once more reduced the need for a large labour force.

By the Dissolution Fountains Abbey had at least 20 deserted villages and hamlets on its estates. The cartulary shows the abbey building up a consolidated property through gifts and purchase at Greenbury near Scorton during the late twelfth century until it was able to remove the remaining inhabitants. It acquired 200 acres of land in Cayton in 1135, and within a decade the village had been replaced by a grange. The same fate befell Herleshow, acquired in 1149 and absorbed into Morker Grange, and Thorpe Underwood, acquired in 1175. At Baldersby the abbey had acquired total control of the township by about 1240, when Hugh of Baldersby surrendered his holding in exchange for another which the monks created for him elsewhere on their lands at Tickhill. Several neighbouring hamlets, Aseby, Birkou and part of Ainderby Quernhow, were also swallowed up. Subsequently the only tax payments from Baldersby were from the grange and from the two demesne servants employed on it, and the 800 acres of arable land there formed the richest single farm in the North Riding. The granges at Marton-le-Moor and Sleningford had respectively absorbed all the lands of the former villages of Caldwell and Ripplington.

Many more examples occur in the midlands. Kirkstead Abbey replaced the village of Cotes with Linwood Grange soon after 1135. Vaudey Abbey swallowed up the village of Little Lavington. The monks of Garendon acquired the manor of Dishley, a place with 33 families in 1086, and by 1180 had converted it to a grange. The manor of Orton-on-the-Hill formed part of the foundation endowment of Merevale Abbey, and its hamlet of Weston soon gave way to a grange. Bruern Abbey was probably responsible for the depopulation of Dunthrop, Sewell and Tangley, where it had granges. The village of Putnoe became a grange of Warden Abbey and the village of Limbersley was also greatly reduced. Beesthorpe became a grange of Rufford Abbey.

In Wales Margam Abbey was responsible for the removal of several substantial settlements in the Vale of Glamorgan. The castle, church and village of Sturmeston, only recently settled on previously uncultivated ground by Geoffrey Sturmi, were granted to the monks at the end of the twelfth century, and soon afterwards were demolished for the creation of Stormy Grange. The monks also acquired a lease of a neglected tract of land at Llangewydd, improved it through intensive cultivation, then sought to reduce its attractiveness to the original holder in order to renegotiate the lease on more favourable terms; before 1218 they had razed the castle to the ground and evicted all the villagers from their houses. Giraldus Cambrensis relates that the monks also dismantled the old village church of Llangewydd by stealth overnight and carted away the stone and timber, so that when the parson rode by some days later he was astonished to find that his church had vanished without trace. The monks of Margam also persuaded the Welsh freeholders of the village of Bradington to sell their holdings, with the consent of their lord, Henry de Umfraville, and their houses were removed piecemeal between c.1190 and 1336 to make the grange of Llanfeuthin. Earthwork remains of several crofts survive here. The church and vill of Caerwigau are mentioned in an early thirteenth-century grant to Margam, and both disappear from the written record soon after.

Occasionally resistance was encountered. Abbot Lambert of Kirkstall (c.1190-3) was required to surrender Cliviger Grange to Robert Lacy, son of the founder and patron of the abbey, in exchange for land at Accrington. When he removed the inhabitants of Accrington to convert it to a grange, some of the men he evicted set fire to the grange buildings and murdered the three lay brothers left in charge there. Lacy forced the offenders to rebuild and to pay compensation before banishing them.

Early desertions on the estates of other orders

The Cistercians were not the only order to seek isolation. The biography of Hugh of Avalon, monk of la Grande Chartreuse and later Bishop of Lincoln, contains a remarkable passage describing his efforts to revive the failing Carthusian foundation at Witham in Selwood Forest. The foundation's first two priors had shown little leadership, only a few wooden huts had been erected, and the few remaining monks were nearly destitute. The silence and solitude required by the Carthusians could not be achieved because about 120 peasant farmers still lived on the site. With the king's consent, Hugh compensated the peasants by buying their houses, offering them comparable fields and dwellings on any other royal manor, or freedom from serfdom to live wherever they chose. He then gave the timber and other building materials back to the peasants, who had the choice of selling them locally or carting them away to rebuild elsewhere. Most of the peasants of Witham settled at Knapp in North Curry, 30 miles away.

Although the Premonstratensians imitated the Cistercians in many ways, their attitude towards adjacent settlements was less consistent. Alongside the site of Croxton Abbey are preserved the earthworks of a village which may have been removed soon after the canons arrived in 1162. However, at Sulby the canons co-existed with a substantial village for well over 250 years. In

1377, 89 contributors to the Poll Tax lived there, but by 1428 payment of tax had been excused because fewer than ten families remained. It was the changing economic conditions of the later Middle Ages, rather than any initial search for isolation, which eventually led the abbey to buy out surviving freeholders in order to enclose.

Some early desertions occurred even near houses of orders with no particular hankering after isolation. At Sempringham virtually the whole of the village community seems to have joined the Gilbertine monastery. The foundation of the Augustinian priory of Haltemprice in 1320 led to the removal of the hamlet of Newton in Cottingham. By contrast, the inhabitants of Ash, a hamlet on the edge of Otmoor granted to Studley Priory around 1176, appear to have been resettled at Studley itself. The village of Fulwell became a grange of Oseney Abbey in 1205, and by the end of the century most of its lands had been converted to sheep grazing and its inhabitants removed to Mixbury. Early settlement desertions occasionally occurred on Benedictine estates. The Lincolnshire vill of Butyate, given by Robert Marmion to Bardney Abbey, had ten villeins and five sokemen in 1086, but it had vanished from the record by the early thirteenth century. The abbey's role in its disappearance is far from clear.

Famine and plague: villages in the fourteenth century

A series of bad harvests in the early fourteenth century caused widespread famine. The Black Death in 1348-9 further reduced the population of many settlements, with subsequent outbreaks of decreasing severity after 1361. The low tax quota for Ingarsby in 1334 suggests that this village was in decay even before the plague, and certainly long before Leicester Abbey undertook the enclosure which resulted in its final extinction. Only rarely did the Black Death wipe entire communities off the map though this did happen to two villages on Eynsham Abbey's lands, Tilgarsley and Coat (**77**). A mortality of between 30 and 50 per cent was widespread. It was reported in 1412 that pestilence had reduced the population of Pipewell Abbey's manor of Elkington to three or four of the abbey's servitors. In 1377 six of the 15 holdings on Tynemouth Priory's land at Monkseaton had been waste since the plague, and the prior had four more holdings in hand with no tenants. Another Tynemouth manor, Seaton Delaval, had once contained 26 holdings, but by 1353 20 of its houses were in ruins.

Peasant tenants who had managed to weather these storms found themselves in a much stronger position, better able to resist pressure from their lords, with new opportunities either to enlarge their farms by taking over vacated holdings, or to abandon unrewarding land to seek an easier life elsewhere. Many monastic houses viewed with alarm their dwindling rent income, and

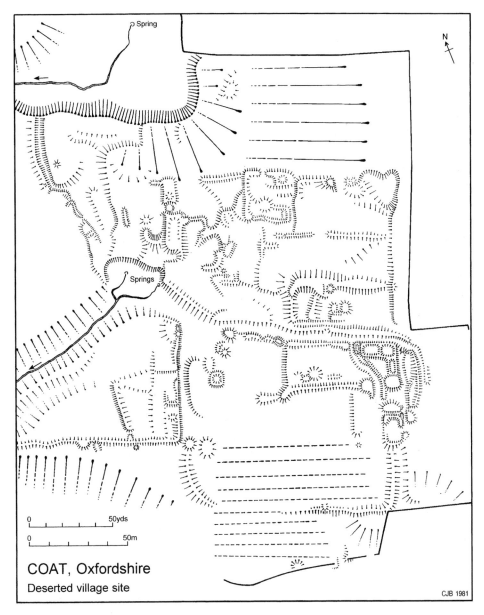

77 *Coat (Oxfordshire), plan of deserted settlement on the Eynsham Abbey estate: tax returns and rentals indicate the existence of 11-13 holdings here between 1279 and 1347, but the abbey failed to collect any rents from the hamlet after 1350, and it is probable that most of its occupants died in the Black Death*

offered considerable inducements to keep tenants on their lands. The Eynsham cartulary tells us that the village of Woodeaton was on the brink of extinction after the plague, with only two tenants remaining, both of whom wished to leave. It may be questioned whether the situation was quite this desperate, since eight families with distinctive personal names recorded in a tax list of

1316 are still there in 1366. There is, nevertheless, no reason to doubt the statement that Abbot Nicholas negotiated a new agreement with his tenants, reducing their rents and manorial services. Eynsham Abbey faced similar problems at Brookend, where initially it had some success in finding new takers for the abandoned crofts. Though 15 tenants remained there in 1363, vacant holdings were again appearing after 1381, and the abbey was once more forced to reduce its rents. Some of the vacated lands were taken over by other resident farmers, who had no need of their houses. Since the retention of a dwelling was critical if the holding was ever to be re-let as a viable unit, the abbey tried to insist on their upkeep; but this soon proved counterproductive since tenants preferred to leave rather than be forced to repair redundant buildings. By 1441 only three permanent tenants remained.

Desertion and enclosure in the later Middle Ages

The famines and plagues of the fourteenth century had reduced both the labour force and the market for grain, and when rent income and labour resources were no longer sufficient to maintain an arable demesne, conversion to pastoral farming became an increasingly attractive option. Surviving tenants clinging on to common rights could then become a nuisance since they were an obstacle to enclosure. Chancery petitions of the early sixteenth century show some monastic lords initially offering to buy out tenants or to exchange lands and then, if this failed, resorting to less legal tactics. The abbot of Hailes was accused of harassing his copyholders at Longborough, hoping to drive them out in order to convert more land to sheep pasture.

Leicester Abbey began to build up a substantial holding in Ingarsby in 1352. By 1469 it owned the entire township and was able to enclose it, so that it became the most valuable pastoral grange on its estates. Earthworks of the former village remain clearly visible in the pasture south of Ingarsby Old Hall (**78**). Selby Abbey systematically acquired lands at Stormsworth from surviving freeholders by various means until it had total control of all land in the manor, which it then enclosed and converted to pasture. From a first small toehold of land in Hampton Gay acquired before 1205, Oseney Abbey had acquired the entire demesne by 1222, and was keeping sheep there. During the fourteenth century it increased its holdings by easing out the freeholders. In this particular case, however, the abbey never achieved total control, and it cannot be blamed for the subsequent enclosure and depopulation of the village, which took place after the Dissolution.

Elsewhere, by the later fourteenth century, a new phase of evictions was beginning. The remaining occupants of West Chirton were removed by Tynemouth Priory some time after 1377 and their arable land converted to two large enclosed cattle pastures. The Knights Hospitallers had almost entirely

78 *Ingarsby (Leicestershire): aerial view of earthworks of deserted village converted to sheep and cattle pasture by Leicester Abbey following enclosure in 1469. The farm lies within a pentagonal moat enclosing the monastic grange buildings on the site of the former manor house*

removed the village of Shingay by 1452, when it was said that 'the preceptor possessed crofts in which once were houses' and the revenues of Shingay church were so diminished that a vicar could no longer be supported, a chaplain being appointed instead. A moat and a few cottages remain here, but the church has long vanished. The village of Whatborough was already in severe decline by 1495, when its remaining occupants were removed and its fields enclosed by Launde Priory, who held it on long lease from All Souls College; in 1539 the prior had 2,000 sheep grazing there.

John Rous' *History of the Kings of England,* written some time between 1486 and 1491, contains a famous diatribe on the impact of enclosure for sheep farming in his own home area, Warwickshire. Rous gave the names of 60 villages and hamlets which he claimed had become depopulated to make way for sheep. He specifically attributed the destruction of Cawston-on-Dunsmore to the greed of the monks of Pipewell, while other places listed included Cryfield, Hurst, Finham and Milburn, all possessions of Stoneleigh Abbey, and Church Honeybourne and Poden on the Evesham estates.

In the wake of agitation by Rous and others about the effects of depopulation and enclosure, Parliament in 1489 passed the first of a series of statutes aimed at curbing these practices. The apparent ineffectiveness of this legislation prompted a Commission of Inquiry, set up by Cardinal Wolsey in 1517, to investigate accusations of continuing evictions. This inquiry's returns on enclosure were discussed in chapter 5, and here we will be concerned primarily with the information it gives on depopulation, though inevitably many of the same places loom large under both headings. About 40 monastic houses and a number of their lessees were blamed for pulling down houses and carrying out evictions. The prior of Daventry held only the rectory estate at Thrupp in Norton but in 1489 he had destroyed 14 houses (to which lands had been attached) and four cottages (without agricultural land of their own) and rendered 100 persons redundant with the result that the church had fallen into ruin. The prioress of Catesby had removed 10 houses and four cottages from Nether Catesby in 1495, displacing 60 persons, though five other houses survived there until the Dissolution.

At Baggrave Leicester Abbey held 216 acres, a little over a quarter of the manor, which had been used time out of mind for corn-growing. In 1501 Abbot John Penny enclosed this land and converted it to pasture, destroying five houses and two cottages, rendering five ploughs idle and forcing 30 people to leave their homes (**79**). The following year the abbey acquired control of five-eighths of the township. Abbot Penny was also accused of pulling down

79 *Baggrave (Leicestershire): aerial view of village depopulated by Abbot Penny of Leicester in 1501. The former village street shows as a hollow-way across the centre of the photograph, with the rectangular moat of the former manor house just above it to the left. Narrow ridge and furrow over the village crofts shows that they have been lightly overploughed since the removal of the houses*

three houses and displacing 18 persons from Kirkby Mallory, where the parish church had, in consequence, fallen into ruin. Abbot Ralph of Kenilworth and a lay lord were together held responsible for the destruction of eight houses and a cottage at Tachbrook Mallory, resulting in 60 people leaving the land, while Abbot Ralph had also destroyed two houses and a cottage at Wood Bevington.

Rarely were these episodes sudden assaults upon a thriving community. Other sources show that evictions recorded in 1517 were just one stage in a protracted process. Bicester Priory had by 1272 become sole lord of the hamlet of Wretchwick, a place occupied by 25 villeins and seven cottagers in 1279. The priory rentals show vacant crofts there from the 1430s. In 1517 local witnesses reported that the prior formerly had five houses and 200 acres of arable at Wretchwick, and that the occupants of each house had been accustomed to plough and sow at least 30 acres of land; the prior had pulled down the houses in March 1489, converting the arable land to pasture, putting three ploughs out of use, and turning out 18 people (**80**). Several of the displaced families were, in fact, able to rent vacant priory land elsewhere.

In many cases the blow to the settlement was not a fatal one. The abbot of Rewley held six houses and four cottages in Yarnton whence nine ploughs had been made redundant and 36 persons removed, while the prior of Great Malvern was said to have destroyed six houses and two cottages at Shuttington; both places are thriving villages today. The majority of the accusations were concerned with the removal of no more than one or two houses. Moreover, not all the statements went uncontested. The Prior of Daventry, accused of destroying three houses in Staverton, was discharged of any responsibility for two of them when he was able to prove that he had no legal interest in them.

Despite the accusations, monastic landlords were not always the initiators of depopulation. When Luffield Abbey acquired the manor of Lillingston Dayrell, the last of its inhabitants had already been removed by its former lord, Thomas Dayrell, in 1493. Sometimes it was monastic lessees who were responsible. John Arden, who leased the manor of Willaston from Rewley Abbey, evicted 42 people there in 1501. Tewkesbury Abbey's tenant at Didcot in Dumbleton had converted to pasture 300 acres in 1491, and it was later said that 30 people had left their homes; though the land remained unenclosed as late as 1540, it had only one farmer. Charwelton in Northamptonshire, largely owned by the abbeys of Thorney and Biddlesden, was leased out by the fifteenth century. John Rous recorded the disappearance of the village of Church Charwelton and claimed that Lower Charwelton too was 'now in great danger of being wholly destroyed by greedy men, and is almost ruined'.

While monastic houses undoubtedly did have a hand in the removal of many villages through forced evictions, this was usually a pragmatic response precipitated by substantial numbers of peasants themselves taking the initiative and deciding to leave. Only when all efforts to keep peasants on their holdings

80 *Wretchwick (Oxfordshire), aerial view of deserted village: the last five houses were destroyed by the prior of Bicester in 1517, and only a single farm remains in the middle of the site*

failed did the monks consider removing the remaining occupants. Enclosure and conversion were usually the consequences and not the causes of depopulation, and by taking such action, monastic owners were simply seeking to minimise their losses.

Resettlement of deserted villages

Depopulations on monastic land were not invariably permanent. Ulceby, on the Lincolnshire Wolds, had become emptied of people through some unknown cause shortly before 1163, and the canons of Thornton were temporarily grazing sheep over its abandoned fields 'until the village shall be resettled and restored'. By 1334 the village had recovered, and its taxpayers contributed over £5 to the Lay Subsidy, though the abbey still retained the right to graze 300 sheep there. As indicated earlier, the decline in the recruitment of lay brothers was sometimes compensated for by the employment of hired labourers supervised by a bailiff, resulting in the re-establishment of small peasant settlements alongside the granges.

Some of the northern abbeys had suffered particular financial stresses in the fourteenth century, not just through pestilence and famine, but also through the devastation of their estates by the Scots after the English defeat at Bannockburn in 1314. Fountains Abbey was itself occupied by the Scottish army in 1318. Over the following half-century the monks of Fountains experimented with three different ways of recouping their losses. Those granges which had suffered least damage were kept in hand and worked by hired labour under ten bailiffs. In 1336 Abbot Coxwold began leasing out many of the ruined granges with strings attached, so that the lay tenants were managing the abbey's livestock. Finally, in 1363 Abbot Robert Monkton began settling new villages on the granges at Aldburgh, Bradley, Bramley, Cayton, Cowton, Kilnsey, Sleningford, Sutton and Thorpe, from which peasant tenants could farm the former monastic demesnes for an annual rent. Jervaulx Abbey also adopted this last solution, dividing Rookwith Grange into 40 separate holdings, Newstead Grange into 30 holdings, Didderston Grange into 24 holdings and Horton-in-Ribblesdale into 16 holdings. Such expedients, however, were often only a temporary measure until yields had recovered. Then it often proved administratively simpler to lease out each grange to a single wealthy tenant, as Jervaulx did at Didderston. By the Dissolution, however, many granges were once again becoming fragmented through subdivision between sons of tenants and detachment of portions to create smaller, more convenient farming units, though the effect was not now to revive vanished villages but to create further separate farms.

Partial resettlement of depopulated villages often occurred after the Dissolution. The village of Pipewell, largely removed by the Cistercian foundation there in 1143, slowly recovered under subsequent lay ownership, the first census of 1841 recording 120 occupants; even today it has a stunted appearance, surrounded by earthworks indicating its former extent.

Dispersed settlement on monastic estates

Extreme dispersal of settlement has traditionally been seen either as an aberration of the Celtic fringes, or as a product of the assarting of waste and woodland. Tenanted monastic lands in Wales or in wooded parts of the English midlands do, indeed, often correspond with this model. Dieulacresse Abbey colonised the sparsely-populated Rossall promontory in Lancashire by transplanting a number of villein families there.

Even in areas where villages were prevalent, progress towards nucleation was not universal. The property of Martinsey, confirmed to Glastonbury Abbey by a spurious charter attributed to King Ine in 725, never seems to have amounted to more than a single farm (**81**). Loose-knit polyfocal settlements, such as the Glastonbury manors of West Pennard or Buckland Newton, can perhaps be seen as an intermediate stage between dispersal and planned nucleation.

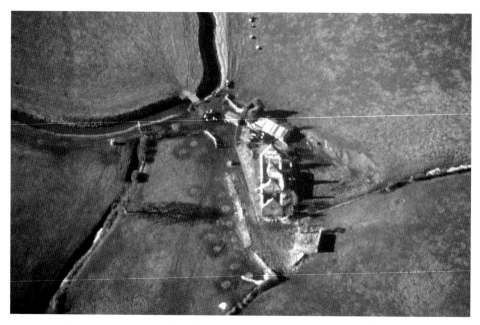

81 *The ruined buildings of Marchey Farm, Wookey (Somerset), preserve the identity of the farm of Martinsey, claimed to have been granted to Glastonbury Abbey in 725*

Depopulation could affect dispersed settlements as well as nucleated villages. Margam had substantial endowments in the uplands north and east of the abbey, with many scattered settlements along the valleys and lower slopes. From the late twelfth century, the monks embarked upon a policy of removing tenants from the abbey's property by revoking their leases and squeezing out the occupants of neighbouring lands, prior to the establishment of granges at Penhydd and Hafod-y-Porth.

14

Monastic boroughs, markets and urban property

Introduction

Two types of monastic foundation are particularly likely to occur in towns, namely Benedictine abbeys and houses of mendicant friars. Some of the earliest monastic communities, including Christ Church in Canterbury, Winchester, Bath, St Peter's in Gloucester and St Werburgh's in Chester, were consciously settled in former Roman towns or, like St Augustine's in Canterbury and St Albans, lay just outside the Roman walls. Many other Benedictine houses were founded in open countryside, but subsequently tolerated, indeed encouraged, settlements of traders and artisans outside their gates. England had become a well-urbanised country when the friars arrived in the thirteenth century and, because their mission was directed towards both the new literate bourgeoisie and the disadvantaged urban poor, they were drawn towards the larger established towns. By contrast, the more austere reformed orders, like the Cistercians and Premonstratensians, shunned towns altogether, while the later Carthusian houses and some types of hospital tended to gravitate towards suburban locations.

Monastic interests in towns operated in various ways. Individual urban plots might be acquired as a trading base or a source of rent. Income might be granted from the profits of a borough or market on a benefactor's land. Monastic houses could themselves acquire rights to hold one or more markets or fairs on their own estates. The most profitable step was to acquire total control of a town, so that all income from borough rents, tolls from markets and fairs, and fines and amercements from courts went to the abbey. This encouraged some monasteries to attempt the creation of planned new towns on their estates, with varying degrees of success.

Urban properties

Many monastic houses found it advantageous to acquire premises in cities, major market centres and ports, initially in order to facilitate trading there, subsequently to lease out for revenue. It has been estimated that up to two-thirds of the properties in London and Southwark were held by religious corporations of various kinds. In the case of abbeys and priories within or near the city, this often formed part of their foundation endowment, or was acquired by gift or purchase very soon afterwards. The Augustinian canons of Holy Trinity in Aldgate held property in over 80 London parishes, which yielded an annual income of over £120 in 1291. The canons of St Mary Overy in Southwark drew 87 per cent of their gross temporal income from property in the capital in 1535, while the canons of St Bartholomew's in Smithfield also had extensive holdings there. In all, at least 17 Augustinian houses held miscellaneous properties of one kind or another in the capital. Despite their aversion to settling in towns, at least 25 Cistercian houses acquired properties in London, Westminster or Southwark, possessions of the more distant abbeys generally being relegated to the urban fringes; Netley, Beaulieu and Waverley had property in Southwark, Vale Royal in the Strand, Westminster and Islington.

Outside London, bases in the eastern coastal and river ports were particularly in demand because of the wool export and fishing trades. Monasteries all over the north of England, up to 180 miles away, held houses in Boston, while Norwich served an even wider range of religious houses in the Midlands and south. Properties in York and Lincoln were also held by many distant monasteries. To expedite the shipping of its wool to Flanders and Italy, Fountains Abbey acquired an extensive urban estate along the riverside in York, also property in Wormgate in Boston, still commemorated by the name 'Fountains Lane'. The monks also had holdings in Grimsby, Scarborough, Redcar and Yarm, which gave them access to the fish markets. St Alban's Abbey had a house in Yarmouth bought by Abbot William Trumpington, later extended in order to provide for the storage of herrings and other fish.

By contrast, the western ports of Exeter, Bristol and Chester, though of regional importance, rarely attracted monasteries beyond a 50-mile radius. In Bristol Margam Abbey had property within the castle bailey by 1153, and acquired further tenements in Smale Street and near St Augustine's cemetery. Margam sold some of its Bristol property in 1216, while the remainder was given to Tewkesbury Abbey in 1484-6 in exchange for Tewkesbury's tithe income from south Wales. Tintern had a house in the merchants' quarter in Redcliffe Street in 1242, and later acquired another tenement, a couple of shops and a plot of empty ground.

Important inland market towns also attracted monastic proprietors. In 1300 a quarter of all tenements in Oxford were owned by six monastic houses, the abbeys of Abingdon, Eynsham, Godstow and Oseney, the priory of St Frideswide and the hospital of St John. Domesday Book records 14 dwellings held there by Abingdon Abbey, eight of which were waste. Later records, the Hundred Rolls of 1279 and the White Book of the City of Oxford 70 years later, identify rents owed to Abingdon from about 25 tenements. Thanks to H.E. Salter's work on the property deeds, most of these can be located with some confidence, and their distribution is of particular interest. Concentrated in the western half of the walled city, they are conspicuously absent beyond the line of Catte Street and Oriel Street, which marked the original eastern defences of the ninth-century town (**82**). The only significant holdings of the abbey outside the earliest defences lie to the south, along the main road to Abingdon, in an area which was settled even before the defences were laid out. This may suggest that the basic pattern of Abingdon Abbey's urban estate in Oxford is of considerable antiquity. In 1008 Abingdon also acquired a property in Cricklade, the next defended borough upstream, which is commemorated in the name of Abingdon Court Farm.

In Cambridge Barnwell Priory was the most prominent owner. Elsewhere in the midlands, Burton Abbey had five houses in Stafford and three houses and two mills in Derby by the late eleventh century. During the fourteenth century Merevale Abbey acquired two houses and three shops in Leicester, six houses in Atherstone, four in Tamworth and one in Norwich. Many of the Welsh houses had property in Monmouth, Shrewsbury and Chester.

During the early Middle Ages properties had often been leased for token rents only. Shrewsbury Abbey, for example, received from various urban tenants a buck carcass, a pound of cummin, a pair of white gloves and a rose. Later on there was a general withdrawal from direct management and maintenance of shops and warehouses in favour of cash rents. It has been estimated that urban property provided about 12 per cent of the entire temporal income of all religious houses recorded in the *Valor Ecclesiasticus* of 1535.

Monastic inns

Many ancient inns are said to have been built by monks to accommodate pilgrims, but such claims do not always stand up to critical examination. Some monastic tenements did nevertheless incorporate taverns and provided rooms for travellers. Several of Abingdon Abbey's properties in Oxford at various times offered these services, including the Blue Boar, Ducklington's Inn, Red Lion Inn and Fleur-de-Luce, all in St Aldate's, the Swan-on-the-Hope in High Street and the Crown in Cornmarket (**82**). In the same city, Oseney Abbey acquired a house on Cornmarket fronted by five shops in 1337, immediately south of another block of tenements which it had owned since the twelfth century. This property was leased out by 1380 and subdivided, with Godstow Nunnery and St Frideswide's Priory holding the three shops at the southern end. The northern part had two chambers above two larger shops at the front, the shops flanking an entry to a courtyard, around which further chambers, a hall and brewhouse were arranged. The whole property was leased out as an

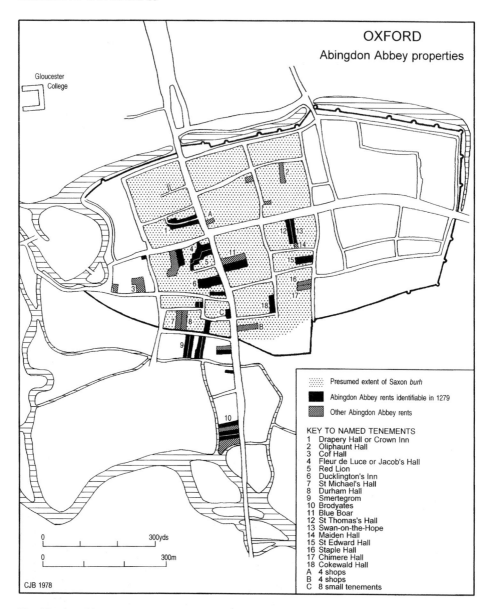

82 *Abingdon Abbey properties in Oxford: the concentration of tenements within the tenth-century* burh *and along St Aldate's to the south, and their absence from the later eastern extension to the walled city, are of interest*

inn named 'the Star' by 1406, and a rental of 1417 assigns the income to the abbey chamberlain. After rebuilding in 1457-8, records of further alterations carried out by the abbey in 1477-8 include the removal of parts of the older house, the making of new fireplaces in a chamber and in the kitchen, and the addition of a new solar.

Many such properties probably differed little from ordinary town houses and shops. From the later fourteenth century, however, some monasteries were investing in more distinctive purpose-built inns. St Peter's Abbey owned several in Gloucester, one of which, the New Inn, survives today (**83**). This is described in a rental of 1455 as recently erected by John Twyning, a monk of the abbey. It is a three-storey, timber-framed structure built around a courtyard. The ground floor of the front range incorporated a wide entry flanked by rooms used as shops. There was a kitchen in one angle of the court, and a rear gate leading through to a stable yard. Galleries run round all four sides of the courtyard at first-floor level, with a further second-floor gallery on one side. These gave access to a series of chambers, originally each about 20ft long by 12-15ft broad. With over 20 chambers to each of the upper floors and with several beds to each chamber, the whole inn could have held up to 200 guests.

The George & Pilgrim Inn at Glastonbury adopted a rather different layout. Here the accommodation was concentrated in the front block facing the street, which had an elaborate panelled stone facade of three storeys (**84**). The initials of Abbot John Selwood and the shield of King Edward IV which decorate the building point to a rebuilding date between 1461 and 1483, and by an agreement dated around 1473 new tenants bought the lease for the large sum of £7 6s 8d plus an annual rent of 12d, the income going to the abbey chamberlain. The Angel Inn at Grantham, once owned by the Knights Hospitallers,

83 *Gloucester: the galleried courtyard of the New Inn, erected by John Twyning, monk of St Peter's Abbey, shortly before 1455*

84 *The street front of the George & Pilgrim Inn at Glastonbury, rebuilt by Abbot Selwood after 1461*

also has an elaborate stone-built facade of similar date. The spandrels of the entrance arch to the George Inn at Winchcombe display the initials of Abbot Richard Kidderminster (1488-1527). The New Inn at Sherborne, built by Abbot Peter Ramsam around 1483, was, sadly, demolished in the middle of the nineteenth century.

The Carthusians of Hinton Charterhouse collected the wool from their Mendip estates at Norton St Philip, and acquired charters to hold markets and two annual fairs there. To accommodate visiting merchants and travellers and to provide storage for wool and cloth, the George Inn was built around 1375, facing the market-place (**colour plate 20**). Its rooms were contained within a single three-storey block, which may have lost a couple of bays from its south-eastern end. The street front was reconstructed in about 1500 with jettied timber-framed upper storeys, while the original rear and north-west gable-end walls are entirely stone-built. An arched doorway at the front gave access to a cross-passage with hall and parlour to the left and buttery and cellar to the right, with the original kitchen probably to the rear.

Monastic town houses in London

Monastic properties in London also included a number of tenements referred to as 'inns' *(hospitia)*, but these were somewhat different in character, resembling large town houses which could accommodate the abbot or his representatives when attending royal councils or visiting the capital on business. They also provided stabling, cartsheds, warehousing, and, sometimes, riverside quays for purchased goods awaiting transport, while some had chapels and gardens. About 40 examples of such 'inns' have been identified, the bulk of them belonging to Benedictine houses, the Cistercians owning up to seven examples, the Augustinians at least four, the Gilbertines one (**85**). Some town houses passed from one monastery to another, Battle Abbey acquiring the prior of Merton's house in Southwark around the end of the twelfth century. The acquisition of such properties by monasteries can be traced from the middle of the twelfth century, gaining further momentum during the fourteenth and fifteenth centuries as more heads of religious houses received regular summonses to Parliament.

The main concentrations of monastic town houses lay in the western suburbs outside Ludgate and Newgate. The Fleet valley became a favoured location because of the availability of wharves and newly-reclaimed land. The abbot of Faversham was the first to acquire a plot west of the Fleet River, in 1147, later enlarging it by purchasing more land from the Knights Templars. A neighbouring tenement in Bride Lane was bequeathed to Tewkesbury Abbey in 1314-15. The prior of Ogbourne, who administered the London properties of the Norman abbey of Bec, built a house lower downstream on the east bank, but dwindling funds forced him to sell this valuable site in 1352. Walter de Wickewane, abbot of Winchcombe (1282-1314), acquired a house on the south side of Fleet Street, near Fleet Wharf. A little further west, on the opposite side of Fleet Street, the abbot of Cirencester had taken over a property called the Popingay (the name is preserved in Poppins Court) before 1216. Further upriver in Westminster, Abingdon Abbey's property is commemorated by Abingdon Street, south of the Houses of Parliament.

To the north, between Newgate and West Smithfield, sites in Cock Lane were acquired by the abbot of Leicester before 1201, and by Glastonbury Abbey in 1426-67. The master of Sempringham acquired a site nearby in Cow Lane (now Smithfield Street) from St Bartholomew's Hospital in 1212-13. In 1377 a fishmonger living in the parish of St Sepulchre outside Newgate bequeathed to Burton Abbey his house called 'Baconsyne', subject to the life interest of his widow; the abbey had entered into possession by 1394 and used it as its town house until the Dissolution. Further out on the southern side of Holborn was the abbot of Malmesbury's house, purchased in 1364. Early in the thirteenth century the abbot of Walden bought land outside Aldersgate to build an inn with its own chapel.

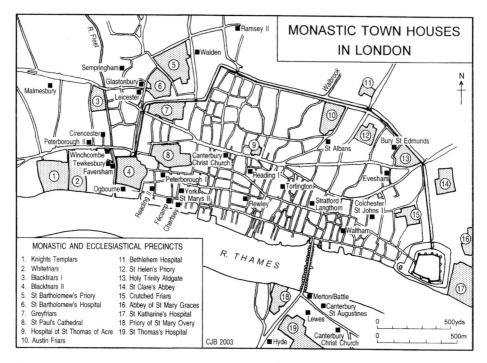

MONASTIC TOWN HOUSES IN LONDON

MONASTIC AND ECCLESIASTICAL PRECINCTS

1. Knights Templars
2. Whitefriars
3. Blackfriars I
4. Blackfriars II
5. St Bartholomew's Priory
6. St Bartholomew's Hospital
7. Greyfriars
8. St Paul's Cathedral
9. Hospital of St Thomas of Acre
10. Austin Friars
11. Bethlehem Hospital
12. St Helen's Priory
13. Holy Trinity Aldgate
14. St Clare's Abbey
15. Crutched Friars
16. Abbey of St Mary Graces
17. St Katharine's Hospital
18. Priory of St Mary Overy
19. St Thomas's Hospital

CJB 2003

85 *Location of monastic town houses and ecclesiastical precincts in London and Southwark*

Inside the walls the abbot of Bury St Edmunds had acquired a property near Bevis Marks before 1156, separated from Holy Trinity Priory, Aldgate, by a lane still called Bury Street today. Walter de Gaunt, abbot of Waltham (1177-1201), accumulated sufficient property south of the church of St Mary at Hill in Billingsgate to begin building an inn there, which included a chapel, gatehouse, great hall, dormitory, kitchen, stable and other domestic offices arranged around a courtyard. Matthew Paris records how William Trumpington, abbot of St Albans (1214-35), bought a house 'as large as a palace' in Old Broad Street, with a chapel, several bedrooms, kitchen, courtyard, stables, garden, orchard and well for his own use, also rents from several adjoining properties. His successor, John Hertford, acquired further 'dilapidated houses' next door which he pulled down and replaced with 'some noble new houses' which he proceeded to let at an increased rent. Dieulacresse Abbey was granted land in London by Everard the Goldsmith in the 1240s, retaining a tenement in Wood Street as its town house and selling the rest. The abbot of Chertsey acquired a property below Thames Street in 1296 with its own wharf. The abbot of Fécamp's inn nearby was confiscated by the Crown in 1346. William of Over, abbot of Croxden (1297-1308), bought a house in the parish of St Peter the Less near Baynards Castle. A mansion in St Swithin's Lane built by the mayor Henry FitzAylwin was left by his grandson to the small Augustinian priory of Tortington in 1286. The abbot of Stratford Langthorn acquired a house on Eastcheap in 1343. Evesham Abbey received a bequest of five houses in 1366, and Stow's survey of 1603 mentions the abbot's 'fair house with diverse tenements adjoining' on the south side of Leadenhall Street.

Another half-dozen monasteries had inns or houses across the Thames in Southwark. By contrast, the less salubrious east end was avoided, and at least five monastic town houses within the walls were later replaced by superior acquisitions further west. The abbot of Ramsey bought a stone house with a cellar off Lime Street in the early twelfth century, but before 1287 had moved outside the walls beyond Cripplegate. The abbot of Reading originally acquired a house in Cheapside, but around 1327 moved to a site near the church of St Andrew by the Wardrobe. The abbot of St Mary's, York, owned a house in the parish of St Dunstan-in-the-East by 1421, but within 30 years had relinquished this in favour of a site south of St Paul's Cathedral. The abbot of Peterborough's first inn was off Carter Lane near the cathedral, but around 1420 he moved outside the walls to the north side of Fleet Street. The abbot of Colchester had land in Mincing Lane before 1230, but his town house there was soon leased out, and by 1277 he had acquired a second property in Castle Baynard ward, though he was again using the Mincing Lane site in the 1390s.

Almost from the outset, parts of each property were rented out. Ringed Hall in the parish of St Michael Paternoster Royal, given to Rewley Abbey by Edmund, Earl of Cornwall, in 1282, was soon being leased to tenants. By the end of the fourteenth century the whole of Faversham Abbey's inn was out on lease for a term of 40 years. The abbot of Cirencester's inn accommodated ten paying guests in the fifteenth century. Several became taverns before the Dissolution; the abbot of Colchester's inn in Mincing Lane became the Bell, the inn of the prior of Lewes in Tooley Street, Southwark, became the Walnut Tree, and part of the abbot of Hyde's town house, also in Southwark, famously became the Tabard Inn of Chaucer's pilgrims. When the abbot of Winchcombe leased out his town house, however, he made the proviso that he or his representative could requisition the lower hall, certain chambers and the stables whenever necessary.

Markets

Trade in the early Middle Ages operated at several different levels. English monasteries were involved in international trade, importing luxury items like gold, wine and spices, and exporting wool. They were also involved in nation-wide trading of necessities with localised production, such as salt and lead, regional trading in corn, cattle and fish, and local trading in more perishable commodities such as eggs, vegetables and fruit. Before the tenth century, commerce was generally unregulated, being conducted by wandering pedlars, but thereafter the law codes of Edward the Elder and Athelstan attempted to channel it through designated market centres where trading standards could be enforced. The acquisition of a market, where provisions and other items of regional and local trade could be bought and sold, was a vital step in urban development, and every successful town held markets on at least one day every week.

During the Middle Ages markets were authorised or held in about 2,170 different places in England and Wales. Some 333 of those markets were initiated or acquired by monastic houses (**86**). Houses of English Benedictine monks possessed markets in over 150 places, another 15 were held by nunneries, while Benedictine houses in Normandy added another dozen to the total. The Cistercians and Augustinians each took income from over 50 markets, but none of the other orders held more than a dozen. Occasionally the grant was only partial; in 1283, for example, John de Vescy gave the Cistercians of Rufford half the profits from his market at Rotherham, before granting them the whole market ten years later.

The Benedictine monks of Canterbury Cathedral Priory held markets in 11 different places, quite apart from those held by the archbishop. In Kent they claimed prescriptive markets at St Mary Cray in 1278-9 and at Westwell in 1312, and acquired charters for markets at Orpington in 1206, Appledore in

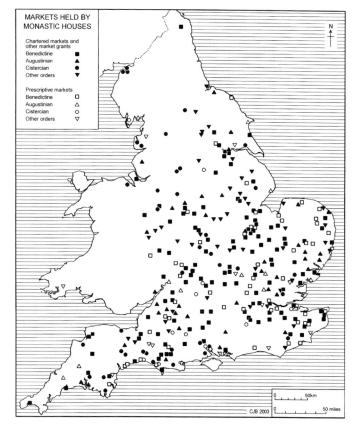

86 *Distribution of markets held by monastic houses in England and Wales*

1358 and Godmersham in 1364. A further charter of 1447 granted them markets at Great Chart, Eastry, Hollingbourne, Meopham and Monkton, while in Surrey they had a chartered market at Merstham, granted in 1338. According to Domesday Book, Bury St Edmunds Abbey had the market in the town of Bury and also took three-quarters of the income from the market of Beccles, the king taking the remainder. By the end of the thirteenth century Bury had five more markets in Suffolk, and others in Norfolk and Essex. Westminster had five markets in the Home Counties and three more scattered across the south Midlands. Of the other wealthy Benedictine abbeys, Glastonbury, St Albans, Peterborough and Ramsey each had markets in half a dozen different places. Even the greatest houses of other orders rarely had more than a couple of markets each.

In the early Middle Ages the best opportunity for barter and exchange occurred when lay people assembled for worship. Many informal prescriptive markets therefore took place in churchyards on Sundays. By the early thirteenth century, the church authorities were attempting to curb the practice of Sunday trading, while the king's lawyers were insisting that markets should be held only under royal licence. Neither change was enforced with complete success, but many Sunday markets were moved to other days and there was a rapid increase in new chartered markets. In 1202 Peterborough Abbey's Sunday market at Oundle was changed to Saturday, while Reading Abbey's Sunday market at Thatcham was moved to Thursdays in 1218. The Abbot of Westminster's Sunday market at Staines was changed to Friday before 1294. Whitby Abbey was still holding a Sunday market as late as 1445, when it was finally changed to Saturday.

Several factors influenced the distribution of markets, some tending to limit, others to increase their spacing (**87**). Customers expected to travel to market on foot and return home the same day, while itinerant traders wished to be able to travel from one market to another on successive days. On the other hand, lords who derived profits from markets wanted a monopoly within as wide a territory as possible and did their best to fend off competitors within their own hinterlands. The thirteenth-century lawyer Henry Bracton wrote that it was not legal to set up a new market within 6⅔ miles of a pre-existing market held on the same day, this distance being reckoned as one-third of a normal day's journey of 20 miles. One-third of the day was thus available for travelling to market, one-third for transacting business there, and one-third for returning home.

Many conflicts arose out of attempts to establish new markets within the hinterland of existing ones. In 1227 the burgesses of Huntingdon objected to competition from the abbot of Ramsey's new market at St Ives and, though the abbot of Thorney's market at Yaxley was 15 miles away, he also complained that many shipmasters were preferring to travel up the River Ouse to dock at St Ives rather than up the River Nene to Yaxley. Occasionally, objections were

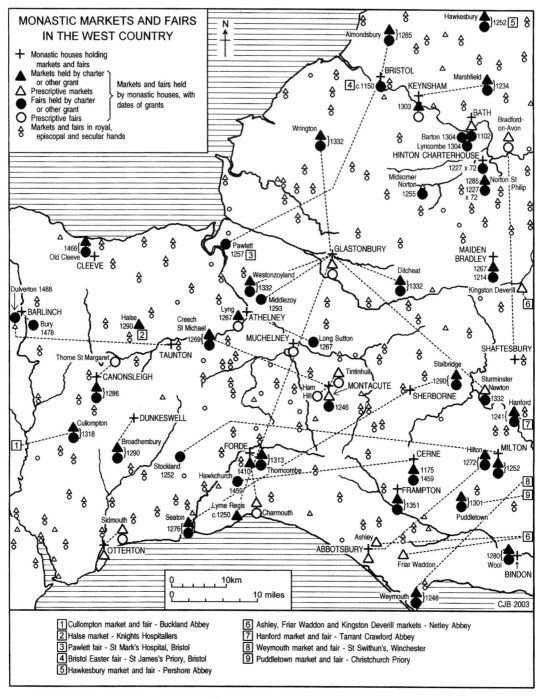

MONASTIC MARKETS AND FAIRS IN THE WEST COUNTRY

N

Legend:
+ Monastic houses holding markets and fairs
▲ Markets held by charter or other grant ⎫
△ Prescriptive markets ⎬ Markets and fairs held by monastic houses, with dates of grants
● Fairs held by charter or other grant ⎭
○ Prescriptive fairs
⌂ Markets and fairs in royal, episcopal and secular hands

Hawkesbury ⎱1252 [5]
Almondsbury ▲}1285
BRISTOL
[4] c.1150
KEYNSHAM
Marshfield ▲}1234
1303
BATH
Barton 1304
Lyncombe 1304 }1102
Bradford-on-Avon
HINTON CHARTERHOUSE
1227 x 72
Wrington ▲}1332
Midsomer Norton 1255
1285 }1227 x 72 Norton St Philip
MAIDEN BRADLEY
1267 1214
Kingston Deverill [6]
Old Cleeve 1466{
CLEEVE
Pawlett 1257 [3]
GLASTONBURY
Westonzoyland }1332
Ditcheat ●}1332
Dulverton 1488
BARLINCH
Bury 1478
Halse 1290 [2]
Creech St Michael
Middlezoy 1293
Lyng 1267 ATHELNEY }1269
MUCHELNEY
Long Sutton 1267
SHAFTESBURY
Thorne St Margaret
TAUNTON
Tintinhull
Stalbridge }1290
Sturminster Newton }1332
Hanford 1241{ [7]
CANONSLEIGH }1286
Ham Hill MONTACUTE
SHERBORNE
1246
DUNKESWELL
Cullompton }1318
Broadhembury }1290
Stockland 1252
Hawkchurch
FORDE
1410{ }1313 Thorncombe
1459{
CERNE
1175 1459
Hilton 1272{
MILTON }1252
[8]
[9]
FRAMPTON }1351
}1301 Puddletown
[1]
Lyme Regis c.1250
Charmouth
Sidmouth
Seaton 1276{
OTTERTON
Ashley
ABBOTSBURY
Friar Waddon
[6]
1280{ Wool
BINDON
Weymouth ●}1248

0   10km
0   10 miles

CJB 2003

[1] Cullompton market and fair - Buckland Abbey
[2] Halse market - Knights Hospitallers
[3] Pawlett fair - St Mark's Hospital, Bristol
[4] Bristol Easter fair - St James's Priory, Bristol
[5] Hawkesbury market and fair - Pershore Abbey
[6] Ashley, Friar Waddon and Kingston Deverill markets - Netley Abbey
[7] Hanford market and fair - Tarrant Crawford Abbey
[8] Weymouth market and fair - St Swithun's, Winchester
[9] Puddletown market and fair - Christchurch Priory

87 *Markets and fairs held by monastic houses in the West Country, set against the total distribution of markets and fairs held by other proprietors*

upheld. The prior of Grove's complaint that traders had been drawn away from his market at Leighton Buzzard by the prior of Snelshall's market set up in 1230 at Mursley, 7 miles away, resulted in the latter's suppression. Ramsey Abbey agreed to give up its market at Barnwell in 1282, following allegations that it was damaging Peterborough Abbey's market at Oundle. The abbot of Furness, however, was unable to secure the suppression of a new market at Ulverston in 1280, although this was within 5 miles of his own at Dalton-in-Furness.

Even ancient and well-established towns feared competition from new markets. The burgesses of Hereford unsuccessfully opposed the abbot of Reading's market at Leominster in 1230. When the abbot of Keynsham applied for a weekly Tuesday market on his manor of Marshfield in 1234, objections raised by the burgesses of Bristol led to its refusal (though one of his successors tried again in 1265 and this time it was unopposed). In 1318 the burgesses of Colchester complained that their trade was damaged by a market at Salcott set up by the abbess of Barking in 1221.

The chronicle of Jocelin of Brakelond records a very unseemly squabble between the Benedictine houses of Ely and Bury St Edmunds in 1201, when the prior of Ely acquired a charter for a new market at Lakenheath. Although this was 16 miles away from Bury St Edmunds, Abbot Sampson decided that it was damaging his market at Bury, and he persuaded the king to suppress it. He also decided to take the enforcement of that decision into his own hands, sending his bailiffs to Lakenheath with 600 armed thugs by dead of night with orders to carry off in chains any buyers or sellers they found there the following morning. Someone gave a warning and those attending the market fled, so the abbot's men contented themselves by smashing up the butchers' shambles and driving away the cattle and other livestock. Despite this setback, Ely secured a new charter for a Wednesday market at Lakenheath in 1309.

Occasionally, conflicts were resolved by moving markets to alternative sites. In 1227 Henry III had granted the Knights Templars the right to hold a market at Walshford, but in 1240 this was replaced by a new market at Wetherby, only for that to provoke opposition in its turn two years later on the grounds that it competed unfairly with the market at Harewood.

Market-places

Markets needed space, and the location, shape and size of market-places provide clues to their origins and function. Livestock markets generally needed more room than provisions markets. Triangular or wedge-shaped market-places immediately outside the abbey gate are particularly characteristic of towns fostered by monasteries before the Norman Conquest (**88**, **89**, **90**), while rectangular market places or single broad main streets are often an intrinsic component of new towns planned after the Conquest. Some markets

88 *Peterborough (Northamptonshire): the pre-Conquest market-place outside the abbey gate*

89 *Abingdon (Berkshire): the market-place; Edward the Confessor granted market rights to the abbey, and Domesday Book records ten traders dwelling outside the Abbey gate*

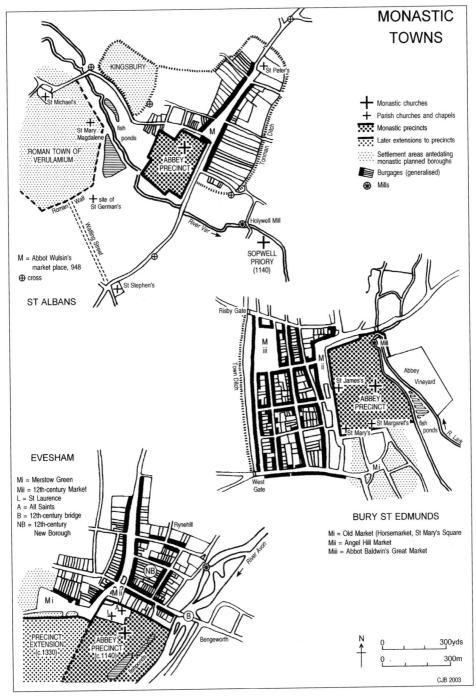

MONASTIC
TOWNS

KINGSBURY

St Michael's

St Mary
Magdalene   fish
             ponds

ROMAN TOWN OF
VERULAMIUM

St Peter's

Watling Street

Roman Wall

site of
St German's

River Ver →

Holywell Mill

M = Abbot Wulsin's
    market place, 948
⊕ = cross

St Stephen's

ST ALBANS

M

ABBEY
PRECINCT

Torman Ditch

SOPWELL
PRIORY
(1140)

✝ Monastic churches
✝ Parish churches and chapels
▦ Monastic precincts
⋯ Later extensions to precincts
⋯ Settlement areas antedating
   monastic planned boroughs
▦ Burgages (generalised)
✺ Mills

Risby Gate

Town Ditch

M
iii

M
ii

St James's

ABBEY
PRECINCT

St Mary's

St Margaret's   fish
                 ponds

Mill

Abbey
Vineyard

R Lark

M i

West
Gate

BURY ST EDMUNDS

EVESHAM

Mi = Merstow Green
Mii = 12th-century Market
L = St Laurence
A = All Saints
B = 12th-century bridge
NB = 12th-century
     New Borough

Rynehill

River Avon

NB

M ii

Mi

A
L

PRECINCT
EXTENSION
(c.1330)

ABBEY
PRECINCT
(c.1140)

B

Bengeworth

Mi = Old Market (Horsemarket, St Mary's Square
Mii = Angel Hill Market
Miii = Abbot Baldwin's Great Market

N

0   300yds
0   300m

CJB 2003

90 *Towns at abbey gates, comparative plans:* (a) *St Albans (Hertfordshire);* (b) *Bury St Edmunds (Suffolk);*
(c) *Evesham (Worcestershire)*

made opportunistic use of a space already in existence, a meeting-place of roads, or a former village green, while in other cases, market places were added to the margins of a pre-existing settlement.

Occasionally a new market-place was imposed over an older settlement by clearing a previously-occupied area. When Bishop Herbert de Losinga of Thetford decided to relocate his see in 1095 by founding a new Benedictine cathedral priory within the town of Norwich, he followed this up by laying out the large rectangular market-place called Tombland just outside its west gate. A number of dwellings and what was then the city's principal church, St Michael's, had to be removed to make way for this new open space.

Some towns, like Norwich, had more than one market-place, which may reflect different proprietorship, or sales of different commodities. The lordship of Coventry was divided between the Benedictine priory and the earls of Chester, and the main market area lay under their joint jurisdiction until about 1230, when the prior won complete control. In 1203 the prior was permitted to move his main general market, presumably to the central market-place of Cross Cheaping, but in 1355 he retained the right to hold cattle and timber markets on Fridays as of old in Bishop Street and Cook Street in the northern part of the city. Kings Lynn has two market-places. The original Saturday market and the adjoining church of St Margaret, both founded by Bishop Herbert de Losinga, were given by him to the monks of Norwich. As the town prospered, adjoining areas of marsh were reclaimed, and a second church and Tuesday market were established, but these were kept in hand by later bishops. At Malmesbury, there is a small market-place with an elaborate late medieval cross just outside the abbey cemetery, and the remains of a much larger market-place in the extra-mural suburb of Westover, part of which retains the name Horse Fair. There is also a big rectangular open space now known as Cross Hayes, which has clearly been created by curtailing the burgage tenements on the eastern side of the High Street. The origins of this intrusive element in the town plan may date from an order in 1223 that the Saturday market, previously held partly in the cemetery and partly outside it, should henceforth take place in the 'Newmarket'.

Shops and market stalls

Monastic ownership of shops, stalls and booths was common. Strata Marcella Abbey owned three shops in the market-place of Shrewsbury by 1225. Vale Royal Abbey owned at least 13 shops in Chester in 1299, most of them apparently occupied by cobblers. A bequest to Evesham Abbey in 1366 included 36 shops off Leadenhall Street in London. Rewley Abbey owned 23 shops in Coventry in 1376. Many urban tenements incorporated arched openings for shops at street level, with undercrofts for storage and domestic rooms behind or above. Shop rows were a distinctive form particularly favoured by monastic

91 *Tewkesbury (Gloucestershire): a fifteenth-century shop row on the edge of the abbey precinct in Church Street*

corporations seeking profits from leasing. A good example survives in Tewkesbury; a speculation built by the abbey in the middle of the fifteenth century comprises a terrace of 23 dwellings with ground-floor shops along the street front (**91**).

Margam Abbey had a stall in Bristol's market and two more stalls in the Goldsmith's Place by St Nicholas' Gate. Market stalls were initially temporary structures, dismantled at the end of each market day. Sometimes, however, they became permanent encroachments, ultimately developing into shops and dwellings. In many places this process was actively encouraged by the town's proprietors because of the extra income which could be extracted; in 1185 the Knights Templars themselves owned a stall in their market-place at Baldock, while tenants paid rent to them for six others. By contrast, the monks of Bury St Edmunds were complaining in 1192 that the burgesses had raised numerous shops, booths and stalls in the market-place without their consent, and that none of the profits came to the abbey because the borough paid only a fixed sum of £40. Objections were also sometimes raised because of the obstruction to traffic. In 1407, Thomas Clive, abbot of Keynsham, was accused of making 'an encroachment in the town of Marshfield by setting up three shops with solars and cellars above and below in the king's highway without licence...to the nuisance of the king and his people. They are worth 6s 4d yearly, and the abbot has taken all the issues since they were set up'. Such encroachments can readily be recognised within the town plan.

Fairs

Whereas markets served for the sale and purchase of locally-produced goods and took place one day a week, fairs took place once a year, lasted for several consecutive days (or longer), and provided an opportunity for the purchase of more exotic goods. They attracted traders and purchasers from a much wider catchment area. Several of England's major international fairs, including St Ives, Westminster and Bury St Edmunds, belonged to Benedictine abbeys. There were also many lesser fairs in England and Wales, at least 400 of which were held by monastic houses (**87**). Some fairs developed special functions, selling horses, sheep, geese, cheese or fish. Although some fairs took place as early as March, the majority fell in the second half of the year, particularly just before, during and after the main harvest. Most of the October or November fairs were held by northern abbeys, in country where the harvest itself was likely to be late.

Many fairs were established by royal grants during the twelfth and thirteenth centuries, though some charters simply endorsed more ancient customary gatherings. Most fairs were held in towns or villages. The abbot of Ramsey's Easter fair at St Ives, established by a charter of 1110, was of international importance by the early thirteenth century, and temporary stalls were erected all along the main street of the town. Others took place outside the town or in open countryside. For six days every September the precentor of Glastonbury held a prescriptive fair in the fields below the Tor, where the name 'Cinnamon Lane' commemorates the exotic goods sold there. London's St Bartholomew's Fair was held in a field between the priory church and Long Lane, where it is commemorated by the street-name 'Cloth Fair'. In 1250 there was an abortive attempt to remove Westminster Abbey's fair from the churchyard out to Tothill. Sempringham Priory revived an ancient fair at Stow Green, the site of a long-abandoned seventh-century nunnery 2 miles to the north. The monks of St Augustine's, Canterbury, were granted rights to hold a fair by their grange at Salmestone in 1225. Tavistock Abbey established an annual fair by its isolated hilltop church of Brentor in 1232 (**92**). Peterborough Abbey acquired the right to hold a fair at Oxney on the edge of the fens in 1249. Waltham Abbey had a chartered fair on Epping Heath from 1253. The nuns of St Mary's, Winchester, had a fair by the Wansdyke on Tan Hill in All Cannings. Montacute Priory claimed the right to hold fairs at St Michael's Chapel on the hill above the town and within the Iron Age fort on Ham Hill, while the nuns of Amesbury held a fair within the ramparts of Danebury hill fort in the later Middle Ages.

During the fourteenth century international trade was disrupted by war and plague, and many of the great fairs went into decline, Ramsey Abbey's fair at St Ives being among the casualties.

92 *Brentor (Devon): John of Rochester, abbot of Tavistock, acquired a charter permitting him to hold an annual three-day Michaelmas fair alongside the isolated church in 1232. The fair was still valued at 6s 8d in 1535*

Monastic boroughs

Another important step in town development was the acquisition of borough status, which conveyed upon the urban community certain exemptions from manorial control as well as rights to govern itself. Over 600 medieval boroughs have been identified in England, of which about 75 were either created or inherited by monastic institutions (**93**). Benedictine houses had interests in about 40 boroughs, Augustinian houses in another dozen, while three boroughs were held by Cluniac priories. Some of these were ancient settlements adjoining monastic precincts, some were planned new towns or promoted villages on outlying estates. About nine boroughs were established or held by the Cistercians, another couple by the Premonstratensians, all at some distance from their respective abbeys.

Borough privileges varied considerably. Even at the bottom end of the scale, burgage tenure conveyed exemption from agricultural services and the right to buy, sell or bequeath tenements freely so that investment in property was a potential source of profit. The usual course of borough development during the Middle Ages was for urban communities to gain increasing independence from their founders. Although monastic lords welcomed the increased profits

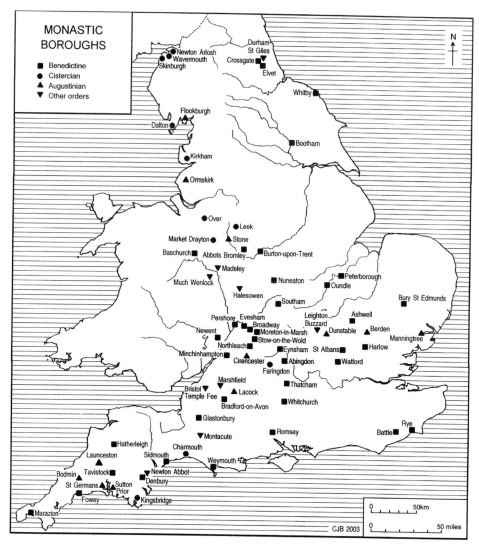

93 *Boroughs founded or acquired by monastic houses in England and Wales*

from burgage rents, tolls and courts which often derived from boroughs, they often tried to hinder moves towards self-government, opposing the setting up of separate town officials, borough courts and merchant guilds. As trade developed, their retention of all commercial tolls often became a particular grievance. The Augustinian abbey of Cirencester was founded within a pre-existing borough and market centre, but in 1190 the abbot purchased from King Richard I the entire manor and town. The abbey received huge profits as the Cotswold wool trade flourished during the thirteenth century, and its clinging control over the town's commerce was deeply resented by local merchants.

On several occasions, grievances broke out into open conflict. Several abbeys suffered violent assaults by townspeople, such as Bury St Edmunds in 1264, St Albans in 1324 and again during Wat Tyler's rebellion in 1381, and Winchcombe in 1360. Two merchants of Abingdon organised an attack upon the abbey's fair in 1295, which they claimed was disrupting their own trade; the abbey fair was disrupted again in 1315, and finally in 1327 when rioting townsfolk burst into the abbey precinct, drove out the monks and looted everything of value they could find. In 1437 a dispute over the position of the parochial font at Sherborne inflamed long-smouldering resentments, and during the ensuing riot the priest of All Hallows, the parish church, shot a burning arrow into part of the abbey roof which was temporarily thatched while rebuilding was taking place, so that the lead and bells melted and the monastic church was ruined. Abbot Bradford compelled the townspeople to contribute to the costs of the splendid fan-vaulted roof which completed the rebuilding.

Monastic town plans before the Norman Conquest

The first generation of towns actually created by monasteries were trading settlements which grew up outside abbey gates during the tenth or eleventh century. Despite the Benedictine aspirations towards self-sufficiency, there were obvious advantages in having traders and craftsmen dwelling close by, to offer goods and services which the monks could not readily provide for themselves. It would be wrong to regard such towns as wholly spontaneous or organic developments, since they can hardly have grown without the support of the monastic community; there is usually little evidence for deliberate planning, however, apart from the designation of an open space for markets. Market-places developed outside monastic gates in many places, including Tavistock, Glastonbury, Romsey, Eynsham, Ely, Peterborough, Evesham, Chester and Hexham (**88, 90c, 94c**).

Matthew Paris, writing in the thirteenth century, attributed the foundation of the town of St Albans to Abbot Wulsin, who acquired the right to hold a market in 948 and laid out the large triangular market-place to the north of the main gate. Wulsin was also said to have built houses there at his own expense, assisting the new settlers with cash and materials, and to have founded three churches at each of the entrances to the town. The market-place at Coventry was probably laid out by Abbot Leofric shortly before the Norman Conquest. Abingdon Abbey's chronicle records the granting of market rights by Edward the Confessor, and the Domesday survey lists ten traders dwelling outside the abbey gate (**89**). It is a conspicuous feature of Abingdon's town plan that the eleventh-century market-place and the roads feeding into it are clearly superimposed over an older pattern of routes aligned upon the more ancient minster church of St Helen at the southern end of the town.

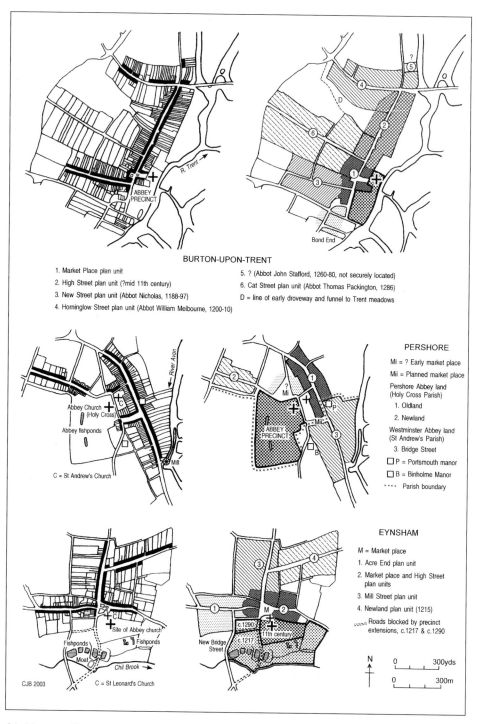

BURTON-UPON-TRENT

1. Market Place plan unit
2. High Street plan unit (?mid 11th century)
3. New Street plan unit (Abbot Nicholas, 1188-97)
4. Horninglow Street plan unit (Abbot William Melbourne, 1200-10)

5. ? (Abbot John Stafford, 1260-80, not securely located)
6. Cat Street plan unit (Abbot Thomas Packington, 1286)
D = line of early droveway and funnel to Trent meadows

PERSHORE

Mi = ? Early market place
Mii = Planned market place
Pershore Abbey land
(Holy Cross Parish)
1. Oldland
2. Newland
Westminster Abbey land
(St Andrew's Parish)
3. Bridge Street
□ P = Portsmouth manor
□ B = Binholme Manor
···· Parish boundary

EYNSHAM

M = Market place
1. Acre End plan unit
2. Market place and High Street plan units
3. Mill Street plan unit
4. Newland plan unit (1215)
····· Roads blocked by precinct extensions, c.1217 & c.1290

N   0   300yds
     0   300m

CJB 2003

94 *Towns at abbey gates, comparative plans: (a) Burton-upon-Trent (Staffordshire) (after Terry Slater, 1996); (b) Pershore (Worcestershire); (c) Eynsham (Oxfordshire)*

Monastic town planning after the Norman Conquest

Monastic houses founded after the Norman Conquest sometimes generated urban growth outside their gates just as their Anglo-Saxon predecessors had done. Soon after his foundation of Battle Abbey, William the Conqueror granted the monks a Sunday market. The abbey chronicle, written a little over a century later, describes what happened next:

> 'A goodly number of men were brought hither out of neighbouring counties, some even from foreign countries. And to each of these the brethren who managed the building allotted a dwelling-place of certain dimensions around the circuit of the abbey; and these still remain as they were apportioned, with their customary rent or service'.

The chronicler goes on to list 115 houses, 65 on one side of the main street leading north from the abbey gate, 21 on the other side, five houses on the east side of St Mary's Church (itself founded between 1107 and 1124 on the town's south-eastern limits), ten more beyond the church, and another 14 facing the church. The standard rent was 7d per house. There were two guildhalls, and the occupants of the town included four shoemakers, three cooks, two bakers, two carpenters, two secretaries, a weaver, a goldsmith and a bell-caster.

Post-Conquest developments of this type were generally on a smaller scale than the towns which had developed outside the greater Anglo-Saxon abbeys. An example is Keynsham, where the Victorine canons acquired rights to hold a market and three-day August fair in 1303. A new triangular market-place was then created outside the south-west corner of the precinct and, probably at the same time, part of the precinct was itself sacrificed to accommodate new burgage plots.

A few planned towns created by monasteries after the Conquest were laid out on a more ambitious scale, using a grid plan. Bury St Edmunds still has the vestiges of its original Anglo-Saxon market-place outside the south gate of the precinct, in the area now called St Mary's Square, with further space available on Angel Hill outside the north-western gate. The Domesday Book records how the town had doubled in value as a result of its considerable enlargement since the Conquest:

> 'The town is now contained within a greater perimeter, including land which used to be ploughed and sown before the Conquest...Whereon are now 30 priests, deacons and clerks together, and 28 nuns and poor people, who pray daily for the king and for all Christian souls...there are 75 bakers, brewers, tailors, washerwomen, shoemakers, robemakers, cooks, porters and bursars...In addition, there are 13 reeves in charge of the abbey estates, who have their houses in the same town...There are

> 34 knights, both English and French...Now altogether there are 342 houses on the demesne of the church of St Edmund which was all under the plough in the time of King Edward the Confessor . . .'

In effect, Abbot Baldwin (1065-97) had laid out an entirely new town over part of the old West Field, with a large new rectangular market-place in the north-west corner, decently removed from the immediate proximity of the abbey. The nucleus of the plan was developed from two straight streets crossing each other at right angles, one, Churchgate Street, leading westwards out of the main abbey gate, the other, Whiting Street, leading north to the market place. Three more streets were then laid out rather more roughly in a north-south alignment and three more in an east-west alignment, one of which entered the market-place at its south-east corner. Though lacking extreme regularity, the level of planning is very evident (**90b**).

The town of Evesham also falls into two very distinct topographical components. The abbey's chronicle attributes its acquisition of a market to a grant of Edward the Confessor in 1055. Outside the main west gate of the precinct is a large open space known as Merstow Green, which almost certainly represents the mid-eleventh-century market-place. Another part of the town is named in the late twelfth-century cartulary as the 'new borough', and this is almost certainly represented by a slightly irregular but nevertheless unmistakeably planned grid of streets north of the abbey precinct (**90c**). A new gate was opened through the precinct wall on this side by Abbot Reginald (1130-49) and he was probably responsible for laying out the new market-place outside it. The main north-south axis, probably itself a much older road, part of an ancient ridgeway coming down to the Avon from the Redditch area, is named as High Street in the early thirteenth century, and other streets within the grid are all recorded by name by the fourteenth century. The Merstow Green market-place was reduced in importance by the creation of the new borough, and probably reduced in size in the early fourteenth century when Abbot William Chiriton extended the precinct wall directly westwards to the river. Evidence of the dual origin of the town survives today, in the curious spectacle of two churches sharing the same churchyard, as mentioned in chapter 12 (**66**).

Several smaller monastic towns have strongly rectilinear plans, including Lacock, where Abbess Ela acquired the right to a market and fair in 1257, and Shipston-on-Stour, where the prior of Worcester received a market and fair charter in 1268. Shipston lay on an outlying monastic estate, where the pre-urban nucleus was not a monastic precinct, but an earlier village, the memory of which is preserved in the name Husbandmans End (**95a**).

The abbey of Burton-on-Trent was founded in 1002-4 alongside an existing village now known as Bond End. By the mid-eleventh century, a borough was established, and Terry Slater has shown that the town then expanded through four more phases, each of which can still be recognised in the plan. Abbot Nicholas (1187-97) began by laying out New Street, running westwards from the abbey precinct. A charter of his successor, William Melbourne (1200-1213), recorded that the king had given him leave to extend the borough by laying out new burgages 24 perches by 4 perches (396ft by 66ft) along Horninglow Street from the Great Bridge to the New Bridge, with all appropriate liberties (the perch, a standard dimension based upon the width of a medieval plough-strip, was commonly used in the planning of new tenements over former open fields). Abbot John Stafford (1260-81) then 'made a borough' of certain outlying districts of the town, widening the road to Wetmoor. Finally Abbot Thomas Packington laid out yet another burghal extension on either side of Cat Street in 1286 as part of a famine relief scheme. This last addition may never have been fully occupied, and much of it was vacated when the town declined in the later fourteenth century (**94a**).

Even in small towns, analysis of the plan may reveal complex phases of development. The market-place outside the former abbey gate at Eynsham still forms the centre of the town, but the street to the west, Acre End Street, probably represents an earlier agricultural settlement. Mill Street, to the north, has a uniform block of tenements with a back lane on its western side, and was clearly developed later. Finally, in 1215, the abbot acquired a charter permitting him to lay out 80 equal-sized plots of a quarter of an acre each on his own demesne land to the north-east of the old town, to be rented at one shilling a year. This extension to the old borough, called Newland, was not an especially successful venture, since even by 1366 only 31 houses had been built there, and some tenements were developed on amalgamated plots of half an acre or more (**94c**). Further thirteenth-century alterations to the town plan on the southern side were described in chapter 11. A similar 'Newland' extension was added by Coventry Priory to its small town of Southam.

Towns under divided proprietorship

The division of Pershore Abbey's estate by Edward the Confessor had given half the town of Pershore to Westminster Abbey, thereby splitting it into two parishes. Domesday Book records 28 burgesses rendering 30s and tolls amounting to 12s on Westminster Abbey's portion, but there is no documentary evidence for any equivalent urban growth on Pershore's portion before the late twelfth century when Henry II granted the local abbey privileges similar to those claimed by Westminster. On the north side of the abbey precinct there are nevertheless signs of a former triangular market space similar to those discussed earlier. The planned town to the east consists of a single main street, divided tenurially between Pershore Abbey's manor of Oldland, which included the northern part, now called High Street, and Westminster's

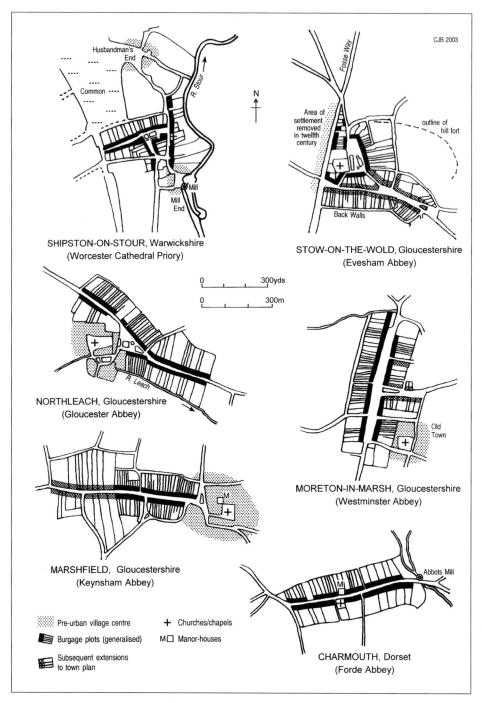

95 *Towns on outlying estates, comparative plans:* (a) *Shipston-on-Stour (Warwickshire) (*after Terry Slater, 1980); (b) *Stow-on-the-Wold (Gloucestershire);* (c) *Northleach (Gloucestershire);* (d) *Moreton-in-Marsh (Gloucestershire);* (e) *Marshfield (Gloucestershire);* (f) *Charmouth (Dorset) (*after Laurence Keen, 1999)

borough to the south, now Bridge Street. Terry Slater's examination of the burgage widths has demonstrated a further distinction between the plots on the east side of Bridge Street, which are generally broader and less regular, and those on the western side of both Bridge Street and High Street, where there is clear evidence of plots with an original standard width of 4 perches (66 feet). These uniform burgages, spanning the tenurial division, may be a product of co-operative replanning after fire destroyed part of the town in 1233. The two abbots jointly held a prescriptive Sunday market which was moved to Tuesday in 1219, and this may have been the occasion when the new rectangular market-place was planned; it is clearly an intrusive element, extending from the main street to the western back lane, with the parish boundary delimiting the separate jurisdictions of the two abbeys passing along its centre, suggesting that it too was developed as a co-operative venture. Also in the early thirteenth century, Pershore's borough was supplemented by an addition called 'Newland', a single street north-west of the abbey precinct, detached from the old town, resembling the previously-mentioned burghal extensions of the same name at Eynsham and Southam (**94b**).

The city of Durham was made up of four separate boroughs by 1200. The principal borough, covering the town centre, was held by the bishop. Across the Framwellgate Bridge, the western suburb of Crossgate belonged to the priory, while east of the Elvet Bridge the suburb of New Elvet, developed by Bishop Hugh de Puisset, was given by him to Prior Bertram (1189-1213), who enfranchised it as a separate borough. The fourth borough, St Giles, straggled along the road leading north-eastwards from the bishop's market-place, and was given by the bishop to the Kepier Hospital. Unusually, only the episcopal borough had its own market.

Other towns were divided between monastic and secular lords, and this has also often left a lasting legacy in the town plan. The division of Coventry between the Benedictine priory and the earls of Chester has already been noted. Here travellers heading for the market place from the west originally had to cross the River Sherbourne by Ram Bridge, where they were immediately confronted by a toll-bar at the entry to the earl's part of the town. To circumvent this, the prior built a new bridge 70 yards downstream, opening up a new street through a waste garden called West Orchard, leading directly into the market place. The borough of Newton Abbot was laid out by the canons of Torre on the extreme north-eastern margin of their manor of Wolborough soon after 1196, but in 1246 the tenant of a neighbouring royal manor planted his own town of Newton Bushel alongside it. Their respective market places were separated only by the little River Lemon, and they have now merged into one town. Towns primarily under lay control sometimes include individual plan units developed by monasteries. Outside the walls of Alnwick the suburb of Canongate grew up along the road leading to the Premonstratensian abbey, containing 36 burgages by the Dissolution.

Towns acquired by monastic proprietors

Not every town adjoining a monastery was itself a monastic promotion. Some monasteries were founded within existing towns, and never acquired control over them, or did so only at a relatively late date. Sherborne, for example, was developed by the bishops of Salisbury, and the abbey had no significant holding in the town before 1122 when Bishop Roger instituted the Abbot's Fee. The abbot built a row of shops in Half Moon Street around 1500, but this was a minor and late contribution to an established town.

Winchcombe was a royal borough and shire town before the Norman Conquest, and nothing in the town plan suggests that the abbey had much influence over its early growth. Although the abbey had 40 burgesses there in 1086, it did not gain control of the whole borough until 1229. The only significant monastic alteration to the town took place in 1289 when the abbot sought to close a lane which ran through the abbey precinct, rerouting it along the present Back Lane. Tewkesbury, too, had a small ancient monastic community, but the borough and market town were established by Matilda, wife of William the Conqueror. When the abbey was refounded in 1102, it lay on the edge of the town, and never achieved total control, though over the following four centuries it acquired many rents from urban properties.

When William, Count of Mortain, founded the Cluniac priory of Montacute in 1102, he endowed it with the existing borough and market of Bishopton. This is represented by the street still bearing that name, lined with burgages on both sides. The expansion of the priory precinct appears to have curtailed its southern end and, perhaps to replace the lost income, Prior Mark created a new borough shortly before 1240. This is represented by a second burgage-lined street to the east, now called The Borough, which includes a planned market square.

Henry I's foundation of Reading Abbey in 1125 gave it the whole borough and manor. Here the abbey developed a new triangular market-place west of its precinct, distinct from the older central crossroads by St Mary's Church, then laid out New Street, entering the north end of the market-place from the west; for some time, rents remained lower here than in the older part of the town.

New towns on outlying monastic estates

In addition to settlements immediately outside their gates, Benedictine abbeys were particularly active in developing towns on their outlying properties. Because their estates so often spanned two or more contrasting types of landscape, they were particularly successful in establishing new markets near junctions between vale and wold, or champion land and woodland, where the products of different regions could be exchanged. Three examples on or near the Roman Fosse Way on the Cotswolds are considered here:

The northernmost town, Moreton-in-Marsh, was held by Westminster Abbey at the time of the Domesday survey, but there is no evidence of anything urban there at that time. The first record of a Friday market occurs in 1226, altered to Tuesday a couple of years later, and then to Saturday in 1241. A six-day September fair was added in 1253. The cartulary ascribes the town's foundation to Abbot Richard Barking (1222-46), who induced the villagers of Batsford to give up their rights of common in the 'new vill of Moreton' in exchange for 4 acres of meadow and two burgages in the new town. Part of the income from the town rents was to be set aside for ringing bells, wine for the convent and bread for the poor to celebrate Abbot Richard's anniversary. The Fosse Way was widened to accommodate a broad market place, with a row of regular burgage tenements on either side (**95d**). The church, which began as a mere chapelry of Bourton-on-the-Hill and did not obtain burial rights until 1512, lies off to the south-east in an area still called 'Old Town', the nucleus of the agricultural hamlet which preceded the town's foundation.

Evesham Abbey had possessed a large estate at Maugersbury since its foundation. Here, the Roman road passed by a prehistoric hill fort, within the ramparts of which a church had been erected by the early eleventh century. This place, originally known as Edwardstow, now Stow-on-the-Wold, probably had a long history as an informal trading centre before Henry I granted Abbot Robert a weekly Thursday market there in 1107-8. The tiny parish of Stow, originally only 33 acres, was clearly excised from Maugersbury at the new town's foundation. By the early thirteenth century the abbey's profits from Stow's weekly market exceeded £10 per annum and its success led to further grants of fairs in 1330 and 1476. The town clusters around the convergence of earlier routes within the hill fort so is less obviously planned than some new towns; it nevertheless has some regular elements, notably its fine market square, now somewhat reduced by infill (**95b** and **colour plate 22**).

Some 8 miles south-west of Stow is Northleach, which had been held by Gloucester Abbey since about AD 780. Again the Domesday survey gives no hint of a town, but the abbot paid Henry III 100s for a market there in 1219, acquiring a new charter for a Wednesday market and three-day June fair in 1227. Two years later, burgages are mentioned for the first time. Here, the axis of the London-Gloucester road was preferred to the Fosse Way, and five distinct blocks of burgage tenements were laid out on either side, part of the road being broadened out into a triangular market-place (**95c** and **colour plate 21**). An extent of 1266-7 records about 80 burgages let at a standard rent of 12d, plus other houses, cottages, workshops and market stalls. Between the thirteenth and fifteenth centuries, Northleach developed as a major marketing centre for wool and cloth.

Some Augustinian houses like Aldgate in London, Cirencester and Dunstable, were founded within existing towns; others, like Royston, established towns outside their gates. Most of the towns established by Augustinian houses on their outlying estates were villages promoted by charters, such as Cartmel Priory's borough of Flookburgh or Burscough Priory's borough of Ormskirk. Occasionally, there are signs that the settlement plan was reorganised. The Victorine canons of Keynsham developed a small town at Marshfield with a single main street lined on either side with burgages (**95e**, **96**), broadening into a triangular market-place at the east end near the church. The dog-leg angles of the two roads entering the town from the east show that they were deliberately rerouted to pass through the market-place.

Income from markets and fairs was forbidden to the Cistercians by their early statutes, but this rule was already being ignored by 1189-90, when Richard I confirmed a market at Hoo St Werburgh to Boxley Abbey. Between 1200 and 1249 four markets and six fairs were acquired by Cistercian houses, and by the Dissolution 35 Cistercian houses in England and Wales had markets or fairs or both in 60 different places. Occasionally, grants were made to compensate abbeys for unexpected losses. Following the ravaging of Basingwerk Abbey's estates during the Welsh wars of 1276-7 and 1282-3, Edward I granted the monks weekly markets and annual fairs on their lands at Holywell and Glossop. In 1467 the monks of Cleeve were permitted a weekly market and two annual fairs in order to repay their expenditure on the rebuilding of an ancient chapel recently destroyed in a flood. This grant probably lapsed once it had fulfilled its original purpose.

Some Cistercian markets belonged to planned new boroughs. Charmouth was created in 1320 by William, Abbot of Forde, who laid out regular burgage plots 20 perches long by 4 perches wide (330ft by 66ft) on either side of the main street and rented them out at 6d a year (**95f**); the burgesses were obliged to use the abbey's mill and attend his court. Initially the Cistercians discouraged settlement directly outside their gates and even when they had a market or borough on their home estate, it usually lay some distance away. An unusually close juxtaposition occurs at Leek, where the town had already acquired its liberties by charter from the earl of Chester before 1214 when the Cistercians of Poulton were resettled at Dieulacresse less than a mile away. Although the town was given to the abbey, they were separated by the flood plain of the River Charnet. By the later Middle Ages, however, a few Cistercian houses were permitting markets in close proximity. In 1410 a complaint was made that the abbot of Forde had 'raised a market at the gate of the abbey...every Sunday...taking tolls, stallages, picages and other profits without licence...to the damage of neighbouring markets', and in 1468, Beaulieu was even holding a market inside the abbey precinct.

A few new towns were founded by the military orders who used their estates primarily as a means of raising funds to support their main purposes in the

96 *Marshfield (Gloucestershire), High Street: a single-street new borough founded by Keynsham Abbey, c.1265-70*

Holy Land. In 1147 King Stephen granted the Essex manor of Witham to the Knights Templars. The canons of St Martin's-le-Grand in London had probably already established a small market town near the church at Chipping Witham, given to them earlier by Stephen's wife. The Templars were claiming market rights there in 1153-4 though it was not until 1199 that King John issued a confirmation. They then decided to create a new town in a more favourable location, a quarter of a mile to the south on the main London-Colchester road, at a place called Wulvesford. In 1212 they acquired a new charter allowing them a Thursday market and annual fair at Wulvesford, which was renamed 'Witham Newland' soon after. A survey of the new town in about 1258 lists a total of 61 plots, of which 53 were occupied and eight vacant. The range of plot sizes suggests that two different planning modules based upon one-quarter and one-sixth of an acre were employed, and Warwick Rodwell's analysis of the burgage patterns has revealed five distinct phases of growth between the late twelfth and mid-thirteenth centuries.

Soon after 1138 Gilbert de Clare, Earl of Pembroke, granted the Templars 150 acres of land at the north end of Weston in Hertfordshire and the survey of Templar properties in 1185 already reveals a flourishing market town there, with 122 tenants rendering only rents and no agricultural services, burgage tenements, 31 houses and seven shops. The names of the tenants imply a wide range of trades and crafts, including a blacksmith, ironmonger, tailor, shoemaker, tanner, mason, cook, carter, reeve, mercer, weaver, saddler, goldsmith, merchant and vintner. The name given to the new town, Baldock, was anglicised from 'Baghdad', the greatest city of the Muslim world. The main London road was diverted from its old course to pass through the market-place and a new church was provided for the town, the parish church of Weston being nearly 4 miles away. Another small borough had been established at Templeton, in Pembrokeshire, by 1283; today this is a compact and regular street-village with long plots behind each house.

Social provisions: education, law and order

Education had been a function of some English monasteries since the eighth century. By the eleventh century, however, access to monastic schools was generally restricted to those intending to enter the cloistered life, while teaching the clergy and laity was undertaken through schools established by cathedrals and collegiate churches. Despite the withdrawal of monks from external teaching, some Benedictine abbeys still encouraged the foundation of schools. Sherborne Abbey continued to support the old cathedral school after 1075, when the see was removed to Old Sarum. One of the most flourishing schools of the twelfth century, at St Albans, operated under that abbey's patronage, while Abbot Samson purchased some stone houses at Bury St Edmunds to provide free lodgings for the master and scholars there. Schools operated by the Augustinian canons of Oseney and St Frideswide's in Oxford and of Barnwell near Cambridge influenced the universities in both cities as did the arrival of the friars in the thirteenth century. By the fourteenth century charitable schools had become attached to monastic almonries at Ely, Norwich, Leicester, Whitby, Durham and elsewhere. In the later Middle Ages grammar schools were often maintained by chantries, guilds and hospitals, but occasional examples were founded through personal bequests of individual abbots such as William Middleton at Milton Abbas and Clement Lichfield at Evesham (**97**).

Monasteries, as landholders, also had responsibilities for the administration of justice, holding various types of courts, including borough courts, and punishing criminals within their own demesnes. The foundation charter of Furness Abbey gave the abbot the right to administer justice throughout his lordship, and two courthouse buildings survive there. In 1292 the abbot claimed rights to a pillory, ducking-stool and gallows at Dalton and the acquisition of further judicial powers in the 1330s may have prompted the building of the existing courthouse, the court-room occupying the top floor of a rectangular stone tower which also contained a guardroom and gaol (**98**). At Hawkshead, manorial courts were held on the first floor of the gatehouse of the grange (**27**). Crowland Abbey maintained a gallows at a crossroads between Dry Drayton and Oakington, where excavations have recovered a dozen human burials, probably of executed criminals.

97 *This porch in Merstow Green, Evesham (Worcestershire), is all that survives of the grammar school founded by Clement Lichfield, last abbot of Evesham (1514-39)*

Failed boroughs and market towns

The acquisition by a monastic proprietor of a borough or market charter was no guarantee of lasting success. Many places where markets were once held acquired no other urban characteristics and subsequently relapsed to village status. The prior of Royston's market at Chesterton, chartered in 1254, Athelney Abbey's market at Lyng, granted in 1267, and Pershore Abbey's 1354 market and fair at Ombersley had all failed long before the Dissolution.

Components of the present village topography may provide a reminder of a decline in status. At Abbot's Bromley Richard de Lisle, abbot of Burton, acquired a royal licence in 1222 to promote the village to a borough, with burgage tenure at 12d a year and the customs of Lichfield. A Tuesday market and three-day fair were confirmed five years later. The timber butter-cross indicates that the market was still functioning into the seventeenth century, but the former market-place is now a large green (**colour plate 23**). In 1251 the abbot of Pershore acquired a charter for a Friday market and midsummer fair on his manor of Broadway, on a promising site where the main road begins to climb the Cotswold scarp from the Vale of Evesham. The wedge-shaped village green is the former market-place with its broader end facing the abbot's grange. The removal of the settlement to this site left the old church isolated, three-quarters of a mile to the south. Here, too, the earliest surviving court roll for 1388 reveals some attempt at borough creation, but the economy of the place by then appears to have been based entirely upon farming.

There is nothing in the documentary record to suggest that Cerne Abbas ever aspired to the dignity of a borough, but the village plan still suggests an attempted urban promotion following the market grant in 1175. The principal street, Long Street, broadens out into a cigar-shaped market place, which has subsequently been reduced by a central block of infill (**99**). Behind the houses along the southern side of the street, vestiges of planned tenements terminate in a back lane. From the centre of the market place, another planned street runs ruler-straight up to the abbey gate.

At East Witton in Wensleydale both church and village were entirely rebuilt at the beginning of the nineteenth century, but the distance of the church from the village, and the very regular plan with two rows of houses lining a broad rectangular green, derive from the replanning undertaken by Jervaulx Abbey following its charter for a market and cattle fair in 1307. A market was still held on the green at least up to 1728.

Town promotions initiated as part of a programme for reclaiming under-utilised land were especially vulnerable, particularly if the improvements failed to live up to expectations. The Knights Templars planted a new village by their

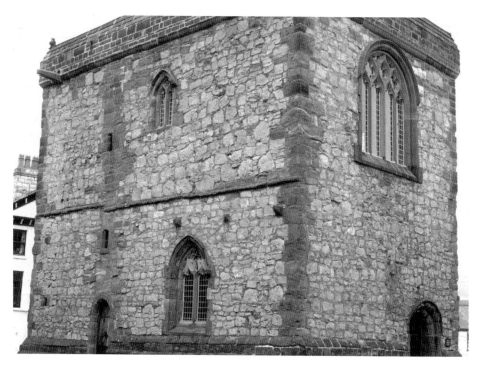

98 *The fourteenth-century courthouse of the abbots of Furness at Dalton-in-Furness (Lancashire)*

99 *Cerne Abbas (Dorset): the 'Royal Oak' (left) forms part of an encroachment over the former market place in Long Street*

preceptory at Temple Bruer, on a wild heathy plateau south of Lincoln, and by 1185 had 37 agricultural tenants there. The acquisition of a weekly market shortly afterwards, however, failed to result in any permanent urban growth, although aerial photographs of the now largely deserted site suggest that some attempt was made to lay out planned tenements around a rectangular green or market-place. The Knights Hospitallers similarly attempted to establish a new town at Eagle on the Fosse Way in 1345, with a weekly market and two annual fairs. Their timing was unlucky, and the Black Death probably destroyed any hopes that the plantation would be successful. A century later the Hospitallers requested the annulment of the charter and a transfer of the market and fair to Swinderby.

Other attempted urban promotions were abortive from the outset. Worcester Priory acquired a market charter for Lindridge in 1236, as did Montacute Priory at Creech St Michael in 1269, the canons of Bradenstoke at their home manor in 1361, Sheen Priory at East Hendred around 1415, and Durham Priory at Greatham in 1445. There is no evidence, however, that any of these markets were ever held.

Finally, one successful monastic town, Milton Abbas, has been lost since the Dissolution. In 1252 Milton Abbey acquired a weekly Thursday market and annual three-day fair in August. A market-place was laid out to the south-east of the abbey, with further streets beyond, perhaps developed in several stages. In 1280 the market day was changed to Monday and the fair to three days in July. The town survived into the eighteenth century, when Joseph Damer, 1st Baron Milton, swept it away in order to provide a parkland landscape setting for his great house. Its inhabitants were rehoused in a neat estate village on the edge of the park.

15

Monasteries and transport

Roads

Roads provided essential lines of communication between monasteries, their estates, and markets and ports. For the most part, monastic traffic used existing routes, but abbeys founded on virgin sites inevitably became the focal points of new networks. Three roads linking Tintern Abbey with its granges to the south and west converged upon the gatehouse, and one of them, known as the Stony Way, still shows signs of ancient cobbling. Symeon of Durham records how Aethelric, a monk of Peterborough who served as bishop of Durham from 1042-56, discovered a great treasure of gold and silver at Chester-le-Street and, returning to Peterborough, used the proceeds in the construction of roads 'of stone and wood' through the Fens.

Considerable movement of livestock took place between upland and lowland pastures and between granges, abbeys and markets. Occasionally this generated distinctive long-distance routes. From Fountains Abbey's grange at Kilnsey, near the head of Wharfedale, a green lane called Mastiles Lane climbs up over the Pennine moors, the first stage on the long journey westwards beyond Ribblesdale to the distant Cumbrian pastures. Before the enclosures of the eighteenth and nineteenth centuries this track traversed open moorland, its course marked at intervals by stone crosses, the bases of some of which still survive.

Monastic shrines attracted pilgrims, but for the most part this was a local traffic using the existing roads. On the continent, the preferred long-distance routes to the greater pilgrimage destinations, such as Santiago de Compostela, were perpetuated by ancient custom, by the availability of accommodation and by the need for mutual protection over dangerous terrain. Improved roads and bridges, chapels, crosses and pilgrim hostels were a feature of such routes. By comparison, even the greatest English pilgrimage venue, Becket's shrine at Canterbury, had little effect upon the wider landscape, though the tour within the precinct was elaborately orchestrated. The so-called 'Pilgrims' Way' running below the scarp of the North Downs between Guildford and

Canterbury is not recorded under that name before the eighteenth century, and its association with medieval travellers is a myth. Most visitors, including Chaucer's pilgrims, approached Canterbury by the old Roman road between London and Dover, which passed through many towns and villages able to provide refreshment and overnight accommodation. Matthew Paris tells us that Abbot Leofstan of St Albans (d.1064 or 1066) cleared back thickets of woodland on either side of the main road from London so that pilgrims and visitors could travel to the abbey without fear of ambush.

The greatest monastic influence on the road system occurred on a more local scale, through diversions necessitated by new buildings and precinct extensions. Abbot Adam of Eynsham acquired licence to stop up the old road to Stanton Harcourt in 1217, replacing it with a new road and new bridge further west. The evidence for this change is clear on the ground (**94c**). In 1225 the prior of Royston was given leave to enclose the road beneath the west wall of the precinct, provided that a new road was made on the prior's own land.

Friaries had a particular impact upon urban street patterns. The friars usually began with a small plot, acquiring neighbouring properties on a piecemeal basis as opportunity offered. When the Franciscans first arrived in England in 1224 their provincial minister, Agnellus of Pisa, permitted them to acquire only the bare minimum of land, forbade unnecessary expenditure on churches, and expected them to beg for their living. Haymo of Faversham, minister-general of the order after 1240, decided, however, that it was preferable for the friars to have gardens large enough to produce their own food, while many Franciscan churches were rebuilt on a bigger scale between 1270 and 1320. In consequence, many friary precincts were enlarged, sometimes absorbing former public roads. In 1258 the Greyfriars of Lincoln received licence to block a postern in the city wall and enclose the lane leading to it. The Franciscans of Canterbury were accused of appropriating a highway 165ft long and 11ft wide in 1275, probably the road formerly known as Pocock Lane, and four years later this enclosure was confirmed by licence. In 1289 the Greyfriars of Coventry were permitted to close part of the main road towards Kenilworth on condition that they replaced it with a new road of equivalent width. Other road diversions by the Franciscans occurred at Chester (1245), Bridgnorth (1247), Great Yarmouth (1271) and Walsingham (1351).

Similarly, in 1246 Henry III gave the Dominican friars of Gloucester money to buy land for their church, to enlarge their churchyard, and to open a new access from Southgate Street, which survives as the lane now called Blackfriars. The Norwich Dominicans began building a new church in 1327, but completion to its full length was baulked by a public lane, and there was a delay of 18 years before they secured consent for its closure. In 1351 the Blackfriars of Hereford acquired a licence permitting them to enclose a road called Frog Lane, 511ft long and 28ft wide, in order to extend their precinct eastwards, though this provoked some local opposition.

Ferries

Ferry tolls could be a source of income, though this had to be offset against the costs of maintaining a boat, paying the ferryman and sometimes paying landing fees where the proprietor did not own both sides of the river. Many monasteries had interests in ferries over the River Thames. Eynsham Abbey operated a ferry at Shifford by the end of the fifteenth century. The ownership and maintenance of a ferry at Swinford was the subject of a prolonged dispute between the abbeys of Eynsham, which held land on the left bank, and Abingdon, whose land lay on the right bank. Finally, in 1299, it was agreed that the ferry should belong to Abingdon, but that Eynsham should receive a landing fee of 12d a year, and that the monks of Eynsham should have free passage, except for the abbot, steward and cellarer, who should pay the ferryman two loaves and 2 gallons of second-best ale on each crossing. Below Oxford the ferry at Sandford was held by the Knights Templar as part of their preceptory in 1279, but was regularly used by the Abingdon monks when they had business on their Wheatley and Cuddesdon manors on the Oxfordshire bank. This ferry claimed the lives of Abbot Richard Clive and several of his officials in July 1315 when they attempted to cross during a flood. The ferry at Goring was given to the Benedictine nuns there by Henry I and continued to contribute a significant part of their income up to the Dissolution. Reading Abbey had an interest in the ferry at Whitchurch.

Birkenhead Priory lay alongside the main road up the Wirral peninsula, which led to a ferry over the Mersey to Liverpool. By 1284 increasing traffic on this road prompted the prior to seek consent to divert it beyond a new wall or hedge. Despite this, the monks continued to find themselves burdened with providing hospitality for many travellers, since there were no inns nearer than Chester. To provide an alternative, the prior built lodgings at the Wirral end of the ferry shortly after 1310, where food could be sold to passengers and those delayed by weather could be accommodated. In 1330 Edward III granted the priory itself the right to transport men, horses and goods over the Mersey, and to charge reasonable tolls for what may previously have been a free charitable service. On several subsequent occasions the prior had to defend this right against allegations of excessive charges. The community itself used the ferry to take surplus produce to Liverpool market, and in the early fourteenth century erected a granary in Liverpool. The ferry and the lodgings contributed £4 6s 8d to the priory's income by 1536.

Bridges

Bridges on monastic property occasionally find mention in pre-Conquest charters. A confirmation of Crowland Abbey's lands with a nominal date of

948 mentions the 'triangular bridge', a predecessor of the existing Trinity Bridge at Crowland, which carried a junction of three streets over a confluence of two tributaries of the Welland. The present bridge is a remarkable structure dating from the later fourteenth century, originally surmounted by a large canopied cross, possibly used as a station by pilgrims approaching the abbey.

Many monastic precincts were intersected or bordered by one or more natural watercourses, and bridges were constructed to provide safe crossings. Two medieval bridges span the River Skell within the precinct of Fountains Abbey, one built around 1147 immediately above the lay brothers' infirmary, the other, of early thirteenth-century date, below the mill. Part of the precinct wall of Bury St Edmunds' Abbey is carried over the River Lark on three pointed arches. Two wide buttresses against the wall's outer face probably carried a plank bridge.

Monastic communities also often took the initiative in constructing bridges on routes which they used regularly for access to their estates. Before 1185 the abbot of Fountains had built new bridges over the Colne and Calder rivers to improve access to its grange at Bradley. Barton Bridge at Bradford-on-Avon linked the estate farm of the abbess of Shaftesbury with the town (**colour plate 24**). Half a dozen bridges over the River Wey between Tilford and Guildford, all of very similar design, with triangular cutwaters on the upstream side and semicircular ones downstream, have been attributed to Waverley Abbey; all were probably reconstructed after the great flood of 1233. Two medieval bridges over the River Nene, at Ditchford and at Irthlingborough, have cutwaters with plaques bearing the crossed keys symbol of Peterborough Abbey (**100** and **colour plate 25**).

Bridges often superseded earlier fords, and on smaller watercourses tended to occupy more or less the same site. However, fords required shallow water which, over larger rivers, might necessitate a crossing of considerable length, whereas bridge-builders ideally looked for the shortest possible span, where the river was deeper. Above Evesham, all the early routes from the east converged upon Twyford, a mile north of the abbey, where the Avon separated into two branches. When Evesham Abbey developed its planned borough outside its northern gate in the early twelfth century, a new stone bridge was constructed across to Bengeworth, necessitating a realignment of all the left-bank roads.

Early bridges were often of timber (**colour plate 30**), but stone bridges were widespread by the later Middle Ages. Oseney Abbey built Hythe Bridge, on the western side of Oxford, as a timber structure between 1200 and 1210, but this was replaced in stone in the later fourteenth century. On the southern side of Oxford Abingdon Abbey was probably responsible for the causeway and wooden bridge which crossed the Thames before the first Norman castellan built the Grand Pont around 1085. The abbey continued to maintain a hermitage and chapel at the southern end of the bridge. Bridges were generally

100 *Irthlingborough Bridge (Northamptonshire): despite its being widened in 1922, the ribbed arches and cutwaters of the bridge built by Peterborough Abbey in the fourteenth century are still clearly visible (see also* **colour plate 25***)*

welcomed by overland travellers, but could be an obstacle to navigation. The Greyfriars in Canterbury were permitted to build two bridges over the Stour in 1264 and 1309, on condition that their arches were high enough to allow laden boats to pass beneath.

Expenditure on bridges is recorded in monastic accounts. Bolton Priory spent £21 12s 9d on the building of Kildwick Bridge over the River Aire in 1305-6, a splendid bridge which still survives. Some ten years later, the same priory received a donation of £6 13s 4d towards the rebuilding of its bridge over the Wharfe. A list of works undertaken in the time of John Fossor, prior of Durham (1341-74), included a bridge over the River Browney at Beaurepaire; the Durham bursar's accounts note 13s 4d spent on repairs to the Aldin Grange Bridge, a mile downstream, in 1370. Contributions to the repair of Kettlewell Bridge over the Wharfe and Summer Bridge over the Nidd are recorded in the Fountains Abbey bursar's book in the mid-fifteenth century. As permanent corporations, monasteries were also seen as suitable custodians for bridges built by others. Horton Bridge over the River Blyth was given to Newminster Abbey by Roger de Merlay in the early thirteenth century, along with endowments for its repair.

Individual abbots sometimes undertook bridge construction or repair as an act of personal charity. Monks' Bridge over the River Dove at Eggington was rebuilt by John Stretton, late thirteenth-century prior of Burton, at his own cost when no-one else would do so. Thomas, abbot of Thornton (1290-1323), agreed to repair Glanford Bridge over the Ancholme at Brigg because it was his birthplace, but the abbey took no further responsibility for it. Abbot Godfrey spent £14 8s on a bridge at Peterborough in 1307, but it was broken down by ice the following winter, and replaced at a cost of £18 5s. This again was a personal benefaction, with the abbey accepting no corporate responsibility. After Godfrey's death, the bridge fell into ruin, but was patched up with timber by Abbot Adam (1321-38) for a later royal visit.

Permitted public use of monastic bridges produced expectations that the monks would keep them in repair. However, upkeep often proved a greater problem than the initial construction, and monastic houses were often on the receiving end of complaints about their condition. John de Braose's charter to Sele Priory in c.1230 allowed the monks timber from his woods for making the bridge at Bramber, but the prior was accused in 1473 of allowing both the bridge and its associated chapel to fall into disrepair. An enquiry held in 1280 claimed that the Abbot of Athelney was bound to repair the bridge crossing the Tone at Lyng, while the abbot of Glastonbury was blamed for the weak construction of a bridge over the Dorset Stour between Stalbridge and Marnhull in 1358. Westminster Abbey was held responsible in 1339 for the repair of Stickledon Bridge over the River Brent near Perivale which had been broken down for 20 years. A short way downstream, Hanwell Bridge was said to be in disrepair in 1398 by default of the prior of Ogbourne St George, English representative of the great Norman abbey of Bec. Powick Bridge over the River Teme was claimed to be the responsibility of Great Malvern Priory in 1336 but, despite many requests, the prior had refused to maintain it and it was then in a dangerous state. The bridge at Deerhurst was broken down in 1378 and it was said that Westminster Abbey was responsible for its repair. In the same year it was decided that the prior of St Oswald's at Gloucester was responsible for the bridges over the Chelt at Norton, which had been broken down for three years, and the abbot of St Peter's, Gloucester, was blamed for the decay of Upleadon Bridge, which was still reported to be in poor condition nine years later.

Sometimes the pressures were evaded. When complaints were made in 1310 that one of the bridges belonging to the abbot of Fountains was broken down, it was concluded that he could not be compelled to repair it since he had built it of his own free will. Responsibility for repairing a wooden bridge at Stratford by Bradwell, where Stane Street crosses the River Blackwater, was imposed upon Coggeshall Abbey in 1308, but the abbot appealed against the decision in 1341 and had it reversed. In 1520 this bridge was swept away in a flood, and the royal authorities made another attempt to place responsibility for its rebuilding upon the abbots of Coggeshall and Westminster and others who held fishing rights in the river. The prior of Kenilworth denied responsibility for Cloud Bridge over the Warwickshire Avon in 1352, claiming that it was redundant since there was another bridge nearby at Stare maintained by Stoneleigh Abbey. The wooden bridge at Edgware, where Watling Street crossed one of the headstreams of the Brent, was claimed in 1370 to be the responsibility of the prior of St Bartholomew, Smithfield, but he too resisted, and the jury found in his favour. Occasionally such reprieves were only temporary. The Abbot of Combe was absolved of responsibility for Chesford Bridge in 1313, but this decision was overturned in 1372, the abbot admitted liability and was fined £1 for his neglect. The abbot of Buildwas was able to persuade a jury in 1318 that he had no responsibility for Buildwas Bridge, though two months later he received a grant for its repair.

The financing of individual bridges was frequently shared by the Crown, monastic institutions, lay benefactors and others. The building of a timber bridge at Caversham appears to have been undertaken jointly by Reading Abbey and the Earl of Pembroke some time between 1163 and 1231. When Pershore Bridge fell into ruin in the early fourteenth century, the townspeople claimed that the obligation to repair it lay solely with the abbot of Westminster, who owned the land on either side. It was decided in 1351 that the costs should be shared between the abbot and the town. When Moulsham Bridge near Chelmsford was broken down in 1351, costs were to be shared between the bishop of London and the abbot of Westminster, and the Westminster treasurer's roll of 1372 records £23 6s 8d paid to the master builder Henry Yevele for work on the new bridge there. Royal gifts sometimes gave support. In 1216 King John granted the abbot of Furness timber for the bridge at Lancaster, and a further grant of 20 oaks was made by Henry III in 1252. Voluntary donations were also solicited. One of the monks of Burton, in his capacity as bridgekeeper, was licensed in 1284 to beg for alms to rebuild the bridge over the Trent, after much of it had been swept away by a flood.

The Crown also made grants of pontage conveying the right to collect tolls for bridge maintenance. The prior of Repton was appointed surveyor of tolls on goods passing over the Trent on Swarkeston Bridge in 1327. The abbot of Merevale received a grant of pontage for three years in 1332 to help maintain Fielden Bridge over the River Anker near Atherstone. Complaints were made against the abbot of Lilleshall in 1221 that he had recently imposed a toll of a penny on every loaded cart crossing the Severn by the bridge at Atcham. The abbot claimed that the bridge was his own construction and that the toll had been agreed in place of the two marks a year which his predecessor had received from the ferry there. Monastic houses however often claimed freedom from toll payments on bridges themselves. In 1263 the abbot of Holm Cultram claimed free passage for his carts over Hexham Bridge. In 1302 the carts and wagons of the prior of Sele were permitted free passage over Mock Bridge north of Henfield, whereas the prior's tenants all had to pay the toll.

There has been relatively little archaeological work on monastic bridges. In 1968, however, Peter Huggins examined the remains of the bridge over the lower millstream at Waltham Abbey. A single arch, reinforced by three chamfered ribs beneath, spanned the stream at an angle. The stone abutments had been set on oak sill-plates and elm piling, and remains of the wooden coffer-dams which had kept water away from the banks during construction were discovered. Dendrochronology pointed to a construction date around 1360. The arch of the new bridge built at Eynsham by Abbot Adam in 1217, when he diverted a road to enlarge the abbey precinct, was rediscovered by Graham Keevill in 1991, beneath the ostensibly Victorian but much-widened Chilmore bridge.

While many abbeys took an active part in building and maintaining bridges, it would be wrong to overemphasise the monastic contribution. The construction of Abingdon Bridge was financed by a local merchant guild in 1416-22, and Abingdon Abbey conspicuously failed to contribute to the costs. Darley Abbey consented to the building of Whatstandwell Bridge over the Derwent in 1390 since the east end encroached 24ft over its land, but it was a local layman who bore the entire cost of construction.

Causeways

On wide flood plains or marshlands, causeways partly took the place of bridges. Matilda, wife of Henry I, built two stone bridges linked by a causeway over the branches of the River Lea between Stratford-le-Bow and Ham Stratford. Believing that a monastic house was likely to survive longer than any arrangement made with laymen and that it would take its responsibilities more seriously, she gave lands to the nuns of Barking, at that time the nearest religious institution, requesting that the income from them should be used for the maintenance of the crossing. In 1135, however, the monastery of Stratford Langthorn was founded closer by, and the abbess seized the opportunity to offload the task to the Cistercians. A dispute over the obligation was resolved in 1315 by the abbot accepting the responsibility and guaranteeing a rent of four marks to Barking in exchange for the abbess paying him £200. In 1317 the abbot received licence to move sand and gravel from another part of the highway to effect the necessary repairs to the causeway. In 1293 the prioress of Higham was held responsible for maintaining a causeway and bridge leading over the Thames estuary marshes to a ferry crossing towards Tilbury; remains of this causeway are still visible.

Several causeways were built on the Glastonbury estates in the late thirteenth century. The Sowy island was connected with the High Ham upland by the Beer Wall running eastwards from Othery, and with the Polden Hills by the Greylake Fosse running north-eastwards over Kings Sedgemoor to Greinton. In 1302 the latter causeway was held to be responsible for severe flooding in the moors above.

Holland Causeway carried the main road from Grantham to Boston over the Lincolnshire fens between Bridge End and Donington. It was the responsibility of Sempringham Priory which, in order to oversee the work, settled a small colony at St Saviour's Chapel at Bridge End. The prior of St Saviour's found the upkeep of a 2-mile-long causeway with 30 floodwater arches no easy task, and despite a string of pontage grants through the fourteenth century, its condition caused much concern. Revesby Abbey was called upon to repair Northdyke Causeway on the main highway from Boston to the Humber at South Ferriby in 1263, but a jury determined in 1316 that the monks had no such obligation.

River transport

Rivers were regularly used by monastic houses for the transport of bulky goods such as building stone and timber and sometimes for bringing in victuals. Transport by water was relatively cheap, carriage by road costing up to six times more. Around 1222 Abbot Alexander of Peterborough confirmed to the abbot and convent of Bury St Edmunds 1 rood of land by the River Nene at Castor where they could make a wharf from which barges could carry Barnack stone to Bury. Two stones, today known as 'Robin Hood and Little John', are believed to mark the bounds of this concession (**101**). Six shiploads of stone for the refectory of Canterbury Cathedral Priory came down the Thames in 1233. In 1276 the abbot of St Mary's in York was complaining that Edmund, earl of Cornwall, was obstructing the free passage of his boats carrying victuals along the Yorkshire Ouse and Ure, a right which he claimed the abbey had enjoyed from time immemorial. In the early fourteenth century goods bought for Durham Priory at Boston Fair were routinely carried by boat up the River Witham to Lincoln, then overland to Torksey, then down the River Trent. After the central tower of Ely Abbey collapsed in 1322, stone and timber for the new lantern was brought in along the Great Ouse, which at some unknown date had been diverted to the west to pass by the town.

Rivers were also used for the export of monastic produce such as wool. Cistercian abbeys possessing sheep pastures over the Wolds and North Yorkshire Moors regularly brought their wool to Clifton, on the outskirts of York, where it could be inspected by continental merchants before being carried on down the Ouse and Humber to the port of Hull. Remains of quays survive on several monastic sites, including the remote Benedictine abbey of St Benet, Hulme, while gates giving access to waterfronts survive at Tintern and Worcester. Town houses in London and Southwark held by monastic houses often had quays and wharves alongside the Thames or Fleet River. The inn of St Augustine's Abbey, Canterbury, had a wharf on the south bank of the

101 *'Robin Hood' and 'Little John': stones marking the bounds of the rood of land granted by Abbot Alexander of Peterborough to Bury St Edmunds Abbey alongside the River Nene at Castor (Northamptonshire) for use as a wharf in c.1222*

Thames by 1330, located by excavation in 1971. In 1296 a fishmonger called Richard de Chigwell gave the abbot of Chertsey land within the city walls, on the river front with a wharf. Within ten years, the abbot had built a stone quay and in 1425 replaced this with a new wharf, extending 10ft further into the Thames.

River transport had its limitations, however. Transfer of goods between barge and wagon was never especially convenient. Rivers were sometimes impassable through flooding, silting or drought, and their passage became increasingly obstructed by fish-weirs, mills and bridges.

Canals

The first construction of artificial navigable waterways, always popularly associated with James Brindley and the Duke of Bridgwater in the 1750s, in fact dates back many centuries earlier. Many pre-Conquest Benedictine abbeys lay close to rivers and marshes, and, although it is sometimes difficult to distinguish navigation cuts from drainage channels (indeed the same channel might serve both purposes), evidence of monastic river diversion and canal construction can be detected from the tenth century. At Glastonbury surviving earthworks and antiquarian accounts suggest that an artificial watercourse once connected the abbey and town with the River Brue, a mile away, following the contour around the north flank of Wirrall Hill. Excavation has recovered twelfth- and thirteenth-century pottery from the upper fill of the ditch and a timber revetment stake from its edge has given a radiocarbon date centred in the mid-tenth century, the very time when Dunstan was reforming and rebuilding the abbey. This watercourse may have been deliberately infilled when it was incorporated into the abbot's deer park of Wirrall in the early thirteenth century.

The River Thames around Abingdon has been much altered. According to the Abingdon Abbey chronicle, in the time of Abbot Ordric (1052-65) the citizens of Oxford requested consent to divert the navigation channel through the abbey's meadow to the south in order to allow their vessels convenient passage upstream, bypassing the dangerous shallows near Barton Court. The watercourse made for this purpose is almost certainly the backwater now known as the Swift Ditch. In exchange for this facility, 100 herring a year were to be paid to the abbey cellarer, and in 1110, the abbot successfully sued some Oxford boatmen who had attempted to evade payment of the toll. The chronicle records a second considerable river diversion to improve navigation just upstream near Thrupp at about the same time. The Thrupp backwater today is a minor ditch, but a sixteenth-century map shows it as a much more considerable stream. John Leland, who visited Abingdon in the early sixteenth century, tells us that the present main stream on the north-western side of Andersey Island was the product of another diversion carried out in the time of Abbot Faricius (1100-17), to bring the navigation channel closer to the abbey, and certainly after the twelfth century the Swift Ditch was the lesser stream. The implication seems to be that both of the streams which surround Andersey Island are substantially artificial and Leland states that in wet periods the old course of the river still flooded so that there were three streams. Indeed, an abandoned meandering watercourse can still be followed in part across the middle of the island in the lowest part of the valley floor.

Where effort went in to digging a new watercourse, it made sense for it to serve as many different purposes as possible. At Waltham Abbey Abbot Walter was authorised to divert the River Lea in 1190 so long as his works did not damage navigation (**colour plate 26**). The primary purpose of his new cut was to work a new overshot mill, but its water was also used to fill the fishponds and to flush the abbey reredorter. The head race was also used by boats bringing grain and other produce to the mill and grange yard, where remains have been excavated of an early medieval dock with an opposed slipway and a timber-framed wharf which succeeded it.

The Cistercian abbey of Meaux was heavily involved in operations to drain the peatlands of the Hull Valley in the twelfth and thirteenth centuries, but some of the new watercourses were clearly more than mere drainage channels. The straight, mile-long *Eschedike*, cut between 1160 and 1182, provided for the carriage of building materials and supplies from the river to the abbey itself. The *Forthdike* may also have been used for water transport, while further up the valley the *Skerndike*, dug between 1249 and 1269, provided access to Skerne Grange. Further works on the Hull were undertaken in connection with the development of the port of Wyke.

The full history of the maze of natural and artificial waterways in the eastern Fenlands has yet to be unravelled, but it is of interest that the Welland, Nene, Great Ouse, Lark, Little Ouse and Nar, all of which show evidence of major early diversions, all had important monasteries on their banks before the mid-twelfth century, while the River Wissey, which lacked any early monastic houses along its course, escaped significant modification. There were also several wholly artificial canals. Cnut's Dyke, extending in a fairly straight line for 8 miles over the fens east of Peterborough, may have been constructed as early as the tenth century for bringing stone to Ramsey Abbey, bypassing the circuitous course of the River Nene through Whittlesey Mere. A little further inland is the Monks' Lode, extending for nearly 5 miles from the Nene to Sawtry Abbey (**102**). This was constructed in the third quarter of the twelfth century. In 1176 the pope confirmed the right of the monks of Sawtry to the watercourse which they had made at their own cost for carrying building stone to their church. The construction occasioned a long dispute with the Benedictines of Ramsey, 5 miles to the east, finally resolved in 1192 when the Ramsey monks conceded to those of Sawtry the right to use the canal and to build a rest-house for the men working the stone barges.

The River Witham shows clear signs of canalisation between Lincoln and the Wash and many of the monastic houses nearby were linked to it by short arms. The construction of such a canal 'for the easy transit of ships' by the Gilbertines of Bullington is recorded around the end of the twelfth century. The Premonstratensian canons of Barlings and the Benedictine nuns of Stainfield appear to have diverted their respective tributaries of the Witham. Another navigable arm from the river was cut by the Benedictine monks of Bardney. Finally, Henry II granted the Premonstratensian canons of Tupholme a watercourse large enough to allow vessels to come and go from the River Witham to allow carriage of stone to the abbey buildings, a distance of a little over a mile. Elsewhere, at Castle Acre, a short length of canal allowed boats to come from the River Nar up to the great court of the priory, terminating by the great granary (**colour plate 28**). At Norwich an arm was cut off the River Wensum, passing through the precinct wall by a water-gate, permitting barge-loads of Caen stone to be brought upriver from the port of Yarmouth. Another cut, about a mile long, linked Butley Priory with the tidal Butley River. At the end of this canal a timber-revetted wharf had been constructed in the late twelfth or early thirteenth century, built up with successive layers of faggots, earth, clay and mortar. In the fourteenth century the timber revetment was reconstructed in stone and a new jetty built.

102 *The Monks' Lode at Sawtry (Huntingdonshire), part of a 5-mile-long canal cut by the Cistercian abbey of Sawtry for the transport of building stone before 1176*

The Rye valley at Rievaulx contains evidence of a succession of natural and artificial watercourses both above and below the abbey. These were first recognised in 1900 by Henry Rye, who drew attention to a series of land grants made to the abbey by local landowners around 1142-6, 1160-70 and 1193-1203, which, he suggested, had been made in order to allow the abbey to cut artificial canals in order to bring in stone from its quarries upstream at Penny Piece and downstream at Hollins Wood. In 1952 the evidence was reassessed by Weatherill, who put forward the view that the canal system antedated the land grants, and suggested a construction date of around 1135-40 when major building works were in progress. Recent opinion has moved away from the canal interpretation, suggesting that the real purpose of the diversions was simply to give the monks of Rievaulx complete control of the valley floor, partly so that the old river course could be used as a leat for a chain of three successive mills and partly in order to have more meadowland on their side of the river. This explanation does not seem entirely convincing, and, although there would be some difficulties in water transport from Hollins Wood, the idea of a canal from Penny Piece is still attractive.

Glastonbury Abbey continued its programme of water management in the Somerset moors into the high Middle Ages. Michael Williams has shown that two substantial projects were carried out in the thirteenth century. Before this time, the River Brue had flowed northwards from Street to join the upper part of the River Axe in the Bleadney gap, which separates the Isle of Wedmore from the mainland. Leland describes the river dividing into two branches at Street, with the old channel still carrying the greater part of the water, but a second channel flowing westwards into Meare Pool. This diversion had been made before 1294, possibly as early as the 1230s. The outlet from Meare Pool originally flowed north-westwards past Mark to join the lower part of the River Axe below Biddisham. This watercourse, now known as the Pilrow Cut (**colour plate 27**), was canalised, possibly in the 1230s and certainly before 1316, and it was described as tidal in the early fourteenth century. The present outlet of the River Brue into Bridgwater Bay below Highbridge may also have been created, either deliberately or by a breakthrough of floodwaters, in the thirteenth or early fourteenth century. Glastonbury Abbey could be reached in the thirteenth century by boats plying up the River Axe to Bleadney and thence by the old course of the upper Brue. Conflict with the bishop of Wells over fisheries in the Axe, however, may have prompted the search for an alternative route. A small port was developed on the Pilrow Cut at Rooksbridge and documentary records show carriage along the canal to Glastonbury continuing at least to 1500.

The earliest monastic canals appear to be associated with new building projects after the tenth-century reform. A further surge of activity began after the Norman Conquest, lasting to the end of the thirteenth century. Then, however, the impulse seems to have died. Often canal construction seems to have been regarded as a short-term expedient and only a few examples were maintained for more than a few decades. Obstructions on the rivers and improvements in roads and bridges resulted in overland transport reasserting its supremacy in the later Middle Ages.

Ships, ports and harbours

At least a dozen Cistercian abbeys had their own sea-going ships, vessels of up to 200 tons engaged in the import and export of wine, fish, grain, wool and other commodities. Ships of Holm Cultram and Furness traded regularly with Ireland and the Isle of Man, while others made crossings to the Low Countries, Normandy and Gascony. A ship of Quarr Abbey laden with wine is recorded entering the port of Southampton in 1252, while William Worcestre noted one of Tintern's ships lying in Bristol harbour in 1453. In 1405 a trading ship and small boat belonging to Neath Abbey were commandeered by the Duke of York, and the abbot had considerable difficulty in securing their return.

For the most part, monasteries traded out of existing ports, but occasionally they created ports of their own. The most successful of these was Wyke-upon-Hull, where, in the late twelfth century, Meaux Abbey straightened out the River Hull and laid out two streets parallel with it as the nucleus of a new town. In 1279 the abbot obtained a grant for a market and fair there, and by

1293 Wyke contained 109 houses. So promising was the site that Edward I persuaded the monks to sell it to him, whereupon he began enlarging the quay, improving the approach roads and laying out more new streets, also giving it a new name, Kingston-upon-Hull. St Mary's Abbey in York was responsible for the development of the small port of Airmyn, near the confluence of the Aire and Yorkshire Ouse.

Holm Cultram Abbey was less successful in its attempts to establish a new port on the Solway Firth. Edward I's use of the Waver estuary for victualling his ships during his Scottish campaign had encouraged the monks to acquire a borough charter for Wavermouth in 1300, giving rights to a Thursday market and annual 17-day fair. This venture failed, perhaps through flooding, and in the following year the abbey acquired a new charter permitting it to develop its grange of Skinburgh on the exposed western side of the estuary. The embryonic borough of Skinburgh and its approach road were themselves soon washed away by the sea. A third attempt was begun further east at Kirkby St John on the abbey's grange of Arlosh, which had been much damaged by the Scots. Here some burgages were laid out at the place now known as Newton Arlosh, and a new church was authorised in 1305 (**colour plate 16**). However, this seems to have enjoyed little more lasting success than its predecessors.

Monastic interests in the fishing industry had encouraged the development of several small ports, some of which later developed a wider role. During the first quarter of the thirteenth century, three huts or 'shiels' were built on the north bank of the River Tyne by fishermen, who kept their nets there and occupied them as seasonal dwellings. The prior of Tynemouth allowed their boats to use his shore on condition that they gave part of their catch to the monks. Subsequently, further cottages were erected by the prior himself, along with mills and bakehouses supplying visiting ships. Within a few decades the new port of North Shields contained a hundred dwellings, and had developed a thriving trade, exporting hides and wool and importing coal and fish. Inevitably this provoked the burgesses of Newcastle-upon-Tyne who, in or around 1267, burned down some of its houses, and confiscated the coal they found there. South Shields developed in a similar way on the land of the priors of Durham.

Torquay may owe its origins to the fishing rights in Tor Bay granted to Torre Abbey by its founder, and a pier and fishing harbour there are mentioned by Leland. Marazion, facing the priory of St Michael's Mount, was developed as a fish market by the parent abbey of Mont St Michel. In 1392 Richard Auncell, prior of St Michael's Mount, built a quay at the small fishing port of Mousehole on the west side of Mounts Bay, while the jetty of the Mount itself was rebuilt by the priory in the late 1420s. In 1310 we find the prior of Plympton attempting to restrict the setting up of fish stalls to his market place in Sutton Prior, a place which was incorporated within the new borough of

Plymouth in 1439. Tavistock Abbey established a quay on the tidal Tamar at Morwellham where ships could offload wine, fish, sand and other cargoes for the abbey's use, and a small port had begun to develop there by 1230. Strata Florida may have developed the port of Aberarth on Cardigan Bay, where the abbey had fishing rights.

Occasionally remains of coastal or estuarine quays have been recorded on former monastic estates. Three massive soleplates of a timber quay, dated by dendrochronology to the mid-twelfth century, were discovered on the foreshore of the Severn estuary near Woolaston. Early in the thirteenth century, the quay had been extended seawards using stone blocks and upright timber posts, so that it could then have accommodated sea-going ships, as well as river craft, at all stages of the tide. Tintern Abbey had held the manor of Woolaston since 1131 and established five granges within its bounds, so it is likely that the abbey built this quay in order to export surplus produce to the markets of Bristol, Gloucester and south Wales.

There are several records of lighthouses being maintained by hermits, and occasionally by more regular monastic communities. A turret at the east end of Tynemouth Priory's church was surmounted by a coal-fired beacon. St Catherine's Chapel at Abbotsbury, built by the Benedictine abbey in the fourteenth century, is also said to have carried a light to warn mariners of the dangerous shore. Some monasteries with coastal properties, however, had rights to salvage from shipwrecks.

16
Monastic mills

Introduction

Grinding grain for meal, flour and malt was a fundamental necessity of medieval life. Querns turned by hand were used by the earliest monastic communities. The search for more efficient alternative sources of power led to the successive adoption of horse mills, watermills, tide mills and windmills. The vast majority of mills on monastic estates were, however, water-powered. Quite apart from their vital role in processing the monastic community's own grain, they also produced an important income through multure, a toll imposed upon tenants for the compulsory requirement of grinding their own corn at their lord's mill. Experiments were also made in applying water power to other industrial applications, such as fulling cloth, iron-working and crushing bark for the tanning industry. Mills also became a significant source of rent income on most estates.

Querns

The most primitive form of mill employed for grinding grain in the Middle Ages was the domestic rotary quern, a pair of stones turned by hand. A quern from a ninth-century context at Whitby is the earliest known from a monastic site in England, though even earlier examples have come from Whithorn in Scotland. Querns may have continued in use for malt milling long after other power sources had become available. Two kitchen servants at Peterborough Abbey were employed to mill grain by hand as late as 1125.

Grinding by hand is hard work and output is small in proportion to the time spent. Resentment against tolls charged at manorial mills nevertheless occasionally resulted in the continuing illicit use of domestic querns by monastic tenants. This often has to be seen in the context of a wider power struggle between lord and tenants, and the monasteries felt obliged to react decisively to enforce their manorial monopolies. In 1274 Abbot Roger Norton of St

Albans fined the townspeople and forced them to surrender the hand mills which they had set up in defiance of the abbey's rights in exchange for his own miller swearing an oath of honesty. When the townspeople again revolted against the abbey's domination in 1324, 80 domestic hand mills were set up in various private houses in the town. By 1331 Abbot Richard Wallingford had regained control of the situation and confiscated them all, setting the quern-stones into the floor of the monks' parlour to prevent their re-use. During Wat Tyler's rebellion 50 years later the townsmen broke into the abbey parlour, tore up the floor and redistributed the now broken and useless querns around the town as a symbol of their re-established liberties. Tenants of Cirencester Abbey complained at the Gloucestershire Assizes of 1301-2 that over the past five years the abbot's bailiff had broken into the houses of five different men and seized their quernstones, breaking up some and taking others away to the abbey. The bailiff countered that all the abbot's tenants in Cirencester were obliged to grind their corn in the abbot's own three mills there and that his confiscation of the stones was therefore justified. The bailiff won the case and the townspeople were required to pay 100 marks (£66 13s 4d) to the abbot for lodging a false complaint.

Horse mills

Animal-powered mills had been widely employed in the classical world, but by the Middle Ages they were used mainly as a supplement to other types of mill, or perhaps for malt grinding. Leicester Abbey acquired a horse mill in Wibtoft in the late twelfth century. John Hertford, abbot of St Albans (1235-63), finding that the abbey's watermill next to the brewhouse no longer functioned adequately because of the reed-beds and summer droughts which hindered the water supply, built a new horse mill in its place. Beaulieu Abbey possessed a horse mill in 1270, the horse being kept at the smithy. Glastonbury Abbey had a horse mill at Westonzoyland by 1301, perhaps built to replace the unsatisfactory windmill then recently abandoned, and this remained in use for grinding malt in 1335 even after a new windmill had been erected. The lessee of Vale Royal Abbey's mill at Kirkham in 1337 had to rebuild the horse mill there whenever the abbot wished. Abbot Thomas Burton (1396-99) built a horse mill within the precinct at Meaux, but used unseasoned timber, with the result that it quickly became ruinous. Coventry Priory had a horse mill and watermill under one roof in 1411. When two laypeople entered the service of the Abbot of Fountains at Warsill Grange in 1526, they undertook to provide a horse for the mill. At the Yorkshire nunnery of Swine the survey made at the Dissolution records the horse mill, bakehouse and boulting-house standing together in the outer yard under a single tiled roof with decayed mud walls, 50ft long by 20ft broad.

As with hand querns, horse mills built by tenants were sometimes seen as an infringement against the abbey's rights. The register of John Wheathampstead, abbot of St Albans, relates an interesting episode in 1455 when one of his tenants, John of Chertsey, set up a horse mill at Watford. The abbot's constable confiscated the millstones and removed them to his own house. John was away at the time and his wife, 'in woman's fashion broke out into execrations and curses and, having gathered together a number of chattering folk of the frail sex with small discretion, went and broke into the constable's house and bore back the stones in triumph'. On his return, John begged the abbot's pardon, and asked for his permission to keep the mill if he undertook to grind only oats; the abbot was unmoved: 'My friend, no-one ever knows when to stop. Experience shows that if you give a man an inch he takes an ell. I will not expose you to such temptation. Anyway, you deserve punishment'. John was forced to pull his mill down.

By the late Middle Ages many monastic houses were no longer able to enforce their manorial monopolies and were finding it increasingly difficult to meet the expense of maintaining watermills and windmills. Horse mills provided a relatively cheap, low-technology alternative. When Coventry Priory's watermill at Sowe fell into disrepair, it was replaced first with a windmill and finally with a horse mill. Abbot Selwood of Glastonbury built a horse mill at Westonzoyland, while further examples were erected at Glastonbury, Middlezoy and Moorlinch under his successor. Some houses licensed private horse mills to their tenants. Around the middle of the fifteenth century, tenants of Ramsey Abbey operated horse mills at Swavesey and Chatteris in Cambridgeshire, both sites where the abbey had found it impossible to maintain its own windmills. A tenant of Nostell Priory paid 3s to have a horse mill on his own land at South Kirkby in the West Riding of Yorkshire in 1466.

Water-powered corn mills

The Benedictine Rule identifies the mill as one of the necessary things which should be located within the monastic enclosure. Many monasteries also acquired and built numerous mills on their landed estates, where they not only served the needs of their tenants, but also provided income through multure (the tolls imposed upon tenants who were obliged to grind their corn there) and through rents.

Water-powered corn mills had existed in Roman Britain, but whether any Roman mills survived long enough to influence the first monastic communities is unknown. There is no clear evidence for their renewed use in England before the seventh century, and it was a long time before they began to supersede the hand quern. Building and maintaining a watermill was costly, and the investment could only be profitable if there was a sufficiently large and assured supply of grain. The earliest examples, in consequence, appear only on royal estates, followed by those of the richer monasteries. The first authentic record of a mill in monastic hands occurs in AD 762, when a charter of King Ethelbert II of Kent records a receipt of half the rent of an already-existing mill at Chart, near Dover, from the minster of SS Peter & Paul in Canterbury, in exchange for rights to graze swine in the Weald.

Not until the late ninth century do charters begin to record mills with any frequency. In 883 a mill-pool is mentioned on the bounds of property at Stoke Bishop surrendered by the monastic community at Berkeley in exchange for exemption from supplying food-rents to the king. Its site can still be recognised amidst the modern suburbs of Bristol above Millpill Bridge, where the Shirehampton road crosses the River Trym. Abingdon Abbey acquired mills at Tadmarton in 956 and at Sutton Courtenay shortly after 1002.

There were two basic types of early watermill. The wheel could be mounted horizontally so that water fell onto angled paddles rotating a vertical spindle which was fixed directly to the upper stone. Since no gearing was involved, this type was small and relatively cheap to construct. The mills held by Burton Abbey shortly before 1120 at Stapenhill and Winhill, specified as 'small mills' and yielding low rents, may have been of this type, as may some of the so-called 'winter mills'. Athelney Abbey had a watermill at Long Sutton which could not grind in summer for lack of water. There is no evidence that horizontal-wheeled mills remained in use in England beyond the thirteenth century.

The more familiar but more complex and expensive vertical-wheeled mill, employing gearing to generate more power, was also in use long before the Norman Conquest. Richard Holt has associated its ultimate triumph over the horizontal mill with the rise of feudal power and the imposition of seignurial monopolies. The vertical wheel was driven by a mill-race flowing at a controllable level. The chronicle of Abingdon Abbey credited Abbot Aethelwold (c.955-963) with the diversion of part of the River Thames into a leat to work his new mill below the great court of the abbey, an artificial watercourse three-quarters of a mile long (103). By the twelfth century water-engineering works of this sort had become commonplace in precinct and estate mills alike. At Fountains Abbey part of the River Skell was diverted into a race by a weir some 200 yards upstream from the mill. At Reading Abbey the mill was driven by a watercourse which diverges from the River Kennett over 5 miles upstream and flows in a wholly artificial course for its lower 2 miles. Excavations here have demonstrated a sequence of realignments of both river and mill leat between the twelfth and fourteenth centuries using dumped clay and post-and-plank revetments.

Vertical mill-wheels could themselves be of several types. The simplest form was the undershot wheel, turned by the kinetic energy of moving water,

103 *The present Abbey Mill at Abingdon (Berkshire), seen here from the tail-race, almost certainly occupies the site of the mill said to have been built by Abbot Aethelwold in the middle of the tenth century*

which could work off streams with a small head of water and rivers of shallow gradient so long as there was a reasonable flow. Wherwell Priory's mill at Winchester had two undershot wheels. Henry I granted Carlisle Priory a mill on the Eden Bridge with its wheel below one arch. A fifteenth-century map of Chertsey Abbey's meadows on the Thames below Laleham shows two undershot mills on either side of a backwater near the abbey (**colour plate 30**). Undershot wheels were unsuited to uncanalised streams with an irregular regime of floods and droughts, and were comparatively inefficient due to the loss of water round the sides of the wheel and the dragging effect as the paddles rose from the water.

The overshot wheel was turned by the potential energy or weight of water led over a trough or launder above the wheel to fall into its buckets. This type required only about a quarter of the water needed to turn an undershot wheel of similar size, and there was no special advantage in a rapid flow, but a significant fall of water was essential, so the choice of possible sites was more limited. At Waltham Abbey a new mill-race was made parallel with the old one, but at a higher level, to work a new overshot wheel, probably in the later twelfth century (**colour plate 26**). The two mills may have worked together for many years, but eventually the lower mill was abandoned. By 1482 the abbot was accused of taking a head of water 16ft broad along the upper leat, which should have been only 4ft broad, thereby diverting too much water off the River Lea.

Domesday Book records many hundreds of mills in monastic tenure, and it is impossible to guess what proportion of these had horizontal or vertical wheels. Where two mills are recorded in the same place, this may sometimes indicate one building containing two vertical wheels and two sets of stones under the same roof, a fairly common arrangement later in the Middle Ages.

Monastic income from mills generally expanded after 1086. In part this was achieved by continuing to build more mills, but there was also some rationalisation, with small mills on unreliable watercourses being abandoned in favour of larger, more profitable enterprises. Domesday Book records 21 mills on 17 manors belonging to Peterborough Abbey, producing a little over £14 per annum. Surveys of those same lands carried out between 1125 and 1128 reveal the same number of mills, but those at Peterborough, Kettering and Collingham had fallen out of use, while new mills had appeared at Alwalton, Castor, Great Easton and Fiskerton, and income from their rents had risen to over £26. In total, 23 of Glastonbury Abbey's manors had 28 mills between them in 1086; half a dozen of the Domesday mills had ceased work by 1189, but the overall total had risen to 31 and the income from them had more than doubled.

The 'high farming' period of the thirteenth century saw the peak of investment in mills on monastic estates. At St Albans the abbey's mills had fallen into disrepair during the long period when they had been farmed out, and Abbot John Hertford (1235-63) spent over £100 in repairing them all with oak timber. On the Glastonbury estates Abbot Michael Amesbury (1235-52) built 16 new mills and there were at least 27 watermills on 31 of Glastonbury's

104 *Newton Mill, Sturminster Newton (Dorset), on the River Stour: the present buildings are mainly of seventeenth- and nineteenth-century date, but the mill formerly belonged to Glastonbury Abbey*

manors by the early fourteenth century (**104**). Abbot John Brookhampton of Evesham (1282-1316) also built 16 new watermills. Prior Henry Eastry augmented the rent income of Christ Church, Canterbury, by £20 through building or acquiring at least eight new mills.

By contrast with Benedictine and Augustinian practices, the Cistercians were forbidden by their early statutes from acquiring manorial mills as a source of revenue, though they were allowed to use mills for grinding their own corn for consumption within the abbey. The first endowments of lands given by secular benefactors often included pre-existing mills, however, and compromises were inevitable. Bordesley Abbey's foundation endowment in 1138 included a mill at Bidford-on-Avon, and Louth Park was given a mill in the following year. The merging of the order of Savigny with that of Cîteaux in 1147 drove a further wedge between theory and practice, since most of the Savignac houses founded in the 1130s already had more than one mill on their lands, and the conditions of the union permitted them to keep them. Later Cistercian statutes maintained the resistance against accepting mills as a source of income, but it is evident that they had little effect.

In order to work a watermill efficiently, control of the water supply was essential. Grants of mills often specified in detail arrangements for access, for the diversion of water and for the maintenance of ponds and dams. Since streams often formed manorial boundaries, agreements for ponds to encroach over neighbouring properties were often required. In 1227 Salley Abbey was allowed to make a mill-pond at Hunslet over land belonging to its neighbours, while in 1301 it negotiated an agreement to make a dam 2ft deep across another layman's land to serve its mills on the River Ribble.

The penning up of water inevitably reduced the flow to other mills lower downstream, while interference with the natural drainage sometimes caused flooding, and mill weirs sometimes obstructed navigation channels. As a result, mills were frequent sources of dispute. In 1066 the bishop of Lincoln's tenants at Great Milton threatened to destroy the weir of Abingdon Abbey's mill at Cuddesdon, but the chronicle records how Abbot Ealdred foiled them with the aid of the miraculous bones of St Vincent. In 1110 Abbot Faricius of Abingdon complained that the miller of Henor Mill on the River Ock used to open his sluices so widely that the abbot's meadows were flooded, while at other times he held back the flow so that the abbot's own mill lower downstream could not work. In 1344 Abingdon Abbey built a new mill at Botley, provoking a complaint from the king that its sluices drew off too much water and reduced the effectiveness of the royal mills at Oxford Castle. Oseney Abbey had several mills on the braided channels of the Thames west of Oxford, and was also involved in prolonged disputes with both the Crown and the civic authorities, being accused of diverting water which should have worked the castle mills, blocking the navigation channel and damaging the fisheries and neighbouring meadows. The abbeys of Beaulieu and Stanley were in conflict from 1213 to 1222 because the weir of Stanley Abbey's mill at Eldey in Worth, near Faringdon, had caused flooding over Beaulieu's land. Fountains Abbey had a protracted dispute with Salley Abbey over Litton Mill, finally resolved in 1279 then in 1301 the abbot of Fountains was accused of diverting a watercourse to his mill at Rigton, though he claimed that he had done no more than repair the mill dam with piles, as was his right. In 1279 the abbot of Westminster protested that his mill and other property in Great Amwell had been flooded and damaged by the raising of the abbot of Waltham's sluices at Amwell and Stansted. In 1307 it was claimed that the River Fleet under Holborn and Fleet Bridges in London had formerly been wide enough to carry ten or a dozen ships, but since the Knights Templars had built mills there access by ship was no longer possible; the Templars lost their case, and the mills had to be pulled down. In 1384 the abbot of Glastonbury was presented because the new mill he had built at Bathpool was undermining the road to Taunton. Occasionally such quarrels broke out into violence. Vale Royal Abbey's mill at Darnhall was attacked by a neighbouring landowner in 1395 and its mill at Onston was wrecked in 1446.

Earthworks of abandoned dams and leats can often be recognised within the monastic precinct, as at Hailes (**colour plate 29**), Stanley and Byland. Many more survive on outlying estates and granges. At Bordesley Abbey's Lye Grange, the mill was given to the abbey by William Baker in 1180 in exchange for an annuity of 12 quarters of wheat and 12 quarters of rye, and the outline of the mill-pond, leats and dam and the footings of the mill building were traced by Mick Aston in the 1960s. Not infrequently, the sites of monastic mills remained in use after the Dissolution, and later buildings now occupy the site, as at Tewkesbury, Rievaulx and Kingswood.

Few upstanding medieval monastic mill buildings remain. The finest example is that in the outer court at Fountains Abbey (**105**). This is a long, three-storey, stone-built range, about 26ft wide and originally over 100ft in length. Much of the existing building, with its two-light pointed windows, dates from the thirteenth century, when the top floor was added as a granary; but Glyn Coppack has shown that parts of an earlier structure from the late 1130s were incorporated into it. At the Dissolution it contained two undershot wheels in a central chamber at basement level. In comparison with other medieval English mills, this is an abnormally large structure, but its factory scale resembles that of some French Cistercian mills where multiple wheels worked several different kinds of machinery. Alterations to a house at Abbotsbury in 1984 resulted in its identification as the medieval abbey mill, again with a wheelpit in the middle of the range. Originally this contained two overshot wheels side by side, but in 1401 it was reported that in summer there was insufficient water to drive the two sets of stones. Subsequently they were replaced by a smaller single wheel driving a single set of stones, and this seems to have worked much better, functioning throughout the year even when there was

105 *The Fountains Abbey mill (Yorkshire North Riding) from the west. The lower floor dates in part from the late 1130s. The mill was extended and the upper floor added as a grain store during the reorganisation of the outer court by Abbot John of Kent, 1220-47. It remained a working mill up to 1939*

little water. The alteration had probably been made by 1469 when the mill's value had doubled. Elsewhere only a few masonry fragments of precinct mill buildings survive, at Shap, Furness, Durham, Jervaulx, Kirkstall, Castle Acre, Waverley and Reading, while others at Coventry and Shrewsbury have been recorded archaeologically. In smaller houses mills were sometimes fairly flimsy structures which may not long have survived the demise of the monastic community. Surveys made of two small Cistercian nunneries in Yorkshire at the Dissolution record at Handale 'a little overshot wheel going with a little water, daubed walls and covered with thatch', while at Basedale the overshot mill by the gate was 20ft long by 14ft broad, stone-walled, part boarded, with a thatched roof, but 'the whole is in decay, so that the said mill goith not'.

Occasionally watermills were removed from one site to another. A grant of Kearby Mill to Salley Abbey before 1246 included the proviso that the monks could move the mill from one end of the dyke to the other. A Fountains Abbey lease of 1527 records an agreement that Bewerley New Mill and its dam could be removed from the west bank of the River Nidd and re-erected further upstream on the east bank.

Most estate mills were rented out for cash from the outset. Sub-leasing also occurred, so that two or more monastic houses obtained an income from the same mill. Fountains Abbey built a mill at Kirkheaton soon after 1200, then leased it to Kirklees Priory, which in turn leased it in 1241 to a lay tenant.

Grants to monastic houses often included just a portion of the income from a mill. Kirkstall Abbey received 12s in rent from a mill at Farnley in 1254, in which two other owners also had interests. Some time between 1257 and 1283 Rufford Abbey acquired a quarter-share of three mills in Rotherham. Leases usually defined the respective responsibilities of abbey and tenant. Sibton Abbey's lease of its mills at Weybread in 1354 required the tenant to maintain them, but undertook to provide the 'good timber needed for planks, beams and mill-wheel'. When Abbot Marmaduke Huby of Fountains leased out Rigton Mill in 1514, he was to provide the millstones and large timber, but the tenant was expected to maintain the iron gear, the timber and thatch of the building, and the dam and leat, at his own expense. Stoneleigh Abbey's Home Grange mill was leased under a similar arrangement in 1367.

The later Middle Ages saw a general decline in the number of mills, as high costs of labour and materials for repairs, lower demand for flour after the Black Death and the difficulty of finding tenants willing to pay an adequate rent resulted in profits becoming increasingly uncertain. A market developed for second-hand parts from abandoned mills: Norwich Priory acquired a used millstone for Hindringham Mill in 1364 for the still considerable sum of £1 6s 10d. Some recovery is however evident before the Dissolution. Abbot Beere (1493-1524) built a new watermill at Glastonbury, which was rented out for £10, while Richard Whiting, last abbot of Glastonbury, was promising to repair the grist and fulling mills at Mells on the very eve of the Dissolution.

Tide mills

The principle of ponding back the incoming tide in coastal creeks to turn mill wheels on the ebb tide was known in Ireland at least since the seventh century. In England monastic tide mills around the east and south coasts are docu-mented from the twelfth century (**106**). Around 1170 the canons of Woodbridge granted land to a certain layman for access to his tide mill on the Deben estuary, which they subsequently acquired. Costs of maintenance and repair were considerable, however, and the mill was blamed for the priory's impoverished state towards the Dissolution. The canons of St Osyth's had a tide mill at the head of the creek below the abbey in 1491. In the Thames estuary Barking Abbey had tide mills at Corringham and Mucking, the Knights Hospitallers had another on the Mardyke at Purfleet, Stratford Langthorn Abbey acquired the tidal mills of Bromley-by-Bow in the thirteenth century, while in 1233 Crashe Mills at Wapping belonged to the Priory of Holy Trinity, Aldgate. On the Medway the chamberlain of St Andrew's Priory, Rochester, is said to have built a tide mill below the castle in the late eleventh century. In the fourteenth century the Abbot of Quarr had a tide mill at the mouth of Wootton Creek on the Isle of Wight. The precinct corn mill at Beaulieu was

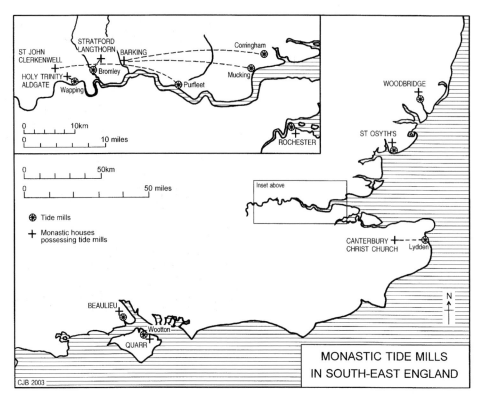

106 *Monastic tide mills in the Thames estuary and south-east England*

also probably a tide mill. A drawback of such mills was their vulnerability to the destructive power of the sea. Henry Eastry, Prior of Christ Church, Canterbury, rebuilt at the astronomical cost of £143 13s a tide mill at Lydden near Sandwich, which had been destroyed in the 1290s. Following damage by flooding in 1316 he paid out a further £74 13s 4d to move it to a safer position, but in 1326 it was again wrecked by high tides, and the venture was abandoned.

The invention of the cam-shaft and trip-hammer opened up the possibility of other industrial applications for vertical waterwheels. In addition to a corn mill, monastic precincts may contain several other watermills with different functions, a fulling mill, iron mill and bark mill. All of these may also occur on the granges and outlying estates.

Fulling mills

Fulling was a process in woollen cloth manufacture whereby the cloth was scoured and pounded in water containing a detergent to cleanse it of super-fluous oil and grease and to mat together the loose fibres. Traditionally this had been done by trampling in wooden tubs, but water power was being applied to this purpose by the late twelfth century. The survey of the Knights Templars' estates in 1185 lists fulling mills at Temple Newsam near Leeds and at Barton by Temple Guiting on the Cotswolds, but there may have been an even earlier example on the lands of Kirkstead Abbey, where a fulling mill at Kirkby-on-Bain is recorded some time between 1154 and 1189.

Fulling mills became most numerous in the western half of Britain where the wetter climate, more constricted valleys and steeper stream gradients with sharper nick-points offered more suitable sites for overshot wheels. They made an early appearance on the estates of Benedictine monasteries in the Cotswolds and Severn valley (**107**). In the south-west, Tavistock Abbey was leasing out a fulling mill at Parkwood in 1388, and during the fifteenth century, Abbot Mey installed fulling-stocks in a derelict corn mill at Crowndale, while several other mills were converted by lessees. By 1500 there were 16 fulling mills operating within 2 miles of Tavistock Abbey. By contrast, in eastern England fulling mills remained generally scarce, although the Prior of Ely had one at Hauxton in 1279, and the Abbey of Bec had another at Blakenham by 1288.

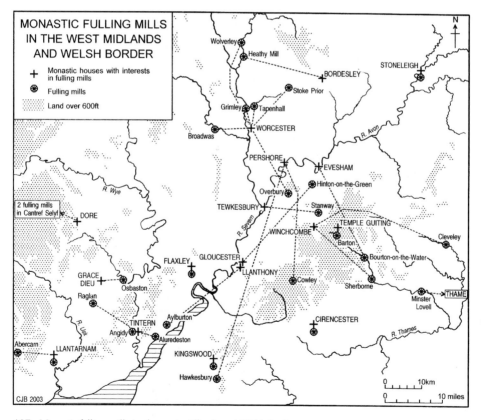

107 *Monastic fulling mills in the west midlands and Welsh border*

Cistercian monasteries drew considerable wealth from wool production but were not generally centres of cloth manufacture. They nevertheless came to hold over 70 fulling mills in England and Wales, at least half a dozen of which date from before the end of the twelfth century. A confirmation of land to Stanley Abbey in 1189 mentions the abbey's fulling mill, also a half-interest in another at Peckingell in Langley Burrell. Thame Abbey received a grant of two mills at Minster Lovell in 1197, one of which was a fulling mill. Quarr Abbey had built an undershot fulling mill at Heasley on the Isle of Wight shortly before the end of the twelfth century. Newminster, Kingswood, Margam, Whitland and Strata Florida all had at least four or five fulling mills on their estates.

Occasionally documentary records tell us something about the buildings and machinery. The Beaulieu account book of 1269-70 records expenditure on timber for the abbey's fulling mill and on repairs to the wheels, even including a schematic sketch. An indenture of 1437 describes in considerably greater detail the building of a new fulling mill at Chartham, capable of fulling three 'dozens', cloths 45ft in length, for William Molash, prior of Christ Church, Canterbury. Two millwrights of Pluckley agreed to build it for 22 marks. The timber was to be of beech and the dimensions of the frame and working parts were closely detailed. The prior was to provide the timber and ironwork and make the earthworks for the dam and the work was to be finished within the year. In the sixteenth century the Abbey Mill at Cirencester contained four pairs of fulling-stocks.

Few examples have yet been recognised archaeologically. At Beaulieu the excavation of a ruined building formerly interpreted as a wine press suggested that it was more probably a fourteenth-century fulling mill, with an adjoining two-storey range serving as a weaving- or drying-shed and store. At Byland Abbey the fulling mill appears to have been just outside the precinct wall, some 700 yards downstream from the corn mill. Stoneleigh Abbey's fulling mill at Cryfield Grange may be represented by one of two surviving dams there. Glyn Coppack's excavations at Fountains led him to suggest that a fulling mill with a narrow undershot wheel was inserted within the woolhouse towards the end of the thirteenth century, lasting only a few decades before being dismantled and replaced by dyeing vats. It is, however, difficult to see how sufficient power can have been generated here for this purpose.

Next to corn mills, fulling mills represent the widest medieval application of water power. Occasionally they proved good investments. Quarr Abbey's fulling mill at Heasley yielded twice the rent of some of the nearby corn mills in the fifteenth century. Few other examples were as profitable, however. During the later thirteenth century Peterborough Abbey's fulling mill at Kettering produced only one-sixth of the income of its corn mills on the same manor. Profits from Ramsey Abbey's fulling mill at Elton were similarly disappointing. Fulling mills on the Glastonbury estates at Wrington and Mells provided only token rents for the use of the water, and these seem to have been built by tenants, the abbey remaining cautious about risking its own capital in such a speculative venture. The number of fulling mills on the Glastonbury estates had risen to six by the end of the Middle Ages, but only the one built at Glastonbury by Abbot Beere himself, and one other, paid rents in excess of £1. The application of water power to fulling is technologically interesting, but the impact it made upon the monastic economy is small.

Iron mills

Water power was also applied to the operation of bellows and trip-hammers for metal-working. The earliest evidence for this is from Bordesley Abbey, where Grenville Astill has excavated an undershot mill first erected in the 1170s and reconstructed several times before the late fourteenth century. The River Arrow had been canalised out of its natural course in order to accommodate the mill and the fishponds above, but increasing difficulties in maintaining the complex water-management system of the valley led to the mill becoming choked up by flood silt and abandoned well before the Dissolution. The Bordesley mill seems never to have operated as a corn mill. A series of hearths and quantities of iron, bronze and lead artefacts and debris indicate that it was used instead for metal-working throughout its lifespan. A mid-fourteenth century water-powered forge for hammering blooms has been excavated at Chingley, on land belonging to Boxley Abbey. Steve Moorhouse has identified a site on Fountains Abbey's Bradley Grange named as 'Smythclough' in a charter of 1240, where substantial earthworks and scatters of slag suggest a water-powered iron-working complex. A blade-sharpening mill, employing a water-powered grindstone, is recorded at Minchinhampton, a manor which belonged to Holy Trinity, Caen, in about 1306. In the late fifteenth century, the canons of Beauchief were leasing out a bloomery hearth with woods for charcoal and a 'smithy dam'. Rents from Merevale Abbey just after the Dissolution include 26s 8d from the iron mill there. Generally, however, iron-working mills remained rare throughout the Middle Ages.

Bark mills

Watermills employed for crushing tanbark are known in England from the early thirteenth century, and occasional examples appear in monastic precincts or elsewhere on the estates. Repairs to the tannery mill at Beaulieu are recorded in 1269-70. Another bark mill is recorded at Kirkstall in 1288. In the early fourteenth century Battle Abbey invested in a bark mill for its Marley tannery at Iltonsbath on the River Brede near Sedlescombe. On the lands of

Tavistock Abbey a tan mill at Taviton was converted to a fulling mill some time between 1400 and 1413. In 1532 Fountains Abbey leased its barkhouse, bark mill, kiln, cisterns, vats and tanning vessels for a 33-year term. Bark mills were never common and no medieval examples have yet been recognised archaeologically.

Windmills

Windmills first appeared towards the end of the twelfth century. They had several advantages over watermills. They were cheaper to build since they only needed about half an acre of land and there were no ponds or leats to be dug. Whereas watercourses could be obstructed or diverted by neighbouring landowners, access to the wind was freely available. Against this, however, the wind was an unpredictable and uncontrollable power source. Windmills might stand idle for long periods in calm weather. They required constant attention to adjust the sails to the changing speed and direction of the wind. They were much more dangerous than watermills; over-rapid rotation of the sails generated sparks which could cause fire, a tail-wind could bowl them over if they were not turned in time, and their hilltop locations rendered them singularly vulnerable to lightning strikes. They were expensive to maintain. Moreover, though windmills were capable of driving several sets of millstones for corn-grinding, they could not be relied upon for more advanced industrial operations such as metal-working.

The appearance of the new technology provoked internal strife in one Benedictine abbey. The chronicle of Jocelin of Brakelond recounts what happened when Herbert, the dean of Bury St Edmunds, set up a windmill just outside the town in about 1190:

> When Abbot Samson heard this, he grew so hot with anger that he would scarcely eat or speak a single word. On the morrow, after hearing Mass, he ordered the sacrist to send his carpenters thither without delay, to pull everything down, and place the timber under safe custody.
>
> Hearing this, the dean came and said that he had the right to do this on his own fief, and that free benefit of the wind ought not to be denied to any man; he said also that he wished to grind his own corn there and not the corn of others, lest perchance he might be thought to do this to the detriment of neighbouring mills.
>
> To this the abbot, still angry, answered:
>
> 'I thank you as I would thank you if you had cut off both my feet. By God's face, I will never eat bread till that building be thrown down. You are an old man, and you ought to know that not even the king, nor his justiciar, can set up anything within the liberties of this town without

the consent of the Abbot and Convent. Why then, have you dared to do such a thing? Nor is this done without detriment to my mills as you claim; for the burgesses will flock to your mill and grind their corn there to their heart's content, and I shall have no right to punish them, since they are free men. Go away...and before you reach your house you shall hear what will be done with your mill.'

However, the dean, shrinking in fear from before the face of the abbot, caused the mill which he had built to be pulled down by his own servants without delay, so that when the sacrist came, they found nothing left to demolish.

When did the windmill first appear, and what part did monastic houses play in its adoption? A survey by Edward Kealey has placed the first English record of a windmill as early as 1137, when King Stephen's almoner granted his Leicestershire manor of Wigston Parva with its mill to Reading Abbey, when he retired to the community as a monk. There is, however, no certain identification of Wigston's mill as a windmill until shortly before 1200, when the monks regained control of it from a lessee. Since a headstream of the River Soar, quite capable of working a horizontal watermill, forms the township's western boundary, it is a dangerous leap of faith to assert that the mill of 1137 must be identical with the windmill mentioned 60 years later. John Stow, writing at the end of the sixteenth century, stated that the benefactor who founded the female Augustinian house at Clerkenwell in about 1144 gave them a site on which to build a windmill. Again, there is no contemporary record of this, though the sisters certainly had a windmill by 1430.

The earliest authentic references date from the 1180s. A windmill is mentioned in the 1185 survey of Knights Templars' properties at Weedley in Yorkshire, and another at Dunwich was granted to the Templars shortly afterwards. Several Benedictine houses had income from windmills before the end of the twelfth century, though, significantly, these were mostly benefactions from lay people, not mills built by the abbeys themselves. Shortly after 1184 Agnes de Mountchesney gave the nuns of Godstow a windmill standing on a mound outside the village of Dinton. By 1194 Reginald Arsic had given to the priory of Hatfield Regis the tithes from his windmill in Silverley. Leaving aside Dean Herbert's ill-fated mill, the abbey of Bury St Edmunds had acquired several windmills before the end of the twelfth century; Walter fitz Robert, the king's steward, gave the monks half an acre at Longbridge in Hempnall on which to erect a windmill, others were acquired at Risby and Timworth, while Abbot Samson was leasing out a windmill with the manor of Elvedon. Wymondham Priory acquired windmills from four different donors during the 1190s, at Flockthorpe, Betwick, Snettisham and at Wymondham itself. Abbot Roger of St Augustine's, Canterbury (1175-1212) acquired from local laymen one windmill on half an acre just north of the city and another at Elmstead, and also built one himself at Chislet. Although something like 80 per cent of the windmills known before the end of the twelfth century had come into monastic ownership, it was mostly local gentry who built them. The monks cannot be seen as pioneering the new invention. Indeed, initially they viewed windmills with caution, accepting them as gifts, but building their own only once they were convinced of their potential profitability.

⌈Despite the Cistercian prohibition on mills as a source of revenue, over 40 windmills held by English and Welsh Cistercian houses have now been traced.⌉ A lost confirmatory charter to Swineshead Abbey granted around 1170, but known only from a recitation in 1316, is claimed to have mentioned a windmill. This early date, however, is unreliable. The first secure references occur in the early thirteenth century. Sibton Abbey had a windmill at Tostock by around 1220, Whalley Abbey had one at Ince by around 1230, and Thame Abbey had one on its grange at Otley by 1237. Windmills are found among the holdings of most of the other major monastic orders: the Augustinian priory of Hickling, for example, had acquired windmills at Hickling, Herringby, Burlingham, Palling, Waxham and Rollesby by the middle of the thirteenth century.

By 1200 monastic windmills were scattered throughout the eastern counties from Northumberland to Kent, and their numbers proliferated during the thirteenth century. By the fourteenth century they were appearing in Cornwall, where the Benedictine monks of Tywardreath Priory held the tithes of two newly-built windmills in 1314. By the Dissolution they had even penetrated into the far north-west, where the *Valor Ecclesiasticus* records a windmill on the home grange of Holm Cultram Abbey.

Windmills had particular advantages over watermills in low-lying areas where streams were sluggish, and in permeable chalk and limestone uplands where water supply was unreliable. In the Cotswolds, for example, records of the taxation of Pope Nicholas IV in around 1291 show windmills belonging to Tewkesbury Abbey at Gotherington, to Eynsham Abbey at Mickleton, to Kingswood Abbey at Hazleton and Tetbury and to Stanley Abbey at Codrington, while later sources show that Cirencester Abbey had a windmill at Througham in Bisley. In Somerset Athelney Abbey's watermill at Upton in Long Sutton was supplemented by a windmill by 1394 because it could not grind in summer for lack of water.

Windmills appeared in some numbers around the fringes of the Fens, Romney Marsh and the Somerset Levels, though even in areas so well suited to their use, the monasteries were slow to adopt them. None are mentioned in surveys of the manors held by Ramsey Abbey around 1200, but by 1279 there were 21 windmills on that estate, compared with 13 watermills. Glastonbury Abbey was preoccupied throughout the late twelfth and early thirteenth centuries, first with the need to rebuild its church after the disastrous fire of 1184, and then with a bitter struggle for independence from the diocesan bishop. It was, therefore, in no position to indulge in technological experiments at that time. During the campaign of Abbot Michael Amesbury (1235-52) to restore the abbey's lost revenues, the rents of ten mills were recovered, four of which, at Westonzoyland, South Brent, Ashcott and Glastonbury itself, were windmills. The Westonzoyland mill does not seem to have worked very well and was abandoned some time after 1274. Two more windmills had appeared on the estates in the 1260s and 1270s. It was nevertheless not until the early fourteenth century that Glastonbury Abbey seems finally to have become convinced of their value and it continued to build or acquire windmills for some time after it had ceased building new watermills. At this time 32 of Glastonbury's manors included 26 watermills, 13 windmills (all but two of which lay around the margins of the flat Somerset moors) and one horse mill. Surviving accounts suggest that the costs of repairs borne by the abbey were small compared with the rent income, and for a while they proved a very good investment.

The commonest form of medieval windmill was the post-mill, in which the entire timber-framed body was rotated on a central post to face the sails into the wind (**108** and **colour plate 31**). These often stood on mounds, which can sometimes be identified by the distinctive cruciform depression made by the setting for the cross-trees at the base of the mill-post. The mound of the mill built on the manor of Littleton by Abbot Brookhampton of Evesham survives in a field called Windmill Hill. Another mound overlying ridge and furrow at East Pennard in Somerset may represent the site of the windmill from

108 *Rievaulx Abbey (Yorkshire North Riding): carving of a post mill from the infirmary*

which the granger of Glastonbury Abbey was receiving tolls in 1361–2 (**colour plate 32**). Building accounts survive for Glastonbury Abbey's new post mill at Walton in 1342–3, detailing the timber, boards, iron fittings, sail canvas and millstones. The Beaulieu Abbey account book of 1269–70 provides similar details of two newly-built post mills on its Berkshire granges. There are several records of post mills being moved bodily from one location to another. The canons of Hickling Priory appear to have relocated their mill at Burlingham before 1200, while Abbot William of Meaux (1372–96) moved a windmill from Beeford in Holderness to a new site at Dringhoe about a mile away, apparently to replace a decayed watermill. By the end of the thirteenth century stone tower mills had also begun to appear in England, but no examples of this type in monastic ownership have yet been recognised.

Windmills were affected even more than watermills by rising maintenance costs and falling profits during the fourteenth century, and many were abandoned. Glastonbury's windmill at Berrow was blown down in 1333, and although the abbey tried to force its tenants to re-erect it at their own expense, and levied an annual fine of £2 in compensation for the lost income, it was never rebuilt. The Walton windmill was in disrepair by 1380, no tenant could be found for it, and it had collapsed by 1393. A similar decline is evident on the Ramsey estates, where the windmill at Brancaster was derelict and untenanted by 1352; the abbey eventually restored this to working order, but it was a long time before the costs of repairs were recovered. Ramsey's windmill at Chatteris had been dismantled by 1379 and its windmill at Holywell was blown down around 1414. Millstones and cogwheels were salvaged from the latter for repairs to Elsworth Mill, 5 miles away, but by 1453 the abbey had decided to abandon this mill too, following fire damage. Only in the sixteenth century, when, for example, Abbot Beere's terrier reveals that he had built new windmills on the Glastonbury estates at East Brent and Winterbourne Monkton, can the beginnings of a recovery be detected.

17

Extractive and manufacturing industry on monastic estates

Introduction

Both extractive and manufacturing industry remained relatively small-scale throughout the Middle Ages, but neither should be underestimated, and monastic communities to some extent depended upon their products. Churches, claustral ranges and estate buildings demanded building-stone, mortar, roofing slates and floor tiles. Ovens and malt kilns were vital for converting the cereal produce of the estates into bread and ale. Cloth looms and tanneries were equally necessary for keeping the monks clothed and shod. Other opportunities were opened up when coal, iron or precious metals were discovered on monastic estates. To what extent were monasteries involved in the development of industry on their lands?

Stone quarries

The earliest monastic foundations often met their building needs by recycling material from redundant Roman ruins. At a time when most buildings were of timber, such reuse may well have been a deliberate evocation of the imperial past and an affirmation of links with the empire's successor, the church in Rome. The first generation of Anglo-Saxon monastic churches, Bradwell-juxta-Mare and Brixworth, and Wilfrid's crypts at Ripon and Hexham, all display much dressed stone or brick of Roman origin. In later years such reuse was more a matter of opportunism in areas lacking good-quality stone. In the early eleventh century Abbot Eadmer of St Albans had begun stockpiling brick dug from the ruins of Roman Verulamium with the intent of rebuilding the abbey church, but it was the Norman builders who made use of it, and it can still be seen in the tower and transepts. Even into the later twelfth century, the canons of Lanercost were robbing stone from Hadrian's Wall for their church.

Alternatively, stone could be imported from abroad. The great Norman rebuilding demanded high-quality masonry, and many monasteries around the south-eastern coast preferred to ship stone over from Normandy rather than risk using unproven materials from local quarries. Lanfranc, appointed arch-bishop of Canterbury four years after the Conquest, had previously been abbot at Caen, and his nephew Paul, abbot of St Albans from 1077, had also been a monk there, so it comes as no surprise to find both of them choosing Caen stone for rebuilding their respective churches. It was used again at Canterbury when the Romanesque choir was reconstructed after the great fire of 1174. The loss of Normandy to France did not end the trade; imports of Caen stone increased after the mid-thirteenth century as new work at Westminster Abbey, Norwich Priory and elsewhere demanded fine stone for gothic mouldings. It commanded a sentimental attachment at Canterbury even into the end of the fifteenth century; when the archbishop and monks decided to complete their central tower, construction was carried out in brick, but over three years they spent £380 on facing stone from Caen, 'from which quarries it is well known that our church was anciently built'.

Few parts of England are more than a few miles from some source of stone. Small-scale quarrying had been renewed by the eighth century. Locally-available liassic rubble characterises some of the earliest buildings excavated at Glastonbury. Building new monastic churches, first during the tenth-century reform, and much more significantly after the Norman Conquest, created demands which could only be met by opening many more quarries. When stone had to be brought from more than about 12 miles away, transport costs exceeded the costs of the stone itself. Rubble, at least, was therefore usually sought locally, even if stone for ashlar facing, mouldings and sculptural detail had to be brought from further afield.

The chronicle of Battle Abbey recounts that, after the first shiploads of stone had arrived from Caen, a pious lady informed the monks that an abundance of good stone could be found if they dug near the projected site of the church in a place revealed to her by a vision, and so it proved. A local source of stone for Finchale Priory was miraculously revealed when the River Wear came down in spate, eroded its banks and dislodged many large blocks. The monks of Fountains found a useful outcrop of Carboniferous Laverton Sandstone on the edge of their precinct, while the monks of Furness found a convenient source of Triassic sandstone immediately south of the abbey.

Many other monasteries found suitable stone on their estates, if not within their precincts. On Evesham Abbey's manor of Offenham, the Domesday Book records the oxen of one plough-team diverted to dragging stone from the quarry for the construction of the abbey church, a couple of miles away. The foundation endowment of Rievaulx gave it access to two types of stone nearby, the Lower Calcareous Grit, usable only for rough walling, and the finer-grained Kellaways Sandstone, available from the Penny Piece quarries less than a mile upstream, which provided plain ashlar for facing the first church. Subsequent acquisitions in Bilsdale included more distant sources of Middle

Jurassic sandstone at Laskill and Weathercote. The former was used for the abbey's woolhouse at Laskill, the latter quarry providing stone for the first claustral buildings. When the east end of Rievaulx's church was rebuilt in the early thirteenth century, oolitic limestone was brought from Griff, less than a mile downstream; the abbey had owned this land since 1131, and it is curious that such an excellent building stone had not been exploited earlier. John Senior has speculated that knowledge of its virtues may have been communicated from Byland Abbey, which quarried the same material at Wass Bank. ⌐

Abingdon Abbey had several quarries providing Corallian and Portland Limestone. The most important of these was at Wheatley, which provided stone for many buildings after the late thirteenth century. In 1346 the Dominican friars were allowed 50ft square of this quarry for their building works at Langley. Another quarry at Cumnor is mentioned in 1383, and a much smaller quarry at Bayworth provided stone for two chimneys at Abingdon Abbey in 1436.

When monastic houses failed to find suitable stone on their own land, they often acquired temporary grants to extract stone from land held by others. Quarrying may originally have been a special royal prerogative, since early medieval monasteries received quarrying rights direct from the king. Ingulph's Chronicle records King Eadred granting stone to Crowland Abbey from quarries on the royal estate of Castor. Quarr on the Isle of Wight, the very name of which reflects its importance as a source of stone, was in the king's hands after the Conquest. A charter of William Rufus to Bishop Walkelin of Winchester granted him land on the Isle of Wight with the right to dig for stone there. The new church of Winchester Cathedral Priory was entirely built of greyish-white limestone from Quarr, and the same material was also used at the abbeys of Romsey, Titchfield and Canterbury and the priories of Christchurch, Lewes and Dover. By about 1120, however, the best of the Quarr stone had been worked out, and its use declined. Ranton Priory was granted quarrying rights in Knightley manor in Gnosall around 1200. A quarry in the Lower Chalk at Totternhoe was granted to St Albans Abbey in the thirteenth century, and Totternhoe stone was also used at Dunstable Priory and Westminster Abbey. Abbot Michael Mentmore of St Albans (1336-49) acquired a stone quarry at Eglemount. Whitby Abbey used a light brown Middle Jurassic sandstone from quarries at Aislaby, 3 miles to the east, which also supplied Guisborough Priory, while a similar stone was quarried on Ingleby Moor for the Charterhouse at Mount Grace, less than a mile away.

Royal support for monastic building works, continuing through the thirteenth and fourteenth centuries, included grants within the royal forests. In 1215 the Cistercians of Stanley were permitted to dig stone within the Forest of Chippenham to build their church, and in 1292-7 they were allowed to work the king's quarry in the Forest of Pewsham for further buildings and their precinct wall. Building accounts for the abbey of Vale Royal over a three-year period (1278-80) record 35,000 cartloads of stone being transported from quarries at Eddisbury, 5 miles to the west in Delamere Forest. Lenton Priory acquired quarrying rights in Sherwood Forest in 1229, and another grant of stone there for the church tower in 1242, while in 1307 the monks of Tintern were granted stone from Wyeswood in the Forest of Wentwood for works at the abbey and its grange of Trelleck.

Other monastic houses had to rely on lay benefactors. The Dale cartulary records quarries in Stanton-by-Dale and Kirk Hallam granted to the abbey by Ralph of Hereford in 1240. Conversely, monasteries occasionally leased their quarries or sold stone to local laymen. In 1434 the canons of Maxstoke sold stone from their home quarry to Sir William Mountford for use at Kingshurst Hall.

Some of the best building stones came from the oolitic limestone belt of the Cotswolds. Local abbeys such as Bruern, which had quarries on its own land at Milton-under-Wychwood, were fortunate indeed. Abbot Serlo, who began rebuilding the abbey church at Gloucester in 1089, brought stone from Painswick, 5 miles away. Cotswold stone was often purchased and carried long distances by monasteries which had no local properties from which they might exploit it directly. The Taynton quarries were supplying stone to St Frideswide's Priory in Oxford by the early thirteenth century and to Abingdon Abbey for its south aisle in 1420-1. Taynton also produced a more fissile limestone which was used for roofing the new refectory at Pershore in 1381-2.

John Aubrey recounts a legend that the oolitic outcrop at Haslebury near Box was miraculously discovered by St Aldhelm while he was seeking a source of stone for the building of Malmesbury Abbey. By the thirteenth century the Cistercians of Stanley and the Augustinian nuns of Lacock had both acquired their own quarries at Haslebury; when the nuns' quarry became worked out, they agreed an exchange with the abbot of Stanley, who gave them a strip 76ft long and of the same width as their original workings in his own quarry. Oolitic limestone was also quarried on Glastonbury Abbey's manor of Doulting by about 1170, and throughout the later fourteenth and fifteenth centuries the abbey derived considerable profits from the concessions which it allowed there to the bishop and canons of Wells.

The source of oolitic limestone most widely employed in monastic buildings was Barnack, where the remains of the medieval quarries may still be seen in the 'hills and holes' adjoining the village (**109**). Barnack owes its pre-eminence to the fact that all the Fenland abbeys had access to its quarries by water. Bury St Edmunds seems to have been the first monastic house to exercise quarrying rights there, but other local Benedictine houses also established early claims. A mid-eleventh-century agreement between the abbots of Peterborough and Ramsey allowed the latter to take dressed freestone from Barnack, while in 1061 Earl Waltheof granted rights in the 'well-known quarry' at Barnack to Crowland Abbey. Almost inevitably, conflicts arose, not just over quarrying

109 *Aerial view of the 'hills and holes' adjoining the village of Barnack (Northamptonshire). Before their abandonment in the early sixteenth century these ancient quarries supplied building stone to many abbeys in eastern England, including Bury St Edmunds, Peterborough, Ramsey, Thorney, Crowland, Norwich and Barnwell*

rights, but also over the transport of the stone. William the Conqueror forced the abbot of Peterborough to confirm the right of the monks of Bury to carry stone from Barnack to the River Nene. Another dispute over the carriage of Barnack stone by water arose between the abbeys of Ramsey and Sawtry in the late twelfth century. Whereas Caen stone was employed in the earliest work at Binham Priory's church, by 1240, when the west front of the nave was completed, Barnack stone had completely superseded it. It was also used at Castle Acre Priory and Thetford Priory.

Other parts of England had more limited sources of stone suitable for high-quality mouldings and sculpture. A fine white limestone from Beer in south Devon was used as far away as Rochester and Westminster in the 1360s. The Upper Liassic Ham Stone from south Somerset was used from the twelfth century by the monks of Sherborne, Cerne and Montacute. By 1478 some of the early quarries had been worked out and new ones opened up, one of which was leased to the Abbot of Forde for 4d a year. In North Yorkshire quarries at Hildenley, on the Howardian Hills, provided a fine light-buff Jurassic limestone used in the twelfth and thirteenth centuries at Kirkham Priory and the Gilbertine house of Old Malton. It also provided stone for a screen at Rievaulx.

Are they quarrying themselves or just buying?

Sources of polished stone

Some stone had special uses. Corfe, on the Isle of Purbeck, produced a hard dark grey limestone capable of taking a polish to resemble marble, and this was in particular demand for decorative work. Shiploads of Purbeck 'Marble' were despatched all over the country after the mid-twelfth century. It first appears in the cloisters of Canterbury Cathedral Priory in about 1150 and in the London Temple by 1161. By 1175 it was being shipped as far north as Durham for use in the Galilee Chapel. Other monastic houses using Purbeck marble include Waltham Abbey in 1229, Westminster Abbey after 1252, Vale Royal in 1287, and Norwich Cathedral Priory, where it was used for the columns of the new cloisters after 1324. Apart from its structural employment, Purbeck marble was widely favoured for effigies, tombs, shrines, altars and piscinae.

Quarries at Alwalton acquired by Peterborough Abbey in the early eleventh century produced a hard grey stone of similar quality, used in effigies in the abbey church, also at Ely and Bury St Edmunds. In the north the distinctively fossiliferous Frosterley 'marble' was already being used at Durham before 1200. Another northern source of polished stone was a quarry owned by the Premonstratensian canons at Egglestone in Teesdale, who permitted the prior of Durham to extract stone there for a new lavatorium in 1432-3 in exchange for a payment of 20s.

suggests they did extracting themselves — not a full-time operation.

Millstone quarries

Stone suitable for millstones could be obtained from the Carboniferous Millstone Grit outcrops of the Peak District and Pennines. A series of grants to Furness Abbey in the first half of the thirteenth century permitted the monks to take millstones from Kellet in Lancashire. Fountains Abbey had rights to quarry millstones from Crossland near Huddersfield and at Sawley (**112**). Elsewhere, the monks of Holm Cultram acquired similar rights at the beginning of the thirteenth century at Hensingham in west Cumberland, where they were also permitted to graze their oxen on the common pasture during the eight days while they were digging and carting the stones.

Limekilns

Limestone could be calcined in coal-fired kilns to produce quicklime, which was then slaked with water and mixed with sand to produce mortar. Limekilns were often set up specifically for particular construction jobs, but burnt lime could also be bought. In 1258 a monk of St Albans received 3s for supplying 'mortar of lime and sand' for building works at Westminster Palace. The nuns of Carrow had a limekiln just outside the walls of Norwich in 1484-5, but by 1530 it was ruined and yielded no rent. Lime was also widely used for rendering rubble walls.

Brick kilns

The Cistercians are believed to have played a major part in the development of the brick industry in the Low Countries and in other parts of northern Europe where building stone was scarce. They may also have been responsible for reintroducing brick manufacture into eastern England after the mid-twelfth century. During the excavation of Coggeshall Abbey church the quoins were found to have been built of distinctive thin, pale orange-brown bricks tempered with coarse sand. Similar bricks appeared in the surviving guest-house, gatehouse chapel and abbot's lodging in the late twelfth and early thirteenth centuries, and they have also been found at the preceptory of Temple Cressing. The resemblance of the Coggeshall bricks to those used at Coxyde Abbey in Flanders is striking, and the Cistercians may have sent over brick-makers from the Low Countries following the acquisition of Coggeshall from the Savignacs in 1148. Thin bricks were appearing at other Cistercian sites, including Rievaulx and Meaux, by the thirteenth century.

Initially brickwork was restricted to quoins, dressings and vaults, specially shaped bricks being made for door-jambs and window mouldings. At the gatehouse of Butley Priory the ribs are of stone, the webs of brick. Brick appears in the late thirteenth-century vault of the refectory undercroft of St Olave's Priory at Herringfleet. Other brick vaults occur at the Augustinian priories of Butley and West Acre, at the Norwich Blackfriars, at the Bridgettine nunnery of Syon and in the reredorter undercroft of Worcester Cathedral Priory. Brick was also employed for firebacks and ovens, and two brick chimneys were listed in the Dissolution survey of Swine Nunnery near Hull.

Entire buildings were being constructed of brick from the fourteenth century, and there was a developing skill in the use of shaped and differently-coloured bricks for decorative purposes. For reasons of ostentation, brickwork was particularly favoured for precinct walls and gatehouses. Thornton Abbey has a magnificent fourteenth-century gatehouse of plum-coloured brick with decorative details in stone, and later examples occur at the Whitefriars in Kings Lynn, at the abbeys of Letheringham and Leiston and at Eye Priory. Waltham Abbey retains a fragment of fourteenth-century brick precinct wall near the gatehouse. The enclosure wall of the Beverley Blackfriars is also of brick. Leicester Abbey retains a half-mile length of wall of diaper-pattern brickwork bearing the initials of Abbot John Penny, built in the last decade of the fifteenth century.

By the later fifteenth century brick was increasingly favoured for domestic ranges, figuring prominently in the lodgings built for Prior Overton of Repton (1437-8), Abbot Sever of York (1485-1502) and Abbot Vyntoner of St Osyth's (1523-33), and in the prior's lodging at Watton and parts of the abbess's lodging at Carrow. Brick also appears in some relatively minor precinct buildings, such as the early sixteenth-century 'Long Gallery' in the outer court of Abingdon Abbey. By contrast, it was rarely chosen for monastic churches or for the main claustral ranges, though it does appear in the tower of the late fourteenth-century Franciscan church at Kings Lynn, while the remains of Reading Abbey include an octagonal brick turret attached to the dormitory. The overall distribution of monastic brickwork is predominantly eastern, with isolated examples extending across the midlands to the Severn valley (**110**). Monasteries in the south-west or north-west of England made no use of it.

Unfortunately we rarely have any direct evidence for the source of the brick used in monastic buildings. Some of the early instances may represent imports brought back as a return cargo by ships carrying English wool to the cloth-manufacturing towns of the Low Countries. Grange buildings at the Augustinian abbey of Waltham were employing distinctive thin bricks before 1200 of a type which have not been found anywhere else in the vicinity. Thicker pale yellow, buff and pink bricks very similar to those manufactured in Flanders in the late thirteenth and fourteenth centuries have been reported from Waltham and from the Whitefriars in Maldon and the Chelmsford Blackfriars.

Once the usefulness of bricks had been recognised, few monastic houses would have had much trouble in locating sources of clay suitable for their manufacture on their own estates. One of the arguments for the Coggeshall bricks being made locally is that bricks of identical type have been recognised by Warwick Rodwell in 16 parish churches in the area, most of which had no tenurial connection with the abbey. Once the abbey had met its own needs, it appears to have sold off subsequent surpluses. Remains of two brick kilns were discovered within a mile of the abbey in the nineteenth century, one of which is said to have contained wasters corresponding with some of the specially-shaped bricks used there. Depressions from clay-digging near Thornton Abbey suggest that the bricks for the gatehouse were made on the spot. A small circular brick-kiln from the early fourteenth century has been excavated at Thornholme Priory. Another kiln is documented on Merevale Abbey's grange

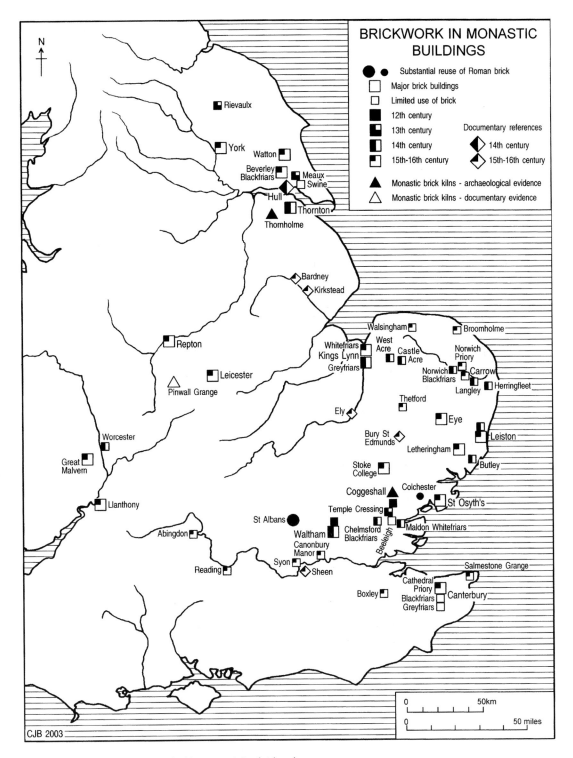

BRICKWORK IN MONASTIC BUILDINGS

● ● Substantial reuse of Roman brick

□ Major brick buildings

□ Limited use of brick

■ 12th century

◧ 13th century

Documentary references

◧ 14th century

◆ 14th century

◧ 15th-16th century

◇ 15th-16th century

▲ Monastic brick kilns - archaeological evidence

△ Monastic brick kilns - documentary evidence

Rievaulx

York

Watton

Beverley
Blackfriars

Meaux
Swine

Hull

Thornton

Thornholme

Bardney

Kirkstead

Repton

Walsingham

Broomholme

Whitefriars
Kings Lynn

West
Acre

Castle
Acre

Norwich
Priory

Leicester

Greyfriars

Norwich
Blackfriars

Carrow

Pinwall Grange

Langley

Herringfleet

Ely

Thetford

Eye

Leiston

Worcester

Bury St
Edmunds

Letheringham

Butley

Great
Malvern

Stoke
College

Llanthony

Coggeshall

Colchester

St Osyth's

St Albans

Temple Cressing

Abingdon

Waltham

Chelmsford
Blackfriars

Maldon Whitefriars

Canonbury
Manor

Beeleigh

Reading

Syon

Sheen

Salmestone Grange

Boxley

Cathedral
Priory

Blackfriars

Greyfriars

Canterbury

0   50km

0   50 miles

CJB 2003

110 *The distribution of monastic buildings containing brickwork*

of Pinwall, for which, in 1498, workmen contracted to bind 8,300 faggots and to provide 30 loads of firewood. Difficulties in obtaining a sufficient supply from the abbey's woods led to most of the faggots being taken from local hedgerows. Some 20,000 tiles and 20,000 bricks were fired at Pinwall in 1499.

Many abbeys, however, elected to purchase their bricks from secular commercial proprietors rather than producing their own. Ralph, Lord Cromwell, who owned a brickworks at Boston, supplied 35,400 bricks to Kirkstead Abbey and 20,000 to Bardney Abbey in 1434. A contract of 1430 between Bury St Edmunds Abbey and two German craftsmen making bricks at the manor of Chevington required the abbot to provide the brickearth. The records of Ely Abbey show that some of the bricks used there in the early fourteenth century were locally made while others were bought from Wisbech and elsewhere in the Fens. Though nothing remains of the Carthusian monastery founded on the outskirts of Hull by Michael de la Pole in 1376-7, Leland recorded that 'Most part of this monastery was builded in brick'. The de la Poles were prominent merchants who had established a brickworks at Trippett just north of the town, and this was almost certainly the source. Henry V employed two brickmakers from Holland during the building of the Carthusian monastery at Sheen.

Tile kilns

Ceramic floor tiles have a wider distribution in monastic buildings than medieval bricks, and were being manufactured from an earlier date. The recognition of late Anglo-Saxon decorated floor tiles at Winchester, Canterbury, Bury St Edmunds, Coventry, Peterborough and St Albans suggests that monastic patronage played a large part in the organisation of their production in the later tenth and eleventh centuries. The use of ceramic tiles then seems to lapse for a couple of centuries. Production was resumed by the northern Cistercian houses of Rievaulx, Fountains, Byland, Meaux and Newminster, all of which had distinctive mosaic tile floors laid in the thirteenth century, probably made from local clays fired on the spot. The church of Meaux Abbey is known to have been paved between 1249 and 1265, and a kiln producing mosaic tiles has been excavated at the North Grange. Finds included a small earthenware mortar and a dish containing ash of lead oxide, which would have been used in the glazing process. Two successive roof-tile kilns were also recorded there.

Much early tile production was carried out by itinerant craftsmen, who set up kilns wherever their products were required. Decorated tiles from identical stamps found at Waltham Abbey and the Norfolk priories of Horsham St Faith and Broomholm probably reflect the wanderings of an individual tile-maker in the third quarter of the thirteenth century.

From the fourteenth century a few monasteries in south-east England, including Boxley and Battle, developed larger permanent commercial tileries. Accounts of Battle Abbey's tileries on its manor of Wye survive for the period 1330–80, and show that it was regularly selling tiles to other monastic houses. In 1355 10 kilns there produced 98,500 flat tiles, 500 ridge or gutter tiles and 1,000 corners; the tasks of clay-digging and firing were contracted out at 11s per kiln, 1,000 faggots were bought for fuel at a cost of 45s, and another 10s spent on carrying the clay and fuel. Profits from sales of tiles that year came to £14 15s. By 1370 there were two tileries at Wye with 13 kilns; a year later, output was greatly reduced because some of the kilns were in poor repair and there was a severe shortage of workmen following an outbreak of plague. In 1441–2, the prior of Earls Colne was hiring men to produce 'plane and hollow tyle' for £3 6s 8d, but sales of surpluses almost recovered the cost.

Excavations at Norton Priory revealed a small temporary double-flued kiln which produced the mosaic tiles used in reflooring the church and chapter-house in the early fourteenth century (**111**). Experiments have shown that the 40,000 tiles needed could have been produced in 54 firings, taking place weekly through two successive summers. A kiln discovered near Great Malvern Priory in the nineteenth century is said to have contained decorative inlaid tiles identical with those used in the church in the 1450s. Other floor-tile kilns have been excavated at Chertsey Abbey, at Repton Priory, and at Dale Abbey. Scientific tests on the floor tiles from Hulton Abbey have shown that they were made on the spot, but the kilns have not yet been located.

111 *Norton Priory (Cheshire): reconstruction of excavated double-flued kiln which produced mosaic tiles for the church and chapter-house in the early fourteenth century*

Potteries

The institutional nature of monasteries meant that the range of pottery vessels used in them was often rather different from that found on secular sites. Cooking-pots tend to be under-represented because catering for a community needed larger metal cauldrons, whereas ceramic jugs for ale are particularly common. The extent to which monastic communities produced their own pottery has been surprisingly little investigated. Fountains Abbey had pottery kilns operating at Winksley on Sutton Grange between the late twelfth and late thirteenth centuries. Production was clearly intended for home use rather than commercial sale, since the pottery commonly occurs around the abbey but is almost absent from the nearby town of Ripon. During the thirteenth and fourteenth centuries Fountains developed another pottery production site on Bradley Grange at Potter Heaton.

Coal-mining

Many abbeys had coal on their estates, and some acquired the right to mine it. There is not always much evidence of those rights actually being exercised, and only occasionally was it extracted on any significant scale. Coal was not suitable for bloomery smelting or for domestic use on open hearths, and its main use was in firing limekilns and, to a lesser extent, brick and tile kilns. It could also be used in iron forging, once the iron was sufficiently consolidated to prevent it absorbing sulphur from the coal. A coalhouse is recorded within the precinct of Meaux Abbey in the late fourteenth century.

The most accessible deposits were the exposures along the Northumbrian coast between Amble and Tynemouth, where coal could be collected from the cliffs and beach. In 1236 Newminster Abbey acquired the right to obtain sea-coal along the shore from the Snook at Blyth. The term 'sea-coal', as opposed to charcoal, derives from the fact that Northumbrian coal was regularly shipped down to the limekilns in east London by the early thirteenth century. Newminster was also permitted to take sea-coal from Middlewood for use at its forge at Stretton near Alnwick.

Further inland open-cast trenching and shallow working by bellpits preceded the excavation of deeper mines in the fourteenth century. The monks of Durham obtained a lease of coal mines in Ferry in 1354 with leave to place pits and watergates where suitable, which presumably implies the use of adits to draw off water. By 1361 they possessed a coalpit at Rainton. The Durham bursar's roll of 1376-7 records £6 6s 6½d spent on sinking a pit at Heworth, along with the cost of picks, buckets and ropes. Another pit there is recorded as 6 fathoms deep. A further source exploited by the monks of Durham was at Aldin Grange, where they sank five more pits and constructed some sort of aqueduct. In 1447 the prior of Durham granted annual leases of land and coalpits to six men in Trillesden and Spennymoor with the proviso that the prior's officials could inspect both sites at any time to ensure that the conditions of the leases were met. At Spennymoor, the lessees were to make adits at their own cost. The monks of Finchale had a coal mine at Lumley in 1348-9 and another at Softley in 1362, the latter yielding a steady income of £6 13s 4d well into the fifteenth century. In 1457-8 another coalpit at Moorhouse Close was rendering £10 a year and supplying 80 chaldrons of coal direct to the priory. It worked right up to the Dissolution. By 1486-7 the miners were venturing below the level of free drainage, and we find the monks of Finchale spending £9 15s 6d on a horse-driven pump to draw water from their mine at Moorhouse. Finchale Priory derived around £30 a year from its coal mines. Elsewhere in the north-east, Hexham Abbey had coal mines on its township of Carraw in 1479, while Tynemouth Priory leased a mine in 1530 for £20 a year.

In the Yorkshire coalfield grants made to the Premonstratensian canons of Beauchief in the late thirteenth century by Sir Thomas Chaworth included full liberty to extract and carry away coal, both for their own use and for their tenants, in their own lands and in the waste grounds lying amidst their lands in the sokes of Norton and Alfreton. In 1368 the canons agreed to release a payment of 13s 4d from the manor of Alfreton, which had been granted to them for a term of 40 years in case the coal mines failed during that period or ceased to work. Jervaulx Abbey had rights to mine coal in Colsterdale, as did Kirkstall in Airedale (**112**). Further south in the Nottinghamshire part of the coalfield the prior of Beauvale was leasing out a mine at Newthorpe in 1380.

In the midlands Hulton Abbey owned coal mines in Hulton and Hanley in the early sixteenth century. Walter Caldebrook paid 6s to Wenlock priory in 1322 to 'dig for seacoal in the Brockholes', below Coalbrookdale. Wenlock Priory had coal mines at Broseley and at Little Wenlock at the time of its suppression. In what later became the Black Country, the abbot of Halesowen granted out two pits of sea-coal at Hill in 1273-4 in return for an annual rent of £7, and in 1307 he made a similar grant in the Coombs to two men, the two pits to be worked with four picks, each man to pay a rent of 40s twice a year. The cartulary of Worcester priory refers to payments for coal from Abberley in the fourteenth century. Nuneaton priory had coal workings along the eastern margins of the Forest of Arden, which were largely exhausted by the fifteenth century. Garendon Abbey acquired land with coal mines in 1270, while Leicester Abbey owned a coal mine of some depth at Oakthorpe in the fifteenth century.

In north Wales Abbot Thomas Pennant of Basingwerk (1481-1519) took a lease of the manor of Coleshill with its mining rights from the Crown. Margam and Neath both operated in the south Wales coalfield. In 1249 Margam secured an agreement with a local landowner to work the coal on his land near

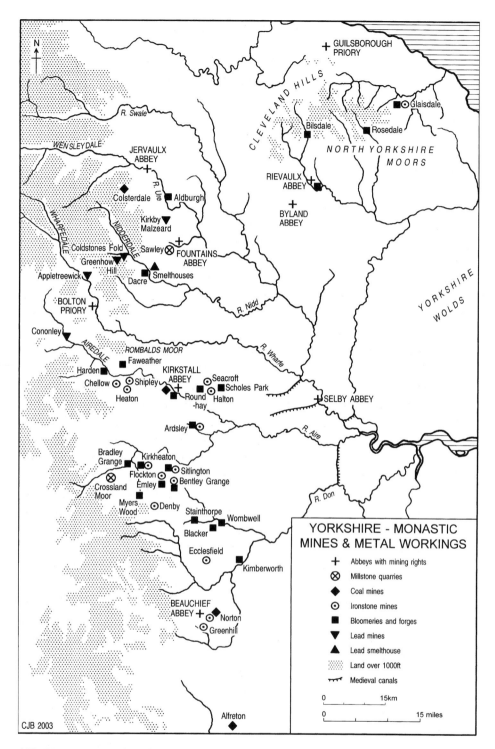

GUILSBOROUGH
PRIORY

N

CLEVELAND HILLS

⊙ Glaisdale

R. Swale

WENSLEYDALE

JERVAULX
ABBEY

Bilsdale ■

NORTH YORKSHIRE
MOORS

■ Rosedale

RIEVAULX
ABBEY

Colsterdale ◆ ■ ■ Aldburgh

R. Ure

BYLAND
ABBEY

WHARFEDALE

NIDDERDALE

Kirkby ▼
Malzeard

Coldstones Fold ◆
Greenhow ▼
Hill
Appletreewick ▼

Sawley ✛
⊗ FOUNTAINS
ABBEY

▲ Smelthouses
Dacre

YORKSHIRE
WOLDS

R. Nidd

BOLTON
PRIORY ✛

R. Wharfe

Cononley ◆

AIREDALE

ROMBALDS MOOR

■ Faweather

Harden ■
Chellow ⊙ ⊙ Shipley
Heaton

KIRKSTALL
ABBEY
◆ ✛
Round
-hay ⊙ Halton

⊙ Seacroft
■ Scholes Park

✛ SELBY ABBEY

Ardsley ⊙

R. Aire

Bradley
Grange ■

Kirkheaton
⊙
Flockton ⊙ ⊙ Sitlington
Émley ■ ⊙ Bentley Grange
⊗
Crossland
Moor
Myers ■
Wood ⊙ Denby

R. Don

Stainthorpe
■ ■ Wombwell

Blacker ■

Ecclesfield
⊙

■ Kimberworth

BEAUCHIEF
ABBEY ✛ ◆ Norton
⊙ Greenhill

Alfreton ◆

YORKSHIRE - MONASTIC MINES & METAL WORKINGS

✛	Abbeys with mining rights
⊗	Millstone quarries
◆	Coal mines
⊙	Ironstone mines
■	Bloomeries and forges
▼	Lead mines
▲	Lead smelthouse
	Land over 1000ft
	Medieval canals

0   15km

0   15 miles

CJB 2003

112 *Monastic mines and metal-workings in Yorkshire*

its grange at Penhydd and to have access for two- and four-wheeled carts in exchange for 5 bushels of wheat a year and compensation for any damage. In 1515 Margam Abbey allowed the lessee of Hafod-y-Porth Grange to dig for coal 'as far as the sea shore'. Neath Abbey had a mine on its grange at Cwrt-y-Carnau and on several other granges in Gower, and retained one coal-mine in its own hands until its suppression.

Ironstone mines and iron forges

Iron was in great demand throughout the Middle Ages for horseshoes, cartwheel rims, ploughs, door latches, hinges, nails, and other tools and equipment. Monastic houses also had more specialised needs; the earliest known iron clock in England was made in 1283 for the canons of Dunstable to regulate the routine of daily services, and elaborate astronomical clocks were made for Norwich Priory and St Albans Abbey in the 1320s. Domesday Book reveals sporadic iron-working activities on some Benedictine estates, for example eight smiths at Glastonbury, and six men on the abbey's manor of Pucklechurch rendering 90 lumps of iron.

Iron ore was available in many parts of the country. Carbonate ores had been exploited in the Weald long before the earliest monastic holdings took shape, and King Oswine of Kent's grant to St Peter's Minster at Canterbury in 689 of land at Lyminge 'where iron had been mined' probably refers to Roman extraction. The Wealden iron industry declined in relative terms during the Middle Ages, and monastic houses with estates there took little part in exploiting local iron resources. Instead, raw material seems to have been bought in when needed. Seven blooms were purchased by Boxley Abbey in 1334 to be worked by estate smiths, while bar iron was purchased by Robertsbridge Abbey for the repair of carts in 1360. In 1308-9, Prior Henry Eastry even bought 15cwt of Spanish iron for works at Canterbury.

Elsewhere Cistercian abbeys took a prominent part in opening up iron ore reserves. Higher-yielding low-phosphorus haematite and limonite ores came from the Forest of Dean, where Flaxley Abbey was permitted to mine iron soon after its foundation and Grace Dieu extracted ore for its forges at Penyard after 1227. In 1267-8 it was reported that the monks of Tintern had long possessed a mine in the same forest, supplying their own smithy, without payment. South Wales, where Margam Abbey was prospecting for iron ore in the thirteenth century, was another source of limonite. Stanley Abbey was allowed to dig ironstone on its demesne lands in the Forest of Pewsham in 1294. Haematite ores were also available in Cumbria, where an iron mine at Egremont was granted to the monks of Holm Cultram. Furness Abbey worked mines in Alinscale, agreeing to pay reasonable compensation for any disturbance to farmland caused thereby.

West and south Yorkshire had particularly extensive, high-quality ore deposits. In the mid-twelfth century Rievaulx acquired exclusive rights to mine iron and take dead wood for fuel around Bingley and Shipley in Airedale, and at Flockton and Sitlington near Wakefield. In 1161 the monks of Kirkstead were allowed to dig for ironstone on the borders of Ecclesfield and Kimberworth near Sheffield. Kirkstall Abbey had open-cast ironstone pits at Seacroft, agreeing to fill them up once the ore had been extracted. Before 1177 Fountains Abbey had acquired rights to dig for ironstone, with wayleaves for access and woodland for charcoal, on its grange at Bradley near Huddersfield. In around 1180, Byland Abbey acquired iron mines at Denby and Bentley (**113**). The canons of Beauchief had iron mines at Norton and Greenhill in the thirteenth century, while the canons of Guisborough acquired exclusive mining rights in Glaisdale (**112**). Other mining concessions such as those granted to Jervaulx, to Fountains Abbey in Nidderdale, and to Salley Abbey at Salesbury, appear never to have been developed.

113 *Iron mines at Bentley Grange, Emley (Yorkshire West Riding). Byland Abbey was extracting iron ore from its grange at Bentley from about 1180, but the visible bell-pits, the spoil-heaps of which overlie narrow ridge and furrow, date from a later phase of working after the 1580s*

114 *Excavation in 2003 of iron bloomery at Oakamoor (Staffordshire), worked by tenants of Croxden Abbey*

Smelting normally took place near the ore source if fuel was also available nearby, since the finished product was less bulky to transport than the ore. The normal method of production was the bloomery. In this process, the ore was first washed, roasted and crushed to remove some of the impurities, then heaped upon a hearth between layers of charcoal, covered with clay, and fired to a temperature of at least 1150°C, with bellows maintaining a continuous draught for many hours. The slag was then tapped off and the resulting spongy iron lump reheated. After being hammered to remove remaining particles of cinder and slag, it was then ready for forging. Early bloomeries were small-scale operations, ore-crushing and the working of bellows and hammers all being undertaken manually (**114**). Monastic experiments with the application of water power to this process will be discussed further below.

The Forest of Dean contained numerous bloomeries and forges. Tintern Abbey was permitted to have a forge in the wood of St Briavels in 1141, and subsequently had two forges in the forest. Around 1147 Roger, earl of Hereford, granted an ironworks at Ardland near Cinderford to Flaxley Abbey. Henry II later amended this grant, permitting the abbey to operate an itinerant forge with the same liberty as the king's own forges. This was later asserted by the abbey as a right to set up a movable forge anywhere in the forest, with concomitant rights to fuel for working it. Inevitably, this provoked conflict with the forest officials charged with the duty of preserving the woodland cover (chapter 6). Grace Dieu Abbey had two itinerant forges at Penyard, but monastic smelting ceased when the abbey sold this manor in 1267. The abbot of Gloucester also had a forge on the east side of the forest in 1282.

In the north midlands, Louth Park Abbey was given a wood at Birley in Brampton near Chesterfield, with the right to take beech and elm wood for fuel for its bloomery and forge; when the bloomery was not working, the monks were allowed to operate two smithies rather than one. Hulton Abbey's smithy at Horton, near Leek, was assaulted by local malefactors in 1528. In the southern Lake District Furness Abbey reputedly had no fewer than 40 forges, and profits from its ironworks in 1291 came to nearly twice the income from its flocks and herds. Several early charters granting mineral rights to Furness included the right to take water from streams for washing the ore. Many slag and cinder deposits in this region can be related to thirteenth-century smelting by Furness Abbey and Conishead Priory. Further north in Cumbria the monks of Holm Cultram had the right to erect a bloomery at Whinfell in the late twelfth century, and to take dead wood from the woodlands between Ennerdale and the Cocker Valley. They also rented land for smelting at Whitehaven from the prior of St Bees.

Yorkshire has the most extensive record of monastic forges (**112**). Before 1150 a benefactor to Rievaulx had given 15 acres at Sitlington for the establishment of forges in which to make iron and necessary utensils. The abbey also had forges by the River Dove at Stainborough, Blacker and Wombwell, and at Faweather on Rombolds Moor above Bingley. The 1161 grant to the monks of Kirkstead allowed them to erect four forges near Ecclesfield. Fountains had rights to operate forges at Bradley Grange by 1177. In 1280-1, when the Earl of Richmond allowed the monks of Jervaulx Abbey to cut wood on his land north of the Ure for smelting, he allowed them to erect two temporary sheds 'without nail, bolt or wall', to shelter the bloomery and smithy, which could readily be dismantled when the ironworkers moved on. By 1228 the Augustinians of Guisborough had several smithies in Glaisdale in the Cleveland Hills, each worth 10 marks a year, and they may have developed a more extensive iron industry on their Eskdale estates, where many medieval slagheaps remain.

Blacksmith's forges were commonly to be found in the home grange or outer court of many abbeys. One example at Waltham Abbey was worked from the late twelfth century to the Dissolution, when the inventory records a smithy with two anvils. Excavation here revealed two hearths on raised firebeds, and five clay-lined pits used either for smelting or as quenching tanks. They were housed in a three-bay aisled building with flint and stone walls. Working debris, including ore, bloomery cinders, slag and hammer scale, was found, along with some of the products, bar iron, chisels, punches, knives, keys, latches, oxshoes, horseshoes and nails. Works carried out at the forge at Beaulieu Abbey in 1269-70 included fitting an iron hoop to a wooden cartwheel and the first shoeing of a colt, as well as routine repairs to ploughs, carts, knives and other tools. The workshops of Bordesley were producing iron knives, tools, nails and tenter-hooks, all of which would have been used by the monastic community itself, but the presence of pieces of weaponry, armour, horse equipment, buckles and brooches suggests that work was also undertaken for lay clients. The canons of Maxstoke also had a large iron-working operation within the precinct, and remains of a smithy have been excavated in the outer court at Tintern.

The first blast-furnaces producing cast iron were beginning to appear in south-east England after 1490, but there is no evidence that monastic houses, by then generally withdrawing from direct demesne exploitation, played any part in their introduction.

Lead-working

Lead was in demand for roofing, water-pipes, brewing vats and window cames. Veins of lead-bearing ore occur around Derwentwater, in Durham, the Yorkshire Dales, the Peak District, several parts of Wales, Shropshire, Mendip and Dartmoor. Monastic houses in those areas were involved in its exploitation long before the Norman Conquest. Lead was employed in roof flashing and glazing at Monkwearmouth and Jarrow as early as the seventh century.

The earliest documentary references come from the Peak District. Ecgburh, abbess of Repton, sent a coffin made of lead from Wirksworth in Derbyshire to Crowland for the burial of St Guthlac in 714. One of her successors, Abbess Cynewaru, was leasing out land at Wirksworth in 835 in exchange for an annual payment of 300 shillings-worth of lead which was to be made to Archbishop Ceolnoth at Christ Church, Canterbury. The ancient abbey of Repton was probably destroyed by the Danes, and its manor of Wirksworth subsequently came to the Crown. Monastic houses seem to have played no later part in the development of the Peak lead industry, except as customers.

In Yorkshire the monks of Fountains and Byland began opening up valuable lead workings on the moors west of Nidderdale in the 1170s, while Jervaulx had rights to mine lead in Wensleydale. Fountains Abbey had a lead-smelting works in Nidderdale at a place still called Smelthouses between Dacre and Pateley Bridge. The canons of Bolton in 1300 purchased the manor of Appletreewick in Wharfedale, which already contained a lead mine worth £2. Considerable expansion of lead-mining in this area followed in the last quarter of the fifteenth century. Bolton was also prospecting over the moors of Storiths, further down Wharfedale, and Cononley in Airedale though there is no evidence that it ever worked ores in either place. By 1480 Fountains Abbey had extended its workings westwards and southwards to Greenhow Hill (an area where many bellpits survive). Here the abbey's miners came into conflict not only with the miners of Bolton Priory, who had been following the veins of ore eastwards from Appletreewick, but also with those of the Duchy of Lancaster, who had been working from Knaresborough Forest. The resulting legal dispute lasted till the Dissolution (**112**).

In Wales outcrops of lead ores are mentioned in a grant to Margam Abbey in 1261. The abbot of Vale Royal had custody of lead mines at Englefield in 1283. Strata Florida had an important lead-mine 6 miles away at Briwnant in Cwmystwyth which it was leasing out in 1505; it had ceased work by the time of Leland's visit in the 1530s.

In the south-west Aethelred, ealdorman of Mercia, obtained from the abbey of Berkeley in 883 an estate at Stoke Bishop, just north of Bristol, which had a lead mine on its bounds. This site was above Walcombe Slade on Clifton Down where traces of workings survive. On Mendip the Carthusians of Witham received confirmation in 1283 of their right to extract lead, and to take the profits without hindrance from the officials of the royal forest. The main centre of their operations became known as Charterhouse Hydon. To the south the Knights Hospitallers, who had inherited the neighbouring land of Temple Hydon from the Templars, also seem to have been working lead ores there in the third quarter of the fourteenth century.

Direct archaeological evidence for medieval lead extraction is limited. The shallow surface trenches following the lead rakes have often been destroyed by later, deeper working. Ore-crushing and washing leaves little trace, and few smelting boles have yet been recognised. Professional plumbers were normally employed as the need arose, but lead workshops sometimes occur within monastic precincts. Part of the outer precinct wall of Reading Abbey was known as the Plummery from the abbey's workshops built against it.

Other metal industries

England was the only significant producer of tin in Europe in the early Middle Ages, so the tin mines of Cornwall and Devon yielded considerable wealth. Monastic estate owners, however, seem to have played little direct part in their exploitation, though Abbot Champeaux of Tavistock was appointed Warden of the Stannaries in 1319, and for a few years leased the revenues of the mines, while Abbot Dynington of Tavistock was disposing of an interest in a tin mine in 1470.

Precious metals were required for candlesticks, censers, chalices, reliquaries and shrines. Professional craftsmen normally supplied the materials and work-manship, though from time to time monastic communities themselves contained skilled men. St Dunstan is said to have been an accomplished metal-worker, while later in the tenth century a monk named Leo made a silver crucifix and gilded statues for the high altar at Ely. Alan of Walsingham, a later prior of Ely, was also a noted goldsmith. Early in the twelfth century a shrine for the relics of St Alban was made by Anketil, goldsmith and former master of the Danish mint, who had become a monk towards the end of his life, while in the 1180s a gold chalice and jewel-encrusted vase were made for St Albans by a monk named Baldwin, who was probably the sacrist. Occasionally metal-working skills were put to less reputable uses. Prior Henry, sent from Tupholme Abbey to establish a colony at Dale, is said to have been 'very cunning in the fabrication of false money', while William Plymouth, abbot of Combermere, was accused in 1414 of counterfeiting gold coins.

The evidence for monastic mining of precious metals is limited. Earl Ranulf of Chester's foundation grant to Basingwerk Abbey included the manor of Fulbrook Greenfield 'on which there are silver deposits', though there is no evidence that the monks ever worked them. Llywelyn ap Iorwerth's charter to Cymer Abbey in 1209 gave the monks 'the right in digging or carrying away metals and treasures free from all secular extraction', and gold could have been mined in small quantities on their Merionethshire estates. In 1378 the prior of Bodmin and the abbot of Buckfast received letters patent enabling them to control the profits arising from gold and silver mines in the far west, requiring them to account for one seventh of the profits to the king.

There is evidence at Tintern for silver being extracted from lead by the cupellation process, whereby the lead was heated to 900°C and subjected to a strong draught, which oxidised it, leaving the silver as a residue. Paul Courtney's excavations in the outer court revealed several mid-fifteenth century bowl hearths lined with ash and containing lead debris. It seems unlikely that the abbey would have found it economical to extract silver from lead ores mined on its own estates, and these hearths may reflect the desilvering of large quantities of sheet lead salvaged from a roof or brought in for a new building.

Bell-founding

Bells were hung in monastic churches from earliest times. When Abbess Hilda died in 680, according to Bede, the tolling of the bell at Whitby was miraculously heard at the nunnery of Hackness, 13 miles away. Dunstan is said to have made a bell or gong for the church at Glastonbury, while Ingulph's Chronicle records Abbot Egelric I (975-84) having six additional bells made for Crowland Abbey to augment the great bell already there. A tenth-century bell-casting pit was identified during excavations at the Old Minster at Winchester. Excavations at Norton Priory have revealed casting-pits both for the first great bell installed in the new church in the twelfth century, and for its successor following the gutting of the church by fire in 1236. Other evidence for bell-casting within monastic precincts has been reported from the abbeys of Kirkstall and Tintern, the priories of Pontefract, Guisborough and Taunton, and the Whitefriars in Ludlow. Occasionally they were transported over long distances. In 1465 John Litlington, abbot of Crowland, paid £160 for the casting of a new set of five bells in London and for their carriage by land and water to the abbey.

Saltpans

Salt was vital for preserving fish, meat, butter and cheese, and was also used in leather preparation and other crafts. It could be obtained by evaporating sea-water, or brine from inland springs. In coastal regions salt-laden sediments were scraped from tidal flats in summer and carted to a filtering trough, where the brine was washed out and the waste sediment dumped. The salt was then extracted by boiling the brine in lead pans in salthouses, which also provided short-term storage. A dubious charter to Milton Abbey attributed to Athelstan includes a grant of a salthouse by the fish-weir at Twyneham. Domesday Book records nearly 1,200 saltpans along the estuaries and marshes of the east and south coasts from Lincolnshire to Cornwall, with the greatest concentrations in Sussex, Norfolk and Lincolnshire. Rights to dig turf and peat or to cut wood for fuel often went with the possession of saltpans.

Herring deteriorates particularly rapidly without salting, and as the importance of the North Sea herring fisheries increased during the twelfth and thirteenth centuries, so did the east coast salterns. Newminster Abbey acquired salterns at Blyth, Tynemouth Priory derived a considerable income from salt-making, Durham Priory had saltpans at South Shields, while Guisborough and Byland both had salthouses at Coatham in the Tees estuary. Interests in salterns around the Lincolnshire shore of the Wash were held by at least 30 monasteries, as far away as Bridlington and Waltham.

On the south coast Bilsington Priory in Kent was endowed with land at Belgar in Romney Marsh which already included productive saltpans. In 1381 the priory's lands here comprised 465 acres, the rent from each acre being 2¼d, two and a half herring, and ¾ bushel of white salt. Coarse salt was used for curing hard cheeses, but the Canterbury Cathedral Priory accounts also refer to the purchase of fine white salt, probably for the production of soft cheese at the Romney dairies. Before 1300 Quarr Abbey had acquired a 'salt pit in a marsh' in Lymington. A fifteenth-century rental of Shaftesbury Abbey records at least 20 tenants holding saltpans at Arne, on Poole Harbour. Some of them were specialist salt-workers, having no share in the arable land of the hamlet, and some owed services of carrying salt to the abbey.

On the Cumbrian coast Carlisle Priory had a grant of four saltpans at the tidal mouth of the Eden between Burgh-by-Sands and Drumburgh. Wetheral Priory acquired saltpans at Burgh-by-Sands and at Salton near Whitehaven around 1088. Holm Cultram Abbey owned saltpans on both sides of the Solway Firth by the end of the twelfth century, and at the Dissolution it had rights to 21 saltpans along the north Cumbrian coast. Calder Abbey also had coastal salterns in this area. St Bees Priory had saltpans on the Duddon Sands, while Furness Abbey had saltworks in Angerton Moss near Ulverston.

Inland brine sources were concentrated around Droitwich in Worcestershire and Northwich, Middlewich and Nantwich in Cheshire. Charters indicate interests in the Droitwich wells held by the church of Worcester, the minster of Hanbury and Evesham Abbey from the seventh or eighth century onwards. When monastic life was restored at Pershore in 972, the community received sites for 18 vats and two furnaces in three places around Droitwich. The Domesday Book also records the monastic communities of Coventry and Westminster holding saltpans or furnaces in Droitwich, while Eynsham Abbey was entitled to 24 measures of salt there through its manor of Mickleton. A number of monastic houses also had rights in the Cheshire saltworks. The foundation endowments of the Cistercian abbeys of Croxden, Dieulacresse and Vale Royal all included saltpits at Middlewich, and Dieulacresse increased its holdings there during the early thirteenth century. Burton Abbey secured a saltpit and saltpan at Nantwich in the 1190s, and Combermere's endowment also included a tithe of its founder's saltpans at Nantwich and a supply of salt. Norton Priory acquired a salthouse at Northwich in the late twelfth century.

Glass-making

Glass was used in monastic churches from the seventh century. Bede describes how Benedict Biscop sent to France for glaziers to provide windows for the church of Monkwearmouth, and how they stayed on to teach the English the art of glass-making, 'which was to prove invaluable in making lamps for the church and many other kinds of vessel'. Archaeological evidence from both Monkwearmouth and Jarrow has confirmed that coloured soda-lime glass was indeed made there. Bishop Wilfrith I of Worcester (718-744) is said to have replaced the wooden lattice windows there with glass. At Glastonbury glass furnaces probably of Dunstan's time were found sealed beneath the twelfth-century cloister.

Although monasteries were major consumers of glass in the later Middle Ages, and although the necessary raw materials – sand and wood-ash – were available in several localities, evidence for direct monastic involvement in glass manufacture is limited. The main centre of English glass-making in the thirteenth and fourteenth centuries was the Weald, and monasteries seem to have played no part in the development of the industry here. In Cheshire, however, Vale Royal Abbey operated a glassworks from 1284 at least up to 1309; the monks had the right to gather ferns from Delamere Forest for burning as a flux and an excavated glasshouse site in Kingswood may have been connected with the abbey.

By the fourteenth century coloured glass was often imported from Burgundy, Lorraine, Flanders and Normandy. Some of the glass for the windows of St Stephen's Chapel in Westminster Abbey was bought from the Hanseatic depot in London in 1351-2, although white Wealden glass was also used there. Glass-painting was undertaken on commission by professionals, and in monastic churches the materials and craftsmen were often provided by lay benefactors. The superb clerestory windows in the choir of Tewkesbury Abbey, for example, were created between 1320 and 1344 through a bequest by Eleanor de Clare.

Cloth-weaving and dyeing workshops

While some monasteries produced cloth for their own needs, there is little evidence that they engaged in this manufacture on a commercial scale. Meaux Abbey had a stone building at Wawne Grange before 1250, where wool was woven and cloth fulled for the use of the monks, lay brothers and poor of the neighbourhood. The Fountains woolhouse appears to have been converted to a cloth-processing and dyeing workshop after the end of the thirteenth century by inserting a succession of vats and furnaces.

Tanneries

Leather was needed for shoes, gloves, belts, saddles, harness, containers and many other items, so tanning and leather-working were among the most wide-spread of medieval industries. Where monastic estates were geared towards cattle-farming, and where beef was consumed in guesthouses and infirmaries, the availability of hides as a by-product encouraged monasteries to develop their own tanneries. Access to oakwoods was also necessary since the tanning process required the raw hides to be steeped for up to two years in a liquor containing oak bark.

Battle Abbey set up a tannery on its nearby manor of Marley in the early fourteenth century, sometimes maintaining it in hand, sometimes leasing it out, and in some years it produced profits of up to £20. Most of the prepared leather was then worked by cordwainers and glovers in the town. Investment in tanneries was especially characteristic of Cistercian houses. Salley had interests in a tannery by 1226. By around 1240 Meaux Abbey's tannery was regarded as sufficiently important for it to be transferred from the North Grange at Wawne into the abbey precinct. An inventory of its contents in 1396 lists various pieces of cow and calf leather in store, 15 tubs, various knives and other tools, 400 tan turves (blocks of bark from which tan had been extracted) and the tan from all the oaks barked that year. Twenty ox- or cow-hides were reserved each year at Meaux for shoes for the poor. The Taxation of *c.*1291 mentions tanneries belonging to Margam, Tintern, Abbey Dore, Hulton and Quarr, and further examples figure in the Dissolution surveys at Rievaulx and Jervaulx. Rievaulx had a tannery with a bark store and tanner's house around a yard in the outer court, and four small brick-lined tanning vats were also

115 *Late medieval tile-built tanning vats in the undercroft of the east range of Rievaulx Abbey (Yorkshire North Riding). Vats for steeping bark for tanning are recorded here in a survey made soon after the Dissolution, and the bark mill, bark store, lime-kiln and tanner's house all stood nearby*

inserted into the dormitory undercroft (**115**). The tannery and barkhouse at Fountains were leased out in 1532, and hides from the Fountains herds were also sent to Newcastle.

Tanneries were relatively rare in areas such as the Cotswolds, where sheep remained much more numerous than cattle. Skins of sheep, horses and deer were tawed with alum and oil, a different process. Sheep- or goat-skins provided parchment for documents, while finer vellum came from calf-, lamb- or kid-skins. Whitby Abbey's accounts even mention the tawing of wolf-pelts.

18
Conclusion

In an age when many people may pass most of their lives without ever seeing a monk, it is difficult to appreciate how pervasive the influence of the monasteries once was. This book has attempted to shed a little light upon their wider social and economic role beyond the cloister, and in particular their impact as landholders upon the landscape. Yet it has barely scratched the surface of a huge topic and many questions remain.

Firstly, in order to maintain a sense of perspective, we need to enquire whether monastic estates did differ from secular estates, and if so, in what ways. It would be easy to overestimate the monastic achievement, simply because of the scale of the documentary legacy left by the religious communities; apart from the Crown, no other class of landholder generated or maintained over such a long period such a wide range of written records. Do sophisticated accounting systems and chroniclers' eulogies on the works undertaken by particular abbots genuinely reflect more investment in monastic estates, or is this an illusion created by the sources? Combining architectural, archaeological and documentary evidence helps to reduce the bias of the written record alone, even if the overall survival of evidence still tends to favour the largest and wealthiest landholders.

We began with the proposal that monasteries had special advantages over most lay landholders in terms of relative security of tenure, scale of holdings and ability as permanent corporations to take the long-term view. In some respects that proposal seems amply supported by the evidence that we have explored. To take just one example, it is surely significant that the evidence for the scale of investment in great barns for crop storage on monastic estates far exceeds anything we can find on secular estates.

That particular example raises another fundamental question: was monastic agriculture any more productive than that on lay estates? It is difficult to generalise about the relative efficiency of monastic and secular farming because of regional and local differences and changes through time. During the early Middle Ages large abbeys were often very successful in accumulating extensive properties, yet this may itself have inhibited attempts at improvement. The relatively low annual value of ploughlands on Glastonbury Abbey's estates recorded in the Domesday survey, compared with those on lands of other holders, has been noted, and at this period the abbey seems to have felt no great need to exploit its holdings more efficiently. During the high farming period, however, when grain prices were high and labour was cheap, monastic proprietors such as Norwich and Battle were in the forefront of agricultural improvement. Careful attention to manuring, use of high sowing rates and, in particular, experimentation with new rotations which included the large-scale cultivation of legumes and made possible the reduction or elimination of fallow courses, all allowed them to achieve much higher yields per acre than their secular neighbours farming similar types of soil. The development of large-scale sheep-farming outside the constraints of a manorial framework was also a feature of monastic estates.

Who actually directed and carried out the work of assarting, woodland management, marshland drainage, enclosure, planting, harvesting, water engineering and building construction? Popular mythology attributes all sorts of undertakings to 'the monks', and I have often been guilty of using the same phrase as a convenient shorthand. In fact, of course, the cultivation, construction and maintenance work on the monastic demesne, even while it was kept in hand, was done through the labour services of peasant tenants, or by lay brothers, or by paid employees under the direction of a bailiff or steward. More important questions concern the extent to which, on the one hand, developments on both the demesne and the leased parts of the estate were directly guided by monastic planning, and, on the other hand, to what extent tenants were able to take the initiative on their own account. On leased lands, tenants undoubtedly played a major role in assarting and reclamation.

Improvement is one thing, innovation quite another. To what extent did monastic houses introduce new techniques into the exploitation of their lands? It is, in fact, quite difficult to identify any specifically monastic 'inventions'. Indeed, monastic proprietors were generally cautious in adopting new ideas. While a few vineyards were in monastic hands before the Norman Conquest, the majority of those documented in the late eleventh century were held by the Crown and the aristocracy, and it is only in the twelfth and thirteenth centuries that monastic vineyards become common. The introduction of fishponds and windmills in the twelfth century also owed far more to secular initiatives. Undoubtedly the monasteries did play an important part in some of the more ambitious marshland reclamation schemes where major reorganisations of the local drainage were involved, but even more extensive piecemeal works had often been undertaken by laymen from an earlier date. Monasteries made effective and extensive use of many forms of technology once they were tried and tested, but they can rarely be seen as pioneers.

Were there significant differences between the ways in which the various monastic orders ran their estates? The Benedictines have loomed particularly large in these pages simply because they had the greatest number of houses and the most extensive landed properties over the longest period. In some respects, for example in the development of towns, the Benedictine contribution is unequalled by that of any other order. There were, however, different approaches to estate organisation which had little to do with scale or longevity. The old-established Benedictine abbeys generally operated within the framework of the feudal system, farming land through peasant services and taking income from feudal dues, while the Cistercians preferred to operate consolidated granges farmed by lay brothers and the Augustinians generally derived a higher proportion of their income through their parochial churches and chapels. Other, more immediately visible, differences perhaps owe more to location than to policy: more great barns are to be found on Benedictine estates because they had a greater tendency to be concentrated in anciently settled areas where arable farming predominated; whereas extensive systems of precinct fishponds may be more characteristic of Cistercian and Premonstratensian abbeys simply because their remote rural settings offered them more space.

When the Cistercians first appeared upon the scene in the twelfth century, they expanded across Europe with a speed and vigour which no other order matched. Did their strongly centralised organisation, with its provisions for an annual general chapter, its familial structure and its system of internal visitation, give the Cistercians an advantage over the more autonomous Benedictine monasteries in terms of the diffusion of ideas for improvement of their properties? Contemporary comments about the efficiency, even ruthlessness, of Cistercian estate management suggest that it may well have done, and the recent work of David Williams has done much to illuminate this on the European scale. Did other orders learn from the Cistercian experience and imitate it? In 1969 Colin Platt was able to show how some aspects of the Cistercian grange were copied, not just by the various orders of regular canons, but even to some extent by the old-established Benedictine and Cluniac communities as they became concerned to make the best out of their landed endowments.

Clearly there were changes in management policy through time, and the general withdrawal from demesne farming in favour of leasing during the later Middle Ages brought the estates of different orders into closer resemblance. Despite the decline of demesne farming, however, there is evidence of continuing capital investment in buildings on some outlying monastic properties up to the eve of the Dissolution. Was leasing seen at the time only as a relatively short-term expedient, the building stock being tended against a time when all might be taken back into hand? Or does the elaboration of selected manorhouses or granges reflect a change of use from estate farm centre to abbot's country retreat?

In order to throw further light upon these questions and to develop a deeper understanding of the monastic contribution to the landscape we need many more case studies of the estates of individual abbeys. For these to be worth-while, they need to be truly multi-disciplinary, co-ordinating the approaches of historians, archaeologists, architectural historians and other specialists. Much remains to be done.

Bibliography

Introductory sources

The literature on monasteries is huge. The following books provide a good introduction and include some information on monastic estates:

Aston, M. (2000) *Monasteries in the Landscape* (Tempus, Stroud)

Coppack, G. (1990) *Abbeys and Priories* (B T Batsford, English Heritage)

Greene, J.P. (1992) *Medieval Monasteries* (Leicester University Press)

Knowles, D. (1948, 1955, 1959) *The Religious Orders in England* (3 vols, Cambridge University Press, reprinted 1974)

— (1950) *The Monastic Order in England, 940-1216* (Cambridge University Press)

Platt, C. (1984) *The Abbeys and Priories of Medieval England* (Secker & Warburg, London)

Chapter 1: Approaches and sources

It is impossible to provide a comprehensive guide to sources here. The following list offers a mere sample of the main classes of records containing information on monastic estates currently available in published form. The English Monastic Archives Project, established in 2003 under the aegis of the History Department of University College, London, and the School of Library, Archive and Information Studies, is aiming to publish a complete list of the records from every monastic house. This promises to become an invaluable resource.

External sources
Domesday Book

Translations of the Domesday text with commentaries have appeared for many counties in the *Victoria History of the Counties of England* (VCH). More recent county editions have been issued by Phillimore and by Alecto Historical Editions. The latter has recently been edited further into a single convenient volume, Williams, A., Martin, G.H. eds, (2002) *Domesday Book: a Complete Translation* (Penguin Books, London)

Pope Nicholas IV Taxation

Astle, T., Ayscough, S., Caley, J. eds, (1802) *Taxatio Ecclesiastica Angliae et Walliae auctoritate P. Nicholai IV, circa AD 1291* (Record Commissioners, London)

Valor Ecclesiasticus

Caley, J., Hunter, J. eds, (1810-34) *Valor Ecclesiasticus* (6 vols, Record Commissioners, London)

Anglo-Saxon wills

Whitelock, D. (1930) *Anglo-Saxon Wills* (Cambridge University Press)

Monastic records
Pre-Conquest charters

A general index is provided by Sawyer, P.H. (1968) *Anglo-Saxon Charters: an Annotated List and Bibliography* (Royal Historical Society, Guides & Handbooks no.8). For fuller transcripts and discussions, see:

Edwards, H. (1988) *The Charters of the Early West Saxon Kingdom* (British Archaeological Reports, British Series, no.198)

Finberg, H.P.R. (1961) *The Early Charters of the West Midlands* (Studies in Early English History II, Leicester University Press, 2nd edn, 1972)

— (1964) *The Early Charters of Wessex* (Studies in Early English History III, Leicester University Press)

Gelling, M. (1979) *The Early Charters of the Thames Valley* (Studies in Early English History VII, Leicester University Press)

Hart, C.R. (1966) *The Early Charters of Eastern England* (Studies in Early English History V, Leicester University Press)

— (1975) *The Early Charters of Northern England and the North Midlands* (Studies in Early English History VI, Leicester University Press)

Hooke, D. (1981) *Anglo-Saxon Landscapes of the West Midlands: the Charter Evidence* (British Archaeological Reports, Oxford, British Series, no.95)

— (1990) *Worcestershire Anglo-Saxon Charter Bounds* (Studies in Anglo-Saxon History II, Boydell, Woodbridge)

— (1994) *Pre-Conquest Charter-Bounds of Devon and Cornwall* (Boydell, Woodbridge)

— (1999) *Warwickshire Anglo-Saxon Charter Bounds* (Studies in Anglo-Saxon History X, Boydell, Woodbridge)

Abingdon: Kelly, S.E. ed. (2000, 2001) *Charters of Abingdon Abbey* (Anglo-Saxon Charters VII & VIII, British Academy, Oxford University Press)

Burton: Sawyer, P.H. ed. (1979) *Charters of Burton Abbey* (Anglo-Saxon Charters II, British Academy, Oxford University Press)

Canterbury, St Augustine's: Kelly, S.E. ed. (1995) *Charters of St Augustine's Abbey, Canterbury, and Minster-in-Thanet* (Anglo-Saxon Charters IV, British Academy, Oxford University Press)

Glastonbury: Morland, S.C. (1986) 'The Glastonbury manors and their Saxon charters', *Proceedings of Somerset Archaeological & Natural History Society,* Vol.130, pp.61-105

Rochester: Campbell, A. ed. (1973) *Charters of Rochester* (Anglo-Saxon Charters I, British Academy, Oxford University Press)

Shaftesbury: Kelly, S.E. ed. (1996) *Charters of Shaftesbury Abbey* (Anglo-Saxon Charters V, British Academy, Oxford University Press)

Sherborne: O'Donovan, M.A. ed. (1988) *Charters of Sherborne* (Anglo-Saxon Charters III, British Academy, Oxford University Press)

Winchester, New Minster: Miller, S. ed. (2000) *Charters of the New Minster, Winchester* (Anglo-Saxon Charters IX, British Academy, Oxford University Press)

Cartularies

A general index is provided by Davis, G.R.C. (1958) *Medieval Cartularies of Great Britain: a Short Catalogue* (London). Published examples include:

Abingdon: Slade, C.F., Lambrick, G. eds (1990, 1991) *Two Cartularies of Abingdon Abbey* (Oxford Historical Society, New Series, Vols 32-33)

Athelney: Bates, E.H. ed. (1899) *Two Cartularies of the Benedictine Abbeys of Muchelney and Athelney* (Somerset Record Society, Vol.14)

Bath: Hunt, W. ed. (1893) *Two Chartularies of the Priory of St Peter at Bath* (Somerset Record Society, Vol.7)

Beaulieu: Hockey, S.F. ed. (1974) *The Beaulieu Cartulary* (Southampton Record Series, Vol.17)

Bilsington: Neilson, N. ed. (1928) *The Cartulary and Terrier of the Priory of Bilsington, Kent* (Records of the Social and Economic History of England and Wales VII, British Academy, Oxford University Press)

Boxgrove: Fleming, L. ed. (1960) *The Cartulary of Boxgrove Priory* (Sussex Record Society, Vol.59)

Bradenstoke: London, V.C.M. ed. (1979) *The Cartulary of Bradenstoke Priory* (Wiltshire Record Society, Vol.35)

Bridlington: Lancaster, W.T. ed. (1912) *Abstracts of the Charters and Other Documents Contained in the Chartulary of the Priory of Bridlington* (Leeds)

Brinkburn: Page, W. ed. (1892) *The Chartulary of Brinkburn Priory* (Surtees Society, Vol.90)

Bristol, St Mark's Hospital: Ross, C.D. ed. (1959) *The Cartulary of St Mark's Hospital, Bristol* (Bristol Record Society, Vol.21)

Bruton: Maxwell Lyte, C.H., Holmes, T.S. eds, (1894) *Two Cartularies of Bruton and Montacute* (Somerset Record Society, Vol.8)

Burscough: Webb, A.N. ed. (1970) *An Edition of the Cartulary of Burscough Priory* (Chetham Society)

Burton: Jeayes, I.H. (1937) 'Burton Abbey: charters and muniments belonging to the Marquis of Anglesey', *Collections for a History of Staffordshire* (Staffordshire Record Society); Wrottesley, G. (1884) 'An abstract of the contents of the Burton Chartulary', *Collections for a History of Staffordshire* (William Salt Archaeological Society, Vol.5.i), pp.1-101

Butley: Mortimer, R. ed. (1979) *Leiston Abbey Cartulary and Butley Priory Charters* (Suffolk Records Society, Suffolk Charters, Vol.1)

Caen Holy Trinity (English estates): Chibnall, M. ed. (1982) *Charters and Custumals of the Abbey of Holy Trinity, Caen* (Records of Social and Economic History, New Series V, British Academy, Oxford University Press)

Canonsleigh: London, V.C.M. ed. (1965) *The Cartulary of Canonsleigh Abbey* (Devon & Cornwall Record Society, New Series, Vol.8)

Canterbury, St Gregory's: Woodcock, A.M. ed. (1956) *Cartulary of the Priory of St Gregory, Canterbury* (Royal Historical Society, Camden 3rd Series, Vol.88)

Carisbrooke: Hockey, F.M. ed. (1981) *The Cartulary of Carisbrooke Priory* (Isle of Wight Record Series, Vol.2)

Chertsey: Giuseppe, M.S. ed. (1915-33), Meekings, C.A.F. ed. (1959-63) *Chertsey Cartularies* (2 vols in 5 parts, Surrey Record Society, Vol.12)

Chester: Tait, J. ed. (1920, 1923) *The Chartulary or Register of the Abbey of St Werburgh, Chester* (Chetham Society, New Series, Vols 79, 82)

Cirencester: Ross, C.D. ed. (1964) *The Cartulary of Cirencester Abbey, Gloucestershire* (Vols 1-2); Devine, M. ed. (1977, Vol 3) (Oxford University Press)

Cleeve: Hugo, T. (1855) 'On the charters and other archives of Cleeve Abbey', *Proceedings of Somerset Archaeological & Natural History Society,* Vol.6.ii, pp.17-73

Cockersand: Farrer, W. ed. (1898, 1900, 1905, 1909) *The Chartulary of Cockersand Abbey* (Chetham Society, New Series, Vols 38-40, 43, 56-7, 64)

Dale: Saltman, A. ed. (1967) *The Cartulary of Dale Abbey* (Derbyshire Archaeological Society, Record Series, Vol.2, Historical Manuscripts Commission Joint Publication no.11)

Darley: Darlington, R.R. ed. (1945) *The Cartulary of Darley Abbey* (2 vols, Kendal)

Daventry: Franklin, M.J. ed. (1988) *The Cartulary of Daventry Priory* (Northamptonshire Record Society, Vol.35)

Dieulacresse: Wrottesley, G. ed. (1906) 'The Chartulary of Dieulacres', *Collections for the History of Staffordshire* (William Salt Archaeological Society, New Series, Vol.9, pp.291-365)

Edington: Stevenson, J.H. ed. (1986) *The Edington Cartulary* (Wiltshire Record Society, Vol.42)

Eynsham: Salter, H.E. ed. (1906-7, 1908) *The Cartulary of the Abbey of Eynsham* (Oxford Historical Soc., Vols 49, 51)

Finchale: Raine, J. ed. (1837) *Charters of Endowment, Inventories and Account Rolls of the Priory of Finchale in the County of Durham* (Surtees Society, Vol.6)

Flaxley: Crawley-Boevey, A.W. (1887) *The Cartulary and Historical Notes of the Cistercian Abbey of Flaxley, otherwise called Dene Abbey, in the County of Gloucester* (Privately printed, Exeter)

Forde: Hobbs, S. ed. (1998) *The Cartulary of Forde Abbey* (Somerset Record Society, Vol.85)

Fountains: Lancaster, W.T. ed. (1915) *Abstracts of the Charters and other Documents contained in the Chartulary of the Cistercian Abbey of Fountains in the West Riding of the County of York* (2 vols, Leeds)

Glastonbury: Watkin, A. ed. (1944, 1948, 1949-50) *The Great Chartulary of Glastonbury* (Somerset Record Society, Vols 59, 62, 64)

Gloucester: Hart, W.H. ed. (1863-7) *Historia et Cartularium Monasterii S.Petri Gloucestriae* (Rolls Series, Vol.33, i-iii)

Guisborough: Brown, W. ed. (1889, 1891) *Cartularium Prioratus de Gyseburne* (Surtees Society, Vols 86, 89)

Harrold: Fowler, G.H. (1935) *Records of Harrold Priory* (Bedfordshire Historical Record Society, Vol.17)

Haughmond: Rees, U. ed. (1985) *The Cartulary of Haughmond Abbey* (Shropshire Archaeological Society, University of Wales Press, Cardiff)

Healaugh Park: Purvis, J.S. ed. (1936) *The Chartulary of the Augustinian Priory of St. John the Evangelist of the Park of Healaugh* (Yorkshire Archaeological Society, Record Series, Vol.92)

Lacock: Rogers, K.H. ed. (1978) *Lacock Abbey Charters* (Wiltshire Record Society, Vol.34)

Lanercost: Todd, J.H. ed. (1997) *The Lanercost Cartulary* (Surtees Society, Vol.203)

Launceston: Hull, P.L. ed. (1987) *The Cartulary of Launceston Priory* (Devon & Cornwall Record Society, New Series, Vol.30)

Leiston: see Butley

Lewes: Salzman, L.F. ed. (1932-4) *Chartulary of the Priory of St Pancras, Lewes* (Sussex Record Society, Vols 38, 40); Bullock, J.H. ed. (1939) *The Norfolk Portion of the Chartulary of the Priory of St Pancras, Lewes* (Norfolk Record Society, Vol.12)

London, Holy Trinity, Aldgate: Hodgett, G.A.J. ed. (1971) *The Cartulary of Holy Trinity, Aldgate* (London Record Society, Vol.7)

London, St Mary Clerkenwell: Hassall, W.O. ed. (1949) *Cartulary of St Mary, Clerkenwell* (Royal Historical Society, Camden 3rd Series, Vol. 71)

Luffield: Elvey, G.R. ed. (1968, 1975) *Luffield Priory Charters* (Buckinghamshire Record Society, Vols 15, 18)

Missenden: Jenkins, J.G. ed. (1938, 1946, 1962) *The Cartulary of Missenden Abbey* (Buckinghamshire Record Society Vols 2, 10, 12)

Monk Bretton: Walker, J.M. ed. (1924) *Abstracts of the Chartularies of the Priory of Monkbretton* (Yorkshire Archaeological Society, Record Series, Vol.66)

Montacute: see Bruton

Muchelney: see Athelney

Newminster: Fowler, J.T. ed. (1878) *Chartularium Abbathiae de Novo Monasterio Ordinis Cisterciensis* (Surtees Society, Vol.66)

Newnham: Godber, J. ed. (1963-64) *The Cartulary of Newnham Priory* (Bedfordshire Historical Record Society, Vol.43, i-ii)

Norwich: Dodwell, B. ed. (1974, 1985) *The Charters of Norwich Cathedral Priory* (2 vols, Pipe Roll Society, New Series, Vols 40, 46)

Oseney: Salter, H.E. ed. (1929, 1931, 1934, 1935, 1936) *The Cartulary of Oseney Abbey* (Oxford Historical Society, Vols 89-91, 97-98, 101)

Oxford: Wigram, S.R. ed. (1894, 1896) *The Cartulary of the Monastery of St Frideswide at Oxford* (Oxford Historical Society, Vols 28, 31)

Peterborough: Brooke, C.N.L., Postan, M.M. eds, (1960) *Carte Nativorum: a Peterborough Abbey Cartulary of the Fourteenth Century* (Northamptonshire Record Society, Vol.20); Martin, J.D. ed. (1978) *The Cartularies and Registers of Peterborough Abbey* (Northamptonshire Record Society, Vol.28)

Pontefract: Holmes, R. ed. (1899, 1902) *The Chartulary of St John of Pontefract* (Yorkshire Archaeological Society, Record Series, Vols 25, 30)

Ramsey: Hart, W.H., Lyons, P.A. eds, (1892-1903) *Cartularium Monasterii de Rameseia* (Rolls Series, Vol.79, i-iii)

Ranton: Wrottesley, G. ed. (1883) 'The Chartulary of Ronton Priory' *Collections for a History of Staffordshire* (William Salt Archaeological Society, Vol.4, pp.264-95)

Reading: Kemp, B.R. (1986, 1987) *Reading Abbey Cartularies* (Royal Historical Society, Camden 4th Series, Vols 31, 33)

Rievaulx: Atkinson, J.C. ed. (1889) *Cartularium Abbathiae de Rievalle Ordinis Cisterciensis* (Surtees Society, Vol.83)

Robertsbridge: Anon. ed. (1873) *Calendar of Charters and Documents Relating to the Abbey of Robertsbridge* (London)

Rufford: Holdsworth, C.J. ed. (1972-81) *Rufford Charters* (Thoroton Society Record Series, Vols 29, 30, 32, 34)

St Albans: Hunn, J.R. (1983) 'A medieval cartulary of St Albans Abbey', *Medieval Archaeology*, Vol.27, pp.151-2

St Benet, Hulme: West, J.R. ed. (1932) *Cartulary of St Benet of Holme, 1020-1210* (Norfolk Record Society, Vols 2-3)

Salley: McNulty, J. ed. (1933, 1934) *The Chartulary of the Cistercian Abbey of St Mary of Sallay in Craven* (Yorkshire Archaeological Society, Record Series, Vols 87, 90)

Sandford-on-Thames: Leys, A.M. ed. (1937, 1940) *The Sandford Cartulary* (Oxfordshire Record Society, Vols 19, 22)

Selborne: Macray, W.D. ed. (1891) *Calendar of Charters and Documents relating to Selborne and its Priory* (Hampshire Record Society)

Shrewsbury: Rees, U. ed. (1975) *The Cartulary of Shrewsbury Abbey* (2 vols, National Library of Wales, Aberystwyth)

Snelshall: Jenkins, J.G. ed. (1945) *The Cartulary of Snelshall Priory* (Buckinghamshire Record Society, Vol.9)

Southwick: Hanna, K.A. ed. (1988, 1989) *The Cartularies of Southwick Priory* (Hampshire Record Series, Vols 9-10)

Stafford: Parker, F. ed. (1887) 'A Chartulary of the Priory of St Thomas the Martyr near Stafford', *Collections for a History of Staffordshire* (William Salt Archaeological Society, Vol.8, pp.125-201)

Stone: Wrottesley, G. ed. (1885) 'The Stone Chartulary', *Collections for a History of Staffordshire* (William Salt Archaeological Society, Vol.6.i), pp.1-28

Thame: Salter, H.E. ed. (1947, 1948) *The Thame Cartulary* (Oxford Record Society, Vols 25-26)

Thurgarton: Foulds, T. ed. (1994) *The Thurgarton Cartulary* (Paul Watkins, Stamford)

Tockwith: Ransome, G.R. ed. (1931) 'The Chartulary of Tockwith, alias Scokirk, a cell to the priory of Nostell', in *Miscellanea III* (Yorkshire Archaeological Society, Record Series, Vol.80), pp.151-206

Trentham: Parker, F.P. ed. (1890) 'A Chartulary of the Augustinian Priory of Trentham', *Collections for a History of Staffordshire* (William Salt Archaeological Society, Vol.11), pp.295-336

Waltham: Ransford, R. ed. (1989) *The Early Charters of the Augustinian Canons of Waltham Abbey, Essex, 1062-1230* (Boydell, Woodbridge)

Warden: Fowler, G.H. ed. (1930) *The Cartulary of the Abbey of Old Wardon* (Bedfordshire Historical Record Society, Vol.13)

Westminster: Mason, E. ed. (1988) *Westminster Abbey Charters, 1066-c.1214* (London Record Society, Vol.25)

Whitby: Atkinson, J.C. ed. (1879, 1881) *Cartularium Abbathiae de Whiteby* (Surtees Society, Vols 69, 72)

Winchcombe: Royce, D. ed. (1892-1903) *Landboc sive Registrum Monasterii de Winchelcumba* (2 vols, Exeter)

Winchester: Hart, C. (1970) 'The *Codex Wintoniensis* and the King's *Haligdom*' in Thirsk, J. ed. *Land, Church and People: Essays presented to Professor H.P.R. Finberg* (British Agricultural History Society, Reading), pp.7-38.

Worcester: Ker, N.R. (1948) 'Hemming's Cartulary', in Hunt, R.W., Pantin, W.A., Southern, R. W. eds, *Studies in Medieval History presented to F.M. Powicke* (Clarendon Press, Oxford), pp.48-75; Darlington, R.R. ed. (1968) *The Cartulary of Worcester Cathedral Priory (Register I)* (Pipe Roll Society, New Series, Vol.38)

Chronicles

Aberconwy: Ellis, H. ed. (1847) 'Register and chronicle of the abbey of Aberconway', *Camden Miscellany Vol. 1*, no.1 (Camden Society, Vol.39), pp.1-23

Abingdon: Stevenson, J. ed. (1958) *Chronicon Monasterii de Abingdon* (Rolls Series, Vol.2, i-ii)

Bermondsey: *Annales Monasterii de Bermundesia*, in Luard, ed., *Annales Monastici* (Rolls Series, Vol.36.iii)

Burton: *Annales Monasterii de Burton*, in Luard, ed., *Annales Monastici* (Rolls Series, Vol.36.i)

Bury St Edmunds: Butler, H.E. ed. (1949) *The Chronicle of Jocelin of Brakelond* (Thomas Nelson, London)

Canterbury, St Augustine's: Hardwick, C. ed. (1858) *Historia Monasterii S.Augustini Cantuariensis, by Thomas of Elmham* (Rolls Series, Vol.8); Davis, A.H. ed. (1934) *William Thorne's Chronicle of St Augustine's Abbey, Canterbury* (Oxford University Press)

Crowland: Riley, H.T. transl. (1854) *Ingulph's Chronicle of the Abbey of Croyland* (Henry G. Bohn, London)

Dale: Saltman, A. ed. (1967) 'The history of the foundation of Dale Abbey, or the so-called Chronicle of Dale', *Journal of Derbyshire Archaeological & Natural History Society*, Vol.87

Dunstable: *Annales Monasterii de Dunstaplia*, in Luard, ed., *Annales Monastici* (Rolls Series, Vol.36.iii)

Durham: Arnold, T. ed. (1882-85) *Symeonis Monachi Opera Omnia* (Rolls Series, Vol.75); Stevenson, J. (1855) *Simeon's History of the Church of Durham* (The Church Historians of England, Seeley, London; facsimile reprint by Llanerch Publishers, Felinfach, 1993)

Ely: Blake, E.O. ed. (1962) *Liber Eliensis* (Royal Historical Society, Camden 3rd Series, Vol.92)

Evesham: Macray, W.D. ed. (1863) *Chronicon Abbatiae de Evesham* (Rolls Series, Vol.29); for a partial translation, see Cox, D.C. ed. (1964) *The Chronicle of Evesham Abbey: an English Translation* (Vale of Evesham Historical Society)

Glastonbury: Hearne, T. ed. (1727) *Adami de Domerham Historia de Rebus Gestis Glastoniensibus* (Oxford); Scott, J. ed. (1981) *The Early History of Glastonbury: an Edition, Translation and Study of William of Malmesbury's De Antiquitate Glastonie Ecclesie* (Boydell, Woodbridge); Carley, J.P. ed. (1985) *The Chronicle of Glastonbury Abbey: an Edition, Translation and Study of John of Glastonbury's Cronica sive Antiquitates Glastoniensis Ecclesie* (Boydell, Woodbridge)

Hexham: Raine, J. ed. (1863, 1864) *The Priory of Hexham: its Chroniclers, Endowments and Annals* (Surtees Society, Vols 44, 46)

Leicester: Lumby, J.R. ed. (1889, 1895) *Chronicon Henrici Knighton vel Cnitthon, Monachi Leycestrensis* (Rolls Series, Vol.92, i-ii); Martin, G.H. ed. & transl. (1995) *Knighton's Chronicle, 1337-1396* (Clarendon Press, Oxford)

Louth Park: Venables, E. ed. (1891) *Chronicon Abbatiae de Parco Lude* (Lincolnshire Record Society publications, Vol.1)

Margam: *Annales Monasterii de Margam*, in Luard, ed., *Annales Monastici* (Rolls Series, Vol.36.i)

Meaux: Bond, E.A. ed. (1866, 1867, 1868) *Chronicon Monasterii de Melsa* (Rolls Series, Vol.43, i-iii)

Oseney: *Annales Monasterii de Oseneia* , in Luard, ed., *Annales Monastici* (Rolls Series, Vol.36.iv)

Peterborough: Mellows, C., Mellows, W.T. (1941) *The Peterborough Chronicle of Hugh Candidus* (reprinted with amendments, Peterborough Museum Society, 1997)

Ramsey: Macray, W.D. ed. (1886) *Chronicon Abbatiae Rameseiensis* (Rolls Series, Vol.83)

St Albans: Riley, H.T. ed. (1863-76) *Chronica Monasterii S.Albani* (Rolls Series, Vol.28, i-xii); extracts from Matthew Paris's *Gesta Abbatum Monasterii S.Albani* are translated by Vaughan, R. ed. (1984) *Chronicles of Matthew Paris: Monastic Life in the Thirteenth Century* (Alan Sutton, Gloucester)

Tewkesbury: *Annales Monasterii de Theokesberia*, in Luard, ed., *Annales Monastici* (Rolls Series, Vol.36.i)

Waverley: *Annales Monasterii de Waverleia*, in Luard, ed. *Annales Monastici* (Rolls Series, Vol.36.ii)

Winchester: *Annales Monasterii de Wintonia*, in Luard, ed., *Annales Monastici* (Rolls Series, Vol.36.ii)

Worcester: *Annales Monasterii de Wigornia*, in Luard, ed. *Annales Monastici* (Rolls Series, Vol.36.iv)

York: Craster, H.E., Thornton, M.E eds (1934) *The Chronicle of St Mary's Abbey of York* (Surtees Society, Vol.148)

Domestic and manorial accounts
Abingdon: Kirk, R.E.G. ed. (1892) *Accounts of the Obedientiars of Abingdon Abbey* (Camden Society, New Series, Vol.51)
Battle: Searle, E., Ross, B. eds (1967) *The Cellarers' Rolls of Battle Abbey, 1275-1513* (Sussex Record Society, Vol.65)
Beaulieu: Hockey, S.F. ed. (1975) *The Account-Book of Beaulieu Abbey* (Camden 4th Series, Vol.16, Royal Historical Society)
Bristol, St Augustine's Abbey: Beachcroft, G., Sabin, A. eds (1938) *Two Compotus Rolls of St Augustine's Abbey, Bristol* (Bristol Record Society, Vol.9); Sabin, A. ed. (1960) *Some Manorial Accounts of St Augustine's Abbey* (Bristol Record Society, Vol.22)
Bromholm: Redstone, L.J. ed. (1944) 'The cellarer's account for Bromholm Priory, Norfolk, 1415-16' (Norfolk Record Society, Vol.17), pp.47-91
Durham: Fowler, J.T. ed. (1898, 1899, 1901) *Extracts from the Account Rolls of the Abbey of Durham* (Surtees Society, Vols 99-100, 103)
Ely: Chapman, F.R. ed. (1907) *The Sacrist Rolls of Ely* (Cambridge University Press)
Harrold: Gilmore, G.D. ed. (1970) 'Two monastic account rolls', *Bedfordshire Historical Record Society*, Vol.49, pp.19-55
Jarrow: Raine, J. ed. (1854) *The Inventories and Account Rolls of the Benedictine Houses or Cells of Jarrow and Monkwearmouth* (Surtees Society, Vol.29)
Lenton: Stitt, F.B. ed. (1958) *Lenton Priory Estate Accounts, 1296-1298* (Thoroton Society, Record Series, Vol.19)
Monkwearmouth: see Jarrow
Newnham: see Harrold
Norwich: Saunders, H.W. (1930) *An Introduction to the Obedientiary and Manor Rolls of Norwich Cathedral Priory* (Norwich)
Pershore: Andrews, F.B. (1933) 'The compotus rolls of the monastery of Pershore', *Transactions of Birmingham Archaeological Society*, Vol.57, pp.1-94
Peterborough: Greatrex, J. ed. (1983) *Account Rolls of the Obedientiaries of Peterborough* (Northamptonshire Record Society Vol.33)
Selby: Tillotson, J.H. ed. (1988) *Monastery and Society in the Late Middle Ages: Selected Account Rolls from Selby Abbey, Yorkshire, 1398-1537* (Boydell, Woodbridge)
Wilton: Crittall, E. ed. (1956) 'Fragment of an account of the cellaress of Wilton Abbey, 1299', in Williams, N.J., Plucknett, T. eds (1956) *Collectanea* (Wiltshire Archaeological & Natural History Society, Records Branch, Vol.12)
Winchester: Kitchin, G.W. ed. (1892) *Compotus Rolls of the Obedientiaries of St Swithun's Priory, Winchester* (Hampshire Record Society, Vol.7); Drew, J.S. (1947) 'Manorial accounts of St Swithun's priory, Winchester', *English Historical Review*, Vol.62, pp.20-41, reprinted in Carus-Wilson, C.M. ed. (1962), *Essays in Economic History*, Vol.2 (London), pp.12-30.
Worcester: Wilson, J.M., Gordon, C. eds (1908) *Early Compotus Rolls of the Priory of Worcester* (Worcestershire Historical Society); Hamilton, S.G. (1910) *Compotus Rolls of the Priory of Worcester of the Fourteenth and Fifteenth Centuries* (Worcestershire Historical Society)

Rentals and lease books
Bolton: Kershaw, I. ed. (1969) *Bolton Priory Rentals and Ministers' Accounts, 1473-1539* (Yorkshire Archaeological Society, Record Series, Vol.132)
Durham: Lomas, R.A., Piper, A.J. eds (1986) *Durham Cathedral Priory Rentals, I:Bursars' Rentals* (Surtees Society, Vol.198)
Fountains: Michelmore, D.J.H. ed. (1981) *The Fountains Abbey Lease Book* (Yorkshire Archaeological Society, Record Series, Vol.140)
Glastonbury: Elton, C.I., Holmes, T.S., Hobhouse, E. eds (1891) *Rentalia et Custumaria Michaelis de Ambresbury (1232-1252) et Rogeri de Ford (1252-1261), Abbatum Monasterii Beatae Mariae Glastonie* (Somerset Record Society, Vol.5)

Kirkstall: Stansfield, J. ed. (1891) 'A rent-roll of Kirkstall Abbey', *Miscellanea* (Thoresby Society, Vol.2), pp.1-21

Miscellaneous sources
Dugdale, W. (1655-73), *Monasticon Anglicanum*, ed. Caley, J., Ellis, H., Bandinel, B., 6 vols in 8, London, 1817-30
Larking, L.B., Kemble, J.M. eds (1857) *The Knights Hospitallers in England, being the Report of Prior Philip de Thame to the Grand master Elyan de Villanova for AD 1338* (Camden Society, Vol.65)
Lees, B.A. ed. (1935) *Records of the Templars in England in the Twelfth Century:the Inquest of 1185* (Records of the Social and Economic History of England and Wales, IX, British Academy; reprinted by Kraus-Thompson Organisation, Munich, 1981)

Burton: Bridgeman, C.G.O. ed. (1916) 'The Burton Abbey twelfth-century surveys', *Collections for a History of Staffordshire* (William Salt Archaeological Society), pp.209-300
Bury St Edmunds: Arnold, T. ed. (1890, 1892, 1896) *Memorials of St Edmunds Abbey* (Rolls Series Vol.96, i-iii); Douglas, D.C. ed. (1932) *Feudal Documents from the Abbey of Bury St Edmunds* (Records of the Social and Economic History of England & Wales, Vol.7)
Canterbury St Augustine's: Turner, G.J., Salter, H.E. eds (1915) *The Register of St Augustine's Abbey, Canterbury, commonly called the Black Book* (Oxford)
Durham: Greenwell, W. ed. (1871) *Feodarium Prioratus Dunelmensis: a Survey of the Estates of the Prior and Convent of Durham compiled in the Fifteenth Century* (Surtees Society, Vol.58)
Fountains: Walbran, J.R. ed. (1862), Walbran, J.R., Raine, J. eds (1876); Fowler, J.T. ed. (1918) *Memorials of the Abbey of St Mary of Fountains* (Surtees Society, Vols 42, 67, 130)
Furness: Atkinson, J.C., Brownbill, J. eds (1886-1919) *The Coucher Book of Furness Abbey* (Chetham Society, New Series, Vols 9, 11, 14, 74, 76, 78)
Glastonbury: Jackson, J.E. ed. (1882) *Liber Henrici de Soliaco Abbatis Glaston': an Inquisition of the Manors of Glastonbury Abbey in the year MCLXXXIX* (Roxburghe Club, London); Stacy, N.E. ed. (2001) *Surveys of the Estates of Glastonbury Abbey, c.1135-1201* (Records of Social and Economic History, New Series, no.33, British Academy, Oxford University Press)
Godstow: Clark, A. ed. (1905, 1906, 1911) *The English Register of Godstow Nunnery near Oxford* (Early English Text Society, Vols 129, 130, 142)
Holm Cultram: Grainger, F., & Collingwood, W.D. eds (1929) *The Register and Records of Holm Cultram* (Cumberland & Westmorland Antiquarian & Archaeological Society, Record Series, Vol.7)
Kingswood: Perkins, V.R. ed. (1899) 'Documents relating to the Cistercian monastery of St Mary, Kingswood' *Transactions of Bristol & Gloucestershire Archaeological Society*, Vol.22, pp.179-256
Kirkstall: Lancaster, W.T., Paley Baildon, W. eds (1904) *The Coucher Book of the Cistercian Abbey of Kirkstall* (Thoresby Society, Vol.8)
Malmesbury: Brewer, J.S. ed. (1879), Brewer, J.S., Trice Martin, C. eds (1880) *Registrum Malmesburiense* (Rolls Series, Vol.72, i-ii)
Peterborough: Raban, S. ed. (2001) *The White Book of Peterborough: the Registers of Abbot William of Woodford, 1295-99, and Abbot Godfrey of Crowland, 1299-1321* (Northamptonshire Record Society, Vol.41)
Selby: Fowler, J. ed. (1891, 1893) *The Coucher Book of Selby* (Yorkshire Archaeological Society, Record Series, Vols 10, 13)
Sibton: Denney, A.H. ed. (1960) *The Sibton Abbey Estates: Select Documents, 1325-1509* (Suffolk Records Society, Vol.2)
Stoneleigh: Hilton, R.H. ed. (1960) *The Stoneleigh Leger Book* (Dugdale Society, Vol.24)
Whalley: Hulton, W.A. ed. (1847-49) *The Coucher Book, or Chartulary, of Whalley Abbey* (Chetham Society, New Series, Vols 10-11, 16, 20)

Worcester: Fegan, E.S. ed. (1913-14) *The Journal of Prior William More* (Worcestershire Historical Society); Hale, W. ed. (1865) *Register of Worcester Priory* (Camden Society, Vol.91)

Vale Royal: Brownbill, J. ed. (1914) *The Ledger Book of Vale Royal Abbey* (Record Society for Lancashire & Cheshire, Vol.68)

Suppression inventories

Brown, W. (1886) 'Description of the buildings of twelve small Yorkshire priories at the Reformation', *Yorkshire Archaeological Journal,* Vol.9, pp. 196-215

Coppack, G. (1999) 'Suppression documents', in Fergusson, P., Harrison, S., *Rievaulx Abbey: Community, Architecture, Memory* (Paul Mellon Centre for Studies in British Art, Yale University Press), Appendix D, pp.226-37

'Inventories of the Religious Houses of Shropshire at their Dissolution', *Transactions of Shropshire Archaeology & Natural History Society,* 3rd Series, Vol.5 (1905), pp.377-92

'Inventories of Goods of the Smaller Monasteries and Friaries of Sussex at the Time of their Dissolution', *Sussex Archaeological Collections,* Vol.44 (1901), pp.55-72

Maps

Mitchell, J.B. (1933) 'Early maps of Great Britain: the Matthew Paris maps', *Geographical Journal,* Vol.81

All the large-scale maps mentioned apart from that at Abingdon are published and discussed in R.A. Skelton & P.D.A. Harvey eds (1986), *Local Maps and Plans from Medieval England* (Oxford University Press)

Chapter 2: Acquisition and exploitation of monastic estates

General works on monastic estates and granges

Bond, C.J. (2000) 'Landscapes of monasticism' in Hooke, D. ed., *Landscape: the Richest Historical Record* (Society for Landscape Studies, Supplementary Series, 1), pp.63-74

— (2003) 'English medieval nunneries: buildings, precincts and estates', in Wood, D. ed., *Women and Religion in Medieval England* (Oxbow, Oxford), pp.46-90

Matthew, D. (1962) *The Norman Monasteries and their English Possessions* (Oxford University Press, reprinted Westport, CT, 1979)

Moorhouse, S. (1989) 'Monastic estates: their composition and development', in Gilchrist, R., Mytum, H. eds, *The Archaeology of Rural Monasteries,* British Archaeological Reports, British Series no.203, pp.29-81

Platt, C. (1969) *The Monastic Grange in Medieval England* (MacMillan)

Surveys of estates and land management of monastic orders

Donkin, R.A. (1978) *The Cistercians: Studies in the Geography of Medieval England and Wales* (Pontifical Institute of Mediaeval Studies, Studies & Texts no.38, Toronto)

Donnelly, J.S. (1954) 'Changes in the grange economy of English and Welsh Cistercian abbeys', *Traditio,* Vol.10, pp.399-458

Golding, B. (1995) *Gilbert of Sempringham and the Gilbertine Order, c.1130-c.1300* (Clarendon Press, Oxford), esp. Part III, 'Resources and their Exploitation', pp.353-443

Graves, C.V. (1957) 'The economic activities of the Cistercians in medieval England (1128-1307)', *Analecta Sacri Ordinis Cisterciensis,* Vol.13, pp.3-60

Robinson, D.M. (1980) *The Geography of Augustinian Settlement in Medieval England and Wales* (British Archaeological Reports, British Series no.80, i-ii)

Williams, D.H. (1998) *The Cistercians in the Early Middle Ages* (Gracewing, Leominster)

Regional surveys of monastic estates and granges

Bishop, T.A.M. (1936) 'Monastic granges in Yorkshire', *Economic History Review,* Vol.51, pp.193-214

Burton, J. (1999) *The Monastic Order in Yorkshire, 1069-1215* (Cambridge Studies in Medieval Life and Thought, 4th Series, no.40, Cambridge University Press), esp. Ch.8, 'Monasteries in the landscape', pp.216-43, and Ch.9, 'Financing the monastery: the management of economic resources', pp.244-76

Coldicott, D.K. (1989) *Hampshire Nunneries* (Phillimore, Chichester), esp. Ch.9, 'The economy of the nunneries: income', pp.105-114

Courtney, P. (1980-81) 'The monastic granges of Leicestershire', *Transactions of Leicestershire Archaeological & Historical Society,* Vol.56, pp.33-45

Cowley, F.G. (1967) 'The Cistercian economy in Glamorgan, 1130-1349', *Morgannwg,* Vol.11, pp.5-26

— (1977) *The Monastic Order in South Wales, 1066-1349* (Studies in Welsh History no.1, University of Wales Press, Cardiff)

Donkin, R.A. (1964) 'The Cistercian grange in England in the twelfth and thirteenth centuries, with special reference to Yorkshire', *Studia Monastica,* Vol.6, pp.95-144

Fletcher, J.S. (1919) *The Cistercians in Yorkshire* (SPCK, London)

Griffiths, W.E. (1982) 'Monastic granges', in Royal Commission on Ancient & Historical Monuments, Wales, *An Inventory of the Ancient Monuments in Glamorgan,* Vol.3: *Medieval Secular Monuments:* part ii: *Non-defensive* (HMSO, Cardiff), pp.245-306

Jack, S. (1965-66) 'Monastic lands in Leicestershire and their administration on the eve of the Dissolution', *Transactions of Leicestershire Archaeological & Historical Society,* Vol.41, pp.9-40

Martin, E.J. (1929) 'The Templars in Yorkshire and a list of Templar lands in Yorkshire, 1185-1308', *Yorkshire Archaeological Journal,* Vol.29, pp.366-85

Moorhouse, S. (1981) 'Monastic holdings', in Faull, M.L., Moorhouse, S.A. eds *West Yorkshire: an Archaeological Survey to AD 1500* (West Yorkshire Metropolitan County Council, Wakefield), Vol.3, pp.781-800

Thompson, A.H. (1913-15) 'The monasteries of Leicestershire in the fifteenth century', *Transactions of Leicestershire Archaeological & Historical Society,* Vol.11.i-ii, pp.89-108

Waites, B. (1962) 'The monastic grange as a factor of the settlement of north-east Yorkshire', *Yorkshire Archaeological Journal,* Vol.40, pp.627-56

— (1997) *Monasteries and Landscape in North-East England: The Medieval Colonisation of the North York Moors* (Oakham)

Williams, D.H. (1965) 'The Cistercians in Wales: some aspects of their economy', *Archaeologia Cambrensis,* Vol.114, pp.2-47

— (1984) *The Welsh Cistercians* (2 vols, Cyhoeddiadau Sistersiaidd, Caldey; revised edn, Gracewing, Leominster, 2001)

— (1990) *Atlas of Cistercian Lands in Wales* (University of Wales Press, Cardiff)

Case studies of individual monastic estates

The 'Religious Houses' sections of the Victoria County Histories normally include at least some consideration of the landed properties and sources of income of each house.

Aberconwy: Hays, R.W. (1963) *The History of the Abbey of Aberconway, 1186-1537* (University of Wales Press, Cardiff), esp. Ch.6, 'The economic history of the abbey to the end of the 14th century', pp.100-24

Abingdon: Stenton, F.M. (1913) *The Early History of the Abbey of Abingdon* (Oxford University Press); Bond, C.J. (1979) 'The reconstruction of the medieval landscape: the estates of Abingdon Abbey', *Landscape History,* Vol.1, pp.59-75

Battle: Searle, E. (1974) *Lordship and Community: Battle Abbey and its Banlieu, 1066-1538* (Pontifical Institute of Mediaeval Studies, Toronto: Studies & Texts, no.26)

Beaulieu: Hockey, F. (1976) *Beaulieu: King John's Abbey: a History of Beaulieu Abbey. Hampshire, 1204-1538* (Pioneer Publications)

Bec: Morgan, M. (1946) *The English Lands of the Abbey of Bec* (Oxford Historical Series, reprinted 1968)

Bolton: Kershaw, I. (1973) *Bolton Priory: the Economy of a Northern Monastery, 1286-1325* (OUP)

Bordesley: Astill, G. (1994) 'The Bordesley Abbey granges project', in Pressouyre, L. ed., *L 'Espace Cistercien* (Comité des Travaux Historiques et Scientifiques, Mémoires de la Section d'Archéologie et d'Histoire de l'Art, no.5, Paris), pp.536-553

Burton: Walmsley, J.F.R. (1972) 'The peasantry of Burton Abbey in the thirteenth century', *North Staffordshire Journal of Field Studies,* Vol.12, pp.47-61

Canterbury, Christ Church: Brooks, N.P. (1984) *The Early History of the Church of Canterbury: Christ Church from 597 to 1066* (Leicester University Press); Mate, M. (1983) 'The farming out of manors: a new look at the evidence from Canterbury Cathedral Priory', *Journal of Medieval History,* Vol.9, pp.331-44; Mate, M. (1984) 'Property investment by Canterbury Cathedral Priory, 1250-1400', *Journal of British Studies,* Vol.33, pp.1-21; Smith, R.A.L. (1943) *Canterbury Cathedral Priory: a Study in Monastic Administration* (Cambridge University Press)

Canterbury, St Augustine's: Tatton-Brown, T. (1997) 'The abbey precinct, liberty and estate', in Gem, R. ed., *St Augustine's Abbey, Canterbury* (English Heritage, B.T. Batsford, London), pp.123-42

Crowland: Page, F.M. (1934) *The Estates of Crowland Abbey: a Study in Manorial Organisation* (Cambridge Studies in Economic History, Cambridge University Press); Raban, S. (1977) *The Estates of Thorney and Crowland: a Study in Medieval Monastic Land Tenure* (University of Cambridge Department of Land Occasional Paper no.7)

Dale: Colvin, H.M. (1939) 'Dale Abbey: granges, mills and other buildings', *Journal of the Derbyshire Archaeological & Natural History Society,* Vol.60, pp.142-55

Dieulacresse: Bayliss, M. (1962) 'Dieulacres Abbey', *North Staffordshire Journal of Field Studies,* Vol.2, pp.78-87; Wagstaffe, J.M. (1970) 'The economy of Dieulacres Abbey, 1214-1539', *North Staffordshire Journal of Field Studies,* Vol.10, pp.83-102

Dore: Williams, D.H. (1997) 'The Abbey of Dore', in Shoesmith, R., Richardson, R. eds *A Definitive History of Dore Abbey* (Logaston Press, Almeley, Herefordshire), esp. pp.29-36

Dunkeswell: Sparks, J.A. (1978) *In the Shadow of the Blackdowns: Life at the Cistercian Abbey of Dunkeswell and on its Manors and Estates, 1209-1531* (Moonraker Press, Bradford-on-Avon)

Durham: Dobson, R.B. (1973) *Durham Priory, 1400-1450* (Cambridge Studies in Medieval Life and Thought no.6, Cambridge University Press); Lomas, R.A. (1978) 'The priory of Durham and its demesnes in the fourteenth and fifteenth centuries', *Economic History Review,* 2nd Series, Vol.31, pp.339-53

Ely: Miller, E. (1951) *The Abbey and Bishopric of Ely: the Social History of an Ecclesiastical Estate from the Tenth to the Early Fourteenth Century* (Cambridge Studies in Medieval Life and Thought, New Series. Vol.1; Cambridge University Press)

Evesham: Bond, C.J. (1973) 'The estates of Evesham Abbey: a preliminary survey of their medieval topography', *Vale of Evesham Historical Society Research Papers,* Vol.4, pp.1-62; Bond, C.J. (1975) 'The medieval topography of the Evesham Abbey estates: a supplement', *Vale of Evesham Historical Society Research Papers,* Vol.5, pp.51-60; Cox, D.C. (1975) 'The Vale estates of the church of Evesham, c. 700-1086', *Vale of Evesham Historical Society Research Papers,* Vol.5, pp.25-50

Fountains: Coppack, G. (1993) *Fountains Abbey* (English Heritage, Batsford, London), esp. Ch.5, 'Agriculture, industry and wealth', pp.78-97; Wardrop, J. (1987) *Fountains Abbey and its Benefactors, 1132-1300* (Cistercian Studies no.91, Cistercian Publications, Kalamazoo, Michigan), esp. Ch.1, 'The lands of Fountains Abbey' and Ch.2, 'The consolidation of the estates', pp.29-131

Glastonbury: Costen, M. (1992) 'Dunstan, Glastonbury and the economy of Somerset in the tenth century', in Ramsay, N., Sparks, M., Tatton-Brown, T. eds, *St Dunstan: his Life, Times and Cult* (Boydell, Woodbridge), pp.25-44; Lennard, R. (1955-6) 'The demesnes of Glastonbury Abbey in the eleventh and twelfth

centuries', *Economic History Review,* 2nd Series, Vol.8, pp.355-363; Lennard, R. (1975) 'The Glastonbury Abbey estates: a rejoinder', *Economic History Review,* 2nd Series, Vol.28. pp.517-23; Morland, S.C. (1970) 'Hidation on the Glastonbury estates: a study in tax evasion', *Proceedings of Somerset Archaeological & Natural History Society,* Vol.114, p.74; Morland, S.C. (1983-84) 'Glaston Twelve Hides', *Proceedings of Somerset Archaeological & Natural History Society,* Vol.128, pp.35-54; Postan, M.M. (1952-3) 'Glastonbury estates in the twelfth century', *Economic History Review,* 2nd Series, Vol.5, pp.358-367; Postan, M.M. (1956-57) 'Glastonbury estates in the twelfth century: a reply', *Economic History Review,* 2nd Series, Vol.9, pp.106-18; both of Postan's papers were reprinted in Postan, M.M. (1973) *Essays in Medieval Agriculture and General Problems of the Medieval Economy* (Cambridge University Press), pp.249-77; Abrams, L. (1996) *Anglo-Saxon Glastonbury: Church and Endowment* (Boydell, Woodbridge)

Gloucester: Hilton, R.H. (1953-4) 'Gloucester Abbey leases in the late thirteenth century', *University of Birmingham Historical Journal,* Vol.4, pp.1-17

Haughmond: Rees, U. (1983) 'The leases of Haughmond Abbey', *Midland History,* Vol.8, pp.14-28

Kirkstall: Barnes, G.D. (1982) *Kirkstall Abbey, 1147-1539: an Historical Study* (Thoresby Society, Vol.58)

Lewes: Blair, J. (1980) 'The Surrey endowments of Lewes Priory before 1200', *Surrey Archaeological Collections,* Vol.72, pp.97-126

London, St Mary's, Clerkenwell: Hassall, W.O. (1948) 'The property of St Mary, Clerkenwell, in the south midlands', *Oxoniensia,* Vol.13, pp.73-4

Margam: Gray, T. (1903, 1905) 'Notes on the granges of Margam Abbey', *Journal of British Archaeological Association,* 2nd Series, Vol.9, pp.161-81, Vol.11, pp.11-29

Maxstoke: Watkins, A. (1996) 'Maxstoke Priory in the fifteenth century: the development of an estate economy in the Forest of Arden', *Warwickshire History,* Vol.10, no.i, pp.3-18.

Merevale: Watkins, A. (1994) 'Merevale Abbey in the late 1490s', *Warwickshire History,* Vol.9, no. iii, pp.87-104

Norwich: Virgoe, R. (1996) 'The estates of Norwich Cathedral Priory, 1101-1538', in Atherton, I., Fernie, E., Harper-Bill, C., Smith, H. eds, *Norwich Cathedral: Church, City and Diocese, 1096-1996* (Hambledon Press, London), pp.339-59

Peterborough: King, E. (1973) *Peterborough Abbey, 1086-1310: a Study in the Land Market* (Cambridge University Press)

Pipewell: John, E.L.T. (1970) 'The Warwickshire estates of the abbey of Pipewell', *Warwickshire History,* Vol.1 no. iii, pp.21-8

Quarr: Hockey, S.F. (1970) *Quarr Abbey and its Lands, 1132-1631* (Leicester University Press)

Ramsey: Raftis, J.A. (1957) *The Estates of Ramsey Abbey: a Study in Economic Growth and Organisation* (Pontifical Institute of Mediaeval Studies, Toronto: Studies & Texts, no.3)

Strata Florida: Bowen, E.J. (1950-1) 'The monastic economy of the Cistercians at Strata Florida', *Ceredigion,* Vol.1, pp.34-37

Tavistock: Finberg, H.P.R. (1951) *Tavistock Abbey: a Study in the Social and Economic History of Devon* (Cambridge University Press, 2nd edn, 1969)

Tewkesbury: Rees, W. (1950) 'The possessions of the abbey of Tewkesbury in Glamorgan', *South Wales & Monmouthshire Record Society,* Vol.2

Thorney: See Raban (1977) under Crowland, above.

Torre: Seymour, D. (1977) *Torre Abbey: an Account of its History, Buildings, Cartularies and Lands* (Torquay)

Westminster: Harvey, B. (1969) 'The leasing of the abbot of Westminster's demesnes in the later Middle Ages', *Economic History Review,* 2nd Series, Vol.22, pp.17-27; Harvey, B. (1977) *Westminster Abbey and its Estates in the Middle Ages* (Oxford University Press); Mason, E. (1996) *Westminster Abbey and its People, c.1050-c.1216* (Studies in the History of Medieval Religion, IX, Boydell, Woodbridge), esp. Chs 10 & 11, pp.189-235

Chapters 3, 4 and 5

The literature on medieval farming is extensive. Important studies and syntheses include:

Baker, A.R.H., Butlin, R.A. eds (1973) *Studies of Field Systems in the British Isles* (Cambridge University Press)

Campbell, B.M.S. (2000) *English Seigniorial Agriculture, 1250-1450* (Cambridge Studies in Historical Geography no.31; CUP)

Finberg, H.P.R. ed. (1972) *The Agrarian History of England and Wales,* Vol.1.ii, *AD 43-1042* (Cambridge University Press)

Hallam, H.E. ed. (1988) *The Agrarian History of England and Wales,* Vol.2, *1042-1350* (Cambridge University Press)

Langdon, J.L. (1986) *Horses, Oxen and Technological Innovation: the Use of Draught Animals in English Farming from 1066-1500* (Cambridge University Press)

Miller, E. ed. (1991) *The Agrarian History of England and Wales,* Vol.3, *1348-1500* (Cambridge University Press)

Thirsk, J. ed. (1967) *The Agrarian History of England and Wales,* Vol.4, *1500-1640* (Cambridge University Press)

Monastic farming

Bailey, M. (1995) 'The prior and convent of Ely and their management of the manor of Lakenheath in the fourteenth century', in Franklin, M.J., Harper-Bill, C. eds, *Medieval Ecclesiastical Studies in honour of Dorothy M. Owen* (Boydell, Woodbridge), pp.1-19

Bond, C.J. (2001) 'Production and consumption of food and drink in the medieval monastery', in Keevill, G., Aston, M., Hall, T. eds *Monastic Archaeology* (Oxbow, Oxford), pp.54-87

Day, L.J.C. (1950) 'The early monastic contribution to medieval farming', *Lincolnshire History,* Vol.5, pp.200-14

Halcrow, E.M. (1954-5) 'The decline of demesne farming on the estates of Durham Cathedral Priory', *Economic History Review,* 2nd Series, Vol.7, pp.345-56

Harrison, B. (1995) 'Field systems and demesne farming on the Wiltshire estates of St Swithun's Priory, Winchester, 1248-1340', *Agricultural History Review,* Vol.43, pp.1-18

Hilton, R.H. (1949) 'Winchcombe Abbey and the manor of Sherborne', *University of Birmingham Historical Journal,* Vol.2, pp.32-52, reprinted in Finberg, H.P.R. ed. (1957), *Gloucestershire Studies* (Leicester University Press), pp.89-113

Keil, I.J. (1965) 'Farming on the Dorset estates of Glastonbury Abbey in the early fourteenth century', *Proceedings of Dorset Natural History & Archaeology Society,* Vol.87, pp.234-50

Kershaw, I. (1973) *Bolton Priory: the Economy of a Northern Monastery,* 1286-1325 (Oxford Historical Monographs, Oxford University Press)

Mate, M. (1984) 'Agrarian economy after the Black Death: the manors of Canterbury Cathedral Priory, 1348-91', *Economic History Review,* 2nd Series, Vol.37, pp.341-54

Oschinsky, D. (1971) *Walter of Henley and other Treatises on Estate Management and Accounting* (Clarendon Press, Oxford)

Smith, R.A.L. (1947) 'The Benedictine contribution to medieval English agriculture', in Knowles, M.D. ed., *Collected Essays of R.A.L. Smith* (Longmans, Green & Co., London), pp.103-16.

Waites, B. (1967) *Moorland and Vale-Land Farming in North-East Yorkshire: the Monastic Contribution in the Thirteenth and Fourteenth Centuries* (Borthwick Papers, No.32, Borthwick Institute of Historical Research, University of York)

Wretts-Smith, M. (1932) 'The organisation of farming at Croyland Abbey, 1257-1321', *Journal of Economic & Business History,* Vol.4, pp.168-92

Chapter 3: Arable farming on monastic estates

Brandon, P.F. (1971) 'Demesne arable farming in coastal Sussex during the later Middle Ages', *Agricultural History Review,* Vol.19, pp.113-34

— (1972) 'Cereal yields on the Sussex estates of Battle Abbey during the later Middle Ages', *Economic History Review,* 2nd Series, Vol.25, pp.403-20

Campbell, B.M.S. (1983) 'Agricultural progress in medieval England: some evidence from eastern Norfolk', *Economic History Review,* 2nd Series, Vol.36.i, pp.26-46

Farmer, D.L. (1983) 'Grain yields on Westminster Abbey manors, 1271-1410', *Canadian Journal of History* , Vol.18, pp.331-47

Fox, H.S.A. (1986) 'The alleged transformation from 2-field to 3-field systems in medieval England', *Economic History Review,* 2nd Series, Vol.39.iv, pp.526-48 [includes discussion of Podimore]

Hogan, M.P. (1988) 'Clays, *culturae* and their cultivation at Wistow', *Agricultural History Review,* Vol.36, pp.117-131

Keil, I.J. (1961-7) 'Account of the granger of Glastonbury Abbey, 1361-2', *Somerset & Dorset Notes & Queries,* Vol.28, pp.86-90

Morimoto, N. (1975) 'Arable farming of Durham Cathedral Priory in the fourteenth century', *Nagoya Gakuin University Review,* Vol.11, pp.137-331

Postles, D. (1979) 'Grain issues from some properties of Oseney Abbey, 1274-1348', *Oxoniensia* , Vol.44, pp.30-37

— (1999) 'Estimates of harvest on Oseney Abbey manors', *Oxoniensia* Vol.64, pp.301-5

Chapter 4: Livestock farming on monastic estates

Cattle farming

Donkin, R.A. (1962-3) 'Cattle on the estates of medieval Cistercian monasteries in England and Wales', *Economic History Review,* 2nd Series, Vol.15, pp.31-53

Fox, A. (1958) 'A monastic homestead on Dean Moor, South Devon', *Medieval Archaeology,* Vol.2, pp.141-157

Sheep farming and wool production

Cunningham, W. (1927) *The Growth of English Industry and Commerce during the Early and Middle Ages* (5th edn, Cambridge University Press) [includes a transcript of the Pegolotti list, pp.628-41]

Donkin, R.A. (1957) 'The disposal of Cistercian wool in England and Wales during the twelfth and thirteenth centuries', *Citeaux in de Nederlanden,* Vol.8, pp.109-131,181-202

— (1958) 'Cistercian sheep-farming and wool sales in the thirteenth century', *Agricultural History Review,* Vol. 6.i, pp.2-8

— (1958) '*Bercaria et Lanaria' Yorkshire Archaeological Journal,* Vol.39, pp.447-450

Evans, A. ed. (1936) Pegolotti, F.B., *La Practica della Mercatura* (Medieval Academy of America, Vol.24, Cambridge, Mass.)

Fowler, R.C. (1930) 'A balance sheet of St Osyth's Abbey', *Essex Archaeological Society,* New Series, Vol.19, pp.187-188

Lloyd, T.H. (1977) *The English Wool Trade in the Middle Ages* (Cambridge University Press)

Postles, D. (1984) 'The Oseney Abbey flock', *Oxoniensia,* Vol.49, pp.141-52

Power, E. (1941) *The Wool Trade in English Medieval History* (Oxford University Press)

Raistrick, A. (1953) *The Role of the Yorkshire Cistercian Monasteries in the History of the Wool Trade in England* (Department of Education of the International Wool Secretariat)

Waites, B. (1980) 'Monasteries and the wool trade in north and east Yorkshire during the thirteenth and fourteenth centuries', *Yorkshire Archaeological Journal,* Vol.52, pp.111-21

Whitwell, R.J. (1904) 'English monasteries and the wool trade in the thirteenth century', *Vierteljahrschrift für Sozial- und Wirtschaftsgeschichte,* Vol.2, pp.1-33

Wroot, H.E. (1930) 'Yorkshire abbeys and the wool trade', *Miscellanea* (Thoresby Society, Vol.33.i), pp.1-21

Pig farming
Biddick, K. (1985) 'Pig husbandry on the Peterborough Abbey estate from the twelfth to the fourteenth century A.D.', in Clutton-Brock, J., Grigson, C. eds, *Animals and Archaeology, Vol.IV: Husbandry in Europe* (British Archaeological Reports, International Series, no. 227), pp.161- 77

Chapter 5: Assarting, reclamation and enclosure

Assarting
Donkin, R.A. (1964) 'The English Cistercians and assarting, *c.*1128- *c.*1350', *Analecti Sacri Ordinis Cisterciensis*, Vol.20, pp.49-75

Marshland holdings and reclamation
Brandon, P.F. (1971) 'Agriculture and the effects of floods and weather at Barnhorne, Sussex, during the later Middle Ages', *Sussex Archaeological Collections,* Vol. 109, 69-83
Darby, H.C. (1940) *The Medieval Fenland* (CUP)
Donkin, R.A. (1958) 'The marshland holdings of the English Cistercians before 1350', *Cîteaux in de Nederlanden*, Vol.9, pp.1-14, 262-275
Eddison, J. ed. (1995) *Romney Marsh: the Debatable Ground* (Oxford University Committee for Archaeology, Monograph no.41)
Eddison, J., Green, C. eds, (1988) *Romney Marsh: Evolution, Occupation, Reclamation* (Oxford University Committee for Archaeology, Monograph no.24)
Rippon, S. (1997) *The Severn Estuary: Landscape Evolution and Wetland Reclamation* (Leicester University Press)
— (2000) *The Transformation of Coastal Wetlands: Exploitation and Management of Marshland Landscapes in North West Europe during the Roman and Medieval Periods* (British Academy, Oxford University Press)
Sheppard, J.A. (1958) *The Draining of the Hull Valley* (East Yorkshire Local History Society, York)
Smith, R.A.L. (1940) 'Marsh embankment and sea defences in medieval Kent', *Economic History Review,* Vol.10.i, pp.29-37
Williams, M. (1970) *The Draining of the Somerset Levels* (Cambridge University Press), esp. Ch.3, pp.25-81
Witney, K.P. (1989) 'Development of the Kentish marshes in the aftermath of the Norman Conquest', *Archaeologia Cantiana,* Vol.107, pp.29-50

Turbaries
Lambert, J.M., Jennings, J.N., Smith, C.T., Green, C., Hutchinson, J.N. (1960) *The Making of the Broads: a Reconsideration of their Origin in the Light of New Evidence* (Royal Geographical Society, Research Series no.3)

Enclosure
Hodges, R. (1991) *Wall-to-Wall History: the Story of Roystone Grange* (Duckworth, London)
Leadam, I.S. (1892, 1893) 'The Inquisition of 1517: inclosures and evictions', *Transactions of Royal Historical Society,* New Series, Vol.6, pp.167-314, Vol.7, pp.127-292
Leadam, I.S. ed. (1897) *The Domesday of Inclosures* (2 vols, Royal Historical Society)

Scientific evidence for environmental change
Moffat, B. (1986) 'The environment of Battle Abbey estates (East Sussex) in medieval times: a re-evaluation using analysis of pollen and sediments', *Landscape History,* Vol.8, pp.77-93
Tinsley, H.M. (1975) 'The vegetation of upper Nidderdale: man's impact in the post-Roman period', in Phillips, A.D., Turton, B.J. eds *Environment, Man and Economic Change* (Longman, London), pp.146-63 [pollen evidence for clearance by Fountains Abbey]
— (1976) 'Monastic woodland clearance on the Dieulacres estate', *North Staffordshire Journal of Field Studies,* Vol.16, pp.16-22

Chapter 6: Monastic woodlands

Woodland management
Linnard, W. (1982) *Welsh Woods and Forests: History and Utilization* (National Museum of Wales, Cardiff), esp. pp.45-50
Preece, P.G. (1990) 'Medieval woods in the Oxfordshire Chilterns', *Oxoniensia*, Vol.55, pp.55-72
Rackham, O. (1980) *Ancient Woodland: its History, Vegetation and Uses in England* (Edward Arnold, London)
— (1982) 'The Avon Gorge and Leigh Woods', in Bell, M., Limbrey, S. eds, *Archaeological Aspects of Woodland Ecology* (British Archaeological Reports, International Series, no.146), pp.171-6
— (1986) *The Woods of South-East Essex* (Rochford District Council)
— (1993) 'Woodland management and timber economy as evidenced by the buildings at Cressing Temple', in Andrews, D.D. ed., *Cressing Temple: a Templar and Hospitaller Manor in Essex* (Essex County Council), pp.85-92
— (1998) 'The abbey woods', in Gransden, A. ed. *Bury St Edmunds: Medieval Art, Architecture, Archaeology and Economy* (British Archaeological Association, Conference Transactions, no.20), pp.139-60.
Wilson, M. (1990) 'Early maps and plans of Tiddesley Wood', *Transactions of Worcestershire Archaeological Society*, 3rd Series, Vol.12, pp.252-7

Monastic consumption of timber
Rackham, O., Blair, W.J., Munby, J.T. (1978) 'The thirteenth-century roofs and floor of the Blackfriars Priory, Gloucester', *Medieval Archaeology,* Vol.22, pp.105-22

Chapters 7 and 8

Monastic granges and estate farms
Aspinall, A., Heron, C., Pocock, J.A. (1994) 'Topographical and geophysical survey of a rural medieval complex' [Cayton Grange, Fountains Abbey], *Medieval Archaeology,* Vol.38, pp.177-82
Clay, T.C. (1929) 'Bradley: a grange of Fountains', *Yorkshire Archaeological Journal*, Vol.29, pp.97-106
Fosbrooke, T.H. (1913-14) 'Newhouse Grange, Sheepy, Leicestershire', *Transactions of Leicestershire Archaeological & Historical Society*, Vol.11, pp.85-86
Hallam, H.E. (1953) 'Goll Grange, a grange of Spalding Priory', *Lincolnshire Architectural & Archaeological Society,* New Series, Vol.5
McDonnell, J. (1975) 'The evolution of a monastic grange: Rievaulx Abbey's grange of Griff, North Yorkshire', *Journal of North Yorkshire County Record Office,* Vol.2, pp.78-95
Mayes, P. (2002) *Excavations at a Templar Preceptory, South Witham, Lincolnshire, 1965-67* (Society for Medieval Archaeology, Monograph Series no. 19)
Nash-Williams, V.E. (1952) 'The medieval settlement at Llantwit Major, Glamorganshire', *Bulletin of Board of Celtic Studies,* Vol.14.iv, pp.313-333
Parkes, L.N., Webster, P.V. (1974) 'Merthyrgeryn: a grange of Tintern', *Archaeologia Cambrensis,* Vol.123, pp.140-154
Price, E.G. (1980) 'Survivals of the medieval monastic estate of Frocester', *Transactions of Bristol & Gloucestershire Archaeological Society*, Vol.98, pp.73-88

Chapter 7: Domestic buildings of monastic manors

General references
There is a vast literature on medieval domestic building. Important general surveys include:
Blair, J. (1993) 'Hall and chamber: English domestic planning, 1000-1250', in Meirion-Jones & Jones eds, *Manorial Domestic Buildings in England and Northern France* (see below), pp.1-21

Grenville, J. (1997) *Medieval Housing* (Leicester University Press)

Meirion-Jones, G., Jones, M. eds (1993) *Manorial Domestic Buildings in England and Northern France* (Society of Antiquaries of London, Occasional Papers, Vol.15)

Wood, M.E. (1948) *Thirteenth-Century Domestic Architecture in England* (Archaeological Journal, Supplement to Vol.105)

— (1965) *The English Mediaeval House* (J.M.Dent, London; reissued by Ferndale Editions, London, 1981)

Domestic buildings on monastic manors and granges

A brief description of most surviving houses formerly in monastic hands will be found in *The Buildings of England* series of county volumes, ed. Pevsner, N. *et al.* (Penguin Books)

Alcock, N.W. (1982) 'The hall of the Knights Templar at Temple Balsall, West Midlands', *Medieval Archaeology*, Vol.26, pp.155-8

Blair, W.J. (1978) 'A late thirteenth-century survey of buildings on estates of Southwark Priory', *Antiquaries Journal,* Vol.58.ii, pp.353-4

Dufty, A.R. (1947) 'Place Farm, Tisbury', *Archaeological Journal* , Vol.104, pp.168-9

Fletcher, J.M. (1975) 'The medieval hall at Lewknor', *Oxoniensia,* Vol.40, pp.247-53

Fletcher, J.M., Spokes, P.S. (1964) 'The origin and development of crown-post roofs', *Medieval Archaeology*, Vol.8, pp.152-83 [includes discussion of Abingdon Abbey's houses at Charney Bassett and Sutton Courtenay]

Godfrey, W.H. (1936) 'Swanborough manor house', *Sussex Archaeological Collections*, Vol.77, pp.3-14

Kipps, P.K. (1929) 'Minster Court, Thanet', *Archaeological Journal,* Vol.86, pp.213-23

Jones, S.R., Smith, J.T. (1958) 'Manor Farm, Wasperton: an early fourteenth-century timber-framed house', *Transactions of Birmingham Archaeological Society*, Vol.76, pp.19-28

Morrey, M.C.J., Smith, J.T. (1973) 'The "Great Barn", Lewknor: the architectural evidence', *Oxoniensia* , Vol.38, pp.339-54

Parkin, E.W. (1962) 'The vanishing houses of Kent, i: Durlock Grange, Minster-in-Thanet', *Archaeologia Cantiana*, Vol.77, pp.82-91

Rigold, S.E. (1965) 'Two camerae of the military orders: Strood Temple, Kent, and Harefield, Middlesex', *Archaeological Journal,* Vol.122, pp.86-132

Robertson, J. (1876) 'The church and Abbot's Grange, Broadway', *Journal of British Archaeological Association,* Vol.32, pp.435-9

Toy, S. (1953) 'Langney Grange, Westham' [a house of Lewes Priory] *Sussex Archaeological Collections*, Vol.49, pp.75-81

Turner, H.L. (1972) 'The "Great Barn", Lewknor: the documentary evidence', *Oxoniensia,* Vol.37, pp.187-91

Moated sites

Aberg, F.A. ed. (1978) *Medieval Moated Sites* (Council for British Archaeology, Research Report no.17)

Allen, T. *et al.* (1994) 'A medieval grange of Abingdon Abbey at Dean Court Farm, Cumnor', *Oxoniensia,* 59, pp.219-448

Le Patourel, H.E.J. (1973) *The Moated Sites of Yorkshire* (Society for Medieval Archaeology, Monograph Series no.5)

Rudkin, D.J. (1971-2) 'The excavation of an early medieval site at Buckminster, Leicestershire', *Transactions of Leicestershire Archaeological & Historical Society*, Vol.47, pp.1-13 [Sewstern Grange, a property of Vaudey Abbey]

Moorhouse, S. (1971) 'Excavation of a moated site near Sawtry, Huntingdonshire', *Proceedings of Cambridgeshire Antiquarian Society,* Vol.63, pp.75-86 [probably the home grange of Sawtry Abbey]

Crenellation

Coulson, C. (1982) 'Hierarchism in conventual crenellation: an essay in the sociology and metaphysics of medieval fortification', *Medieval Archaeology*, Vol.26, pp.69-100

Chapter 8: Monastic farm buildings

Barns

Bond, C.J., Weller, J.B. (1991) 'The Somerset barns of Glastonbury Abbey', in Abrams, L., Carley, J.P. eds, *The Archaeology and History of Glastonbury Abbey* (Boydell, Woodbridge), pp.57-87

Bond, R. (1993) 'Great Tomkyns barn, Upminster, and the sequence of assembly in timber-framed aisled barns', *Vernacular Architecture,* Vol.24, pp.32-9

Brady, N. (1997) 'The gothic barn of England: icon of prestige and authority', in Smith, E.B., Wolfe, M. eds, *Technology and Resource Use in Medieval Europe: Cathedrals, Mills and Mines* (Ashgate, Aldershot), pp.76-105

Castle, S.A. (1973) 'The aisled barn at Parsonage Farm, Abbots Langley', *Hertfordshire Archaeology*, Vol.3, pp.131-134

— (1973) 'The medieval aisled barns at Kingsbury Manor Farm, St Albans, and Croxley Hall Farm', *Hertfordshire Archaeology,* Vol.3, pp.134-8

Charles, F.W.B., Horn, W. (1973) 'The cruck-built barn of Leigh Court, Worcestershire', *Journal of Society of Architectural Historians,* Vol.2, pp.5-29.

—, — (1983) 'The cruck-built barn of Frocester Court Farm, Gloucestershire', *Journal of Society of Architectural Historians,* Vol.42, pp.211-37

Everett, A.W. (1965) 'The monastic barn at Shiphay, Torquay', *Reports & Transactions of the Devonshire Association for the Advancement of Science, Literature & Art,* Vol.97, pp.157-160

Gibson, A.V.B. (1994) 'The constructive geometry in the design of the thirteenth-century barns at Cressing Temple', *Essex Archaeology & History,* Vol.25, pp.107-12

Hartshorne, A. (1874) 'The Great Barn, Harmondsworth', *Transactions of London & Middlesex Archaeological Society,* Vol.4, pp.417-18

Hewett, C.A. (1967) 'The barns at Cressing Temple, Essex, and their significance in the history of English carpentry', *Journal of Society of Architectural Historians,* Vol.26.i, pp.48-70

Heyworth, P.L. (1971) 'A lost Cistercian barn at Shilton, Oxon.', *Oxoniensia,*Vol.36, pp.52-54

Holdsworth, C. (1994) 'Barns at Cistercian granges in England and Wales', in Pressouyre, L. ed., *L'Espace Cistercien* (Comité des Travaux Historiques et Scientifiques, Mémoires de la Section d'Archéologie et d'Histoire de l'Art, no.5, Paris), pp.353-63

Horn, W. (1963) 'The great tithe barn of Cholsey, Berkshire', *Journal of Society of Architectural Historians,* Vol.22.i, pp.13-23.

Horn, W., Born, E. (1965) *The Barns of the Abbey of Beaulieu at its Granges of Great Coxwell and Beaulieu St Leonards* (Berkeley & Los Angeles)

Horn, W., Charles, F.W.B. (1966) 'The cruck-built barn of Middle Littleton in Worcestershire, England', *Journal of Society of Architectural Historians,* Vol.25.iv, pp.221-39

Rigold, S.E. (1966) 'Some major Kentish timber barns', *Archaeologia Cantiana*, Vol.81, pp.1-30

Roberts, J.H. (1979) 'Five medieval barns in Hertfordshire', *Hertfordshire Archaeology,* Vol. 7, pp.159-80

Stenning, D.F. (1993) 'The Barley Barn, the Wheat Barn and the early development of barns in south-east England', in Andrews, D.D. ed., *Cressing Temple: a Templar and Hospitaller Manor in Essex* (Essex County Council, Chelmsford)

Thompson, M.G. (1998) 'The building of a barn, byre and carthouse on Glastonbury Abbey's manor of Street between 1340 and 1343', *Proceedings of Somerset Archaeological & Natural History Society,* Vol.141, pp.103-14

Weaver, O.J. (1970) 'A medieval aisled barn at St Julian's Farm, St Albans', *Hertfordshire Archaeology,* Vol.2, pp.110-112

Wood-Jones, R.B. (1956) 'The rectorial barn at Church Enstone', *Oxoniensia,* Vol.21, pp.43-47

Dendrochronological dating
Reports of new dendrochronological dates appear annually in *Vernacular Architecture*.
Siebenlist-Kerner, V., Schove, D.J., Fletcher, J.M. (1978) 'The barn at Great Coxwell, Berkshire', in Fletcher, J.M. ed., *Dendrochronology in Europe* (British Archaeological Reports, International Series, no.51), pp.295-302
Tyers, I. (1993) 'Tree-ring dating at Cressing and the Essex Curve', in Andrews, D.D., ed., *Cressing Temple: a Templar and Hospitaller Manor in Essex* (Essex County Council), pp.77-93

Livestock housing and other farm buildings
Fox, A. (1958) 'A monastic homestead on Dean Moor, South Devon', *Medieval Archaeology*, Vol.2, pp.141-157
Haslam, J. (1984) 'Bradford-on-Avon, Barton Farm', *Medieval Archaeology*, Vol.28, pp.246-247
Hawkes, J. (1986-90) 'Excavations on the site of the Reading Abbey stables, 1983', *Berkshire Archaeological Journal*, Vol.73, pp.66-87
Huggins, P.J. (1972) 'Monastic grange and outer close excavation, Waltham Abbey, Essex', *Transactions of Essex Archaeological Society*, Vol.4, pp.30-127
Jobey, G. (1967) 'Excavation at Tynemouth Priory and Castle', *Archaeologia Aeliana*, 4th Series, Vol.45, pp.33-104

Sheepcotes
Dyer, C. (1995) 'Sheepcotes: evidence for medieval sheep farming', *Medieval Archaeology*, Vol.39, pp.136-164

Woolhouses
Coppack, G. (1986) 'The excavation of an outer court building, perhaps the woolhouse, at Fountains Abbey, North Yorkshire', *Medieval Archaeology*, Vol.30, pp.46-87
Faulkner, P.A. (1975) 'The surviving medieval buildings', in Platt, C., Coleman-Smith, R. eds, *Excavations in Medieval Southampton, 1953-1969* (Leicester University Press), i, pp.56-124 [Beaulieu Abbey's Southampton woolhouse is described on pp.72-5]
McDonnell, J. (1988-9) 'The Rievaulx Abbey woolhouse remains at Laskill', *Ryedale Historian*, Vol.15, pp.51-52

Dovecotes
Bond, C.J. (1989) 'Shapwick Manor dovecote', *Proceedings of Somerset Archaeological & Natural History Society*, Vol.133, pp.161-4
McCann, J. (1991) 'An historical enquiry into the design and use of dovecotes', *Transactions of Ancient Monuments Society*, Vol.35, pp.89-160
— (1998) *The Dovecotes of Suffolk* (Suffolk Institute of Archaeology and History)
— (2000) 'Dovecotes and pigeons in English law', *Transactions of Ancient Monuments Society*, Vol.44, pp.25-50
Webb, J. (1846) 'Notes upon a preceptory of the Templars at Garway, in the county of Hereford...', *Archaeologia*, Vol.31, pp.182-197

Chapter 9: Monastic gardens, orchards and vineyards

Gardens
Amherst, A. (1896) A *History of Gardening in England* (2nd edn, London)
Blunt, W., Raphael, S. (1979) *The Illustrated Herbal* (Frances Lincoln, Weidenfeld & Nicolson, London)
Bond, C.J. (1998) 'Somerset gardens in the Middle Ages', in Bond, *Somerset Parks and Gardens: a Landscape History* (Somerset Books, Tiverton), pp.32-43
Dyer, C. (1994) 'Gardens and orchards in medieval England', in Dyer, C., *Everyday Life in Medieval England* (Hambledon Press, London), pp.113-31

Harvey, J.H. (1981) *Mediaeval Gardens* (Batsford, London)
— (1984) 'Vegetables in the Middle Ages', *Garden History*, Vol.12 no.ii, pp.89-99
— (1992) 'Westminster Abbey: the infirmarer's garden', *Garden History*, Vol.20 no.ii, pp.97-115
Keil, I. (1959-60) 'The garden at Glastonbury Abbey', *Proceedings of Somerset Archaeological & Natural History Society*, Vol.104, pp.96-101
McLean, T. (1981) *Medieval English Gardens* (Collins, London), esp. Ch.1, 'The monastic garden', pp.13-58
Meyvaert, P. (1986) 'The medieval monastic garden', in MacDougall, E.B. ed., *Medieval Gardens* (Dumbarton Oaks Colloquium on the History of Landscape Architecture, no.9, Trustees for Harvard University, Washington DC), pp.23-53

Bee-keeping
Crane, E. (1983) *The Archaeology of Bee-Keeping* (Duckworth)
Vernon, F.G. (1979) 'Bee-keeping in 1260-70 at Beaulieu Abbey in England', *Bee World*, Vol.60.iv, pp.170-5

Orchards
Roach, F.A. (1985) *Cultivated Fruits of Britain: their Origin and History* (Basil Blackwell, Oxford)

Vineyards
Barty-King, H. (1977) A *Tradition of English Wine* (Oxford Illustrated Press)
Seward, D. (1979) *Monks and Wine* (Mitchell Beazley, London)

Chapter 10: Monastic deer parks and rabbit warrens

Deer parks
Bond, C.J. (1994) 'Forests, chases, warrens and parks in medieval Wessex', in Aston, M., Lewis, C. eds, *The Medieval Landscape of Wessex* (Oxbow Monograph no.46), pp.115-158
— (1998) 'Medieval deer parks in Somerset', in Bond, *Somerset Parks and Gardens: a Landscape History* (Somerset Books, Tiverton), pp.22-31
Cantor, L.M. (1965) 'The medieval parks of south Staffordshire', *Transactions of Birmingham Archaeological Society*, Vol.80, pp.1-9
— (1971) 'The medieval parks of Leicestershire', *Transactions of Leicestershire Archaeological & Historical Society*, Vol.46, pp.9-24
— (1983) *The Medieval Parks of England: a Gazetteer* (Department of Education, Loughborough University of Technology)
Cantor, L.M., Wilson, J.D. (1961-9) 'The medieval deer parks of Dorset', parts 1-9, *Proceedings of Dorset Archaeology & Natural History Society*, Vols 83, pp.109-16; 84, pp.145-53; 85, pp.141-52; 86, pp.164-78; 87, pp.223-33; 88, pp.176-85; 89, pp.171-80; 90, pp.241-8; 91, pp.196-205
Coulton, G.G. (1960) 'Monks and hunting', Appendix 29 of Coulton, *Medieval Village, Manor and Monastery* (Harper Torchbooks Academy Library, New York), pp.508-12
Squires, A.E., Humphrey, W. (1986) *The Medieval Parks of Charnwood Forest* (Sycamore Press, Melton Mowbray)
Wilson, J.D. (1970-4) 'The medieval deer parks of Dorset', parts 10-14, *Proceedings of Dorset Archaeology & Natural History Society*, Vol.92, pp.205-11; 93, pp.169-75; 94, pp.67-9; 95, pp.47-50; 96, pp.76-80

Rabbit warrens
Bailey, M. (1988) 'The rabbit and the medieval East Anglian economy', *Agricultural History Review*, Vol.36, pp.1-20
Fuller, E.A. (1890-1) 'Cirencester Castle', *Transactions of Bristol & Gloucestershire Archaeological Society*, Vol.15, pp.103-119 [rabbit warren at the Crundles, p.114]
Rigold, S.E. (1979) 'Thetford Warren Lodge', in Raby, F.J.E., Baillie Reynolds, P.K. *Thetford Priory, Norfolk* (HMSO, London)
Sheail, J. (1971) *Rabbits and their History* (David & Charles, Newton Abbot)

Chapter 11: Monastic fisheries and fishponds

Aston, M. (1972) 'The earthworks of Bordesley Abbey, Redditch, Worcestershire', *Medieval Archaeology*, Vol.16, pp.133-136

Aston, M. ed. (1988), *Medieval Fish, Fisheries and Fishponds in England* (British Archaeological Reports, British Series, no.182)

Aston, M., Munton, A.P. (1976) 'A survey of Bordesley Abbey and its water control system', in Rahtz, P.A., Hirst, S. eds, *Bordesley Abbey* (British Archaeological Reports, British Series, no.23), pp.24-37

Bond, C.J. (1988) 'Monastic fisheries', in Aston, *Medieval Fish, Fisheries and Fishponds in England,* pp.69-112

— (1989) 'Water management in the rural monastery', in Gilchrist, R., Mytum, H. eds, *The Archaeology of Rural Monasteries* (British Archaeological Reports, British Series, no.203, pp.83-111, esp. pp.100-2.

Currie, C.K. (1988) 'Medieval fishponds in Hampshire', in Aston, ed., *Medieval Fish, Fisheries and Fishponds in England,* pp.267-290

— (1989) 'The role of fishponds in the monastic economy', in Gilchrist, R., Mytum, H. eds, *The Archaeology of the Rural Monastery* (British Archaeological Reports, British Series, no.203), pp.147-72

Hickling, C.F. (1971) 'Prior More's fishponds', *Medieval Archaeology* , Vol.15, pp.118-23

Hoffman, R. (1994) 'Mediaeval Cistercian fisheries, natural and artificial', in Pressouyre, L. ed., *L'Espace Cistercien* (Comité des Travaux Historiques et Scientifiques, Mémoires de la Section d'Archéologie et d'Histoire de l'Art, no.5, Paris), pp.401-14.

James, T. (1978) 'A survey of the fishponds, watercourses and other earthworks at the site of Whitland Abbey and iron forge', *Carmarthenshire Antiquary*, Vol.14, pp.71-8

Kemp, R. (1984) 'A fish-keeper's store at Byland Abbey', *Ryedale Historian*, Vol.12, pp.44-51

Lucas, G. (1998) 'A medieval fishery on Whittlesea Mere, Cambridgeshire', *Medieval Archaeology*, Vol.42, pp.19-44

Mackay, D.A., Swan, V.G. (1989) 'Earthworks at Marton and Moxby Priories', *Yorkshire Archaeological Journal*, Vol.61, pp.71-84

McDonnell, J. (1981) *Inland Fisheries in Medieval Yorkshire, 1066-1300* (University of York, Borthwick Papers no.60)

McDonnell, J., Goodall, G.W.(1974) 'More about Byland Abbey fishponds', *Ryedale Historian*, Vol.7, pp.75-78

Shackley, M., Hayne, J., Wainwright, N. (1988) 'Environmental analysis of medieval fishpond deposits at Owston Abbey, Leicestershire', in Aston, ed., *Medieval Fish, Fisheries & Fishponds,* pp.301-8

Swan, V.G. (1991) 'Marton Priory fishponds: a postscript', *Yorkshire Archaeological Journal*, Vol.63, pp.219-20

Chapter 12: Churches and chapels on monastic estates

There are numerous books on the architecture of churches, but the following examine parish churches in their tenurial and landscape setting:

Blair, J. ed. (1988) *Minsters and Parish Churches: The Local Church in Transition, 950-1200* (Oxford University Committee for Archaeology, Monograph no.17)

Morris, R. (1989) *Churches in the Landscape* (J.M. Dent, London)

Platt, C. (1981) *The Parish Churches of Medieval England* (Secker & Warburg, London)

Churches and monastic houses
Burton, J.E. (1987) 'Monasteries and parish churches in eleventh- and twelfth-century Yorkshire', *Northern History*, Vol.23, pp.39-50

Colvin, H.M. (1951) *The White Canons in England* (Clarendon Press, Oxford), esp. pp.272-88, 'Parochial Responsibilities'

Constable, G. (1964) *Monastic Tithes from their Origins to the Twelfth Century* (Cambridge University Press)

— (1988) 'Monasteries, rural churches and the *Cura Animarum* in the early Middle Ages', in Constable, *Monks, Hermits and Crusaders in Medieval Europe* (Variorum Reprints, London), pp.349-89

Dickinson, J.C. (1950) *The Origins of the Austin Canons and their Introduction into England* (SPCK, London), esp. pp.224-41,' The Regular Canons and Parish Work'

Dunning, R.W. (2001) 'The abbot of Glastonbury saves money', *Somerset & Dorset Notes & Queries,* Vol.35, no.354, pp.51-2 [West Pennard chapel]

Kemp, B.R. (1980) 'Monastic possession of parish churches in England in the twelfth century', *Journal of Ecclesiastical History*, Vol.31, pp.133-160

Mason, E. (1991) 'Westminster Abbey and its parish churches, *c*.1050-1216', in Loades, J. ed., *Monastic Studies: the Continuity of Tradition* (Headstart History, Bangor), pp.43-65, reprinted as Appendix 4 in Mason, *Westminster Abbey and its People, c.1050-c.1216* (Boydell, Woodbridge, 1996), pp.318-42

Postles, D. (1986) 'The acquisition and administration of spiritualities by Oseney Abbey', *Oxoniensia*, Vol.51, pp.69-77

Tatton-Brown, T. (1989) 'Church building on Romney Marsh in the later Middle Ages', *Archaeologia Cantiana*, Vol.107, pp.253-65

Priests' houses
Pantin, W.A. (1957) 'Medieval priests' houses in south-west England', *Medieval Archaeology*, Vol.1, pp.118-46

Chapter 13: Monasteries and rural settlement

Village origins and planning
Anon. (1997) 'The Shapwick project', *Current Archaeology*, Vol.13 no. vii (no.151), pp.244-54. Eight interim reports on work at Shapwick have been issued (Aston, M., Costen, M., Gerrard, C.M. & Hall, T. eds, (1988-98) *The Shapwick Project,* Vols 1-8 (University of Bristol Department for Continuing Education), and the final report is in preparation.

Aston, M., Austin, D., Dyer, C. eds, 1989 *The Rural Settlements of Medieval England: Studies dedicated to Maurice Beresford and John Hurst* (Basil Blackwell, Oxford)

Campey, L. (1989) 'Medieval village plans in County Durham: an analysis of reconstructed plans based on medieval documentary sources', *Northern History*, Vol.25, pp.60-87

Corcos, N. (1982-3) 'Early estates on the Poldens and the origin of the settlement at Shapwick', *Proceedings of Somerset Archaeological & Natural History Society*, Vol.127, pp.47-54

— (2002) 'Bourne and Burrington: a *Burnantun* estate?' *Proceedings of Somerset Archaeological & Historical Society*, Vol.144, pp.117-38

Costen, M. (1991) 'Some evidence for new settlements and field systems in late Anglo-Saxon Somerset', in Abrams, L., Carley, L.P. eds, *The Archaeology and History of Glastonbury Abbey* (Boydell, Woodbridge), pp.39-56

Everson, P.L., Taylor, C.C., Dunn, C.J. (1991) *Change and Continuity: Rural Settlement in North-West Lincolnshire* (Royal Commission on the Historical Monuments of England)

Hall, T. (2000) *Minster Churches in the Dorset Landscape* (British Archaeological Reports, British Series, no.204), esp. Ch.4, 'The layout of minster settlements', pp.49-78

Hayfield, C. (1984) 'Wawne, East Riding of Yorkshire: a case study in settlement morphology', *Landscape History*, Vol.6, pp.41-67

Lewis, C., Mitchell-Fox, P., Dyer, C. (1997) *Village, Hamlet and Field: Changing Medieval Settlements in Central England* (Manchester University Press)

Oosthuizen, S. (2002) 'Ancient greens in "midland" landscapes: Barrington, South Cambridgeshire', *Medieval Archaeology*, Vol.46, pp.110-15

Watts, D.G. (1958-60) 'The villages on the manors of Titchfield Abbey', *Proceedings of Hampshire Field Club,* Vol.21, pp.31-37

Williams, E.H.D., Penoyre, J., Penoyre, J., Hale, B.C.M. (1986) 'New Street, Mells: a building survey of an uncompleted late medieval planned development', *Proceedings of Somerset Archaeological & Natural History Society,* Vol.130, pp.115-125

Deserted villages

Barley, M.W. (1957) 'Cistercian land clearances in Nottinghamshire: three deserted villages and their moated successor', *Nottingham Medieval Studies,* Vol.1, pp.75-89

Beresford, M.W. (1945) 'The deserted villages of Warwickshire', *Transactions of Birmingham Archaeological Society,* Vol.66, pp.49-106

— (1951, 1952, 1953, 1954) 'The lost villages of Yorkshire', *Yorkshire Archaeological Journal,* Vol.37, pp.474-91; Vol.38, pp.44-70, 215-40, 280-309

— (1954) *The Lost Villages of England* (Lutterworth Press, London)

Beresford, M.W., Hurst, J.G. eds, (1971) *Deserted Medieval Villages* (Lutterworth Press, London)

Donkin, R.A. (1960) 'Settlement and depopulation on Cistercian estates in the twelfth and thirteenth centuries, especially in Yorkshire', *Bulletin of Institute of Historical Research,* Vol.33, pp.141-65

Farmer, D.H. (1992) *St Hugh of Lincoln* (Darton, Longman & Todd, London) [for Witham, Somerset, pp.16-17]

Hoskins, W.G. (1944-5) 'The deserted villages of Leicestershire', *Transactions of Leicestershire Archaeological Society,* Vol.22, pp.241-63, revised and extended in Hoskins (1950), *Essays in Leicestershire History* (Liverpool University Press), pp.67-107

— (1956) 'Seven deserted village sites in Leicestershire', *Transactions of Leicestershire Archaeological Society,* Vol.32, pp.36-52, reprinted in Hoskins (1963) *Provincial England* (MacMillan, London), pp.115-30

Leadam, I.S. (1892-3, 1897) – see references listed for 'Monastic Enclosure' under chapter 5

Lloyd, T.H. (1964-5) 'Some documentary sidelights on the deserted Oxfordshire village of Brookend', *Oxoniensia,* Vol.29-30, pp.116-28

Owen, D.M. (1957-8) 'Thornton Abbey and the lost vill of Audleby', *Lincolnshire Architectural & Archaeological Society Reports & Papers,* Vol.7, pp.112-16

Thompson, F.H. (1960) 'The deserted medieval village of Riseholme, near Lincoln', *Medieval Archaeology,* Vol.4, pp.95-108

Chapter 14: Monastic boroughs, markets and urban property

Monastic urban property

Donkin, R.A. (1959) 'The urban property of the Cistercians in medieval England', *Analecta Sacri Ordinis Cisterciensis,* Vol.15, pp.104-131

Steer, J. (1988) 'Medieval holdings of Burton Abbey in Derby, part i: the identification of the holdings of Burton Abbey', *Derbyshire Miscellany,* Vol.11.vi, pp.118-39

Monastic inns

Jope, E.M., Pantin, W.A. (1958) 'The Clarendon Hotel, Oxford', *Oxoniensia,* Vol.23, pp.1-129 (archaeological and architectural investigation of the Star Inn site)

Pantin, W.A. (1961) 'Medieval Inns', in Jope, E.M. ed., *Studies in Building History* (Odhams, London), pp.166-191

Williams, E.H.D., Penoyre, J., Penoyre, J., Hale, R. (1987) 'The George Inn, Norton St Philip', *Archaeological Journal,* Vol.144, pp.317-327

Monastic town houses in London

Gadd, D. (1983) 'The London inn of the abbots of Waltham: a revised reconstruction of a medieval town house in Lovat Lane', *Transactions of London & Middlesex Archaeological Society,* Vol.34, pp.171-8

Honeybourne, M.J. (1947) 'The Fleet and its neighbourhood in early and medieval times', *London Topographical Record,* Vol.19, pp.13-87

— (1952) 'The abbot of Waltham's inn', *London Topographical Record,* Vol.20, pp.34-46

— (1965) 'The reconstructed map of London under Richard II', esp. 'The religious foundations and the town houses or inns of provincial bishops, abbots and priors', *London Topographical Record,* Vol.22, pp.31-5

Lobel, M.D. ed., (1989) *The City of London* (British Atlas of Historic Towns, Oxford, Vol.3)

Norman, P. (1896-7) 'The Tabard Inn, Southwark', *Surrey Archaeological Collections,* Vol.13, pp.28-38

Markets and fairs

Donkin, R.A. (1962) 'The markets and fairs of medieval Cistercian monasteries in England and Wales', *Cistercienser Chronik,* Vol.69, pp.1-14

Letters, S. (updated 21.1.2003) *Gazetteer of Markets and Fairs in England and Wales to 1516* (www.ihrinfo.ac.uk/cmh/gaz/gazweb2.html)

Morimoto, N. (1983) *Monastic Economy and Medieval Markets* (Kyoto)

Palliser, D.M., Pinnock, A.C. (1971) 'The markets of medieval Staffordshire', *North Staffordshire Journal of Field Studies,* Vol.11, pp.49-63

Boroughs

Beresford, M., Finberg, H.P.R. (1973) *English Medieval Boroughs: a Hand-List* (David & Charles, Newton Abbot)

Palliser, D.M. (1972) 'The boroughs of medieval Staffordshire', *North Staffordshire Journal of Field Studies,* Vol.12, pp.63-73

Trenholme, N.M. (1927) *The English Monastic Boroughs* (University of Missouri Studies, Vol.2, no. iii, Columbia)

Monastic new towns and town planning

Baker, N. (2002) Chs 11-13, 'The changing precinct', 'The abbey and its suburb' and 'The abbey and the town', in Baker, N. ed., *Shrewsbury Abbey: Studies in the Archaeology and History of an Urban Abbey* (Shropshire Archaeological & Historical Society, Monograph Series no.2), pp.193-226

Beresford, M.W. (1967) *New Towns of the Middle Ages: Town Plantation in England, Wales and Gascony* (Lutterworth Press, London)

Bond, C.J., Hunt, A.M. (1977) 'Recent archaeological work in Pershore', *Vale of Evesham Historical Society Research Papers,* Vol.6, pp.1-76

Keen, L. (1999) 'Monastic urban speculation: the Cistercians and medieval Charmouth', *Proceedings of Dorset Natural History & Archaeology Society,* Vol.121, pp.17-22

Lilley, K.D. (1994) 'Coventry's topographical development: the impact of the priory', in Demidowicz, G. ed., *Coventry's First Cathedral: the Cathedral and Priory of St Mary* (Paul Watkins, Stamford), pp.72-96

— (1998) 'Trading places: monastic initiative and the development of high-medieval Coventry', in Slater, T.R., Rosser, G. eds, *The Church in the Medieval Town* (Ashgate, Aldershot), pp.177-208

Slater, T.R. (1980) *The Analysis of Burgages in Medieval Towns* (Department of Geography, University of Birmingham, Working Paper Series, no.4) [includes Pershore and Shipston-on-Stour]

— (1996) 'Medieval town-founding on the estates of the Benedictine order in England', in Eliassen, F.-E., Ersland, G.A., *Power, Profit and Urban Land: Landownership in Medieval and Early-Modern Northern European Towns* (Scolar Press, Aldershot), pp.70-93.

— (1998) 'Benedictine town planning in medieval England: evidence from St Albans', in Slater, T.R., Rosser, G. eds, *The Church in the Medieval Town* (Ashgate, Aldershot), pp.155-76

Schools

Orme, N.I. (1973) *English Schools in the Middle Ages* (Methuen, London), esp. pp.224-51

— (1977) 'Evesham School before the Reformation', *Vale of Evesham Historical Society Research Papers*, Vol.6, pp.95-100

Chapter 15: Monasteries and transport

Roads

Hindle, B.P. (1993) *Roads, Tracks and their Interpretation* (B.T. Batsford, London), esp. Ch.4, 'Medieval routes', pp.48-63

Bridges

Huggins, P.J. (1970), 'Excavation of a medieval bridge at Waltham Abbey, Essex, 1968', *Medieval Archaeology*, Vol.14, pp.126-47.

Jervoise, E. (1930) *The Ancient Bridges of the South of England* (Westminster)

— (1931) *The Ancient Bridges of the North of England* (Westminster)

— (1932) *The Ancient Bridges of Mid and Eastern England* (Westminster)

— (1936) *The Ancient Bridges of Wales & Western England* (Westminster)

Monastic canals and water transport

Bond, C.J. (forthcoming) 'Canal construction in the early Middle Ages: an introductory review', in Blair, J. ed., *Water Transport and Management in Medieval England* (Oxford University Press)

Glastonbury: Hollinrake, C., Hollinrake, N. (1991) 'A late Saxon monastic enclosure ditch and canal, Glastonbury, Somerset', *Antiquity*, Vol.65, pp.117-8; Hollinrake, C., Hollinrake, N. (1992) 'The abbey enclosure ditch and a late Saxon canal: rescue excavations at Glastonbury, 1984-1988', *Proceedings of the Somerset Archaeological and Natural History Society*, Vol.136, pp.73-94

Meaux: Sheppard, J.A. (1958), *The Draining of the Hull Valley* (East Yorkshire Local History Society, York)

Rievaulx: Rye, H.A. (1900) 'Rievaulx Abbey, its canals and building stones', *Archaeological Journal*, Vol.57, pp.69-88; Weatherill, J. (1954) 'Rievaulx Abbey: the stone used in its building, with notes on the means of transport and a new study of the diversion of the River Rye in the twelfth century', *Yorkshire Archaeological Journal*, Vol.38, pp.333-354

Monastic wharves and quays

Butley: Ward Perkins, J.B. (1933) 'The priory wharf or landing stage', in Myres, J.N.L., Caroe, W.O., Ward Perkins, J.B., 'Butley Priory, Suffolk', *Archaeological Journal*, Vol.90, pp.260-4

London: Sheldon, H. (1972) 'Excavations at Toppings and Sun Wharves, Southwark, 1970-72', *Transactions of London & Middlesex Archaeological Society*, Vol.25, pp.1-116

Waltham: Huggins, P.J. (1972) 'Monastic grange and outer close excavations, Waltham Abbey, Essex, 1970-1972', *Transactions of Essex Archaeological Society*, Vol.4, esp. 'Dock and wharf', pp.81-8

Woolaston Grange (Tintern): Fulford, M.G., Rippon, S., Allen, J.R.L., Hillam, J. (1992) 'The medieval quay at Woolaston Grange, Gloucestershire', *Transactions of Bristol & Gloucestershire Archaeological Society*, Vol.110, pp.101-22

Lighthouses

Hague, D.B., Christie, R. (1975) *Lighthouses: their Architecture, History and Archaeology* (Gomer Press, Llandysul), esp. pp.9-20

Chapter 16: Monastic mills

General references

Bennett, R., Elton, J. (1898-1904) A *History of Corn Milling* (4 vols, Simpkin Marshall, London)

Bond, C.J. (1994) 'Cistercian mills in England and Wales: a preliminary survey', in Pressouyre, L. ed., *L'Espace Cistercien* (Comité des Travaux Historiques et Scientifiques, Mémoires de la Section d'Archéologie et d'Histoire de l'Art, no.5, Paris), pp.364-77

Drinkwater, C.H. (1894) 'The abbot of Shrewsbury versus the burgesses thereof in the matter of the mills', *Transactions of Shropshire Archaeological & Natural History Society*, 2nd Series, Vol.6, pp.341-57

Holt, R. (1987) 'Whose were the profits of corn milling? An aspect of the changing relationships between the abbots of Glastonbury and their tenants, 1086-1350', *Past & Present*, Vol.116, pp.3-23

— (1988) *The Mills of Medieval England* (Basil Blackwell, Oxford)

Keil, I.J. (1961-7) 'Mills on the estates of Glastonbury Abbey in the later Middle Ages', *Somerset & Dorset Notes & Queries*, Vol.28, pp.181-4

Lindley, E.S. (1954, 1955, 1956) 'Kingswood Abbey, its lands and mills', *Transactions of Bristol & Gloucestershire Archaeological Society*, Vol.73, pp.115-91; Vol.74, pp.36-59; Vol.75, pp.73-104

Williams, D. (1998) *The Cistercians in the Early Middle Ages* (Gracewing, Leominster), 'Milling', pp.332-5, 'Fulling mills', pp.360-1

Water-powered corn mills

Coppack, G. (1998) 'The water-driven corn mill at Fountains Abbey: a major Cistercian mill of the twelfth and thirteenth centuries', in Lillich, M. ed., *Studies in Cistercian Art & Architecture*, Vol.5 (Cistercian Studies no.167, Kalamazoo, Michigan), pp.270-296

Graham, A.H. (1986) 'The Old Malthouse, Abbotsbury: the medieval watermill of the Benedictine abbey', *Proceedings of Dorset Natural History & Archaeology Society*, Vol.108, pp.103-25

Luckhurst, D. (1964) *Monastic Watermills: a Study of the Mills within English Monastic Precincts* (Society for Protection of Ancient Buildings, Wind- & Watermill Section, Booklet no.8)

Slade, C.F. (1971-2) 'Excavation at Reading Abbey, 1964-1967', *Berkshire Archaeological Journal*, Vol.66, pp.65-116

Tide mills

Minchinton, W.E. (1982) 'Tidemills of England and Wales', *Transactions of the Fourth Symposium of the International Molinological Society*, 1977, pp.339-53

Wailes, R. (n.d.) *Tide Mills* (Society for Protection of Ancient Buildings, Wind- & Watermill Section, Booklet nos 2-3)

Fulling mills

Barton, K.J., Burns, R.B., Allen, D. (1997) 'Archaeological excavations at the 'Wine Press', Beaulieu Abbey, 1987-1989', *Proceedings of Hampshire Field Club & Archaeology Society*, Vol.52, pp.107-149

Carus-Wilson, E.M. (1941) 'An industrial revolution of the thirteenth century', *Economic History Review*, Vol.11, pp.39-60, reprinted in Carus-Wilson, *Essays in Economic History*, i (London, 1954), pp.41-60

Jack, R.I. (1981) 'Fulling-mills in Wales and the March before 1547', *Archaeologia Cambrensis*, Vol.130, pp.70-130

Pelham, R.A. (1958) *Fulling Mill* (Society for Protection of Ancient Buildings, Wind- & Watermill Section, Booklet no.5)

Industrial watermills

Astill, G.G. (1993) *A Medieval Industrial Complex and its Landscape: the Metalworking Watermills and Workshops of Bordesley Abbey* (Council for British Archaeology, Research Report no.92)

Crossley, D.W. (1975) *The Bewl Valley Ironworks, Kent, c.1300-1730 AD* (Royal Archaeological Institute Monograph, London)

Windmills

Bond, C.J. (1995) *Medieval Windmills in South-Western England* (Society for Protection of Ancient Buildings, Wind- & Watermill Section, Occasional Publication no.3)

Kealey, E.J. (1987) *Harvesting the Air: Windmill Pioneers in Twelfth-Century England* (Boydell, Woodbridge)

Keil, I.J. (1961-2) 'Building a post windmill in 1342', *Transactions of Newcomen Society*, Vol.34, pp.151-4 [Glastonbury Abbey's mill at Walton, Somerset]

Chapter 17: Extractive and manufacturing industry on monastic estates

General references

Blair, J., Ramsay, N. eds (1991) *English Medieval Industries* (Hambledon Press, London)

Crossley, D.W. ed., (1981), *Medieval Industry* (Council for British Archaeology, Research Report no.40)

Salzman, L.F. (1913) *English Industries in the Middle Ages* (Constable, London)

Building stone

Alexander, J.S. (1995) 'Building stone from the east midlands quarries: sources, transportation and usage', *Medieval Archaeology*, Vol.39, pp.107-35

Jope, E.M. (1948) 'Abingdon Abbey craftsmen and building stone supplies', *Berkshire Archaeological Journal*, Vol.51, pp.53-64

— (1956) 'The archaeology of Wheatley stone', in Jope, *Wheatley Records, 956-1956* (Oxfordshire Record Society, Vol.37), pp.17-26

— (1964) 'The Saxon building-stone industry in southern and midland England', *Medieval Archaeology*, Vol.8, pp.91-118

Parsons, D. ed. (1990) *Stone Quarrying and Building in England, AD 43-1525* (Royal Archaeological Institute, Phillimore, Chichester)

Senior, J.R. (1999) 'The stonework and quarries', in Fergusson, P., Harrison, S., *Rievaulx Abbey: Community, Architecture, Memory* (Paul Mellon Centre for Studies in British Art, Yale University Press), pp.215-9

Brick-making and brick building

Gardner, J.S. (1955) 'Coggeshall Abbey and its early brickwork', *Journal of British Archaeological Association*, 3rd Series, Vol.18, pp.19-32

Lloyd, N. (1925) *A History of English Brickwork* (Greville Montgomery, London; reprinted by Antique Collectors' Club, 1983)

Wight, J. (1972) *Brick Building in England and Wales from the Middle Ages to 1550* (John Baker, London)

Tiles and tileries

Beulah, G.K. (1993) 'Thirteenth-century square-tile mosaic pavements at Cistercian houses in Britain', *Studies in Cistercian Art & Architecture no.4* (Cistercian Studies Series no.134, Kalamazoo, Michigan), pp.1-14

Drury, P.J. (1981) 'The production of brick and tile in medieval England', in Crossley ed., *Medieval Industry*, pp.126-42

Gardner, J.S., Eames, E.S. (1954) 'A tile kiln at Chertsey Abbey', *Journal of British Archaeological Association*, 3rd Series, Vol.17, pp 24-42

Gem, R., Keen, L. (1981-4) 'Late Anglo-Saxon finds from the site of St Edmund's Abbey', *Proceedings of Suffolk Institute of Archaeology* Vol.35, pp.1-30

Greene, J.P. (1980) 'Tile-making at Norton Priory', *Popular Archaeology*, June 1980, pp.41-4

— (1989) *Norton Priory: the Archaeology of a Medieval Religious House* (Cambridge University Press), pp.132-44

Greene, J.P., Johnson, B. (1978) 'An experimental tile kiln at Norton Priory', *Medieval Ceramics*, Vol.2, pp.30-41

Eames, E.S. (1961) 'A thirteenth-century tile kiln site at North Grange, Meaux, Beverley, Yorkshire', *Medieval Archaeology*, Vol.5, pp.137-68.

Eames, E.S., Beulah, G.K. (1956) 'The thirteenth-century tile mosaic pavements in the Yorkshire Cistercian houses', *Cîteaux in de Nederlanden* Vol.7, pp.264-77

Smallwood, J. (1978) 'A medieval tile kiln at Abbey Farm, Shouldham', *East Anglian Archaeology*, Vol.8, pp.45-54

Potteries

Bellamy, C.V., Le Patourel, H.E.J. (1970) 'Four medieval pottery kilns on Woodhouse Farm, Winksley, near Ripon, West Riding of Yorkshire', *Medieval Archaeology*, Vol.14, pp.104-25

Ironstone mines and iron forges

Cleere, H., Crossley, D. (1985) *The Iron Industry of the Weald* (Leicester University Press), esp.Ch.5, 'Iron in the Weald in the Middle Ages', pp.87-110

Crossley, D.W. (1981) 'Medieval iron smelting', in Crossley, ed., *Medieval Industry*, pp.29-41

Geddes, J. (1991) 'Iron', in Blair & Ramsay, eds, *English Medieval Industries*, pp.167-188

Goodall, I.H. (1981) 'The medieval blacksmith and his products', in Crossley, ed., *Medieval Industry*, pp.51-62

Huggins, P.J., Huggins, R.M. (1973) 'Excavation of monastic forge and Saxo-Norman enclosure, Waltham Abbey, Essex, 1972-3', *Transactions of Essex Archaeological Society*, Vol.5, pp.127-84

Tylecote, R.F. (1981) 'The medieval smith and his methods', in Crossley, ed., *Medieval Industry*, pp.42-50

Waites, B. (1964) 'Medieval iron working in northeast Yorkshire', *Geography*, Vol.49.i (no.222), pp.33-43

Other metals

Courtney, P. (1989) 'Excavations in the outer precinct of Tintern Abbey', *Medieval Archaeology*, Vol.33, pp.99-143

Duncan, H.B., Wrathmell, S. (1986) 'Bell moulds from Kirkstall Abbey', *Journal of Historical Metallurgy*, Vol.20.i, pp.33-5

Greene, J.P. (1989) *Norton Priory* [bell-casting pit described on pp.118-22]

Hawkes, J.W. (1991-3) 'Archaeological observations along the line of the Plummery wall, Reading Abbey', *Berkshire Archaeological Journal*, Vol.74, p.147

Raistrick, A., Jennings, B. (1965) *A History of Lead Mining in the Pennines* (London)

Salt-making

Vollans, E. (1995) 'Medieval salt-making and the inning of the tidal marshes at Belgar, Lydd', in Eddison, J. ed., *Romney Marsh: the Debatable Ground* (Oxford University Committee for Archaeology, Monograph no.41), pp.118-126

Index

If you are interested in purchasing other books published by Tempus,
or in case you have difficulty finding any Tempus books in your local bookshop,
you can also place orders directly through our website

www.tempus-publishing.com

or from

BOOKPOST, Freepost, PO Box 29, Douglas, Isle of Man IM99 1BQ
Tel 01624 836000   email bookshop@enterprise.net